Mississippi Women

Mississippi Women

THEIR HISTORIES, THEIR LIVES

EDITED BY

Martha H. Swain, Elizabeth Anne Payne,

and Marjorie Julian Spruill

Associate Editor, Susan Ditto

FOREWORD BY ANNE FIROR SCOTT

The University of Georgia Press   *Athens and London*

© 2003 by the University of Georgia Press
Athens, Georgia 30602
All rights reserved
Designed by Kathi Dailey Morgan
Set in Minion by Bookcomp, Inc.
Printed and bound by Sheridan Books
The paper in this book meets the guidelines for
permanence and durability of the Committee on
Production Guidelines for Book Longevity of the
Council on Library Resources.

Printed in the United States of America
07 06 05 04 03 C 5 4 3 2 1
07 06 05 04 03 P 5 4 3 2 1

Library of Congress Cataloging-in-Publication Data

Mississippi women : their histories, their lives / edited by Martha H. Swain,
Elizabeth Anne Payne, Marjorie Julian Spruill ; associate editor, Susan Ditto.
p. cm.
Includes bibliographical references (p.) and index.
ISBN 0-8203-2502-3 (alk. paper) — ISBN 0-8203-2503-1 (pbk. : alk. paper)
1. Women—Mississippi—Biography. 2. Mississippi—Biography. I. Swain, Martha H.,
1929– II. Payne, Elizabeth Anne, 1943– III. Spruill, Marjorie Julian, 1951–
CT3260 .M57 2003
920.72'09762–dc21   2003008776

Quotations from the Burnita Shelton Matthews oral history are used with permission
of the Bancroft Library of the University of California at Berkeley.
"Eudora Welty (1909–2001): En Route to *A Curtain of Green*"
reprinted by permission of Louisiana State University Press
from *One Writer's Imagination: The Fiction of Eudora Welty,* ed. Suzanne Marrs.
Copyright © 2002 by Louisiana State University Press.
Portions of "Hazel Brannon Smith (1914–1994): Journalist under Siege"
were originally published in the *Journal of Mississippi History* (February 1992)
and are used with permission. "I Want to Write" and "For My People" appear
in *This Is My Century: New and Collected Poems* by Margaret Walker, © 1989
by Margaret Walker Alexander (Athens: University of Georgia Press, 1989).

British Library Cataloging-in-Publication Data available

Contents

Foreword

This book and its soon-to-come companion volume are new steps on a long, long road. While the systematic study of women's role in the past has only recently become a recognized part of academic history, for centuries women have been interested in establishing the fact that women did indeed belong in "history." To make that point they most often resorted to biography.

Collections of essays about famous women sold briskly in the United States in the nineteenth century. Titles such as *Lives of Celebrated Women* or *Noble Deeds of American Women* abounded. Others, such as the successive volumes edited by Sarah Josepha Hale, the prolific editor of *Godey's Ladies Book,* covered the history of the world from creation to the time of publication. Year by year Hale published a new edition, moving the end date forward. The authors of these works did not always distinguish clearly between documented fact and legend. Heroine worship was rife, and part of the announced purpose was to inspire young women. Elizabeth Ellett, preparing to write about women in the American Revolution came closest to serious scholarly research. She searched for letters and other documents, and she foreshadowed modern oral history when she interviewed survivors.

Other works concentrated on contemporary women. Some were created by feminists interested in seeking precedents for their own social activism; others were by women and an occasional man who saw a market and attempted to supply it. One intriguing volume included essays by women leaders about other women leaders. Toward the end of the century three collections appeared that would be of great use to posterity: Jennie June Croly's history of women's clubs, Frances Willard and Mary Livermore's work on contemporary women, and the intriguing collection of biographies of graduates of the Troy Female Seminary based on questionnaires sent to as many survivors as the editors could find.

Whatever the editors had in mind, and no matter how brisk the sales, few of these works attracted the attention of the handful of historical scholars, those talented amateurs, most of whom were men, who were at work in this country from the earliest European settlements until the study of history began to become a recognized profession in the late nineteenth century. Henry Adams was a notable exception. In his *Education,* as well as in his novel *Democracy,* he recognized women as shapers of society and politics. Adams, however, was only briefly an academic historian, and those who became such, concentrating usually on wars, diplomacy, constitutions, and legal systems, paid no attention to women's influence on society.

In the 1970s, just as the new feminism was creating an interest in women's past, the tradition of women's biography was brought up to date with the publication of the first three volumes of *Notable American Women,* a work of serious scholarship and one that has inspired the publication of a number of studies of women of individual states.

Of course states are man-made entities with somewhat artificial boundaries, but some at least tend to develop a unique culture. Certainly this is true of certain southern states of which Mississippi is a most striking example. In one state after another, groups of women have undertaken to create their own history of notables. Some have collected essays by different hands. In a few cases a single author or a handful of authors has written not simply a collection of biographies but a social history narrative in which the lives of individuals can be seen in context. One result of this approach has been that the definition of *significance* expanded, and women not known to fame are seen as worthy of attention. Suzanne Lebsock's *Share of Honor,* published in conjunction with the Virginia Museum, is an outstanding example of this genre, as is the history of North Carolina women written by Emily Herring Wilson and Margaret Supplee Smith. Similar work has been initiated in other states.

Now the Mississippi Women's History Project combines both approaches. This volume contains essays by a wide range of authors, including not only historians but also scholars in English, political science, science, art history, and literature, as well as one individual whose chief experience has been as a social activist. The range of subjects is equally wide—reaching from a woman as well known as Eudora Welty to women long forgotten and only brought back to memory by recent scholarship.

As we survey the long history of women's biographical collections, it is clear that in creating such works each generation not only enriches our understanding of the past but also reveals something of its own values and concerns. It is intriguing to imagine what Sarah Josepha Hale, for example, would make of this collection, which includes several African American women, a social activist "flapper," a woman who made significant medical discoveries, and a woman whose claim to attention was that she became an icon that bore little resemblance to her real self. It is safe to say that Hale would have been startled, but probably she would also have been intrigued. So, too, will be the reader who opens this volume.

ANNE FIROR SCOTT

Preface

This collection of essays by the Mississippi Women's History Project is the first of two volumes that seek to present to new readers recent scholarship on the achievements and experiences of women in Mississippi over a period of four centuries. This compilation is biographical, focusing on the lives of individuals; the second volume will be topical, covering themes as diverse as Mississippi women themselves.

What these women had in common is the shared experience of attaining womanhood with all the attendant challenges, pains, and privileges that entailed. Sometimes upholding traditional notions of gender and race, sometimes striving to overcome tradition, none were free from the constraints of social hierarchies. Neither were they free from what Mississippi writer Eudora Welty once called "the crossroads of circumstance" that defined and still shapes the lives of Mississippi women.

There are fascinating stories here that range from that of a "black" slaveholder in old Natchez to that of a mother hoping to finally loose the bonds of slavery for her children in the mid-twentieth century. There is a daughter of privilege and position who basked in the glory of a Lost Cause. And there are women who fought the restrictions placed upon them by a patriarchal society that sought to deny to them the vote and the right to obtain a higher education leading to self-support. There are women who escaped Mississippi because they refused or were unable to live within the social and political constructs they believed prevented them from reaching their full potential. But then there are those who remained in a closed society, facing the daily struggle known as life, hoping simply to create a better future for themselves and their families. Some lived for a time outside the state, but ultimately returned to the place that was home.

A word of explanation is due to readers about the selection of the subjects in this volume. In soliciting essays, the editors faced the reality that sources available to scholars on individual women are seriously lacking for the state's early history. Hence, most of the biographical essays are on late-nineteenth- and twentieth-century women. Suffragists, artists, and educators left their records in abundance. The history of individual African American women in Mississippi to date is mainly that of participants in the civil rights movement, a period when many ordinary and a few extraordinary black women stepped out from the shadows of anonymity to claim their rightful place in history. We are grateful to those women who were involved in that struggle who have released their papers or allowed folklorists and historians to record their activities and their unique, largely unsung, contributions and perspectives on that movement.

Despite these challenges, there proved to be riches beyond expectation in both sources and present literature on the experience of Mississippi women, both individually and collectively. A chief goal of the Mississippi Women's History Project is to encourage further scholarship on the women and issues presented herein, further tapping the sources from which these biographies are drawn. Toward that goal, we have foregone a traditional bibliography in favor of a list of important manuscript collections and other resources of use to historians and other researchers.

We have made a deliberate effort to strike a balance between essays on renowned women, such as Eudora Welty and Fannie Lou Hamer, and sketches of little-known women, like Sadye Wier and Elizabeth Lee Hazen, whose so-called ordinary lives radiated extraordinary meaning. It was also our calling to capture a broader audience than many other scholarly volumes achieve—particularly to interest people who may be new to the area of women's studies. College undergraduates, advanced high school students, and general readers should find these essays engaging and enlightening, while scholars will find them useful teaching tools, as well as fertile ground for further study.

Half of the women whose lives are described in this volume never married, by choice or by chance. Most did not confide to others the conflicts they may have felt about pursuing a career over a family, and most did not speak about matters pertaining to sexuality. But a few made no secret of their opinions regarding men and marriage and their restraints on an independent life, while others appear to have found fulfillment in relationships with other women. On the other hand, half of the women in this volume were married. Some depended on emotional and economic support from their husbands or fathers to further their goals. Others succeeded in spite of the men in their lives. A select few were inspired by the awesome responsibilities of motherhood to help create a better world for their children and grandchildren.

We make no claim that the despair or triumphs that these women experienced in their private or public lives are unique to Mississippi women. What we hope is that the history written by our contributors will expand knowledge of and appreciation for women's history everywhere. We anticipate that our volumes will join the many recent studies that have come into print as a result of other statewide women's history projects.

More than a decade ago the Mississippi Women's History Project first began primarily through the efforts of the late Joanne Varner "Jan" Hawks, long-time director of the Sarah Isom Center for Women Studies at the University of Mississippi. Subsequently, an interested group attended a one-day symposium in Jackson in 1990 on the subject "Exploring the Archives for Women's History." In August 1991 the *Journal of Mississippi History* published the results of this symposium in a special issue. Jan Hawks made a major contribution to the field when she brought forth her *Mississippi's Historical Heritage: A Guide to Women's Resources in Mississippi Repositories* (1993). It is because of her pioneering efforts and our deep friendship with her that we dedicate this volume to Jan.

Now we have brought to new life a Mississippi Women's History Project. We intend for any royalties realized from our publications to go toward activities that will further the study of women in Mississippi: conferences, exhibits, workshops, research grants, and publications. After a two-year stay at the McDonnell-Barksdale Honors College at the University of Mississippi, the project will again be housed at the Sarah Isom Center for Women's Studies.

My coeditors, Elizabeth Anne Payne and Marjorie Julian Spruill, and I wish to acknowledge with much gratitude the work of our authors and their patient participation in this project. We also appreciate the encouragement of the Department of History at the University of Mississippi, especially the support of its chair, Robert Haws. We are grateful to Sally McDonnell Barksdale and Jim Barksdale, whose support of the McDonnell-Barksdale Honors College provided resources and an institutional base for the final production of this project. Costa Osadov of the MBHC provided invaluable technical assistance. We thank Elizabeth Propes, Clayton Andrew James, and Donna Buzzard for their logistical and technical help. And we thank Vanderbilt University for its generous support for the anthology in its final stages of preparation. Most of all we appreciate our associate editor, Susan Ditto, for her historical frame of mind, computer literacy and editing skills, and extreme diligence in bringing this volume to closure. We are thankful that she will join us as a coeditor for our second collection. And finally, we are grateful for the work of our copyeditor, Courtney Denney.

MARTHA H. SWAIN

Part One

Confronting Challenges

This anthology begins with an essay on Felicité Girodeau, a remarkable figure in the early history of Mississippi, a woman of color, and one of the few women of this early period about whom there are sufficient sources for a biographical essay. There follow in part 1 several essays focusing upon several prominent white women of the second half of the nineteenth century and the early twentieth century, an era in which such women were entering public life and therefore generating ample records for the use of researchers. Much research remains to be completed. But the Mississippi Women's History Project is pleased to offer as a beginning the compelling stories of these five notable women.

Felicité Girodeau played a major role in the development of the Catholic Church in Natchez, the center of antebellum settlement in Mississippi. The essay explores the intricacies of racial identity in the territorial period and the tightening of racial policies in the years leading up to the Civil War. Ironically, Girodeau, a free woman of color who became a slaveholder, so embodied the ideal of the southern lady that she was later revered as such by a member of the United Daughters of the Confederacy who was unaware of Girodeau's race.

Few were more affected by the war than Winnie Davis, the daughter of Varina and Jefferson Davis, the first couple of the Confederacy. Winnie, embraced by Lost Cause devotees who venerated the Confederate cause, was made into a cultural icon and became known as the "Daughter of the Confederacy." Significantly, she lived only a fraction of her life in the South, was educated abroad, developed an accent more German than southern, and fell in love with a Yankee. Yet her life was severely circumscribed by this role as symbol of ideal southern womanhood, which she cultivated and exploited while declining to embrace it in most aspects of her private life.

Nellie Nugent Somerville was a member of a wealthy and influential family that played a major role in shaping the institutions of Mississippi beginning in

the territorial period and continuing into the early twentieth century. Somerville became prominent in the emerging women's club movement, following a
path familiar to many middle- and upper-class women of the South in the late
nineteenth century as she moved from church organizations to civic groups to
the Woman's Christian Temperance Union (WCTU) and to the movement for
female enfranchisement. The social prominence of her family made it possible for Somerville to engage in a level of social activism contrary to prevailing
assumptions about woman's role and to play a pioneering role in such an unpopular reform as woman suffrage.

Belle Kearney, also from a wealthy Mississippi family, followed a similar trajectory of participation in women's voluntary organizations and became a professional lecturer for the WCTU before taking up the suffrage cause. Unlike
Somerville's family, the Kearneys were impoverished by the war, though they re-
tained their social standing. Both women were proud to be southern ladies while
seeking to expand woman's prerogatives and power, and both ran successfully
for higher office in Mississippi as soon as women were enfranchised. Both used
conservative arguments to advance a progressive cause and demanded equality
for white women but not for African Americans. Both women, born during the
Civil War, believed that the war had played a transformative role in the lives of
southern white women, jolting them out of the domestic sphere and into lives
of public service.

All of the above Mississippi women, including Girodeau, carved out a life
for themselves by pressing the limits of prevailing ideals about woman's sphere,
making use of these ideals to accomplish their goals even while refusing to be
totally constrained by them. They maneuvered within the complex matrix of
ideas about woman's nature and proper role to live the fullest lives they could
without bringing down the wrath of society. Indeed, in many respects they embraced conventional values and profited from them.

Pauline Van de Graaf Orr, on the other hand, offered a more direct challenge
to conventional thinking and public policies regulating women's lives in late-
nineteenth- and early-twentieth-century Mississippi. And she did so within the
fascinating social milieu of the amazing institution of higher education created
by the state for white women of Mississippi in 1884. Having enjoyed opportunities for education far superior to those enjoyed by most women of her era, Orr
brought these skills to bear as a pioneering member of the faculty at the Industrial Institute and College for the Education of White Girls. With the support
of an impressive group of students and alumnae, she fought for full support for
women's education of the highest quality. She believed that higher education
should radically change women's role and propel them into positions of leader-

ship and authority. Active in the woman suffrage movement in Mississippi, Orr served as an officer of the Mississippi Woman Suffrage Association, influencing countless numbers of young students and alumnae to embrace this cause. Not surprising, Orr did indeed attract the wrath of society, or at least of male leaders she defied. This did not, however, deter her from acting on her beliefs and touching many lives in Mississippi, including those of many of the women covered in part 2.

Felicité Girodeau

(1791–1860)

Racial and Religious Identity in Antebellum Natchez

EMILY CLARK

The parishioners of St. Mary's Cathedral in Natchez gathered on a November night in 1991 to celebrate the 275th anniversary of their congregation with a pageant dramatizing the church's history and the four individuals remembered as having made the greatest contribution to it. As the house lights went down and the stage lights came up, a woman appeared in the spotlight. "This is Felicité Girodeau," the narrator's voice intoned. "At St. Mary's, she is known most simply as 'Grandma.' " Grandma. Grand-mère. The mother of the parish.[1] We might allow ourselves to follow Felicité's pageant appearance through to its conclusion, but instead, let us begin again and see Grandma first as she was seen through the eyes of a child.

Laura Edwards set out with her mother one afternoon in antebellum Natchez to pay the kind of call that knit together the fabric of polite white society. Her mother took care that day to warn her daughter to "be very nice and precise," because their destination was special: the home of Felicité Girodeau. In a town that epitomized the wealth and gentility that lend the mythic plantation South a stubborn whiff of glamour, Madame Felicité represented a paragon of refinement for mother and daughter as they made their way to her gracious home.[2] Laura recalled Girodeau through the lens of memory more than sixty years after the end of the war that irrevocably altered the South of her childhood. With the passage of time, Girodeau became a touchstone for Laura, a synecdoche of the benighted rituals of politesse, honor, and elegance that were the essence of the way of life that had passed. This was no small matter, because the chief

4

feature of Laura's public identity in postbellum Natchez was her "special interest in the ideals of the old South." She expressed that identity through leadership of the local Daughters of the Confederacy and the Confederate Memorial Association, guided by Girodeau's antebellum example of genteel activism. Feted on her eightieth birthday as a "grand old lady of Natchez," Laura Edwards Monteith looked back on her childhood and recalled Madame Felicité with a phrase freighted with meaning for the survivors of the Old South's demise. Madame Felicité was, Laura pronounced in 1932, "a woman of culture."[3] She was also a woman of color.

This chapter bypasses the straightforward path of biography to engage two allied pursuits: a meditation on the historical forces that shape identity and memory, and the challenge of restoring to visibility a lost passage in Mississippi's history. Historical research reveals Felicité Girodeau to have been a free woman of color well aware of the identity ascribed to her by the official keepers of racial categories. Popular memory in Natchez presents a woman who appears to have "passed" as white in a culture where a strict "one drop rule" dictated that any person with a tiny fraction of "black blood" was a second-class citizen, regardless of skin color. Such instances of double identity are not unusual in the history of the Lower Mississippi Valley. Racial phenotyping as a basis for identity was ill adapted to a region marked by multigenerational racial mixing, making the assignment of race on the basis of appearance a slippery business.[4] But Girodeau's case is both more interesting and more important than most. She was evoked by Laura Edwards Monteith in a way that bound her to the project of memorializing the slave regime of the Old South, erasing or ignoring Girodeau's racial complexity in the process. In that erasure, a crucial episode in Mississippi history is lost. Girodeau's story breaks through the thick layers of Protestantism and Confederate pageantry that obscure the region's Catholic roots and its cultural and social indebtedness to people of African descent. In order to recover that story, we must unpick the threads of Girodeau's identity that were woven into popular memory and reweave them into a fabric of more complicated design.

We begin with the Girodeau of Laura Edwards Monteith's post-Confederate memory. "Mrs. Girodeau was either the daughter or a close relative of Governor Guion of Louisiana," Monteith averred to an interviewer in 1932. Conferring a fitting pedigree upon the woman of culture for whom she was supposed to have been "very nice and precise" during her childhood visits, Monteith established Girodeau's whiteness with a single stroke. In the imagination of the segregated South of the 1930s, the daughter of a governor could be nothing but a white woman. The interviewer duly added the information to the notes he was gathering to write a history of St. Mary's Parish, of which he was pastor. But when another elderly lady of Natchez remembered differently and told him that Girodeau's maiden name was Pomet, he turned to sources in his keeping to test the two stories. A manuscript recording an interview with Girodeau in 1859 and sacramental records in Natchez both contained information that gave "at least a suspicion of her belonging to the Pomet family." Although he knew that she had come to Natchez from New Orleans, the priest sought no further enlightenment on Girodeau's lineage.[5] Had he consulted the sacramental registers kept by his counterpart in the diocese downstream, he would have been able to confirm Pomet as Girodeau's maiden name. And he would have encountered evidence of much more.

The sacramental records of New Orleans note that the marriage of Felicité Pomet to Gabriel Girodeau took place on 3 July 1817 at St. Louis Cathedral before three witnesses. The ceremony was recorded in the marriage register reserved for whites, inscribed and signed with the customary care that was the hallmark of the cathedral's pastor, Antonio Sedella. Immediately below the original inscription, a correction was penned in another hand. "This matrimonial act of Gabriel Girodeau with Felicité Pomet was recorded by error, improperly entered in this register since the said contractors are people of color." Father Antonio signed the entry correcting his mistake.[6]

Here, in the first appearance of Felicité Girodeau in a surviving historical source, we encounter the elusive and ambiguous nature of her racial identity. If anyone in New Orleans was equipped to discern the boundary between black and white, it was Antonio Sedella. It was Sedella, who came to the city in 1781 as pastor of St. Louis Church, who combed through the ill-kept sacramental registers he found in the city to weed out and rectify careless slippages in the ascription of racial identity. His task was made necessary by a significant difference in practice between French and Spanish sacramental record keeping. French clergy maintained single registers for the two sacraments of baptism and marriage. Black or white, enslaved or free, all the baptisms and marriages of Louisiana inhabitants were inscribed in strict chronological order in a single book. Open the pages of a French register at random, and one is likely to encounter the record of the baptism of a French official's son sharing the page with the records of several slave baptisms, and that of a *fille de coleur libre,* or free person of color. The Spanish, by contrast, kept strictly segregated records. Only sacraments administered to those recognized by Spanish legal and social practice as white were to be recorded in the *libro de blancos,* the book of whites. All others, from newly arrived enslaved Africans to free quadroons of property and status, were consigned to the volume recording the *bautizados negros y mulatos,* the baptisms of blacks and mulattoes. When they took control of Louisiana from the French in 1763, the Spanish were appalled at the racial mélange presented in the French sacramental records. Sedella was zealous in his efforts to remediate this transgression of Spanish practice and soon effectively instituted the racially segregated Spanish system. He also became its vigilant enforcer.[7]

In the early days of Sedella's ministry, this was no easy task. New Orleanians of African descent understood quite well that the sacramental registers served as the principal record of status in the city. They recorded one's birth as legitimate, or not. They recorded parentage. It was in the sacramental records that white fathers often took the step of recognizing their mixed-race offspring, paving the way for inheritance and other advantages. And they recorded and revealed the composition of one's race with relentless precision. Under the Spanish, this became a crucial function of the registers, because certain admixtures were preferable to others.[8]

By the late eighteenth century, when Sedella presided over the sacramental registers of New Orleans, Spanish racial phenotypes were well delineated, if not codified. The label *negro* was applied to persons of unmixed African descent, *moreno* or *morena* to those of mixed race with less than half white ancestry, and *pardo* or *parda* to those of at least half white ancestry. A *grifo* in New Orleans was an individual born of a *pardo/a* and a *morena/o*, a *cuarterón* the offspring of a white and a *pardo/a*. *Mestizo* or *mestiza* was a label applied both to the offspring of a white and an *indio/a* and to that of a *negro* and an *indio/a*.[9] The least restrictive of these labels was *mestizo*, because Spain had outlawed Indian slavery in the late sixteenth century, and in 1769 Louisiana's Spanish colonial governor issued a decree explicitly extending the ban to the colony. If an enslaved person could prove mestizo status through the maternal line, it provided a route to freedom. Over time, descent from a mestiza in combination with several generations of white paternity could supply the basis for claiming the privilege of having one's baptism or marriage recorded in the register reserved for whites.[10] Sacramental records were an essential documentary source for racial status not only for those of mestizo descent, but for all New Orleanians who might want to demonstrate the racial purity that was essential to hold public office or enter the ranks of the clergy.[11] The city's sacramental records were deemed by all to be authoritative references on an individual's racial status.

Antonio Sedella was uniquely positioned to monitor the racial lineage of the city's free people of color because he baptized most of them and recorded the acts personally. Such ceremonies were often performed in the presence of the children's white fathers. One such man was Santiago Lemelle, who fathered three daughters by a *parda* named Jaquelina. One of those daughters,

Adelaida, entered a long-term liaison with a Frenchman, Bruno Girodeau. Six of the children she bore him were baptized at St. Louis Cathedral. All, beginning with Gabriel in 1788, were identified as people of color—although they could have been no more than *octoroon*, the term for a person of one-eighth African ancestry—and had their baptisms recorded in the register reserved for nonwhites.[12] When Gabriel Girodeau stood before Antonio Sedella in 1817, the priest should have been well aware of the groom's racial status from his own experience at the baptismal font. He had other clues as well. Two of the couple's three witnesses, Esteban Larieux and Rosalia Juan-Maria, were free people of color, both from large families who would likely have been as well known to Sedella as the Girodeau clan. While it was not uncommon for white people to act as witnesses at the weddings of free people of color in New Orleans, the opposite appears never to have been the case. By context, the Girodeau nuptials were a celebration of free black community and social ties.[13]

Perhaps Sedella's error can be attributed to his unfamiliarity with Felicité. She was not a New Orleanian, but had been born in 1791 in nearby West Florida, in what would later be known as Adams County, Mississippi.[14] Did Sedella look at Felicité and decide that she must be white, and in an absentminded moment assume that her husband was, too? Perhaps. He was, after all, an elderly man in 1817, who had been ministering to New Orleanians off and on for nearly forty years.[15]

Whatever the reason for the mistake, it was apparently corrected quickly. Many sacramental records bear corrective emendations, but these are usually written in tiny, cramped script in the margins or between the lines of the original entry. The correction of the Girodeau record follows the main entry and is written in freehand. It was made at some point after the initial entry, but before the next record was inscribed, perhaps as a consequence of something that Felicité and Gabriel did themselves. When people moved from one place to another, it was common to take certified copies of their marriage and baptismal records with them for both legal and religious purposes. This would have been especially true for free people of color, who might be asked to document their free status.[16] All of this suggests that when Felicité and Gabriel left New Orleans for Natchez shortly after their wedding, the error in their marriage record was caught and corrected. And it suggests that the official documentation they brought with them to Mississippi made clear the partial African ancestry of the couple. If it had been their intention to "pass" when they moved to Natchez shortly after their marriage, Felicité and Gabriel Girodeau would have had to do so without benefit of the sacramental evidence that most people used to establish their whiteness.

This convoluted probe of the Girodeau marriage record echoes the kinds of analyses pursued by some of the legendary custodians of vital records who attempted with manic resolve to preserve the boundaries of racial purity in the era of Jim Crow. Today, however, recovering racial genealogies serves a very different purpose. If history were to allow Felicité Girodeau to rest in peace with the identity of a white woman, the history of Catholicism in Natchez would be unnaturally bleached. It would remain a comfortable narrative of white achievement, the credit for its early years of success shared by male clergy and a genteel "woman of culture" revered in the untroubled memory of a stalwart member of the Daughters of the Confederacy. By "outing" Felicité Girodeau, we recover the central black contribution to the religious life of Natchez and draw attention more generally to the substantial role played by women of color in the development of Catholicism throughout the Lower Mississippi Valley.

Girodeau is not only a central figure in that historical process; she was among its first historians. In 1859, William Henry Elder, the new bishop of Natchez took down Girodeau's detailed account of the development of St. Mary's Parish, Natchez. In a narrative peppered with vivid characterization and attentive to the political and economic forces that bore upon the Church, Girodeau provided a methodical chronicle of Catholicism in antebellum Natchez. In so doing, she depicted the fragility of a religious institution caught in the shifting sands of territorial identity. Natchez became an American territory in 1798 and occupied a prominent perch on the uneasy border with Spanish Louisiana for the next five years. Dependent for decades on the intermittent ministry of French and Spanish clerics on the west bank of the Mississippi, Natchez relied in the opening years of the nineteenth century on the distant administration of America's first bishop, John Carroll of Baltimore.[17] With a few telling strokes, Girodeau sketched the marginality of the Natchez church at the turn of the nineteenth century and the provisional nature of life along the Mississippi before the arrival of the steamboat.

The first priest to cross Girodeau's field of historical vision made a brief appearance that was typical of clerical attentions paid the fledgling Natchez congregation. Despite the fleeting nature of the priest's ministry in Natchez, Girodeau captures this episode of church history with a combination of colorful detail and awareness of broader context that betrays a keen historical sensibility. A "tall thin man," Father Boudin loped into town from Baltimore in 1802, Girodeau recounted to her amanuensis. His feet barely touched the red earth of Natchez before world events called him to a larger stage. When Louisiana's retrocession to France was made public in 1803, the Ursuline nuns in New Orleans were terrified that they would meet the fate of their sisters in the homeland

and be disbanded or executed by the republican government. Half of them insisted on fleeing to Cuba as refugees, and the good Father Boudin was called upon to serve as escort. When Boudin returned to the banks of the Mississippi a few months later, the Stars and Stripes flew over New Orleans, and he was sent to pastor the flock across the river from Natchez, at Pointe Coupee, Louisiana. Before the good Catholics of Natchez could petition for his return to their orphaned congregation, he drowned in a Louisiana bayou, paddling a canoe on his way to visit the sick.[18]

Girodeau's sophisticated awareness of the larger political events of her day was remarkable for a woman at the turn of the nineteenth century. Her eye for colorful narrative detail enlivens a chronicle that might otherwise have lapsed into a dull catalog. She was also an astute observer of the personal qualities of the clerics who passed through Natchez, especially as they bore on their engagement with the town's mixed Creole and American Catholic community. Father Chandorat was dispatched from Bardstown, Kentucky, in 1819 to minister to the Natchez faithful. "He was rather high tempered and spoke bad English," Girodeau reported frankly. When several French members of his parish taunted him on this point, he "told them he could speak good French and preached a severe sermon in that language." Girodeau was equally fearless about passing judgment on poor decisions made by the Natchez congregation. An Irish priest named Kinderling offered to remain without salary after the church burned in 1832. His offer to stay in Natchez was declined, as was his offer of a four-hundred-dollar contribution to the parish. He went on to New Orleans where, Girodeau related pointedly, "The Irish built him a church. . . . He started the boys' asylum in New Orleans. He was very generous."[19]

The fire of 1832 inaugurated a particularly difficult period for the Natchez church, and Girodeau modulated her pronouncements on both the clergy and the congregation of this period. She was charitable in her assessment of the itinerant priests sent occasionally by Bishop Blanc of New Orleans to say mass in the city hall chambers located above the Market House. With such telling details as their willingness to sleep on sofas, hear confession in a closet, and say mass in a parlor, Girodeau sketched a benediction to their dedication. Such heroic clerics found a congregation lapsed in the proper observance of their faith but hungry for a return to the rubric of Catholic ritual, according to Girodeau. When a priest visited for ten days in the winter of 1839, he "brought a great many to communion—one man had not been to communion for fifty years, and another not since her first communion."[20]

During this period of intermittent pastoral care, Girodeau was clearly the key force preserving and sustaining the fragile fabric of the Natchez congregation. The priest who visited briefly that January heard confession in her closet, slept on her sofa, and said mass in her parlor. She took special interest in one particular aspect of his visit: his administration of communion to many who had lapsed in their sacramental observance. For Girodeau, the sacraments were the ligaments that bound the Church together and preserved it. They, and the priests, who alone had the power to confer them, form the focus of her story. Therein lies a central irony embedded in the chronicle of Natchez church history that Girodeau dictated to Bishop Elder.

The clergy are front and center in Girodeau's account. Each successive priest enjoys his moment in the spotlight and takes his place as a narrative building block. Yet, for many of the fifty-seven years over which Girodeau ranged in her recollections, there was no priest in residence in Natchez. Spain relinquished its claim to the Natchez District in favor of the United States in 1798, and three years later Spanish clergy were withdrawn, taking everything with them from vestments to communion vessels. Many Catholic residents appear to have left with them. Those who remained never enjoyed the services of a resident priest for more than a few months. Thirteen different priests passed through Natchez on brief tours of duty in the first four decades of the nineteenth century; for most of that time there were periods of up to six years with no priest.[21] Throughout this era, the survival of the Catholic community in Natchez depended on a mortar rendered all but invisible by Girodeau's pious account: the lay Catholics of Natchez.

The lay leadership that sustained Catholicism in Natchez did its work in both formal and informal ways. In 1818, seven men organized the Roman Catholic Society of Christians in the City of Natchez and Its Vicinity. This group of lay trustees managed the financial affairs of the parish and issued a succession of urgent petitions to the American Catholic hierarchy pleading for the assignment of a resident priest to Natchez. This formal organization tended the clerical and physical infrastructure of St. Mary's. It fell to an informal but no less vital arm of the laity to develop and maintain the essential foundation of the Natchez church: its congregation. This is the realm in which Felicité Girodeau made her most significant contribution to Natchez's Catholic community, acting in concert with a well-established pattern in the Lower Mississippi Valley that places women of African descent at the center of Catholicism's development.

A thriving congregation is fundamental to the success of any denomination. As a sacramentally based religion, Catholicism charts its membership not through attendance at services, but through the ritual of baptism. The baptism of an infant or an adult convert is thus an act of primary significance in church-building. It is also an enactment of the communal nature of Catholic piety.

Unlike baptism in certain Protestant denominations, Catholic baptism is not an individual act. The one who is baptized must be sponsored by godparents, who not only are expected to be devout Catholics themselves but are to take "lasting interest in their spiritual child, and to take good care that he leads a truly Christian life."[22]

Girodeau was a virtuoso godmother. She sponsored some thirty-two infants, children, and adults for baptism between 1836 and 1860. Her godchildren were drawn from every segment of Natchez's heterogeneous population: people of unmixed European descent, free people of color, and slaves. Her bondwomen, Betty, Alexandrine, and Anne, in what was perhaps an extension of her project, stood as godmothers to numerous enslaved children.[23] The prominence of people of African descent among Girodeau's godchildren is significant. Mississippi's population grew by leaps and bounds in the antebellum decades. Between 1820 and 1840 it quadrupled, and much of the increase was attributable to a dramatic growth in the slave population as American planters pushed westward into the state's fertile cotton country. People of African descent constituted a majority by 1840 and even in the urban space of Natchez made up a substantial proportion of the population.[24] The new black majority posed both an opportunity and a threat to the Catholic community. As the fastest-growing segment of the population, its participation was essential to the church's future. The addition of a significant proportion of the enslaved to Natchez's Catholic community would help secure its vitality. But the bondpeople pouring into Mississippi in the antebellum years also held the potential to foreclose that rosy future. Nearly all of them came from the upper South, where evangelical Protestantism had made substantial progress in conversion. When they arrived in Natchez, slaves who had embraced the Baptist or Methodist denomination were greeted by established biracial congregations with resident pastors and permanent buildings. Wooing them, and their unchurched brethren, to Catholicism would require no small effort.[25]

That effort could not have been placed in better hands than those of Felicité Girodeau. Godmothers, particularly when they sponsored adults, were the primary proselytizers for Catholicism among people of African descent during the colonial and early national periods in the Lower Mississippi Valley. Women of color, particularly free women of color, played an especially crucial role in church-building through this mechanism. When Girodeau took her place as sponsor at the baptismal font with an adult slave or held the infant of an English-speaking slave from the upper South in her arms, she stood in solidarity with several generations of other women of African descent who played an instrumental role in enlarging and sustaining the region's Catholic community.

The centrality of African and African American women's contribution to the growth of Catholicism in the Lower Mississippi Valley has emerged from recent research on early New Orleans. There, several factors combined over the course of the eighteenth century to encourage the participation of women of African descent in Catholicism. The presence of a female missionary endeavor, West African traditions favoring female religious leadership, the peculiar rhythms of the slave trade to colonial Louisiana, and the growth of a free black population all helped shape a prominent role for women of African descent in Catholicism in and around New Orleans.

A community of Ursuline nuns established a convent and school in New Orleans in 1727. The Ursulines were the first order of teaching sisters, a product of the French Catholic reformation of the seventeenth century. Growing to prominence on the heels of the late-sixteenth-century French Wars of Religion between Catholic and Protestant partisans, the Ursulines responded to France's desire to find a peaceful way to return the nation to universal Catholicism. They essentially mounted an internal missionary campaign with a rather radical strategy: educate girls—the future mothers of France—to be good Catholics and literate in order to ensure an orthodox Catholic future. A central feature of their project was to include all girls, not just the wealthy and socially prominent, in their educational dragnet.[26] This feature of their mission was to have signal consequences in Louisiana, where the girls they encountered included Indians and Africans, along with French inhabitants.

From the outset, the New Orleans Ursulines extended religious education to girls of all races at their free school. The impact of the relatively small band of nuns, averaging only six to ten sisters during their first forty years in Louisiana, was amplified by a group of laywomen who formed an association known as a confraternity. Calling itself the Children of Mary and growing to include eighty-five women and girls between 1730 and 1744, this confraternity took as its special mission the evangelizing of enslaved people. Although most of its members were white women, there were also a few women of color among the Children of Mary. Together with members of their families, the Children of Mary were extremely active as godparents to enslaved people.[27]

The historical record of these two female ministries, the Ursuline nuns and the Children of Mary, reveals that enslaved people were the object of substantial attention from pious women in the colony. Attention, however, does not necessarily produce conversion. In order to understand why Catholicism took root among people of African descent in and around New Orleans, it is essential to take into account factors that may have rendered enslaved people, particularly women, open to participation in Catholicism.

A tradition of female religious leadership in West Africa may have been one such factor. In Senegambia, the region of West Africa from which most of Louisiana's first generation of enslaved people came, religious observance and rites of induction generally followed a gendered division of labor and leadership. Women oversaw religious initiation for girls, men for boys, with each operating within their own sacred spaces. Senegambian women finding themselves in bondage in Louisiana may have recognized similarities with their own religious culture in the female sacred space of the Ursuline convent and in the rite of baptism encouraged by the laywomen and girls of the Children of Mary. Their initial attraction to Catholicism may well have been based on the culturally comfortable feature of a female ministry.[28]

Another influence on the growth of Catholicism among the enslaved was the unusual trajectory of the Louisiana slave trade. After 1744, no new shipments of enslaved people arrived in the colony from Africa for a period of over thirty years. This meant that traditional African religion could survive only through preservation among those already in Louisiana; it would not be revitalized by successive waves of newly enslaved Africans arriving with religious knowledge and ceremonial skill still fresh in their minds. Catholicism had a better chance of taking hold because competition from traditional African religion was suppressed during a long period of time, allowing a generation to be born and attain adulthood without the renewal of African religious influence.[29]

The transfer of Louisiana from France to Spain in 1763 also had a significant effect on the course of Catholicism among people of African descent. Under French law, emancipation was a complicated and difficult process that few slave owners undertook. Spanish slave law not only simplified manumission, requiring only a routine notarial act, but extended the right of self-purchase to all slaves. The result was a veritable explosion in the free black population of New Orleans. In 1771, free people of color in New Orleans numbered 97, constituting 3.1 percent of the total population and 7.3 percent of the nonwhite population. By 1791, free people of color numbered 862, 17 percent of the total population and one-third of the nonwhite population.[30]

Free people of color found in the church a venue for the expression of status and the creation of community. When they paid fees for weddings, funerals, and memorial masses, they demonstrated their financial success and free status in an easily recognizable way. Through networks of godparenting and witnessing at weddings of free blacks, they constituted and strengthened the fabric of the free black community. The church was thus a major institution of colonial society that was open to free blacks and provided them with certain social benefits. Some free men of color belonged to a special arm of the Spanish military, the free black militia, which gave them access to another major public institution. For most free black men, however, and for all free black women, the church was the only major public institution that allowed such extensive participation. Significantly, nearly two-thirds of the free people of color in New Orleans at the end of the eighteenth century were women, amplifying the importance of this institution for the free black female population.[31]

All of these factors combined to foster the development of a large, vital Afro-Catholic community in New Orleans that was dominated by women. Women of African descent were baptized in greater numbers than were men and appeared more frequently in leadership roles. For example, women were more likely than men to become frequent godparents. They were especially prominent in sponsoring adult enslaved Africans for baptism and so became crucial agents of creolization and socialization for the newly enslaved Africans who began to pour into Louisiana in the last three decades of the eighteenth century. In the early nineteenth century, they were prominent as godparents to enslaved people who came to Louisiana from the Anglophone, Protestant South.[32]

Among the religiously active women of African descent in late colonial and early national New Orleans, free women of color were especially conspicuous. They stood frequently as godmothers to free and enslaved men, women, and children of African descent. At least one of them sent her granddaughter to be educated at the elite boarding school of the Ursuline nuns at the turn of the nineteenth century. And one family produced a particularly distinguished lineage of religiously active women. An enslaved African woman named Nanette was evangelized shortly after her arrival in Louisiana, probably by the mistress of her household, who was a member of the Children of Mary. Nanette's great-great-great-granddaughter was a free woman of color, Henriette Delille. Delille founded a Catholic religious order for free women of color in antebellum New Orleans called the Sisters of the Holy Family.[33]

Although Felicité Girodeau was born outside of New Orleans, in Adams County, Mississippi, her religious activism makes the most sense when interpreted as part of the larger phenomenon of female Afro-Creole piety in the Lower Mississippi Valley. While there is no direct evidence linking her to Henriette Delille and other pious free women of color in New Orleans, it is clear that her social network was rooted in the larger community of free people of color that extended along the Gulf Coast and upriver from New Orleans. In her study of the free black Johnson family, Virginia Gould delineates the ties of blood and commerce that bound people of color in New Orleans and Natchez. Felicité's marriage to Gabriel Girodeau was only the most obvious and formal of the bonds that linked her to the city to the south of her home county. The appearance of her relatives as baptismal sponsors to free children of color in New Orleans reveals other strands in the web of relationships that bound her to the port city.[34] Such ties brought her into fellowship with the community of devout Afro-Creole women who, by the end of the eighteenth century, had assumed significant religious leadership in the New Orleans Catholic Church.

When we unpack Girodeau's racial identity we are able to enlarge our field of vision beyond the borders of New Orleans to other parts of the Gulf South and see the crucial role played by women of African descent in the development of one of the region's major social institutions. This is the prize that lies at the end of her tangled historical identity, but the exercise produces a sobering realization, as well. Girodeau's counterpart in New Orleans, Henriette Delille, survived her passage through historical memory with her racial identity intact.

When Girodeau crossed the state line into Mississippi after her wedding, she seems to have crossed the color line, as well. The year that Mississippi was admitted as a state, 1817, was also the last year that Girodeau was identified as a woman of color in the historical record. The only official historical records produced after that year that mention her race are the decennial U.S. censuses. In the 1830 census, three years after the death of her husband, she is named as the head of a household comprising one white man, three white women, three adult slaves, and no free people of color. Subsequent decennial censuses continue to identify her as a white woman. We cannot reconstruct the exchanges that occurred between Girodeau and the census taker, but the social and legal circumstances in antebellum Mississippi would have encouraged her complicity in the suppression of her African ancestry.

Within three years of Mississippi's admission to statehood, its laws began to constrain the lives of its free black population. In 1820, people of color were presumed to be slaves unless they could certify otherwise, and an elaborate certification and registration process was initiated. Emancipation was restricted so severely in the 1820s that it became impossible to achieve without a special act of the legislature. Laws limited the types of economic activities in which free people of color could engage and restricted their movement outside their localities. Free people of color were forbidden to move into Mississippi from other states, and after the Nat Turner Rebellion of 1831, a draconian law called for the forced out-migration of all free blacks between the ages of sixteen and fifty. Those remaining risked being enslaved. Formal exceptions could only be obtained for those with the financial means to obtain secured bonds and whose "good character and honest deportment" were vouched for by whites.[35] The tightening ligatures of Mississippi's race laws had a tangible impact on the free black community, whose population declined 33 percent, from 1,366 to 913, between 1840 and 1850.[36] In such a climate of racial oppression, Girodeau may well have purposefully orchestrated her racial passage from black to white.

With that passage, Girodeau's extraordinary story shrinks into the contours of the ordinary. The outlines of her life are commonplace for a southern woman of the slave-owning class who traversed the first half of the nineteenth century. She was born in the twilight of the colonial age, in 1791, and married at the age of twenty-six. She and her New Orleans–born groom took up residence in Natchez in the quiet years before the town blossomed in the wake of the cotton boom. Her husband, Gabriel, who was apparently also very light-skinned, made a good living as a goldsmith, and their prosperity enabled them to keep three slaves as domestic servants. When she was left a childless widow at the age of thirty-six, her religion, always important to her, became the focus of her life. She became, to her community, an exemplar of piety and graciousness. This life, punctuated with the markers of marriage, slave-ownership, religious devotion, and social grace, matches the idealized standard of antebellum southern white womanhood at every turn.[37]

Girodeau's role in constructing the historical racial identity that obscures the significance of her achievement is less interesting than the processes of memory and memorialization that constructed and reconstructed that identity in the years after her death. The ways that she has been publicly remembered expose the hazards of assuming a foundation of whiteness for the remembered virtues of the Old South. From the cultural fortress of the Jim Crow 1930s, Laura Edwards Monteith, stalwart Daughter of the Confederacy and "grand old lady of Natchez," venerated Girodeau as the southern epitome of graciousness, a "woman of culture." A keeper of the southern shrine, in the literal as well as the figurative sense, Monteith's memory revered Girodeau as a model of southern white womanhood. It fell to a churchman to memorialize her as a model slaveholder. Bishop Richard O. Gerow takes pains in his 1941 history of St. Mary's to point out that Girodeau treated her three bondwomen, Betty, Alexandrine, and Anne "kindly, and long before her death she made them free." Sealing Girodeau's reputation for posterity, Gerow noted that the three freed women "continued to live with her as before." Gerow called upon the memory of Girodeau to bear out the postbellum South's insistent Lost Cause mythology that the enslaved preferred the state of bondage under a good mistress to freedom. Her example is offered as proof of the virtuous face of the white slave-owning race.[38]

If presented with the revealing marriage record, would either of these memorializers have been able to adjust their memories to accommodate Girodeau's Afro-Creole identity? One suspects not. Memory is a product of the historical circumstances that mold it and is less susceptible to modification on the basis of a few circuitous Spanish phrases written in a church register than the rational among us like to think. Happily, the discovery of the critical passage occurred in another age, nearly thirty years after the events of Freedom Summer changed the hearts, minds, and memories of many Mississippians. When historian Charles Nolan sat down with the committee planning the 275th anniversary celebration of St. Mary's Parish of Natchez and told them that he had discovered that "Grandma" Felicité Girodeau was a free woman of color, "they didn't bat an eye."[39]

On stage, the actress playing Girodeau faces the pageant audience and says: "You see before you a white woman. I am not white, I am passing. I think there are those here who suspect the truth, but were too kind to say the words. When you write about the past, write the truth about me."[40]

NOTES

The author wishes to extend special thanks to Charles E. Nolan, Robert and Sarah Shumway, and Jeanne Gillespie, for their assistance with this chapter.

1. *Bless this House*, prod. and dir. Tommy Jackson, 24 November 1991, Archdiocese of New Orleans Archives, videocassette.

2. Laura Edwards Monteith, interview by Richard O. Gerow, 18 September 1932, photocopy, Archdiocese of New Orleans Archives; "Grand Old Lady of Natchez Given Honor by Friends," *Natchez Democrat*, 19 September 1933.

3. Monteith, interview.

4. Winthrop D. Jordan, *White over Black: American Attitudes toward the Negro, 1550–1812* (Chapel Hill: University of North Carolina Press, 1968), 165–78; Jennifer Michel Spear, " 'Whiteness and the Purity of Blood': Race, Sexuality, and Social Order in Colonial Louisiana" (Ph.D. diss., University of Minnesota, 1999), 36–37; Gwendolyn Midlo Hall, *Africans in Colonial Louisiana: The Development of Afro-Creole Culture in the Eighteenth Century* (Baton Rouge: Louisiana State University Press, 1992), 15, 128, 239–41, 258–60, 264–66.

5. Elizabeth Ann Reddy Carroll, interview by Richard O. Gerow, 18 September 1932, photocopy; William Henry Elder, "Copy of notes written Sept. 2d 1859 from the account given by Mad. Felicité Girodeau. Written originally in her presence by me," photocopy, Archdiocese of New Orleans Archives.

6. St. Louis Cathedral Marriages, 1806–1821, entry no. 675, 3 July 1817, Archdiocese of New Orleans Archives. Translation from Spanish by the author, with assistance from Jeanne Gillespie.

7. Roger Baudier, *The Catholic Church in Louisiana* (New Orleans: A. W. Hyatt, 1939), 209; St. Louis Cathedral Baptisms, 1731–1733; "Libro donde se asientan las partidas de baptismos de negros esclavos y mulatos que se han celebr[a]do en esta Iglesia parroquial de Sr. San Luis de la ciudad de la Nueva Orleans desde el día 1 de enero de 1777 que empezó hasta el año de 1781 que es el corrente," Archdiocese of New Orleans Archives.

8. Kimberly S. Hanger, *Bounded Lives, Bounded Places: Free Black Society in Colonial New Orleans, 1769–1803* (Durham: Duke University Press, 1997), 93–94, 204 n. 11; Spear, 225–46.

9. Hanger, 16.

10. Spear, 233.

11. Ibid., 195–224.

12. Earl C. Woods and Charles E. Nolan, *Sacramental Records of the Roman Catholic Church of the Archdiocese of New Orleans* (henceforth SRNO), 13 vols. (New Orleans, La.: Archdiocese of New Orleans, 1987–), 4:144; 5:186, 187; 6:135; 8:155.

13. SRNO, 7:174; 8:186, 198; 9:195; 10:245; 13:221, 248; 10:266.

14. Charles E. Nolan, *St. Mary's of Natchez: The History of a Southern Catholic Congregation, 1716–1988* (Natchez: St. Mary's Catholic Church, 1992), 97.

15. J. Edgar Bruns, "Annotating for Posterity: The Sacramental Records of Father Antonio de Sedella," in *Cross Crozier and Crucible: A Volume Celebrating the Bicentennial of a Catholic Diocese in Louisiana,* ed. Glenn R. Conrad (Lafayette, La.: Archdiocese of New Orleans, 1993), 350.

16. Virginia Meacham Gould, introduction to *Chained to the Rock of Adversity: To Be Free, Black, and Female in the Old South* (Athens: University of Georgia Press, 1998), xxix–xxx.

17. Nolan, 82–103.

18. Elder.

19. Ibid.

20. Ibid.

21. Nolan, 82–103.

22. James A. Coriden, Thomas J. Green, Donald E. Heintschel, eds., *The Code of Canon Law: A Text and Commentary* (New York: Paulist Press, 1985), canon 874; Stanislaus Woywod, *A Practical Commentary on the Code of Canon Law,* rev. ed. (New York: Callistus Smith, 1957), 393–95.

23. St. Mary's Sacramental Records, 1836–1862, transcription by Robert Shumway, Archdiocese of New Orleans Archives.

24. U.S. Census Office, *Fourth Census of the United States, 1820* (New York: N. Ross, 1990); U.S. Census Office, *Sixth Census of the United States* (New York: N. Ross, 1990); U.S. Census Office, *Census of the United States, Population Schedules, 1820, 1830, 1840, 1850, 1860, for Adams County, Mississippi* (Washington, D.C.: National Archives, 1946), microfilm.

25. Nolan, 93; Sylvia R. Frey and Betty Wood, *Come Shouting to Zion: African American Protestantism in the American South and British Caribbean to 1830* (Chapel Hill: University of North Carolina Press, 1998), 118–208.

26. Linda Lierheimer, "Female Eloquence and Maternal Ministry: The Apostolate of Ursuline Nuns in Seventeenth-Century France" (Ph.D. diss., Princeton University, 1994); Elizabeth Rapley, *The Dévotes: Women and Church in Seventeenth-Century France* (Montreal: McGill-Queen's University Press, 1990), 48–60.

27. Marie Madeleine Hachard, *The Letters of Marie Madeleine Hachard, 1727–28,* trans. Myldred Masson Costa (New Orleans: Laborde, 1974), 59; Emily Clark, " 'By All the Conduct of Their Lives: A Laywomen's Confraternity in New Orleans, 1730–1744," *William and Mary Quarterly,* 3d ser., 54 (October 1997): 769–94.

28. Emily Clark and Virginia Meacham Gould, "The Feminine Face of Afro-Catholicism in New Orleans, 1727–1852," *William and Mary Quarterly,* 3d ser., 59 (April 2002): 419–21.

29. Ibid., 422–23.

30. Hanger, 18, 22.

31. Clark and Gould, 428; Hanger, 109–35, 140–42.

32. Clark and Gould, 429–37, 445–48.

33. Ibid., 407–48; General Accounts, 1797–1812, Ursuline Convent of New Orleans Archives, 317, 321.

34. Nolan, 96; Gould, xix–lii.

35. Hutchinson's Code of Mississippi, 1798–1848, 514, 524, 533–34, 948; Revised Code of Laws of Mississippi, 1857, 255.

36. Gould, xxix.

37. Nolan, 97; St. Louis Cathedral Marriages, 1806–1821, entry no. 675, 3 July 1817; Anne Firor Scott, *The Southern Lady: From Pedestal to Politics, 1830–1930* (1970; reprint, Charlottesville: University of Virginia Press, 1995), 3–21.

38. R[ichard] O. Gerow, *Cradle Days of St. Mary's at Natchez* (Marrero, La.: Hope Haven Press, 1941), 68.

39. Charles E. Nolan, interview by author, 21 August 2001.

40. *Bless This House,* videocassette.

Winnie Davis

(1864–1898)

The Challenges of Daughterhood

CITA COOK

In the fall of 1898, white southerners who celebrated their version of the Confederacy as a Lost Cause experienced a new disappointment when they learned of the death of thirty-four-year-old Winnie Davis. In resolutions such as the following, her mourners explained why she meant so much to them.

> She was the embodiment of all that is great and noble in southern womanhood and her life made her an exemplar for the women of all nations, and the uncrowned queen in the hearts of her own people. Adopted as the daughter of the Confederacy by those old veterans who had carried the government upon their arms . . . she possessed in her early childhood the spirit of their heroism. She was our idol, our representative as the Confederacy went down without a stain upon its honor, so its daughter, "Winnie" Davis (1864–1898), yielded up her bountiful life, with a name that will live in song and story, fadeless and pure![1]

Confederate veterans like the author of this eulogy often wrote about the woman known as the "Daughter of the Confederacy" as if she had led a similar, if purer, life than that of many other daughters of Mississippi planters. Such eulogists, of course, recognized that she had received special honors granted to her as the youngest child of the only president of the Confederate States of America. They never discussed the significance of her having lived outside the United States for half of her first seventeen years and in the Northeast for most of the last decade of her short life. Winnie Davis was a child of Mississippi who spent only one-fourth of her thirty-four years in her official native state. She was a symbol of southern femininity who developed a German accent and a goal of earning enough money to live in Bar Harbor, Maine. While the veterans and her

WINNIE DAVIS
"Daughter of the Confederacy," circa 1898.
From the Papers of Jefferson Davis,
Rice University, Houston, Texas.

other admirers projected onto her the traits they most wanted to see in a public icon and her parents praised her for being a devoted daughter, Winnie Davis tried to please everyone without totally abdicating her interest in intellectual and social pleasures. She learned as well to identify with the top rank of a social hierarchy. She learned that she had to pay for the special privileges that came with her elite heritage by always submitting to the wills of her birth and her symbolic parents, even when she was old enough to move out of daughterhood into adult maturity.

The youngest child of Mississippians Jefferson and Varina Howell Davis, Varina Anne Jefferson Davis, usually known as Winnie, was born in the Confederate White House in Richmond, Virginia, on 27 June 1864. At that point the Davis family, including Maggie (nine years old), Jeff Jr. (seven), and Billie (two), was mourning not only the losses of the Confederate military but also the death of Joe, a five-year-old son who had fallen from a balcony at the executive mansion two months earlier. The Davis household and their public, in classic Victorian fashion, looked to the new baby to bring sunshine into their beleaguered lives. The end of the war only increased this need. After the capture of Jefferson Davis in May 1865, a newspaper reporter covering the family's arrival in Macon, Georgia, under an armed guard described the "sweet little girl" looking out "upon the vast throng of soldiers and citizens . . . with a pleasing smile."[2] Most statements about Winnie's first years rhapsodized about the young girl's happy, loving nature, but she was often sick and had a volatile temper. Whenever she did not get her way, she would butt people with her head, leading at least one child to complain that she was "too mean." Concerns about Winnie's "lack of self-control" would be scattered among her parents' words of praise for her for the next fifteen years or so. A proper daughter could not put her will ahead of others'.[3]

During the first several months of Jefferson Davis's two-year imprisonment in Virginia, his wife became so disturbed by United States soldiers taunting her sons that she sent her three oldest children to Montreal, Canada, with her mother and sister. Once she received permission to visit her husband, she took Winnie with her, confident that she was too young to understand her father's plight. In 1866, Varina, Winnie, an Irish American nanny, and two African American servants moved into the fort with the prisoner where, with the encouragement of both her mother and her father's supporters, Winnie's reputation as a source of joy continued to grow. During a whistle-stop in Oxford, Mississippi, Varina allowed a crowd to pass around the three-year-old child.[4] Various people, including a Sunday school class in Richmond, sent her dolls and other gifts. At "a little tea party" Varina held for "the little children in the Fort," her daughter "danced and entertained them to the best of her ability."

Winnie's recitations of poems such as "Cock Robin" convinced everyone that she was unusually precocious.[5] She was learning both how to please others and that she might expect special attention from them in return.

On 1 May 1867, Jefferson Davis received a writ of habeas corpus and permission to live in Montreal until the U.S. government decided in February 1869 not to try him for treason. During these months of uncertainty, he taught his children to pray daily for the suffering people of the South like the "many little children" who had "prayed every night" for his safety and release, a lesson that could add to Winnie's sense that she was a member of a royal family.[6] In August 1868, the family went to England, where they remained for several years. Trips to British historical sites and tales tinged by the Irish Catholic sympathies of her nanny stimulated Winnie, when she was almost five, to hate "that nasty old hypocrite Henry the Eighth" and "that bloody old dreadful Elizabeth who killed the blessed saintly queen Mary of the Scotch," a displaced ruler like her father.[7] Jefferson Davis had not yet regained ownership of his Mississippi plantations, so he returned to America alone in the fall of 1869 to try his luck in Memphis as the president of a life insurance company. He reminded Winnie that while he was preparing a home for them she was "to make [her] Mother happy and to keep her amused."[8]

As Winnie grew from six to twelve, the Davis family lived in Memphis in small rented houses that Jefferson Davis admitted did not live up to "the grand expectations" of his daughters and probably also of his wife. The insurance company did not last, and none of his other attempts at earning money were successful. Economic uncertainties combined with political disappointments gave Winnie's life a bittersweet aura of loss that tended to displace any awareness of how privileged the family was in comparison to most southerners, white as well as black. Although Winnie followed her mother's lead in constantly "torment[ing] their absence from England," the six years in Memphis were the one period in her life when she lived much as other southern white girls of her class. She attended a school across the street from their house and made occasional visits to relatives in Mississippi.[9]

One of Winnie's Memphis playmates later recalled how they had named individual oaks for southern generals and fought over who got to play under "Robert E. Lee." After Jefferson Davis read Scott's "Lady of the Lake" to them, they named their favorite stick horse Roderick Dhu for the hero of the epic poem, but they also imagined themselves to be Miss Betty Vance, a well-known belle in the region. In a picture taken when Winnie was about eight, she is dressed to look like an eighteenth-century aristocratic woman, complete with a tall wig.[10]

One of her lessons in being a southern lady was how to greet guests properly. At nine, Winnie decided that "it was 'not such a very easy thing to receive,' " but her mother heard her say to a man who had taken her to a benefit performance, "Farewell Sir I am indebted to you for very much pleasure and hope I have not troubled you in return."[11] For Winnie, formulas of politeness were replacing childish recitations as the most effective methods for charming adults.

However well Winnie adapted to the life of southern girlhood in Memphis, she and her mother became ill so often there that Jefferson Davis took them back to Europe in 1876 in the hope that they would "grow strong and active in England, Scotland, and France." Disillusioned with education in America, the Davises enrolled their twelve-year-old daughter in the Friedlander Institute, a Protestant girls' school in Carlsruhe, Germany. In one letter after another, they stressed their conviction that only at such a school would she develop the "self-control" and "systematic methods" of studying that they believed she needed.[12] When Jefferson Davis moved to the Mississippi coast, Varina wrote him from England, "the place where you desire to live seems to render an education of the higher sort impossible."[13] They therefore left Winnie in Germany for five years.

As an adult, Winnie would write an article criticizing European education for American girls because it alienated them from their own culture, but the Friedlander sisters apparently molded her in much the way her parents wished them to. Two years after Winnie's arrival in Germany, her mother was impressed with how well she was "learning to live with people and to obey strictly & without questioning authority." She added that the "nervously irritable dreamy child" had turned into "an active hearty little gay girl."[14] Winnie also became accomplished in German, French, art, and music and developed an admiration for European elite society. On several occasions she wrote with great excitement about seeing the Grand Duchess Luise of Baden, the patron of her school, at a concert or in a procession. She thought her daughter, Princess Victoria, who was about her age, "looked good natured." Some Europeans may have encouraged her to identify with the princess further by equating Jefferson Davis with royal and aristocratic figures. When Winnie was about to return to America, the German Minister-Resident in Mexico wrote a poem in German for her in which he encouraged her to hold her name high, since she would never travel incognito. The final line of each stanza was "Noblesse oblige!"[15]

Before leaving Europe in 1881, Winnie spent a few months in Paris working on her music and "Parisian graces" under the guidance of Miss Emily Mason, an old friend of her parents. According to Mason, Winnie's greatest desire was to prepare for life in America by learning "all that happened to [her] parents just after the war" and the songs her father loved most. She committed herself to making him happy and adapting to a society that was somewhat foreign to her. Even her accent was more German than southern. At Beauvoir, the new family home on the Mississippi Gulf Coast, she read to her father and took walks with him, but after making her social debut at Mardi Gras in 1882, she also socialized frequently in New Orleans and elsewhere.[16] When she requested permission to extend a visit in a nearby community, her father agreed because "it would be very dull for her here with me alone." A few years later she complained of the "strange sleepy atmosphere" of the Gulf Coast where "the gayety" was "of the mildest description." As she moved into her twenties, Winnie's choices of pleasure were understandably different from those of a man in his mid-seventies.

For almost five years, Winnie was relatively free from public attention, but her lessons in symbolic daughterhood continued. People wishing to pay court to her father often showed up at Beauvoir with no previous notice, requiring Winnie, no matter how "neuralgic" she felt, to put the hostess skills she had learned as a child into practice, particularly when her mother was visiting her married daughter in Memphis. When General Jubal A. Early asked her to go to Virginia in 1883 for the unveiling of a statue honoring Robert E. Lee, her mother responded that Winnie needed to stay home "to get over the New Orleans gaieties" she had been enjoying. Early then asked her father if "Miss Winnie" would make "by her own hands" two flower wreaths "to be placed in the tombs of Generals Lee and Jackson as a tribute of your family to the merits of our great leaders." His requests reflected the growing practice of highlighting the symbolic presence and actions of girls and virginal young women in ceremonies honoring the Lost Cause of the Confederacy. Winnie sent "two little battle flags and two bay wreaths" and a modest apology that they were not grander.[17] She thanked General Bradley T. Johnson for a ribbon badge from the Association of the Army of Northern Virginia in a gracious fashion guaranteed to please veterans:

> Born in Richmond in our darkest days, when the very name of Gen Johnson's Maryland Line gave confidence to the helpless noncombatants, it is a great pleasure to me to know that I have ever so small a place in the memories of the gallant men whose courage patriotism and endurance have become fireside traditions on both continents.[18]

In the spring of 1886 Jefferson Davis returned temporarily to public life when asked to speak at several Lost Cause events in Alabama and Georgia. He took his twenty-one-year-old daughter with him, introducing Winnie to a public acclaim for both of them that was (except for the rebel yell) similar to that offered to the nobility she had observed in Europe. When her father was too ill to appear at some of the whistle-stops the train made, Winnie came out in his place and smiled. Whatever she was thinking, she apparently projected the perfect blend of warmth, modesty, and regal distance. At West Point, Georgia, General John B. Gordon, a candidate for the governorship of Georgia, introduced her as "*the* Daughter of the Confederacy." The crowd reacted with such enthusiasm that the politician and reporters repeated the phrase at every opportunity. They honored Winnie as the representative of their old commander but also as a feminine symbol, akin to Lady Liberty, that they could mold according to their individual beliefs. Whereas Jefferson and Varina Davis had occasionally upset people, an iconic Daughter of the Confederacy could do no wrong.

Jefferson Davis was evidently not opposed to the new attention his daughter received. In a speech in Macon, Georgia, he asked Winnie to come forward and, with his arm around her, proclaimed, "This is my daughter, the child of the Confederacy. . . . She exults in the fact that she was born in the southern Confederacy." The two of them then "reverently" kissed an old battle flag.[19] Possibly following his lead, some people at first spoke of "The Child of the Confederacy," but General Gordon's title won out. The more journalists and speakers praised the charm and modesty of the Daughter of the Confederacy, the more her fame spread to all ages. The *Atlanta Constitution* and a patent medicine company were among those who distributed copies of her picture, and veterans increasingly wore buttons and badges honoring her. In 1893, when a four-year-old girl first saw her baby sister, she exclaimed, "Oh, Mama, can we name her Winnie Davis?"[20] Over the years, many parents did just that and wrote Winnie about her new namesakes.

Whenever Winnie appeared at a Lost Cause celebration, she divided her time between truly public appearances before people of all ages and classes and more private social functions similar to the parties she enjoyed in New Orleans. Physical descriptions tended to emphasize her beauty as coming more from the loveliness of her smile than from her looks, although they also praised her "willowy, graceful form," olive skin, hazel eyes, black hair, and "patrician" face. She had a sharp wit and enjoyed intellectual debate but always supported the basic tenets of the Lost Cause when in public. She reacted to a stranger's comment about how young she had been during "the rebellion" by saying, "I know of no rebellion, but I know all about the war between sovereign states." When the Lee Camp of Confederate Veterans in Richmond made her an honorary member, Dr. J. William Jones was pleased to discover that "she was a typical southern woman of the old school," so opposed to women speaking in public that she asked him to read for her a statement assuring the veterans that their fight had been honorable.[21]

With people she related to as peers, however, Winnie sometimes expressed more independent political opinions. She wrote one male friend, for example, that she hoped to see him in person so she might "discuss the franchise question better than is possible by letter." [22] Her mother complained that whenever she tried to urge her daughter "to rearrange some half worn dress," Winnie would change the subject to "the woes of the Irish, the labor question, or some system of philosophy which she has been studying with intense interest." [23] The lessons in "systematic" study in Germany had had unintended consequences.

About six months after Winnie was first proclaimed the Daughter of the Confederacy, she visited various family friends in New York state, thus making her debut in northern society. Some of the social elite were not ready to greet the daughter of the commander-in-chief of the military they had once fought, but most, including society columnists, were converted by her genial personality and proper femininity. [24] While in Syracuse, Winnie Davis met and fell in love with a young patent lawyer named Alfred Wilkinson, whom she called Fred. She kept the relationship a secret for almost two years, not only because Fred was a northerner but also because his maternal grandfather was abolitionist leader Samuel May. Winnie was so anxious about what her parents might feel about the match that, by the fall of 1888, she had become "a shadow of her former self, thin to attenuation," with "dinner & breakfast sometimes both going untasted." She was also suffering from a bruised bone in her foot, the result of an accident while dancing at Bar Harbor, Maine, possibly with Fred. [25]

In spite of her various maladies, Winnie's public life did not come to a halt. In May 1888 she was a last-minute replacement for her father at the laying of the cornerstone of a Confederate monument in Jackson, Mississippi. Determined to wear all of the badges that different veterans' groups had bestowed upon her, she asked her mother how to put on one "precious old soldier's badge" without marking her dress. According to a newspaper report of the ceremony, "thousands of Mississippi's great and near-great, people in all walks of life, proudly shook hands with Winnie Davis, the South's most beloved woman." When Governor Robert Lowry, "in behalf of the ladies of Jackson, presented her with a diamond ring with a star resting on a crescent," she charmed the crowd by announcing that the visit would "be a 'bright particular star' in her memory." That year she also transformed papers she had presented at a New Orleans literary society into two published works—"Serpent Myths," in the *North American Review* and a booklet on Irish patriot Robert Emmet titled *An Irish Knight of the Nineteenth Century,* which some interpreted as an allusion to her father as an equally noble martyr. [26]

After Winnie returned to Mississippi from another trip to the Northeast,

Fred followed to ask her parents for permission to marry her. Varina first told Fred that they could never allow a "union with a yankee." Winnie agreed to honor her parents' wishes but declared that she could never love anyone else. Varina questioned Fred closely about his financial situation and warned him that Winnie did not know how to "sew or economize." Unlike other southern women, the daughter of Jefferson Davis could not be expected to succumb to a total loss of class privileges. Encouraged by reassurances of his solvency, Varina eventually decided that Fred was a "refined well born yankee, full of energy, spirit, and love" for Winnie and that it would be wrong to ask her daughter to sacrifice any more to the memory of the Confederacy. When she suggested this to her husband, he answered, "Death would be preferable. I will never consent." But after getting to know Fred better, he allowed Winnie to hope that they might marry someday. She agreed to keep the engagement secret, but one Mississippi neighbor later reported that she had rushed, with great pride, to give them the good news.[27] Enough information leaked out to stimulate some critical letters. In response to the controversy, Winnie's chronic physical and emotional ailments increased so markedly that she went to Europe in the fall of 1889 with the wife of the newspaper publisher Joseph Pulitzer to try to calm her nerves.

In December 1889, two months after Winnie's departure, Jefferson Davis became extremely ill but did not allow Varina to inform their daughters how serious his situation was. The day he died, Winnie wrote him a letter from Paris revealing the strength of her attachment to her father.

> I think of you all the time Dearest darling Father, when as now, I want to tell you how much I love you I grow bewildered. . . . When I am away from you I can only think, and think, and love you for your goodness and tenderness, with which you covered me as with a cloak, all through my little childhood, screening my faults and answering my unreasonable questions with always an honest reply, the rarest thing given to a child in the world.[28]

The news of his death overwhelmed Winnie so much that she had a nervous breakdown. Varina asked Fred to travel to Europe to help her recover; he reported back that although Winnie was doing better, she would need six months or a year to return to normal. He explained that "the least little thing" could make her believe he was "trying to deceive her," but she longed "all the time to have her friends love her."[29] Fred may have alienated his prospective mother-in-law when he asserted firmly where he thought Winnie should be. Fred was apparently another person ready to treat Winnie like a daughter, at least while she was in emotional distress.

After refusing to discuss marriage for some months, Winnie finally consented to renewing their engagement. Her mother began notifying friends in March 1890, stressing that Jefferson Davis had approved of the match out of recognition that Wilkinson had been only a little boy during the war and had long been a confirmed states' rights Democrat. Formal announcements followed in April in newspapers across the country.[30]

By the summer of 1890 Wilkinson and the Davis family were receiving letters opposing the marriage of the Daughter of the Confederacy with a Yankee. When Varina sent one to her friend John Gordon, he advised her not to worry because, while at a Confederate reunion in Chattanooga, Tennessee, he had heard no "unkind criticism."[31] However, one letter from a man claiming to have been a colonel under Robert E. Lee indicates how important Winnie's symbolic role had become for some.

> The very sleeping dead southern soldiers would rise from their graves, and hustle you back to Yankeedom ere they would see the daughter of Jefferson Davis ruined, and shame-covered forever, by marrying one whose desire in marrying her is to get a southern woman—preferring such an one with warm feelings to the Salamander-like girl of Yankeedom. No, Sir, a thousand balls would be shot into your Negro-loving heart ere we would permit such an humiliating outrage consummated in our own Southland—and even should Miss Winnie whom we so deeply love as infinitely purer than any Yankee woman on earth, consent to go North, then we will bind ourselves together to lay you in the dust.[32]

To the extent that the veterans considered Winnie Davis special because she carried the blood of her father, they would not be able to forgive Wilkinson for being the descendant of a northern radical. A symbol, apparently, could only marry another symbol and, in this case, some felt she had chosen the wrong one. The angry letters had to have been disturbing to the couple, but they also heard from supporters of the marriage and began making plans for a wedding in June 1891, after a suitable period of mourning for Winnie's father.[33]

Lost Cause advocates have tended to proclaim that the marriage was called off so that Winnie Davis could honor the South and keep her father's name.[34] The actual end to the engagement, however, developed in reaction to financial problems that persisted after the failure of Fred's father's bank in the mid-1880s and a fire that burned his family home to the ground in August of 1890, killing a servant and almost killing Fred and a brother. Fred may have been at least partially responsible for the fire because he had left some extremely flammable benzene in the basement. A newspaper also reported that a southern gentleman had questioned some leading men in Syracuse about the financial status of Fred and the Wilkinson family.[35]

In the early fall of 1890, Varina questioned Fred on the veracity of earlier statements he had made about his ability to support either his mother or Winnie and his judgment in the use of the benzene "in such quantities." Fred, in turn, seemed surprised that Winnie did not have enough money "to be self-sustaining." Winnie met with him briefly, but the main interaction seems to have been between Fred and Varina. Winnie was not prepared to put her love for Fred and her opportunity to have a life beyond daughterhood ahead of her loyalty to her mother. Whatever the exact sequence of events that day, an article in the *New York Times* in early October declared that the engagement had been called off.[36] It suggested that money was probably the primary cause, but Winnie's poor health was generally the reason given in southern newspapers. Although Lost Cause emotions had strained the nerves of both Winnie Davis and Alfred Wilkinson, they probably would have married if they had had enough money and mutual trust.

Neither Winnie nor Fred ever became engaged again, but she led an active social life after she and her mother moved to New York City where they could enjoy cooler weather, closer access to publishers, relief from the expenses of welcoming pilgrims to Beauvoir, and the society that both of them preferred. While some people in Mississippi were openly critical of Varina Davis for leaving her native state, there is no record of any of Winnie's admirers expressing disapproval of her for not remaining in the South. Shortly after the breakup with Fred, she turned down a request that she represent Mississippi at the World's Fair because she feared becoming "at once the source, and victim of contention," but she soon resurfaced at Lost Cause events.[37] For the last eight years of her life, Winnie divided her time between attending Confederate commemorations in the South, caring for her mother's physical and emotional needs, trying to earn money by publishing articles and books, and enjoying the theater and parties. There are no records of her participating in any charitable functions, even in a symbolic role, and she apparently did not know the growing cadre of female progressive activists in New York such as Lillian Wald. Her sense of noblesse oblige extended only to the men who had served under her father.

In 1893 Winnie, along with her sister, accompanied her father's body as it was moved from New Orleans to be reinterred in Hollywood Cemetery in Richmond. Newspapers commented on how taxing the trip was for her but also on how gracious she remained when greeted by the people who came to see her train pass even before it had reached New Orleans. She later commented that the "great crowds" who had thrown flowers on the track had made the trip "a progress of a conqueror, more than the burial of a man who had failed." In 1895 she was the main honoree at Confederate Reunion ceremonies held in the new Winnie Davis Auditorium in Houston, Texas.[38] She did not, however, always have to go South to appear as the Daughter of the Confederacy. In spite of their genteel poverty, her mother welcomed supporters to what became a Lost Cause salon in her hotel suite and the New York Southern Society always gave both women a standing ovation when they arrived at their dinners. Although Winnie reigned as Queen of Comus in the 1892 New Orleans Mardi Gras, most of her private socializing was in the North. She wrote a friend, for example, that after a "most beautiful time" at the resort at Tuxedo, New York, she had found it hard to return to New Orleans "even with a dinner party at Delmonico's as an inducement." Her address book had many more New York than southern addresses.[39]

Winnie took seriously her responsibility to support her mother financially as well as emotionally although she never succeeded in making them totally independent of gifts from relatives and close friends. She was disappointed when they had to settle for summering at "some cheap place," explaining to a friend that "patriotism does not pay very well anywhere, and we belong to a family who 'have done the State some service.' " She then added that when "her ship" came in, she wanted, above all, to have a house at Bar Harbor, Maine, where she had visited wealthy friends like Joseph and Kate Pulitzer and Burton and Constance Harrison.[40] Jefferson Davis had left some of his property to Winnie, so she had to handle some business matters by mail. She wrote a levee commissioner that she could not "spare out of my narrow means the amount required to recoup my lessee" for the expense of draining land inundated because of levee work, and she asked him to make sure that the parish authorities settled the matter as he had promised her father that he would do.[41]

Both Winnie and her mother depended, in part, on retainers they received from their friend Joseph Pulitzer's *New York World*. Some of her articles, such as a critical review in *Belford Magazine* in 1891 of *The Prototype of Hamlet* by William Preston Johnston, reflected her bluestocking interest in intellectual debate; others were similar to those written by many descendants of southern planters ready to believe the best about an allegedly paternalistic Old South. "The Ante-Bellum Southern Woman," relying on her mother's version of the past, described the typical mistress of "the great river properties before the war" as a busy household manager whose "gentle and sincere piety" made her "the best model for the half-civilized souls entrusted to her care." She spent so much time with "her sable dependents" that she, more than any other white people, was able to "penetrate the interesting but bewildering tangle of 'tergiver-sations' which the plantation negro calls his thoughts." In "Home Life of Jeffer-son Davis," she praised her father for having been so "tender and considerate" to children, animals, and "the negroes, who would appeal to him from the over-seer with the assured confidence of children, relying on the loving partisanship of a father."[42] She never drew the parallel between the poor Irish nationalists with whom she identified and southern African Americans, both groups being denied basic rights, nor did she question the existence of a social hierarchy that distinguished between elite and nonelite white people.

Winnie wrote two novels that received fair reviews but did not lead to the fi-nancial rewards she had dreamed of. Neither took place in the South. *The Veiled Doctor,* based on a story her mother had told her about the failed marriage many years earlier of a Pennsylvania doctor and a self-centered beauty, appeared in 1895. In Winnie's often-preachy version, Isabel (as in "is a belle"), in a manner similar to some Jane Austen characters, turned to officers in local barracks to escape the boredom of life in a backwater town until she realized too late that she wanted her husband's love. Considering herself a professional author, Winnie founded a literary club, the Little Sisters of the Quill, only for women who had already published a book.[43] She spent two years researching Chinese society so she might write a novel about life in Hong Kong and published an article on Chinese money. She, nevertheless, kept the characters in her next book on a ship cruising the Asian seas rather than letting them land where she would have to describe a society she had never observed in person. This posthumous novel, *A Romance of Summer Seas,* which some consider her best work, revealed the tensions that shipboard gossip could cause.[44]

Throughout her life, Winnie Davis, like both her parents, had suffered from various physical and emotional ailments, but her bouts with "nervous pros-tration" and "rheumatic gout" seemed more serious by 1895. The Lost Cause events she attended in the South invariably took a toll on her body and nerves.[45] She discovered the joy of bicycle riding in 1896 only to be crippled for an ex-tended period by an accident.[46] In 1898, although Winnie begged to stay with her mother, Varina persuaded her to spend several months in Egypt and Eu-rope with the Joseph Pulitzers, assuming, like most people in the nineteenth century, that travel had a healing effect. Winnie returned in time to participate in a Confederate Reunion in Atlanta but told her mother that she "had a strong foreboding that she would not come back alive." While riding in a carriage in an Atlanta storm, she began to feel ill with "a cold in her stomach," which pro-gressed into severe gastritis, possibly worsened by the existence of malaria in her system. She returned to her mother in Narragansett Pier, Rhode Island, where she became steadily weaker until she died on 18 September 1898.[47] The official cause of death was recorded as "malarial gastritis."

The Lost Cause community immediately mobilized for what may have been the largest funeral for any American female up to that time. Both United States and Confederate veterans volunteered to escort her body to Richmond. After a crowded service in St. Paul's Episcopal Church in Richmond, the body traveled to Hollywood Cemetery in front of a mile-long procession; thousands of mourners lined the streets. As the sun set on 23 September 1898, Winnie Davis, the Daughter of the Confederacy, was buried next to her father with full military honors. Newspaper magnate and long-time benefactor of the Davises, Joseph Pulitzer, paid for many of the funeral expenses.[48]

In the days and weeks following the death, mourners across the nation expressed their sorrow in a variety of ways. Chapters of the United Confederate Veterans and the United Daughters of the Confederacy organized memorial services and wore mourning badges for a month. The flag flew at half-mast over the Mississippi capitol and at many other locations. Within about a year, a seven-foot-tall marble statue entitled *The Angel of Grief* stood over her grave.[49] Stained glass windows honoring her were placed in the churches she had attended in Biloxi, Mississippi, and Narragansett Pier, Rhode Island.

The hundreds of paeans for the dead Daughter of the Confederacy that Varina Davis received indicate that Winnie Davis, in her allegedly perfect femininity, had become a female counterpoint to the idealized Robert E. Lee. Some Texas veterans resolved, for example, that she had "a spirit that made her the model of every woman and the uncrowned queen of her southern home." At least two groups of veterans stated that they looked to a portrait of her to inspire them "to better deeds and purer lives."[50] On the surface, the life of Winnie Davis had been different in many ways from that of most southern women. The veterans who encouraged their daughters and granddaughters to emulate her did not want them to leave the South or, even when they praised Winnie's literary efforts, to put most of their energy into becoming published intellectuals. On the other hand, Winnie did behave like their image of a proper female when she was reluctant to rebel directly against any of the people who considered her their daughter. She, like many other southern women, praised the paternalistic males in her life for being knightly protectors while quietly trying to support herself by publishing works in which the heroines focused on relationships with men rather than on learning how to be independent.

The limits on the financial capital available to the Jefferson Davis family led them to rely more openly on the symbolic capital that came with their celebrity status as a means to economic and social security.[51] Following a similar path to that of Jefferson Davis when he gave up on his career in business to write his memoirs, when Varina and Winnie accepted a retainer from the *New York World* and when Winnie published novels that received more attention because of her name, they were seeking both to spread their ideals and to transform their fame into material wealth. Winnie was sincerely moved by the veterans' adoration of her and their respect for her father. She wanted to honor them, but if she had not periodically replenished her symbolic capital by making sometimes taxing public appearances as the Daughter of the Confederacy, she would have become simply another struggling daughter of a planter politician unable to adapt to the ways of the New South. If she had been willing to seek a blood and money marriage with a wealthy southerner or northerner, she might have been more physically secure. If she had decided to go against her mother by marrying Alfred Wilkinson when he was still at the start of his career as a lawyer, she might have been more emotionally fulfilled. Instead, she remained torn between her commitment to being a devoted daughter to her parents and to the men who had served under her father and her desire to be an intellectual able to enjoy some of the pleasures of northeastern society. Mississippi and the South were not yet ready to encourage their white daughters to become mature adults able to move beyond the limitations and the protection of daughterhood.

NOTES

1. Resolution, Pat Cleburne Camp, no. 222, United Confederate Veterans, Waco, Texas, 7 October 1898, Eleanor S. Brockenbrough Library, Museum of the Confederacy, Richmond, Va.

2. *Macon Telegraph*, 14 May 1865, clipping in an anonymous scrapbook, 1885–1896, Duke University Library, Durham, N.C.

3. Varina Davis to Jefferson Davis, 23 October 1865, 7 November 1865, Jefferson Davis Papers, Amelia Gayle Gorgas Library (henceforth ALA), University of Alabama, Tuscaloosa.

4. Ishbel Ross, *First Lady of the South: The Life of Mrs. Jefferson Davis* (New York: Harper and Brothers, 1958), 260; Bell Wiley, *Confederate Women* (Westport, Conn.: Greenwood Press, 1975), 125; Jeanette Blount, "The Littlest Rebel and Recollections of the Days That Were," clipping from an unnamed newspaper or magazine, n.d., Jefferson Davis Papers, Mississippi Department of Archives and History (henceforth MDAH), Jackson.

5. Varina Davis to Maggie Davis, 15 February 1867; Varina Davis to Mary Stamps, 17 February 1867, Jefferson Davis Papers, ALA; Varina Davis to Burton Harrison, 8 January 1867, Jefferson Davis Papers, Library of Congress (henceforth LC), Washington, D.C.

6. Jefferson Davis to his children, 15 February 1868, Jefferson Davis and Family Papers, MDAH.

7. Varina Davis to Lise Mitchell, 20 April 1869, typescript, Jefferson Davis Papers, Tilton Memorial, Tulane University, New Orleans, La.

8. Jefferson Davis to Winnie Davis, 1 June 1870, Jefferson Davis Papers, ALA.

9. Jefferson Davis to Pollie [Margaret] Davis, 26 October 1871, Jefferson Davis Papers, Transylvania University, Lexington, Ky.; Jefferson Davis to Mrs. Blandy, 6 August 1872, typescript, Massachusetts Historical Society, Boston; Jefferson Davis to Mollie Stamps, 28 May 1872, typescript, Mary Stamps Papers, Southern Historical Collection (henceforth SHC), Chapel Hill, N.C.

10. Blount; "Death of the Daughter of the Confederacy," clipping in Winnie Davis subject file, MDAH.

11. Varina Davis to Jefferson Davis, 1 January 1874, 8 March 1874, Jefferson Davis Papers, ALA.

12. Jefferson Davis to Maggie Davis Hayes, 4 April 1876, Jefferson Davis Papers, Transylvania University; Jefferson Davis to Winnie Davis, 21 September 1876, 17 March 1877, 17 October 1877; Varina Davis to Jefferson Davis, 18 February 1877, 9 September 1877; Varina Davis to Winnie Davis, 27 June 1880, Jefferson Davis Papers, ALA.

13. Varina Davis to Jefferson Davis, 2 August 1877, Jefferson Davis Papers, Transylvania University.

14. Varina Anne Davis, "The American Girl Who Studies Abroad," parts 1 and 2, *Ladies' Home Journal*, February 1892, 99; March 1892, 6; Varina Davis to Jefferson Davis, 4 February 1878, Jefferson Davis Papers, ALA.

15. Hudson Strode, ed. *Jefferson Davis: Private Letters, 1823–1889* (New York: Harcourt, Brace and World, 1966), 434; Winnie Davis to Varina Davis, December 1876, 9 December 1877, Jefferson Davis Papers, ALA; Gustav Enzenbert, 28 January 1881, autograph book of Winnie Davis, Jefferson Davis Presidential Library, Biloxi, Miss.

16. Myrta Lockett Avary, *Dixie after the War* (New York: Doubleday, Page, 1906), 416; Thomas Joseph Gaughan, "Memorable Visit to Jeff Davis Made by Camden Man in 1887," unpublished transcript, n.d., Museum of the Confederacy; Jefferson Davis to J. Addison Hayes, 23 February 1882, Jefferson Davis and Family Papers, MDAH.

17. Jefferson Davis to Varina Davis, 1883, Jefferson Davis Papers, ALA; Varina Davis to Jubal Early, 5 May, 22 June 1883, Jubal A. Early Papers, LC; Jubal A. Early to Jefferson Davis, 15 June 1883, Jefferson Davis Papers, Transylvania University.

18. Winnie Davis to General Bradley T. Johnson, 13 March 1885, McGregor Collection, University of Virginia, Charlottesville.

19. "A Triumphal Tour," newspaper clipping, May 1886, scrapbook of anonymous Georgia woman, 1885–1896, Duke University.

20. "The Child of the Confederacy," *Richmond Dispatch*, 21 September 1886; Henry W. Grady to Jefferson Davis, 15 November 1886, Museum of the Confederacy; F. M. Sterrett to Jefferson Davis, 15 July 1888, Jefferson Davis Papers, Rice University, Houston, Tex.; Otis S. Tarver to the *Confederate Veteran*, 1 (March 1893): 74.

21. *New York Sun*, quoted in the *Atlanta Constitution*, 7 September 1886; clipping from a southern newspaper, 10 September 1996, Museum of the Confederacy; "The Daughter of the Confederacy," *Macon Telegraph*, November 188[6], scrapbook of an anonymous Georgia woman, Duke University; Gaines Foster, *Ghosts of the Confederacy: Defeat, the Lost Cause, and the Emergence of the New South* (New York: Oxford University Press, 1987), 97.

22. Varina Anne Davis to Gaston Ahi Robbins, 27 September, William McKendree Robbins Papers, SHC.

23. Varina Davis to Connie [Constance Cary] Harrison, 20 December 1886, Harrison Family Papers, University of Virginia.

24. *New York Sun,* September 1886, reported in the *Denver Tribune-Republican,* 17 September 1886.

25. Anita Monsees, "How the Daughter of the Confederacy Almost Became a Daughter of New York," *Heritage* (January/February 1991); Varina Davis to Major Morgan, September 1888, Jefferson Davis Papers, LC; Varina Davis to Jubal Early, 7 September 1888, Jubal A. Early Papers, LC.

26. Annabel Power, "When Winnie Davis Came to Jackson 54 Years Ago," *Jackson Clarion-Ledger,* 25 May 1942, based on articles in the *Jackson Clarion-Ledger* in May 1888; Chiles Clifton Ferrell, "The Daughter of the Confederacy, Her Life, Character, and Writings," *Publications of the Mississippi Historical Society* 2 (1989): 74; A. Dudley Mann to Winnie Davis, 31 July 1888, Museum of the Confederacy; Mildred Lewis Rutherford, *The South in History and Literature* (Atlanta: Franklin-Turner, 1907); Varina Anne Davis, "Serpent Myths," *North American Review* 146 (February 1888): 161; Varina Anne Davis, *An Irish Knight of the Nineteenth Century* (New York: J. W. Lovell, 1888).

27. Varina Davis to Major Morgan, September 1888, Jefferson Davis Papers, LC; Ross, 358.

28. Winnie Davis to Jefferson Davis, 5 December 1889, Jefferson Davis Papers, ALA.

29. Fred [Wilkinson] to Major Morgan, 1 March 1890, Jefferson Davis Papers, LC.

30. Varina Davis to Margaret Davis Hayes, 8 November 1889, Jefferson Davis Papers, ALA; Fred Wilkinson to Varina Davis, 25 February, 1 March 1890; Fred Wilkinson to Major Morgan, 1 March 1890; Varina Davis to Major Morgan, 9 March 1890, n.d., Jefferson Davis Papers, LC; Varina Davis to Jubal Early, 20 April, 27 April 1890, Jubal A. Early Papers, Virginia Historical Society, Richmond; *New York Times,* 27 April, 10 August 1890; *Fort Worth Daily Gazette,* 24 April 1890; [Richmond?] *Times,* n.d., in anonymous scrapbook, Museum of the Confederacy.

31. John B. Gordon to Varina Davis, 7 July 1890, Jefferson Davis Papers, Transylvania University.

32. Letter to Alfred Wilkinson, 10 June 1890, reprinted in *Southern Belle: The Personal Story of a Crusader's Wife,* by Mary Craig Sinclair (Phoenix, Ariz.: Sinclair Press, 1957), 60.

33. M. Hoover to Winnie Davis, 20 May 1890, Museum of the Confederacy; *New York Times,* 10 August 1890.

34. Resolution of the Ben McCulloch Camp, United Confederate Veterans, Rockdale, Tex., 20 September 1898, Museum of the Confederacy; "In Her Memory," unnamed Louisville, Ky., newspaper, September 1898, subject file, MDAH.

35. Varina Davis to William H. Morgan, 26 August 1890, Jefferson Davis Papers, LC; *New York Times,* 7 October 1890.

36. Varina Davis to Major Morgan, 5 October 1890, Jefferson Davis Papers, LC; *New York Times,* 7 October 1890.

37. Ross, 382–84; Winnie Davis to Major Morgan, 3 November 1890, in Ross, 374.

38. *New York World,* [28?] May 1893; Winnie Davis to Marquis de Ruvigny, 27 September [1893?], Museum of the Confederacy; William Bledsoe Philpott, ed., *The Sponsor Souvenir Album and History of the United Confederate Veterans' Reunion, 1895* (Houston: Sponsor Souvenir, 1895).

39. Daniel E. Sutherland, *The Confederate Carpetbaggers* (Baton Rouge: Louisiana State University Press, 1988), 131, 290; Winnie Davis to Ella Mehle, February 1894, Historic New Orleans Collection; address book of Winnie Davis, Jefferson Davis Presidential Library.

40. Winnie Davis to Marquis de Ruvigny, 21 March 1893, Museum of the Confederacy; W. A. Swanberg, *Pulitzer* (New York: Charles Scribner's Sons, 1967), 187; Sutherland, 67, 131.

41. Varina Anne Davis to Judge C. C. Cordell [Cordill], 30 January [1895], Historic New Orleans Collection.

42. Winnie Davis, "The Antebellum Southern Woman," *Confederate Veteran* (March 1893), 73–74; Varina Anne Davis, "Home Life of Jefferson Davis," reprinted in *Houston Daily Post,* 18 August 1895.

43. Varina Anne Jefferson Davis, *The Veiled Doctor: A Novel* (New York: Harper and Brothers, 1895); Ferrell, "The Daughter of the Confederacy," 75–81; *New York Times,* 20 September 1898.

44. Chiles Clifton Ferrell, "Varina Anne Jefferson Davis" in *Library of Southern Literature,* vol. 3, ed. Edwin Anderson Alderman and Joel Chandler Harris (New Orleans: Martin and Hoyt, 1907), 1335; Varina Anne Davis, *A Romance of Summer Seas* (New York: Harper and Brothers, 1898).

45. Varina Davis to Col. Henry K. Ellyson, 1 May 1895, 25 June 1896; Varina Davis to Varina H. D. Hayes, 15 June 1895, Joel A. H. Webb Private Collection; Varina Davis to John H. Reagan, 14 February 1897, Dallas Historical Society; Varina Davis to Anne Grant, 3 May 1897, Museum of the Confederacy.

46. Ross, 391.

47. Varina Davis to Anne Grant, 26 February, 29 August [1898], Museum of the Confederacy; Varina Davis to Cassie, 24 May 1898, Jefferson Davis Papers, Duke University; Varina Davis to Mary Belle Morgan, 14 September 1898, Jefferson Davis Papers, LC.

48. *Richmond (Va.) Dispatch,* 24 September 1898, reprinted in *Varina Anne "Winnie" Davis: The Daughter of the Confederacy,* by Tommie Phillips LaCavera (Athens, Ga.: Southern Trace, 1994), 34–48; check for $543 from Joseph Pulitzer to J. P. Case, 14 November 1898, Joseph Pulitzer Personal Account, Pulitzer Family Papers, Columbia University, New York, N.Y.

49. LaCavera, 73–75.

50. Resolution, Albert Sidney Johnson Camp, no. 70, United Confederate Veterans, Paris, Tex., 2 October 1898, Museum of the Confederacy; Laurence Thomsen Dickinson for the Nathan Bedford Forrest Camp in Chattanooga, Tenn., to Varina Davis, 31 October 1898; J. M. Wright for the Joseph E. Johnston Camp in Gainesville, Tex., to Varina Davis, 30 November 1898, Museum of the Confederacy.

51. See Pierre Bourdieu, *The Logic of Practice* (Stanford: Stanford University Press, 1990), 112–21.

Nellie Nugent Somerville

(1863–1952)

Mississippi Reformer, Suffragist, and Politician

MARJORIE JULIAN SPRUILL

Nellie Nugent Somerville played a major role in Mississippi history as a reformer, suffragist, and politician. A woman of exceptional ability who was determined to right wrongs as she saw them, she adamantly rejected the prevailing view that women should confine their activities and influence to their homes and families. Particularly from the 1880s through the 1920s, Somerville contributed much to her church, her community, her state, and to a certain extent her nation. Through the reforms she supported and her personal example, she helped pave the way for women, including her own daughter, Lucy Somerville Howorth, to make meaningful contributions to society as activists, voters, and elected officials.

Somerville's keen interest in serving society as well as her confidence in her ability to do so despite her gender owed much to her family background. The daughter of William Lewis Nugent and Eleanor Smith Nugent of Greenville, Mississippi, she was reared in a family long interested in law and politics. Her paternal great-grandfather, Seth Lewis, had been the second chief justice of the Mississippi Territory and organized its judicial system; her maternal grandfather, Abram F. Smith, had been a lawyer and member of the Mississippi legislature. Her father, William Lewis Nugent, who became one of the most respected jurists as well as Methodist laymen in the state, read law with Abram Smith and married Smith's daughter Eleanor, also called Nellie.[1]

Nellie Nugent Somerville was born on her grandparents' plantation in the Mississippi Delta in 1863 in the midst of the Civil War. Her father was serving as a colonel in the Confederate Army. Shortly thereafter, Union troops killed her grandfather Smith, a civilian, and burned their home. In her early childhood,

NELLIE NUGENT SOMERVILLE

From *The Official and Statistical Register of the
State of Mississippi, 1924–1928*. Courtesy of Mississippi
Department of Archives and History.

following her mother's death and before her father remarried and moved to Jackson, young Nellie Nugent was reared largely by her grandmother, S. Myra Smith. Nugent was devoted to Smith, who was known for exceptional piety, "unselfish and heroic service" to her church and community, and her intelligence and strong will.[2]

In fact, the Smith/Nugent family was accustomed to strong, capable women as well as men, and the women of the family received more opportunities for education than most women of the era. Both of Nugent's grandmothers studied at academies: Myra Smith attended Nazareth Academy in Bardston, Kentucky, the first boarding school for girls west of the Appalachian Mountains, and Anne Lavinia Lewis graduated from Elizabeth Female Academy in Washington, Mississippi, in 1827. Nellie Nugent's father, William Lewis Nugent, was influenced in favor of women's education by his mother, who was a woman "of great intellectual power" with "a great feeling for learning" and was often compared to Queen Victoria. As a result he sent his bright young daughter to Whitworth College, a Methodist school for women in Brookhaven, Mississippi, when she was only twelve years old. At age fourteen, having learned all that the school had to offer (according to its president), Nugent was then sent to Martha Washington College in Abingdon, Virginia, from which she graduated as valedictorian in 1880. For the rest of her life she read voraciously and amassed an impressive personal library that after her death enriched the holdings of several colleges.[3]

After Nugent's graduation, her father took the unusual step of inviting his daughter to read law in his Jackson law offices, but she declined, explaining that as the only descendent of her grandmother Smith, she must return to Greenville and be with Smith in her last years. Nellie's daughter Lucy later speculated that her mother loved studying the law but had "what you call now a sociological urge to do some good and that reading law in her father's office . . . was a little more on the side of pure business than her nature would respond to." In addition, Nugent was eager to be financially independent and soon took a job as tutor for a Greenville family.[4]

There is no doubt, however, that Nugent was very attached to Myra Smith and shared her grandmother's sectional loyalty. Nugent's father had been willing to send Nellie to Vassar instead of Martha Washington. Nellie, however, decided against it out of allegiance to her grandmother, who might feel that she was deserting the South. Clearly the young woman had a strong sense of southern identity: late in her life she told her daughters that it was not "until she went to a meeting in Boston . . . after World War I . . . and stood on Plymouth Rock [that] she felt for the first time that she was an American" rather than a Mississippian or a southerner.[5]

The experiences of Nugent's family during the Civil War and Reconstruction clearly shaped her perspective. In his wartime letters, William Nugent made it clear that he fought to the bitter end out of fear that a Confederate defeat would usher in a period of vindictive "Yankee despotism" in which the best classes of white southerners would be ruined and "denied all the privileges of a freeman" and the South turned into "a howling waste" abandoned "to the *freed negroes* & the wild beasts." He declared, "Never will I be content to submit to Yankee rule." His daughter, too, wanted white political supremacy maintained, defended the rights of the states, and revered her father for the role he played in the overthrow of the Republican government in Mississippi in the 1870s. Throughout her life she regarded political power as the rightful privilege as well as responsibility of the most "able" people and supported restrictions on voting that had the effect of limiting the franchise to those she regarded as the best qualified.[6]

In addition, Nellie Nugent's family background contributed to the fact that, as she became involved in promoting reform, even in the controversial area of women's rights, she continued to enjoy the respect and cooperation of white citizens in her community. After her marriage in 1885, she continued to live in Greenville and from there began her career as a social and political activist while also launching a family. Between 1886 and 1895 she bore four children. Unlike her husband, Robert Somerville, a civil engineer educated at the University of Virginia who had come to Mississippi to work on flood control, she was fully at home in the Delta and felt a vital connection with others shaped by their Delta heritage. Robert Somerville, according to his daughter Lucy, "lacked the imagination" to understand his wife's "inner drive" and desire to reform things, but like many others in the community he not only tolerated but supported Nellie Nugent Somerville's reformist endeavors and admired her ability "to get the community moving."[7]

According to Howorth, her mother had a "faithful, strong, and devoted following . . . composed of the people who had lived in Greenville before and immediately after the Civil War and who were all of a bond," possessing "a deep understanding that no one of their own kind would be rejected or severely criticized for anything, no matter what they did, because they had stood together under great tribulation and they would continue to." As a result, said Howorth, "my mother could get away with a great deal."[8]

Somerville's social activism began through her work in the Methodist Episcopal Church, South. In the 1890s she served as district secretary for Women's Foreign Mission work, as a member of the Board of Missions, and as the first president of the North Mississippi Conference Parsonage and Home Mission Society. In her 1893 presidential address, Somerville exhorted these women to expand their social usefulness, reminding them that they belonged "not only to one family but to the great human family." Furthermore, she urged them to "thank God for your freedom, accept the opportunity, and help in this work," and rejoice that the sympathies and activities of a woman no longer had to be "limited by the walls of her own home."[9]

Somerville's nascent feminism was inadvertently stimulated by the leading men of the church who infuriated her by their attempts to establish male authority over the rapidly expanding enterprises of Methodist women. She remained a devoted Methodist throughout her life, but the subordinate status of women in the church was a constant irritant to her and she was eager to see them rise up against it. As she wrote in a church magazine, "What long-suffering creatures women are anyway. They consent to hold office in a sort of sub rosa way, doing all the hard work; but as soon as some immature stripling or reformed drunkard joins the Church he gets the office, while the women keep on doing the work."[10]

From the early 1890s to 1898, Somerville also belonged to a women's social and literary society in Greenville, named, significantly, for Hypatia, a learned woman of ancient Egypt, stoned to death by a mob. This invitation-only association of the Delta's female intelligentsia met to read and discuss literary and historical selections and hear occasional speakers, but they soon began to research, write, and present their own papers for discussion. According to the *Greenville Times,* it was a matter of great regret to locals that these presentations were for members only. In one of her Hypatia Club speeches, Somerville addressed the delicate subject of "woman's right to her person," by which she meant the right to decide when to have sex with her husband and therefore control her fertility. In other speeches she discussed the evolution of southern womanhood and advances in the industrial, educational, and legal position of women and the work that remained to be done. In "The Progress of Women," Somerville charged that every improvement in women's status had been "hotly contested" by men who considered it their most cherished privilege to "define woman's place and keep her in it."[11]

Somerville was inspired to work for increasing women's influence in politics by Frances Willard, national president of the Woman's Christian Temperance Union (WCTU), who was convinced that women must be directly involved in politics in order to inject morality. Willard came to Mississippi in 1889, inspiring both Somerville and Mississippi's other well-known suffrage leader, Belle Kearney, to become lifelong supporters of women's rights as well as temperance. According to Howorth, although there were many factors that converted her mother to woman suffrage, Willard convinced Somerville that "the women couldn't get anything done until they had the right to vote" and "that is really what pinned my mother's mind to that point." Somerville considered Willard to be the greatest person of all time and used to say "if Frances Willard called upon the women of the country to follow her into the Atlantic Ocean they would do it." Somerville presided over the Greenville chapter of the WCTU in 1894 and 1895 and became corresponding secretary for the state WCTU in 1896.[12]

Although Willard convinced Somerville of the importance of woman suffrage, Somerville was recruited into the suffrage movement by leaders of the National American Woman Suffrage Association (NAWSA), who recognized her ability and valued her social and political influence in Mississippi. Laura Clay of Kentucky, a NAWSA leader who took upon herself the task of "bringing in the South," first contacted Somerville in the early 1890s, but Somerville initially declined to work for suffrage, saying she was "up to [her] eyes in WCTU work to say nothing of a family."[13] When suffrage organizers came into the state in 1895 and again in 1897, however, she came to their assistance, even though she was slightly critical of the NAWSA for launching an organizing drive in the state without first consulting Mississippi women. Yet sympathetic to their cause, aware of the shortage of state suffrage supporters, and not wanting to see their efforts fail, she gave them her full support, even giving up her WCTU post to become the president of the Mississippi Woman Suffrage Association (MWSA) when it was formed in 1897.[14] NAWSA organizer Ella Harrison proudly informed Carrie Chapman Catt: "At last our work in Mississippi is done, and I believe it is *well done,* because I know the new officers of the 'Mississippi Woman Suffrage Association' are capable, prominent women. The Pres., Mrs. Robert Sommerville [*sic*] of Greenville, Miss. is a daughter of the late Col. Nugent of Jackson, a man of rare ability and great prominence. Mrs. Somerville has long been the Corr. Sec. of the WCTU and was elected again this year but resigned. She is businesslike and has read law and I am sure the State is well provided for in the selection of its chief. There are few women to compare with her."[15]

The new president went right to work. Well aware of the unpopularity of their cause in the South, where the suffrage movement was widely regarded as an offshoot of the abolitionist movement and incompatible with southern traditions, Somerville sent an appeal "to Members and Friends of the Mississippi Woman Suffrage Association" stating, "The public, and especially the editorial public will be quick to see and use against us any mistakes that may be made. An unpleasant aggressiveness will doubtless be expected from us. Let us endeavor to disappoint such expectations and spend the year in learning what to do and how to do it."[16]

In her 1898 presidential address, Somerville described the MWSA's systematic efforts, including research to inform themselves and others about "such fragments of suffrage" as were already granted to women and encourage their exercise. It also included research to find out "who our friends and enemies are." Part of this effort was sending letters of inquiry to men who had been delegates to the 1890 Mississippi constitutional convention that had considered enfranchising women with property as a means of re-establishing white political supremacy. Somerville implied that she expected to find few "friends" among ministers, but would be "surprised if we do not meet with sympathy from lawyers who best know the legal injustices under which women have suffered and from newspaper men who are most keenly alive to the signs of the times."[17] She was resourceful in her use of tactics, and generous with her own funds. Soon thereafter, when one newspaper editor charged that there was only slight interest in suffrage in the state and little about it in the press, Somerville subscribed to every county paper in the state for six months; she asked her young daughter, Lucy, to cut out every clipping on suffrage and pin them on a piece of fabric large enough to go around most rooms, and then took it with her on speaking tours to decorate the halls and demonstrate interest in the suffrage movement.[18]

Despite the best efforts of Somerville and her supporters, however, the suffragists made little headway between 1897 and 1899, when she resigned the presidency for health reasons. Belle Kearney took over as president but, as a professional speaker often out of the state, found it difficult to continue and resigned after two months. Without strong leadership, the MWSA was dormant until Belle Kearney's efforts resulted in its revival late in 1906 with Kearney as president and Somerville as vice president. Somerville succeeded Kearney in 1908 and served as president until 1912, followed by Lily Wilkinson Thompson, Annie K. Dent, and Pauline V. Orr. But Somerville continued to be a force in the state, regional, and even national suffrage organizations until the movement ended in the ratification of the Nineteenth Amendment in 1920.[19]

From the very beginning, Somerville's suffrage speeches reflected her combined sense of religious and patriotic duty as well as her tendency to invoke widely shared, even conservative ideas in support of reform. She insisted that women's ability to perform successfully their traditional role of training sons for citizenship required their own enfranchisement and full exercise of civic responsibility. In her 1898 presidential address, delivered as her country was at war, Somerville stated,

> In a republican country, patriotism must find its truest expression in politics . . . [and] a disenfranchised class can never be truly patriotic. If today, our political life is controlled by selfish and corrupt men, if good men, to a great extent, hold themselves back from politics the cause may be found in a disenfranchised moth-

erhood. The mother's influence is extolled to the highest degree, how we ask, can disenfranchised mothers teach their sons the patriotic use of the ballot? When we ask for the ballot, we ask for the privilege of assisting in perpetuating the traditions and images of freedom.[20]

Somerville was convinced that, for the sake of the nation, the best people must serve as leaders and voters and that religion must be injected anew in the politics and schools of the land. Quoting Frances Willard, she declared, "The Ten Commandments are voted up and down on election day." Like Willard, Somerville believed it was woman's Christian duty to enter politics. By 1900 she wrote, "Beginning as a demand for rights—the right to education, to business opportunities, property rights," the women's movement has become increasingly "a plea for power to help in righting wrong conditions."[21]

Throughout her suffrage career, Somerville worked simultaneously to promote woman suffrage and improve the quality of life in her native Greenville and in Mississippi. It was her philosophy that women should practice good citizenship, ameliorating conditions in their communities and in the process demonstrating what they would do with the vote. In that spirit, Greenville's suffrage club renamed itself the Greenville Civic Club, established a public library, petitioned for sanitation and health measures, and launched the state's first antituberculosis campaign, which included ladies handing out cards to expectorating men warning of the health risks they were creating. They secured the first public health nurse ever employed in Mississippi and insisted that she serve the whole community, including its African American citizens, a step Somerville believed in for "humanitarian" reasons but justified to skeptics as necessary because blacks came into contact with whites as servants. As president of the state suffrage organization, Somerville worked with suffragists statewide on behalf of public health measures, for example, persuading the president of the state railroad commission to place antispitting signs in all passenger coaches and stations and getting laws passed requiring that Argyrol drops be placed in the eyes of all newborns to protect against blindness from venereal disease.[22]

These efforts were similar to those of many middle- and upper-class women reformers in the late-nineteenth- and early-twentieth-century South who were gradually expanding the role of women. They stretched as far as the public would allow the traditional idea of the benevolent southern lady ministering to the needs of her extended household and the "unprivileged" in her community in the spirit of noblesse oblige. Unless the reforms they advocated came into conflict with powerful foes like the liquor or cotton textile industries, people seemed to find their activism unsurprising, especially advocacy of improvements in public health, education, or "culture" in their own communities.

Somerville and other suffragists had less success, however, as they lobbied for more opportunities and better conditions for women and children. Somerville chaired the MWSA Legislative Committee, which sought legislation to make women eligible to serve as school trustees and members of the state boards of trustees of educational and benevolent institutions, to make women eligible to serve as county superintendents of education, to give mothers equal guardianship rights to their children, and to provide for a woman assistant physician in the state's hospital for the insane. The MWSA also supported establishing "equal pay for equal work"; adding women to the state's college board; and raising the age of consent for girls from twelve to eighteen as a means of ending the double standard of morality. Among their other concerns were promoting the "Biblical standard of purity"; employing women probation officers, matrons, and physicians in the "great work of juvenile reform"; establishing a state reformatory for criminals under age twenty-one; and hiring women factory inspectors especially where women and children were working. Somerville was strongly influenced by her friends the New Orleans Progressive reformers Jean and Kate Gordon; they came to Mississippi frequently and Somerville visited them during her annual visits to New Orleans. Somerville became active in the Southern Conference for Women and Child Labor, founded largely through the efforts of the Gordons, and attended its 1909 conference in New Orleans. In 1909, the MWSA endorsed a resolution adopted at that conference calling for uniform child labor legislation in all of the southern states. In 1912 she joined the Southern Sociological Conference, an organization established by leading southern philanthropists and reformers to seek solutions to a variety of social problems in the region.[23]

Somerville was passionate in her opposition to child labor, and she wrote numerous articles on the subject, publicizing conditions in the cotton mills, shrimp and oyster processing plants, and other industries in Mississippi that employed young children. Somerville was convinced that in meeting the challenge of eradicating child labor and in other issues involving morality and politics, the nation must allow its women to provide assistance through their ballots. "Divine Providence has opened the domain of moral leadership to the Christian women of this nation," she wrote. "This is the reason political power is being given and must be given to women; because, if the blessing of God is upon the nation, moral power and political power must be together."[24]

Somerville was adamant that the franchise must be extended to women because it was just, not because an enfranchised womanhood "will bring about great reforms." As she told one Mississippi editor, "the orthodox suffragists do not base their claims on any such argument" but on the Declaration of Independence; "governments derive their just powers from the consent of the governed."[25] Although she supported suffrage restrictions that would limit the vote to the "best qualified," she considered women like herself to be among that group and regarded the denial of the privilege as a "degradation" as well as a major liability. She declared herself "exasperated" with suffrage opponents who tried to "sugarcoat" the denial of the vote to women by claiming that it was in woman's own best interests or that women were protected and did not need the vote. In a 1898 letter to the editor of the *Sardis (Miss.) Southern Reporter,* she took him to task, saying: "we do not believe that you, and many other men, oppose woman suffrage because you believe it best for women themselves. You will pardon us, however, if we fail to feel complimented by an opinion which virtually says women will not conduct themselves properly unless kept under certain restrictions and held perpetually within fixed limitations. We should be glad if you were able to believe that no amount of freedom and no amount of rights and privileges could cause us to lose our dignity and good sense."[26]

Somerville railed against "civilization" for having encouraged in women helplessness, ignorance, and reliance on beauty, and denounced the claim that "pain is woman's curse and heritage, endurance and submission her highest virtues." She hated the term "auxiliary" in the titles of women's organizations and persuaded at least one organization to change the wording in its title from "ladies" to "women's." And, unlike many other southern suffrage leaders, she consistently signed her articles and correspondence with her own name, as Nellie Nugent Somerville and not Mrs. Robert Somerville. She attacked the widespread assumption that the women of her era were all pampered and dependent and had no need of the vote to represent their interests.[27]

In a flyer entitled "Who Takes Care of Mississippi Women?" written by Somerville and distributed by the Civic Improvement Club in 1915, she offered statistics from the 1910 census to prove that large numbers of white, native-born women in the state were working for a living and therefore ought to have the right to vote in order to "protect their own positions." She stated, "Opposition to woman suffrage in the South seems to be based upon the theory that men are the real burden bearers, that women are a highly privileged, supported class, and because of special and peculiar exemptions from work they should be willing to leave the government in the hands of men." The statistics she cited revealed that one-fifth of white, native-born women worked for wages, that many "girl orphans" and "a large number of nurses and teachers" were gainfully employed. In a similar flyer she discussed the high numbers of women workers throughout the South and concluded, "The theory is that all southern women occupy pedestals; [but] these are the facts."[28]

Although Somerville certainly made use of the argument embraced by suffragists all over the nation that women would inject morality into politics, according to her daughter, she did not share the widespread assumption that there were innate differences in character between the sexes. It appears that, like Jane Addams, Somerville believed that women's life experiences—not inherent characteristics—led women to support reform legislation. Yet, she once observed in jest that if the sexes did indeed have different natures, "reason rebels against placid submission to the rulership of the more degraded class of citizens."[29]

Nellie Nugent Somerville, according to Lucy Somerville Howorth, was a woman of shrewd political instincts who advanced whatever arguments would be most appropriate and persuasive in a given situation. Generally speaking, this did not include the argument common among first generation suffragists of the South, including Mississippi's Belle Kearney, that the South should enfranchise women (with literacy or property qualifications that would limit the vote largely to white women) as a means of restoring white political supremacy. This significant omission was not, as Howorth explained, because of "any feeling of what is now called 'civil rights.' " Rather, said Howorth, her mother "didn't think that it was a good, sound argument." Given the political realities in Somerville's home state, where African Americans had been virtually removed from the electorate since 1890, white rule was not in jeopardy. Like most white southern suffragists in the years after disfranchisement of the region's African American men, Somerville was quick to dismiss as absurd the antisuffragists' claim that woman suffrage would endanger white supremacy, insisting that the vote would be "applied" to "the American negress . . . just as it applies to the American negro."[30]

After its revival in 1908 with Somerville as president, the MWSA stepped up its educational activities in hopes of increasing suffrage sentiment in the state and eventually winning enfranchisement by a state constitutional amendment. Again, they followed her strategy of trying to "make friends without making enemies." Seeking to defuse the idea that woman suffrage was a radical idea from the North, the MWSA produced much of its own promotional literature rather than relying on the NAWSA press service. As Lily Wilkinson Thompson put it, "An ounce of Mississippi was worth a pound of Massachusetts." Somerville, who often headed the legislative committee, wrote many of the pamphlets; she made a deal with the antisuffrage editor of the *Greenville Democrat* to edit his "woman's page" for several months without pay if he would print up her suffrage pamphlets in large quantities at cost. But the MWSA also made use of national suffrage publications like the moderate-in-tone *Woman's Journal*. In 1911 Mississippi suffragists sent the paper to editors and other important public figures. In 1913 and 1914, Somerville sent copies of the *Woman's Journal* at her own expense to all members of the state legislature for three months.[31]

Although Somerville and most Mississippi suffragists disapproved of picketing and many of the methods embraced by Alice Paul and the Woman's Party, they did not regard parades or open-air speaking as unladylike or counterproductive. In 1914 the suffragists were a major attraction at the state fair, marching in the opening parade and addressing large crowds from the cotton bale "platform" at their booth. And they persuaded every gubernatorial candidate to address the suffrage question from their booth. The suffragists also brought in nationally famous orators, particularly NAWSA president Dr. Anna Howard Shaw, an ordained Methodist minister and physician whom Somerville much admired. Kate Gordon was invited periodically to add oratorical power, and Mississippi's own Belle Kearney lent her internationally acclaimed speaking ability to the suffrage cause in her home state. Somerville herself was described as an accomplished orator and debater who could "play an audience just like a musical instrument" and advance her pragmatic, persuasive arguments in a voice capable of "moving a thousand people" in an era before the invention of the microphone.[32]

Especially as she grew older, Somerville was regarded by some as "fierce" and "stern," and younger suffragists sometimes complained that she was domineering and lacked confidence in them. In 1915 Mary P. Crane wrote to Pauline Orr, "Mrs. S. does not realize that her complaint of the weakness of this organization is made a reality by her own assumption of all power. She does not dare let it go."[33] But veteran suffragists described Somerville, publicly at least, as having, "an exceptional combination of talents, a brilliant mind, a pleasing personality, a veritable gift for organization, unusual executive ability, and a tact and devotion that has accomplished wonders for the cause."[34] Family members insisted that she had a good sense of humor and could laugh at herself. She once told her daughter that she was elected many times but never unanimously. She could be generous and impulsive. When on a train full of Millsaps College "boys" who began jeering and "cutting up" at the sight of her suffrage banners, she bought the porter's entire cartload of candy and drinks, telling him to deliver it to the students, who at once began yelling, "Votes for Women! Hurrah! Hurrah!"[35]

Anna Howard Shaw, who came to Mississippi partly out of a sense of obligation to support suffrage workers where "they were having the hardest struggle and making the bravest fight," was certainly a Somerville fan. Surprised by the huge crowds who filled the halls wherever she spoke, Shaw wrote, "Too much praise cannot be given to the state officers and the local helpers, but more particularly to Mrs. Somerville. Her enthusiasm and tireless service, added to the prominence of her family in the state, make her an ideal president. If Mississippi does not show a marked increase in sentiment during the coming year it will not be the fault of Mrs. Somerville and her corps of splendid assistants." [36]

State suffrage conventions began to attract large crowds and an increasingly larger number of supporters. By 1916, many members of the DAR, the UDC, and the WCTU were working for suffrage; in 1917 the Mississippi Federation of Women's Clubs officially endorsed it. A growing number of editors and politicians showed sympathy for their cause, including Governors James K. Vardaman and Edmund Noel. In 1914, the year that the MWSA ran its strongest campaign for a state constitutional amendment for woman suffrage, Somerville and other suffragists were invited to address a joint session of the state legislature. But in 1914, as in 1918, the legislators voted down the measure. [37]

Because of her strong sense of identification with her state, Somerville, like many southern suffragists, was very disappointed at the MWSA's failure to attain a state suffrage amendment. In 1915 the MWSA passed a resolution stating that they did not oppose other methods but preferred "to obtain the ballot at the hands of Mississippi men." The suffragists were eager to convince the people with whom they must work in state politics that women should be enfranchised, rather than have woman suffrage forced upon the unconverted by federal mandate. Some suffragists, including Kate and Jean Gordon, were such strong proponents of states' rights that they shared the antisuffragists' belief that the federal government in the 1860s had had no constitutional right to "force" black suffrage on the South and now had no right to "interfere with" state suffrage requirements regarding women. In 1913, as support grew nationally for a federal woman suffrage amendment, Kate Gordon led the way in establishing the Southern States Woman Suffrage Conference (SSWSC), demanding that all southern suffragists rally under its banner, eschew NAWSA leadership, and work for suffrage by state action only. [38]

Here Somerville parted ways with her old friend and ally. Somerville joined the SSWSC and the MWSA endorsed it; but when Gordon began denouncing the NAWSA and demanding that southern suffragists actually oppose the federal amendment, Somerville refused. Although a strong believer in states' rights, Somerville was even more committed to woman suffrage and had become convinced that her only hope for women's enfranchisement in her lifetime was through federal action. In 1914 she accepted the invitation to serve as a NAWSA vice president, and although Gordon denounced her as a traitor, Somerville made a major contribution to NAWSA by actively supporting the federal amendment and urging key southern suffrage leaders to remain in the NAWSA fold. In 1915, speaking for herself and other southern supporters of the federal amendment, Somerville declared, "We all believe in [the federal amendment] and we are gradually convincing thoughtful men and women in the South that it holds no menace for the institutions of any State or any group of States." Following the "Winning Plan" devised by Carrie Chapman Catt, Mississippi suffragists, like those in other states Catt deemed hopeless, did not launch further state campaigns, but worked for adoption and ratification of the federal amendment.[39]

To no one's surprise, Somerville and other Mississippi suffragists were no more successful in winning ratification of the federal amendment than they were at attaining a state suffrage bill. They gained some support in the press and among some leading politicians, but issues of race and states' rights plus a strong conservatism regarding woman's role contributed to Mississippi's continued rejection of woman suffrage. As the legislature considered the ratification issue, Somerville listened from the gallery as Kate Gordon, in Jackson at the invitation of the *Clarion-Ledger,* urged defeat of the amendment in order to preserve white supremacy and states' rights and honor those "patriotic sons who had fought for southern civilization and for Mississippi." The state legislature refused to ratify the amendment, despite the plea of Governor Theodore Bilbo that ratification by a Democrat-controlled legislature would assist President Woodrow Wilson and the national Democratic party. Furthermore, Mississippi did not allow women to vote in the 1920 election. As women elsewhere voted for the first time, an all-male Mississippi electorate voted on whether or not to amend the state constitution to allow women to vote. The measure was approved by a majority but failed to get the required two-thirds necessary for passage.[40]

Despite Mississippi's intransigence on woman suffrage, in one of the first elections in which women were allowed to vote (1923), Nellie Nugent Somerville was elected to the state legislature. Somerville had long been active in partisan politics, and by 1920 she had earned a reputation as a political leader, the head of one faction (the "dry" or prohibition faction) within the Democratic party in her county. Somerville was convinced that NAWSA President Carrie Chapman Catt and other national leaders made a terrible mistake in converting the NAWSA to the nonpartisan League of Women Voters, and she insisted that to be effective women must plunge directly into party politics and run for office.[41]

Somerville had a distinguished career in the legislature, where she served until 1927. She studied the issues and her fellow legislators with great thoroughness, knowing the interests, the record, the motivation, the family, friends, supporters, and intentions of each legislator and using this knowledge so effectively

the newspapers "considered it a matter for comment when a bill she supported failed to pass." She chaired the committee on charitable institutions, sponsored a number of social welfare proposals, and was responsible for major reforms in the state's mental hospital.[42] She also supported a bill to prevent the trial of a delinquent girl in open court, believing the society was far more forgiving of youthful mistakes among young men than women.

Despite her long-time advocacy of child labor laws, Somerville's states' rights views resurfaced in 1924 when she opposed ratification of the proposed federal amendment giving Congress the power to regulate the labor of persons under eighteen. Somerville explained that although she had worked hard for protection of women and children, she thought the age of eighteen was too high, and "such a sweeping grant of power" could "bring the long arm of federal law into any home and fireside in our state." She announced for re-election, but withdrew when the campaign promised to be a nasty and probably unsuccessful one in which she expected the gender issue to be raised against her. She insisted that her district did not need a divisive political struggle while trying to recover from the disastrous flood of 1927 and threw her support to one of her male supporters (ironically, a "reformed alcoholic"), who won the election. On the closing day of her last legislative session, according to the *Clarion-Ledger,* Washington County's "lady member" was escorted to the podium and, while the representatives rose, a Mr. George eulogized Somerville "for her work in the legislature and as an exponent of southern womanhood, binding the old fashioned woman of the South, which he described as the greatest in all history, with the modern woman."[43]

As a former WCTU leader, Somerville was delighted with the adoption of national prohibition, and throughout the 1920s she was committed to its enforcement and retention. She served as a delegate to the Democratic National Convention in 1924, one of the few delegates financially able to remain in New York for the extraordinarily long convention. She was instrumental in getting the Mississippi delegation to support the "dry" candidate, William McAdoo. Once again she served as president of the state WCTU, promoted prohibition through the state's Federation of Women's Clubs, and was the Mississippi representative on the National Woman's Democratic Law Enforcement League. She broke with the Democratic party in 1928 to back the dry Republican Herbert Hoover over the "wet" Democrat Al Smith for president.[44]

In the 1930s and 1940s, Somerville lived mainly in Cleveland, Mississippi, but spent considerable time in Memphis and in the Methodist mountaintop retreat at Monteagle, Tennessee, where she had owned a cottage since the 1890s. After her husband died in 1925, she developed a strong interest in real estate and in her last decades enjoyed tremendous success as an investor, quadrupling the estate left after her husband's death. She continued to take a lively interest in public affairs and took an active interest in her daughter Lucy's successful campaign for the state legislature in 1931.[45]

Never a radical on any issue other than woman suffrage, Somerville took a progressive stand on many issues throughout her public career. As she aged, however, her views remained largely unchanged as the nation changed dramatically, and she became increasingly disturbed by new developments in national affairs. Having fought for prohibition for most of her life, she was upset by the repeal of the Eighteenth Amendment in 1933. She was displeased by the reunification of the Methodist Church in 1935 and the growing support for desegregation and civil rights among some Methodists. She once chastised Greenville newspaper editor Hodding Carter for praising the southern Methodist Church for its work for racial tolerance and spent several months each year in Memphis so that she could attend an Independent Methodist Church there in which she felt at home.[46]

In the 1940s Somerville also publicly protested revisionist scholarship on women's history and the race issue. In 1944 she wrote to the *Memphis Press-Scimitar* objecting heatedly to an article giving the National Woman's Party credit for the victory of the woman suffrage amendment: "Shades of Susan B. Anthony!" she wrote. "The enfranchisement of American women was due to half a century of devoted work by the National American Woman Suffrage Association with auxiliary state associations in every state" and "I cannot be silent when credit due so many devoted workers is given to others." She was far more upset, however, over revisionist views concerning Reconstruction. After reading an account of a black communist leader praising the accomplishments of the Reconstruction legislatures, she wrote to the *Memphis Commercial Appeal:* "My father, the late Col. W. L. Nugent of Jackson, Mississippi, was one of the men who led the campaign to free Mississippi from the debauchery of Reconstruction politics. The presumptuous statements of the negro Communist and Mr. DeLacey [a Congressman] move me to burning indignation." She also wrote a pamphlet on this subject entitled "Lest We Forget" in which she defended what she considered her family heritage, stubbornly adhering to what historians today refer to as "the myth dogma of Reconstruction."[47]

Finally, the 1940s saw Somerville publicly defending the poll tax and denouncing the 1944 Supreme Court decision *Smith v. Allwright,* which ended the white primary. In letters to numerous newspapers, Somerville insisted—as she had in the 1890s—"The United States is not a Democracy it is a Republic with a government based upon principles of representation. It is to be noted that thousands who support pernicious theories as to the government of the United States base their theories on the assertion that the United States is a Democracy." Apparently, after 1920 when the franchise was extended to women, with (as Somerville predicted) most African American women of the South excluded by the same methods that excluded most African American men, Somerville thought further expansion of the electorate was unnecessary and unwise. In 1942 she insisted "those who are so enamored of democracy as to be willing to tear down restrictions on the exercise of the franchise should consider where that road leads before they decide to walk in it." By 1948 she was a states' rights, segregationist Democrat.[48]

Nellie Nugent Somerville died of cancer in 1952 at age eighty-eight, still busily reading, thinking, and writing about public affairs.

NOTES

1. Lucy Somerville Howorth, interview by Constance Ashton Myers, Monteagle, Tenn., 20–23 June 1975, no. 4007, Southern Oral History Collection, University of North Carolina, Chapel Hill, 41; Mary Louise Meredith, "The Mississippi Woman's Rights Movement, 1889–1923" (master's thesis, Delta State University, 1974), 24–27; William M. Cash and Lucy Somerville Howorth, eds., *My Dear Nellie: The Civil War Letters of William L. Nugent to Eleanor Smith Nugent* (Jackson: University Press of Mississippi, 1977), 3–6, 237–42.

2. Cash and Howorth, eds., 238–39; Anne Firor Scott, "Nellie Nugent Somerville," in *Notable American Women: The Modern Period,* ed. Barbara Sicherman and Carol Hurd Greed (Cambridge: Harvard University Press, 1980), 654, 655; Meredith, 25.

3. Howorth, interview, 1975, 29, 84; Lucy Somerville Howorth, interview by author, Cleveland, Miss., 15 March 1983, and Hattiesburg, Miss., 6 March 1984, vol. 297, Mississippi Oral History Program, University of Southern Mississippi, Hattiesburg, 2, 3, 7, 9; Cash and Howorth, eds., 3, 6; Scott, 654, 655; on Somerville's early education, see Meredith, 25, 26.

4. Howorth, interview, 1975, 7, 30.

5. Ibid., 7, 8, 32.

6. William L. Nugent to Eleanor Smith Nugent, 13 June 1862, 27 August, 7 September 1863, 8 August 1864, in Cash and Howorth, eds., 86–89, 128–30, 196–99; see also William A. Link and Marjorie Spruill Wheeler, *The South in the History of the Nation: A Reader* (Boston: Bedford/St. Martin's, 1999), 278–89; on Nugent's role in ousting the Reconstruction government, see Cash and Howorth, eds., 240–42; Howorth, interview, 1983, 1984, 19–22; Nellie Nugent Somerville, brochure defending the poll tax, 1942; newspaper clippings in which Somerville opposed the 1944 Supreme Court decision against white primaries, Somerville-Howorth Family Papers, Arthur and Elizabeth Schlesinger Library (henceforth AESL), Radcliffe Institute for Advanced Study, Cambridge, Mass.; Somerville, "Democracy and the Poll Tax," *Cleveland (Miss.) Enterprise,* n.d., reprinted from *Jackson Daily News,* 24 April 1942, Somerville-Howorth Family Papers.

7. Howorth, interview, 1975, 3–6, 124–28; Howorth, interview, 1983, 1984, 4, 5; Meredith, 27, 28.

8. Howorth, interview, 1975, 5, 6.

9. John Patrick McDowell, *The Social Gospel in the South: The Woman's Home Mission Movement in the Methodist Episcopal Church, South, 1886–1939* (Baton Rouge: Louisiana State University Press, 1982), 118, 119; Meredith, 28–30.

10. Howorth, interview, 1983, 1984, 6–8; Howorth, interview, 1975, 8; McDowell, 134–35.

11. Meredith, 32–34; Howorth, interview, 1975, 43–44; Howorth, interview, 1983, 1984, 1–2; Somerville, "The Progress of Women," 1898, Somerville Papers, Mississippi Department of Archives and History (henceforth MDAH), Jackson; Meredith, 33, 34.

12. Howorth, interview, 1975, 7; Meredith, 30–32; Howorth, interview, 1983, 1984, 9, 10.

13. Somerville to Laura Clay, 16 February 1895, Laura Clay Papers, Special Collections and Archives, Margaret I. King Library, University of Kentucky, Lexington.

14. Wheeler, *New Women of the New South: The Leaders of the Woman Suffrage Movement in the Southern States* (New York: Oxford University Press, 1993), 63; Somerville to Laura Clay, 28 November 1897, Laura Clay Papers.

15. Catt to "Dear Girls," 1 April 1897, Ella Harrison Papers, AESL, copy in Somerville Papers.

16. Lily Wilkinson Thompson, corresponding secretary for Somerville, appeal "to Members and Friends of the Mississippi Woman Suffrage Association," Crystal Springs, 1897, reel 3, vol. 8, Somerville-Howorth Family Papers.

17. Somerville, "President's Address," Mississippi State Suffrage Convention, 1898, Somerville Papers.

18. Howorth, interview, 1975, 12.

19. Howorth, interview, 1983, 1984, 12; A. Elizabeth Taylor, "The Woman Suffrage Movement in Mississippi, 1890–1920," *Journal of Mississippi History* 30 (February 1968): 9–10; Wheeler, "Belle Kearney," in *American National Biography,* ed. John A. Garraty (New York: Oxford University Press, 1999).

20. Somerville, "President's Address," Mississippi Woman Suffrage Association Convention, 1898, Somerville Papers.

21. Somerville, "Christian Citizenship," [1898 or 1899]; Somerville, "President's Address," 1898, Somerville Papers; Carolyn DeSwarte Gifford, "Frances Willard and the Woman's Christian Temperance Union's Conversion to Woman Suffrage," in *One Woman, One Vote: Rediscovering the Woman Suffrage Movement,* ed. Marjorie Spruill Wheeler (Troutdale, Ore.: NewSage Press, 1995), 117–33; Somerville, "Expediency vs Natural Right," clipping, [ca. 1900], Somerville-Howorth Family Papers.

22. Meredith, 50–60; on public health nurse and African Americans, see Howorth, interview, 1975, 43; Somerville, "History of the Mississippi Woman Suffrage Association, 1897–1919," Somerville Papers; Report on the 1911 MWSA convention in Cleveland, Miss., Somerville-Howorth Family Papers.

23. Meredith, 71, 74–75; Somerville, "History of Mississippi Woman Suffrage Association 1897–1919"; Somerville, "1898 President's Address to the MWSA," Minutes of the 1913 Annual MWSA Convention; Somerville, handwritten list of her activities as she announced as a candidate for the House of Representatives, Somerville Papers; list of MWSA resolutions adopted 1909–1911, reel 4, vol. 20, Somerville-Howorth Family Papers; Dewey Grantham, *Southern Progressivism: The Reconciliation*

of Progress and Tradition (Knoxville: University of Tennessee Press, 1983), 198, 199; James E. McCulloch, ed., *The South Mobilizing for Social Service* (Nashville: The Southern Sociological Congress, 1913), 679–91.

24. Somerville, "Factories and Child Labor," n.d., clipping from a Women's Home Mission Society publication; Somerville, "Child Labor in Mississippi"; Somerville, "Moral Leadership: The True Basis of Woman Suffrage," *Greenville (Miss.) Democrat-Times*, n.d., Somerville Papers.

25. Somerville to the editor, 16 May, scrapbook, Somerville Papers.

26. Somerville, "Are Women Too Good to Vote?" [ca. 1914], Somerville-Howorth Family Papers; Somerville to editor of *Sardis* (Miss.) *Southern Reporter*, 20 June 1898, Somerville Papers.

27. Somerville, "Christian Charity," n.d.; Somerville, handwritten notes, [ca. 1900], reel 3, vol. 9, Somerville-Howorth Family Papers; Howorth, interview, 1975; Somerville, handwritten notes, [ca. 1900], reel 3, vol. 9, Somerville-Howorth Family Papers.

28. "Who Takes Care of Mississippi Women?" Somerville Papers; handbill, n.d., scrapbook, reel 3, Somerville-Howorth Family Papers.

29. Howorth, interview, 1983, 1984, 17, 18; Victoria Bissell Brown, "Jane Addams, Progressivism, and Woman Suffrage," in *One Woman, One Vote*, ed. Wheeler, 179–95; clipping, n.d., reel 3, vol. 8, Somerville-Howorth Family Papers.

30. Wheeler, *New Women of the New South*, 100–132; clipping from *Jackson Evening News*, n.d., Belle Kearney Papers, MDAH; Somerville, "Arguments to Be Met: MWSA"; "Report of Legislative Work, 1914"; letter to the editor, *Greenville (Miss.) Times-Democrat*, n.d., in scrapbook, 1909–1912, Somerville-Howorth Family Papers.

31. Meredith, 72; Somerville, "History of Woman Suffrage in Mississippi"; 1911 Report of State Work, Somerville Papers.

32. Howorth, interview, 1983, 1984, 22–24; Meredith, 67; Somerville, note in yearbook diary, 1943, reel 3, vol. 15, Somerville-Howorth Family Papers; Howorth, interview, 1983, 1984, 10; Howorth, interview, 1975, 29, 41.

33. Howorth, interview, 1975, 28, 29; Mary P. Crane to Pauline Orr, 22 April 1915, Pauline V. Orr Papers, MDAH.

34. Dell Kelso Mohlenoff, clipping, August 1910, reel 4, folder 20, Somerville-Howorth Family Papers.

35. Howorth, interview, 1975, 19, 28, 29, 129.

36. Anna Howard Shaw, "Report on Southern Trip," n.d., box 22, Somerville-Howorth Family Papers.

37. Meredith, 63, 73–74, 79.

38. Meredith, 69; Wheeler, *New Women of the New South*, 133–71.

39. Howorth, interview, 1983, 1984, 21, 22; Somerville to Barbara Bynum Henderson, 2 February 1916; Somerville, "Comment on Letter to Members of National Board," [1915], Somerville Papers; Kenneth R. Johnson, "Kate Gordon and the Woman Suffrage Movement in the South," *Journal of Southern History* 38 (August 1972): 381; Wheeler, *New Women of the New South*, 162–65, 170–71.

40. Wheeler, *New Women of the New South*, 174–75; Meredith, 80–85; Taylor, 226–33.

41. Scott, 655–56; clipping from *Jackson (Miss.) Clarion-Ledger*, 28 July 1924, reel 3, Somerville-Howorth Family Papers; Howorth, interview, 1975, 33.

58

42. Scott, 655.

43. Clippings, reel 3, vols. 11 and 14, Somerville-Howorth Family Papers; Howorth, interview, 1983, 1984, 15, 16, 51; clipping from the *Jackson (Miss.) Clarion-Ledger*, n.d., reel 3, vol. 8, Somerville-Howorth Family Papers.

44. Clippings, Somerville scrapbook, Somerville-Howorth Family Papers.

45. Howorth, interview, 1975, 46–48, 129, 133, 134; Scott, 656.

46. Howorth, interview, 1975, 6, 47; Lucy Somerville Howorth, biographical sketch of Nellie Nugent Somerville, Somerville Papers.

47. Somerville, "Honor and Credit," *Cleveland (Miss.) Enterprise*, 3 May 1944; clipping from *Memphis Press-Scimitar*, n.d., Somerville Papers; Howorth, interview, 1983, 1984, 22–24; clippings, reel 3, vols. 11 and 14, Somerville-Howorth Family Papers; Somerville, "Lest We Forget," in subject files, MDAH.

48. Clippings, reel 3, vol. 14, Somerville-Howorth Family Papers; Scott, 655.

Belle Kearney

(1863–1939)

Mississippi Gentlewoman and Slaveholder's Daughter

JOANNE VARNER HAWKS

❁   ❁   ❁

Belle Kearney's publicists, no doubt with her permission, described her as a "Mississippi gentlewoman," "tall and dignified, with a gracious, queenly bearing."[1] Yet she believed that nineteenth-century southern ladies were nonentities, locked in a prison of "pent up possibilities," and she desired for herself a "higher life."[2] She credited the Civil War and the Woman's Christian Temperance Union (WCTU) with her opportunity to create a more satisfying life for herself. Who was this Belle Kearney who chose as the inscription for her gravestone the words "Lecturer—Author—Senator"?

Carrie Belle Kearney was born two months after Abraham Lincoln issued the Emancipation Proclamation and four months before Union victories at Vicksburg and Gettysburg sealed the fate of the Confederate cause. Her parents were children of the Old South, and Kearney was imbued with their customs and sensibilities. Kearney said in her autobiography that she was born "just two months and six days too late for [her] to be a constitutional slaveholder."[3] But she also realized that the South was changing rapidly and that she must adapt to realities that her parents found daunting.

Kearney's father, Walter Guston Kearney, came to Madison County, Mississippi, with his family in 1829 when he was two years old. He graduated from Centenary College in Louisiana in 1847 and went to Kentucky to study law. Deciding that his future lay in planting rather than law, he returned to Madison County, where a generous father endowed him with a home, land, and slaves. In 1849 he married Susannah Owens, also an heir to land, slaves, and furniture, and

BELLE KEARNEY

From her autobiography, *A Slaveholder's Daughter* (1900).

they set up a household at Vernon Heights, near Flora, Mississippi.[4] In her auto-biography, Kearney observed that her father was more interested in books than planting and spent much of his time in his library. She described her mother as "intensely literary" and the whole family as noted for intelligence.[5]

Belle Kearney remembered both of her parents as being ill-fitted for the con-ditions of life after the war. Not realizing the "terrible change that had come into their fortunes," they continued to live extravagantly for a few years.[6] Mortgage foreclosures deprived them of most of their property, and the loss of most of their laborers caused her father to seek other means of supporting his family. But neither an insurance business nor a law practice was successful.

Kearney was the family's third child, but by the mid-1870s her older brother and sister had died, leaving her as the oldest child with three younger brothers.[7] Because of their precarious financial situation, her father could hire very little help, and the family had to take care of the rest of the work. When another baby was born in 1874, Kearney was indignant, believing her parents should have known they were too poor to have another child. Her mother was often "prostrated by neuralgia," which left much of the cooking and housework to Belle.[8] To enlist the assistance of her brothers, Kearney offered to read to them and tell them stories at night in return for their help. They became her first audience.

Kearney received her early education from young women who boarded with them.[9] Later she attended public school taught by Mrs. Bettie Fenderson, who had come from Maine to Mississippi, where she lived with her widowed sister Mrs. Woodman. Visits to their home gave Kearney her "first wide out look upon humanity."[10] When she was thirteen, she went to Canton to live with her uncle Kinchen Kearney so that she could attend the Canton Female Institute. After two years her father could no longer pay the monthly tuition of $5.00. Kearney was in despair, believing that her formal schooling was at an end. She had never heard of a woman working her way through college. Even if she had thought of it, her family would have considered it a disgrace for her to work publicly. "I was fairly bound to the rock of hopelessness by the cankered chains of a false conventionality, and sacrificed for lack of a precedent," she wrote.[11]

At fifteen Belle felt aimless. She wondered, if living meant no more for her than it did for the women around her, what was the use of reading? But she did read avidly. She wanted to study law, but her father was opposed. Because they needed the income, she and her mother began sewing for the black families who lived around them, charging fifty to seventy-five cents for a ruffled dress. For a "slaveholder's daughter," this was a sign of extreme desperation. At this time Kearney also suffered a crisis in her faith. She described herself later as haunted by unbelief for ten years. She tried to avoid the Methodist ministers who were frequent visitors in their home even while her curiosity about the world led her to seek out the Democratic politicians who came to see her father.

Despite their dire financial straits, the Kearney family remained members of Mississippi's white elite, and at sixteen Kearney made her "first entrance into society as a young lady," participating in social activities surrounding commencement at the University of Mississippi, croquet and fashionable calls by day, cards and other entertainments at night.[12] During the next few years she visited cousins in Canton and Jackson, "drift[ing] with the tide," and engaging in the "gaities" that occupied the privileged youth of her day.[13] She had serious reservations about her lifestyle, doubting that card playing, dancing, and wine drinking were proper and feeling that she was not living up to her own "high conceptions of life."[14]

Kearney decided to give up her "shallow" life and find appropriate work.[15] When she proposed to become a teacher, her father objected but finally agreed for her to hold classes in an upstairs room of their home. She enrolled seven children from the surrounding area but found the monthly tuition of $12.00 inadequate and the lack of interest of most of the students discouraging. Her decision to teach in a public school was even more alarming to her father, who considered such work unbecoming to one of her social standing and an indication that he could not support his family. Nevertheless, she taught for several years, working for part of the year at the public school and another few months at a private school held in a Methodist church building. She used money from her first session to attend the Normal School at Iuka, where she studied pedagogy and bookkeeping. She also studied math with a private tutor in Canton.

In 1889, when the famed leader of the WCTU, Frances Willard, came to Mississippi, Kearney's father urged her to go to Jackson to hear Willard speak. Kearney was captivated by Willard's dynamic presence and disappointed when she did not have the opportunity to meet her personally. Willard went on to Crystal Springs for the state convention, however, and friends arranged for Kearney to attend that meeting, where she was asked to lead the young women's department. After being assured that she would be furnished materials needed to prepare her for her duties, Kearney agreed to become state superintendent of the Loyal Temperance Legion, a juvenile society, and the Young Woman's Christian Temperance Union. She set out on a tour of Mississippi towns, speaking wherever a group could be assembled. She organized her first unit in Flora near her home, a second in Port Gibson, and another on the Gulf Coast near Biloxi. During the first year she claimed to have organized over one hundred unions of young women and juveniles.

When Kearney entered the Methodist church at Washington near Natchez, a surprise awaited her. Her audience consisted of young men from the local academy, and she realized that neither of her prepared speeches, one aimed at children, the other at young women, would suffice. After a moment of panic, she improvised a presentation, which persuaded many of those present to sign a pledge against the use of alcohol and tobacco.

Kearney attended a national convention in Chicago in 1889 and national and international conventions in Boston in 1891, where she was commissioned as a national lecturer and organizer. She traveled widely in the South from Delaware to Texas speaking in many different settings, including to black audiences. She claimed to have encountered little opposition to women's public work, even in the South: "Southerners, though tenacious of social traditions, are hospitable to new ideas and are chivalrous toward a woman who wishes their cooperation provided that she comes to them also as a lady," she later wrote.[16] Kearney's work greatly impressed WCTU president Frances Willard, who described Kearney as the "most gifted young woman I have met in the whole South" and "one of the most remarkable I have met anywhere."[17]

Belle enrolled in a Bible study course in 1887 at evangelist Dwight L. Moody's Bible Institute in Chicago but left the six-month course after one month, claiming physical exhaustion. She continued with voice lessons and instruction in physical training, however. While in the North she spoke at an international convention of the newly formed youth organization the Christian Endeavor Society in Canada, and the prominent prohibitionist John G. Woolley invited her to attend a Minnesota convention of men who wanted to break the alcohol habit.

In the fall of 1893 Kearney resumed her work in the southern states. At a state convention in Natchez in 1895 Kearney was elected president of the Mississippi WCTU. She resigned almost immediately, however, when Frances Willard invited her to attend an international conference in London and asked her to consider becoming a "round-the-world missionary" for the WCTU. Kearney was sorely tempted by the offer, as she clearly enjoyed the limelight and delighted in being given this opportunity to visit places she might not otherwise see. But she was also conflicted over the time away from her parents, feeling that she might be needed at home. After careful consideration, she concluded that it was not God's will for her to make the tour. God's will or not, her return home seemed providential, for she arrived to find her brother Guston Thomas Kearney near death. Within a week he was gone.

Kearney traveled widely during 1896 and 1897, lecturing in the Northeast, the far west, and Alaska. She was at home in 1898 when Harry Kinchen Kearney, her brother, made a rare visit, however. Later that year she received word that he had died, shot by an outlaw in New Mexico. In three years she had lost two brothers who were only twenty-nine and thirty-one years old at the time of their deaths.[18]

Kearney continued her support of the temperance movement for the remainder of her life, serving as a national WCTU lecturer for twenty-one years. Later, as part of the popular Chautauqua adult education movement, she became a traveling lyceum lecturer. She spoke on a number of topics but always managed to bring up the importance of temperance no matter what her chosen subject. After the passage of the Eighteenth Amendment to the Constitution, which prohibited the "manufacture, sale, or transportation of intoxicating liquors," she urged its strict enforcement.[19]

Kearney also became an advocate and spokesperson for woman suffrage. While attending the national WCTU convention in Boston in 1891, she attended a reception hosted by members of the Massachusetts Woman Suffrage Association and the Woman Suffrage League of Boston. National leaders Lucy Stone and Julia Ward Howe invited those present to express their beliefs regarding woman suffrage. Two southern women, Lide Meriwether of Tennessee and Frances Griffin of Alabama, were among those who supported equal rights. Kearney later wrote in her autobiography that she had always believed in the rights of women although initially she did not think they should ask for the ballot. Yet, like many other temperance workers, she came to recognize women's need for enfranchisement as a means of achieving other goals. Later, during another trip to the North, Kearney spent a night in the home of Susan B. Anthony, who encouraged the Mississippian to push for woman suffrage in her home state.

Several local suffrage clubs were organized in 1895 after Carrie Chapman Catt and Elizabeth Upham Yates toured Mississippi.[20] The Mississippi Woman Suffrage Association (MWSA) was formed in Meridian on 5 May 1897 following a WCTU convention. Nellie Nugent Somerville was elected president; Belle Kearney, vice president; and Lily Wilkinson Thompson, corresponding secretary.[21]

Kearney attended a convention of the National American Woman Suffrage Association (NAWSA) 1898 in Washington, D.C. While at the convention, Kearney learned that Frances Willard, the woman Kearney described as "the leading inspiration of my life," had died. Kearney traveled from Washington, D.C., to New York to attend Willard's funeral service and then returned to Washington to make a speech before the NAWSA. Kearney "lectured on social changes in the South, 'depicting in a rapid, magnetic manner, interspersed with flashes of wit, the evolution of the southern woman and the revolution in customs and privileges which must inevitably lead up to political rights.'"[22] Back in Mississippi she addressed a meeting of the MWSA on the subject "Come Let Us Reason Together."[23] In June she organized a local club in Flora. Her seventy-one-year-old father and sixty-seven-year-old mother attended the meeting with her, and her father, who had apparently come to terms with and even grown to support his daughter's unconventional career, agreed to serve as president.[24]

Kearney's association with some Mississippi supporters of temperance and woman suffrage was strained because of her peripatetic ways. Nellie Nugent Somerville complained that Kearney would come home long enough to stir things up and then would be gone again.[25] Somerville later referred to Kearney as "too selfish and egotistical for real usefulness."[26] National suffrage leader Anna Howard Shaw had a similar reaction, considering Kearney to be "brilliant" but "erratic."[27] Kearney was a flamboyant person who promoted herself, probably at times taking more than her share of the credit for accomplishments. And she annoyed other suffrage leaders at times by requesting payment for her suffrage lectures. Kearney's critics, many of them affluent women, may not have sufficiently taken into account her more precarious financial situation and need to support herself through her work. Paid lecture tours provided most of that support and therefore were her scheduling priority.

Whatever suffrage leaders may have thought of Kearney, she was widely recognized as a great orator. In 1903 she was invited to give the keynote address at the NAWSA Convention in New Orleans. She chose as her subject "The South and Woman Suffrage." Kearney used this national stage to promote woman suffrage as a means of maintaining the "political supremacy of Anglo-Saxonism" in the South. Kearney and many other southern suffragists had come to believe that their most effective means of gaining support for woman suffrage in their states was to offer it as an answer to the "negro problem." Although she expressed relief that slavery had been abolished, Kearney was incensed that "illiterate and semi-barbarous" freedmen had been granted the vote. "The South is slow to grasp the fact that enfranchisement of women would settle the race question in politics," she wrote.[28] She brushed aside the fears of those who thought that opening up the question of woman suffrage was wrong because black women as well as white women would gain the vote. She reassured opponents that the same methods that prevented black men from voting could be used to control the votes of black women, including literacy tests. According to Kearney, the idea of promoting woman suffrage as a way of preserving white supremacy was suggested to her by *Woman's Journal* editor Henry Blackwell of Massachusetts. Blackwell, a former abolitionist, nonetheless urged the South to enfranchise literate women only, although he realized that most literate women in the region were white.[29]

The 1903 convention was "perhaps the high-water mark of the southern strategy" of promoting woman suffrage as a solution to "the negro problem."[30] Believing that southern states might be convinced to adopt woman suffrage to help preserve white supremacy in politics, national leaders accepted the racist arguments made by Kearney and others. And in NAWSA policy they officially adopted "the principle of State rights, leaving to each State Association to determine the qualification for membership in the Association and the terms upon which the extension of suffrage to women shall be requested of the respective State Legislatures."[31] It soon became clear, however, that the southern states were not likely to approve woman suffrage on any grounds.

In the year following the New Orleans convention, Kearney began her long awaited world tour, giving lectures on temperance and woman suffrage and authoring a series of newspaper articles about her experiences. It is not clear how she was able to afford the trip, but she no doubt drew upon her southern charm, her renown as a temperance lecturer, and her acquaintance with prominent people in England and on the Continent. She had the opportunity to meet such notables as Prince Bernhard Von Buelow in Berlin, the empress's sister and Count Leo Tolstoy in Russia, Queen Wilhelmina in Holland, and King Leopold in Belgium. She organized chapters of the WCTU in Damascus and Cairo and addressed the National Educational Association of China in Shanghai and the National Convention of Japanese Women in Yokohama. Always an avid observer of new places and people, Kearney gathered material for many future lectures.[32]

Upon her return to the South, Kearney found the woman suffrage movement in the doldrums in Mississippi as well as other southern states. She called for a meeting of southern suffragists to be held in Memphis in December 1906. The dozen or so women who attended organized the Southern Woman Suffrage Conference and recommended enfranchising all literate women. At a similar meeting in Jackson those in attendance sought to rejuvenate the dormant MWSA. Kearney then toured the state organizing local suffrage clubs wherever she could, bringing the number in the state to eleven.[33]

In addition to temperance and woman suffrage, Kearney supported the social purity or sex hygiene movement, an effort closely allied with the WCTU to wipe out prostitution and venereal diseases. She served for a time as the field secretary of the World Purity Foundation, encouraging sex education beginning in the home for young children and continuing in school.[34] Her weightiest contribution to the cause was a 576-page novel published in 1921. Its title described its purpose: *Conqueror or Conquered: or The Sex Challenge Answered. A Revelation of Scientific Facts from the Highest Medical Authorities, Based upon the Relations of Sex Life to the Mental, Moral and Physical Welfare of Both Sexes—Young and Old. A Dramatic Story of Real Life Written in a Fascinating and Entertaining Style, Describing the Tragic Results of Ignorance Surrounding the Mysteries of Sex.* Set in the post–Civil War South, the book tells the story of two young aristocrats. One learned to control his sexual urges and maintained his chastity until marriage while the other brought ruin to himself and others by his promiscuity. Included in the book, by means of conversations between a physician and others, was explicit information about the risks of sex and the causes and effects of venereal disease.[35]

Belle Kearney spent much of her time outside the South after 1910. She participated in lyceum and Chautauqua lecture tours, and she lobbied in Washington for the passage of the prohibition and woman suffrage amendments. During World War I she spent time as a volunteer in England and France and also toured army camps in the United States, encouraging the soldiers.[36] Following the war, Kearney saw her two cherished causes guaranteed by federal amendment. The prohibition amendment was ratified in 1919, and the Nineteenth Amendment, giving women the right to vote, was ratified in 1920. Mississippi was the first state to ratify the Eighteenth Amendment. Despite the efforts of Kearney and others, however, the legislature refused to ratify the woman suffrage amendment, denying supporters the pleasure of receiving the vote by the action of their own state. Although legal prohibition did not have the effect its supporters had hoped for and was repealed in 1933, temperance advocates, especially Kearney, were gratified to have gained the amendment.

Four months after the ratification of the national suffrage amendment, Belle Kearney announced her intention to seek the U.S. Senate seat being vacated by John Sharp Williams in 1922. Politics was in her blood. Democratic politicians had frequented her home when she was growing up, and her father had served in the Mississippi House of Representatives in the early 1880s and in the state senate in the early 1890s. Kearney had long considered herself a member of the Prohibition party, a one-issue party that was extremely popular during the 1880s and 1890s but lost steam after 1920. By 1922 she was in the Democratic fold. Her opponents in the senatorial race were former governor and U.S. Senator James K. Vardaman and U.S. Representative Hubert D. Stephens.

Kearney's platform reflected her belief in activist government and a preference for federal legislation over a strict adherence to the philosophy of states' rights, a position that put her at odds with most southern politicians of her day. The yearbook of the Mississippi Federation of Women's Clubs for 1920–21 printed her statement: "I stand for: Education; Law Enforcement; Restricted Immigration; Child Welfare; Protective Legislation for Women in Industry;

Ownership of Homes; Public Health and Social Morality; Economy in Government; Reduction in Taxation; Federal Co-operation for Aid of Farmers; Labor Legislation; Commission for Mediation, Conciliation and Arbitration; A League of Nations."[37] Accustomed to lecture tours, she campaigned actively. Often she would choose a subject designed to draw a crowd, such as "Our Country and Others" or "The World's New Republics."[38] People who did not intend to vote for her would come to hear her speak, for the novel opportunity of hearing a woman orator or because of her reputation as an interesting and entertaining speaker.

Never one to be overly modest, Kearney claimed "the political allegiance of every woman in Mississippi."[39] Yet she failed to take into account the apathy of much of the female population, the poor level of organization among activist women, and the fact that some of her sister reformers were not as supportive as she may have expected. Nellie Nugent Somerville, for example, confided to a friend that she would never vote for Kearney.[40] Kearney received just over 18,000 votes in the first primary in August 1922, putting her well behind Vardaman's 74,597 votes and Stephens's 65,980 and eliminating her from the race.

In the second primary, Kearney encouraged her supporters to vote for Stephens because she considered Vardaman and his cronies a disgrace. She especially objected to Vardaman because of his opposition to the United States support of the Allied cause in World War I. Although Vardaman had favored woman suffrage and Stephens had not, Kearney felt that his lack of patriotism was a more important issue. When Stephens won, she prided herself for having helped (she believed) to bring about the defeat of Vardamanism. She spent the rest of the year lecturing about her experiences, referring to herself as a "heroine in the fight against factionalism."[41]

The following year Kearney ran for a seat in the Mississippi Senate representing the Eighteenth District. She was amazed when three men entered the race against her. She told a campaign audience that she did not dream that any man in Madison County who knew of her record of service would oppose her. She was certain no woman would "because of her sex loyalty."[42] As in her campaign for the U.S. Senate, she emphasized issues she had espoused for many years, including strict enforcement of prohibition; programs to benefit women, children, and persons with special needs; governmental reform; improvement of schools and charitable institutions; and appointment of women to state boards and agencies. She led in the first primary and easily won election in the second. Nellie Nugent Somerville, who had won a seat in the Mississippi House of Representatives in the first primary that year, earned the title of the first woman elected to the Mississippi state legislature. Not one to be outdone, Belle Kearney labeled herself the South's first woman state senator.

As might be expected, Kearney's entrance into the Senate chamber caused a stir. When her new colleagues presented her a bouquet of roses, she "rose instantly and with a bow and a gesture of appreciation that brought up visions of Queen Bess and Queen Anne expressed her thanks in effective manner."[43] Kearney uncharacteristically indicated that she intended to "be very quiet as a member of the Senate of the Legislature of Mississippi. Those who expect great things of me, I fear, will be disappointed."[44] She told her colleagues in the Senate that she had determined not to speak unless she "felt the absolute necessity of doing so," because men expect women to have something to say on every subject.[45] It was not long, however, before she began to feel the necessity. When it was proposed that the Senate adjourn on Thursday of the first week to await the inauguration of the governor on the following Monday, she regretted the valuable session time that would be lost and protested the adjournment in vain. Later she suggested successfully that Jackson clergy be invited to open each day's session with prayer. Her attempt to ban smoking in the chamber was not successful, however, nor was her attempt to prevent Alabama Senator Oscar Underwood from speaking to the legislature because of his antiprohibition views.

Only four of the twenty bills Kearney introduced became law. Several passed the upper house but were not acted on favorably in the lower house. Others failed in the Senate. Two of her successful bills dealt with her county, one of them authorizing the Board of Supervisors to borrow money to maintain a consolidated school. A third bill established bird and game sanctuaries in Mississippi, and a fourth, cosponsored with two other senators, provided for the appointment of directors for the Old Soldiers' Home at Beauvoir. Other bills, concerning eleemosynary institutions, prohibition laws, and governmental reform all failed.[46]

When her four-year term came to an end, Kearney did not seek reelection. She resumed her former activities, undertaking a lecture tour to California. She soon decided that she no longer had the stamina for the exhausting schedule, however. She worked hard for the enforcement of prohibition, including supporting efforts of the National Woman's Democratic Law Enforcement League to prevent Democrats from selecting New York Governor Al Smith as their nominee for president on the grounds that he was a "wet."

After the repeal of the Eighteenth Amendment in 1933, Kearney was much less active in the public arena. She spent time organizing materials regarding her career and gave personal and family mementos to the Industrial Institute and College and the Mississippi Department of Archives and History. She even rejoined the Methodist Church.

Kearney was ill during the last few years of her life and died of cancer on 27 February 1939. On the day of her funeral her body lay in state in the Capitol rotunda, and the state flag flew at half-mast. Following services conducted in Jackson by the Reverend W. J. Ferguson, her Flora minister, she was buried in the Kearney family cemetery. An article in the *Jackson Clarion-Ledger* described her as a "gentle-woman for all her progressive ideas about the emancipation of woman."[47] The woman who desired a significant life would have been pleased with the ceremonies surrounding her death. For one who relished travel and new experiences but always loved to come home, her burial with other family members at the old home place was fitting.

NOTES

1. Brochure, n.d., Belle Kearney Papers, Mississippi Department of Archives and History (henceforth MDAH), Jackson.

2. Belle Kearney, *A Slaveholder's Daughter* (New York: Abbey Press, 1900), 166, 169. Details about Kearney's early life not otherwise cited come from this source.

3. Ibid., 9.

4. *Biographical and Historical Memoirs of Mississippi*, vol. 1 (Chicago: Goodspeed Publishing, 1891), 1066–67; Dunbar Rowland, comp., *The Official and Statistical Register of the State of Mississippi* (New York: J. J. Little and Ives, 1924–28), 147–50.

5. Death notice of Susannah Owens Kearney, *New Orleans Christian Advocate*, 7 November 1918, Kearney Papers.

6. Kearney, *Slaveholder's Daughter*, 20.

7. Nancy Carol Tipton, " 'It Is My Duty': The Public Career of Belle Kearney" (master's thesis, University of Mississippi, 1975), 7.

8. Kearney, *Slaveholder's Daughter*, 24.

9. Kearney, "School Days," Kearney Papers.

10. Kearney, *Slaveholder's Daughter*, 31.

11. Ibid., 41.

12. Ibid., 66–67.

13. Ibid., 68–70.

14. Ibid., 69.

15. Ibid., 70.

16. Ibid., 185.

17. Frances E. Willard to My dear sister [Mrs. Frank Parker, Englewood, Ill.], 10 December 1892, Kearney Papers.

18. Tipton, 7.

19. Rowland, 147–50.

20. A. Elizabeth Taylor, "The Woman Suffrage Movement in Mississippi, 1890–1920," *Journal of Mississippi History* 30 (February 1968): 6–7.

21. Susan B. Anthony and Ida Husted Harper, eds., *The History of Woman Suffrage*, vol. 4, *1883– 1900* (1922; reprint, New York: Arno Press, 1969), 783–89; Taylor, 7.

22. Kearney, *Slaveholder's Daughter*, 266; Anthony and Harper, eds., 293.

23. Tipton, 40.

24. Kearney, *Slaveholder's Daughter*, 109; Taylor, 8–9.

25. Marjorie Spruill Wheeler, *New Women of the New South: The Leaders of the Woman Suffrage Movement in the Southern States* (New York: Oxford University Press, 1993), 192.

26. Ibid.

27. Ibid., 121.

28. Kearney, "The South and Woman Suffrage," *Woman's Journal* (4 April 1903), reprinted in *Up from the Pedestal, Selected Writings in the History of American Feminism*, ed. Aileen S. Kraditor (Chicago: Quadrangle Books, 1968), 263–64; Kearney, *Slaveholder's Daughter*, 97.

29. Kearney, *Slaveholder's Daughter*, 97–100.

30. Wheeler, 118.

31. Ibid.

32. Tipton, 49–51; lecture brochure, n.d., Kearney Papers; Ian Tyrrell, *Woman's World, Woman's Empire: The Woman's Christian Temperance Union in International Perspective, 1880–1930* (Chapel Hill: University of North Carolina Press, 1991), 87–88.

33. Taylor, 11–14.

34. Rowland, 150.

35. Kearney, *Conqueror or Conquered* (Cincinnati: S. A. Mullikin, 1921).

36. Lecture brochure, n.d., Kearney Papers; Anne Firor Scott, "Belle Kearney," in *Notable American Women, 1607–1950, A Biographical Dictionary*, ed. Edward T. James, vol. 2 (Cambridge: The Belknap Press of Harvard University Press, 1971), 309–10.

37. Tipton, 95.

38. Ibid., 99.

39. Ibid., 93.

40. Wheeler, 192.

41. Flyer, n.d., Kearney Papers; Tipton, 113.

42. Tipton, 114.

43. *Jackson Clarion-Ledger*, 9 January 1924, quoted in Tipton, 121.

44. Kearney to Dunbar Rowland, 12 January 1924, Kearney Papers, quoted in Tipton, 119.

45. Tipton, 123.

46. Ibid., 123–37.

47. Ibid., 141–51.

Pauline Van de Graaf Orr

(1861–1955)

Feminist Education in Mississippi

SARAH WILKERSON-FREEMAN

In 1885, Pauline Van de Graaf Orr joined the founding faculty of the state Industrial Institute and College for the Education of White Girls (II&C). Over the next twenty-eight years, as head of the English and Literature Department, she earned a reputation as a fierce defender and promoter of women's higher education. When she resigned in May 1913 from her position at the college, which later became the Mississippi University for Women, she explained the principal goals of her work: "I have desired, above everything else, the mental enfranchisement of the girls of Mississippi. I have tried to help them to realize and express themselves; and whatever success I have attained in this direction, I count my best service to my day and generation."[1] Orr had been elected to an office in the Mississippi Woman Suffrage Association and her resignation from the faculty represented the next step in her life-long challenge to traditional views regarding the subjugation and education of women. Her stature as a brilliant thinker and revered teacher brought many II&C students, alumnae, and club women to the suffrage cause. Orr was twice elected to serve as president of the Mississippi suffragists, and the impact of her work in Mississippi, as a feminist and an educator, would be felt for generations.

Pauline Orr was born in Chickasaw County, Mississippi, in 1861. Her parents, Cornelia Van de Graaf (1833–1917) and Jehu (J. A.) Orr (1828–1920), came from prominent southern families. Cornelia, originally from Mobile, Alabama, learned from her lawyer father to hate slavery and was sent to New Haven, Connecticut, to be educated in a girls' boarding school. J. A. Orr, a lawyer from a politically connected South Carolina family, earned a master's degree at Princeton University and was a widower with three small children when he married

Cornelia in 1857. He was a devoted Democrat prior to the Civil War and was appointed secretary of the state senate and United States Attorney for Mississippi's northern district. Although he was a reluctant secessionist, J.A. served in the Secession Convention and the Provisional Congress of the Confederacy and raised and commanded a regiment of 1,400 men. As a member of the Confederate Congress during the last eighteen months of the war, J.A. and his brother, Confederate Senator James Orr of South Carolina, tried unsuccessfully to convince Confederate President Jefferson Davis to negotiate for peace.[2]

The hard circumstances of the war and postwar years blurred gender roles, strained domestic relations, and threatened patriarchal traditions of the Old South. The Orr household was a laboratory for these forces. Shortly after their marriage, J.A. purchased a plantation with his new wife's fortune and, against her wishes, used her money to buy slaves. During the war, and J.A.'s long absences, Cornelia bore two children, Pauline and her younger sister, Corinne, cared for three stepchildren, and managed the plantation and family business interests. Her husband's heavy investment in "negro property," as many as sixty-five slaves, would have financially ruined the family if Cornelia's mother had not intervened and paid a large portion of J.A.'s debt.[3] As an adult, Pauline remembered her mother taking charge of the finances and credited her with "saving" the family in the face of a difficult and uncertain future. In the late 1860s, when Union soldiers occupied Mississippi and Republicans ruled the legislature, J.A. accepted a judicial appointment in the sixth district and the family's economic situation improved. Pauline watched her parents, especially her mother, struggle in this period, and she became determined to be economically independent and resourceful.

Pauline also responded to the years of crisis by losing herself in books. Her mother taught her to read before she was old enough to attend grammar school. For endless hours she read books from her father's library, a vast room walled with shelves containing English literary classics. After briefly attending a girls' grammar school, Pauline "respectfully but emphatically . . . refused to attend school altogether, unless she were allowed to go to the 'big school,'" a local boys' preparatory school. For a year, she secretly studied the school's curriculum, mastered the advanced English and Latin, and memorized geometric theorems and algebraic principles. After demonstrating her skills to the school's headmaster, and her surprised parents, Pauline was allowed to enroll even though she was female and ten years younger than most of the students. In the waning days of Reconstruction, Pauline graduated at the top of her class from the "boys' school," an accomplishment of which she would be proud all her life.[4]

PAULINE VAN DE GRAAF ORR

1910. From *Meh Lady*, yearbook of the
Mississippi University for Women.
Special Collections, Mississippi University
for Women.

In 1876, the family's position shifted dramatically once again. Mississippi's conservative Democrats refused to reappoint Pauline's father to the bench despite the fact J.A. never supported a radical Republican agenda and fought to exclude African American men from politics.[5] Stung by the rejection, he channeled his energies into establishing a successful legal practice. Perhaps to soften the blow, Pauline and her father traveled to the 1876 Sesquicentennial Exhibition in Philadelphia, where the exhibits whetted her appetite for cultural and intellectual life beyond Mississippi.[6] Two years later, she rejected her mother's choice of a traditional "finishing school" and instead insisted on attending Packer Collegiate Institute in Brooklyn Heights, New York, a girls' boarding school with a rigorous and innovative curriculum. At age sixteen, Pauline left Columbus for Brooklyn Heights, a short trolley ride from the nation's largest city. In 1878, she was the only Packer student from the Deep South.

Pauline's years at Packer, where women's intellectual abilities were held in high regard, had a profound impact on her. She studied geometry, theology, "Moral Science" (ethics), chemistry, botany, and English literature, especially Milton, Chaucer, and Shakespeare's *Merchant of Venice* and *Hamlet.* Packer promised in its promotional literature to prepare women "to enter the larger sphere of citizens of the United States, and . . . citizens of the world, with all the wider social[,] national, and international interest implied in that term." Several female faculty members advocated expanding women's "sphere," especially Professor Mary Lowe Dickinson, who was a nationally recognized author, woman suffragist, and temperance activist. Dickinson took Pauline under her wing, guided her development as a scholar and feminist, and encouraged her to become a professional writer.[7]

For all of the excitement and intellectual inspiration Pauline experienced in the North, her time away from home was not easy. During these years, she periodically suffered from severe migraine headaches that signaled the onset of "dark" periods later described as depression. She went home to Columbus during such an episode but returned to Packer in 1881 accompanied by her sister. At this point, Pauline's self-styled advanced studies focused on literature and writing, supplemented by private lessons in German and public speaking at the Diehl School for Oratory. She fully immersed herself in the Gilded Age culture of the city's theatres and galleries.[8] Entering her twenties, Pauline set her sights on becoming a New York City journalist. But home and family had a strong hold on her affections, and Mississippi was changing in ways that would offer Pauline unexpected and attractive alternatives to life in the North.

When Mississippi's legislators in 1884 debated a bill to establish a state college for white women, supporters argued that, like it or not, times had changed.

Mississippi's farmers in particular could not afford to delude themselves that white women could depend on financial support from husbands, fathers, or brothers who were themselves dependent on the unstable cotton market. For the sake of their daughters, they needed to provide white women with the means to support themselves if necessary. Some legislators, including Orr's half-brother William, a state representative, opposed the bill, but a powerful coalition, led by the Woman's Christian Temperance Union (WCTU) and the Grange, suc-ceeded in passing the legislation. The establishment of the Industrial Institute and College for the Education of White Girls in 1885 marked the creation of the first state-supported women's college in the nation. Georgia, North Carolina, Alabama, Texas, Florida, South Carolina, and Oklahoma, where the Grange, the Farmers' Alliance, and the WCTU also wielded political influence, followed Mississippi's lead and founded similar institutions.[9]

The decision to locate the II&C at Columbus proved fortuitous for Pauline. Unhappy with his daughter's desire to stay in New York, J.A. persuaded her to apply for a position at the new college. Pauline had rejected offers to teach from several excellent private women's colleges and coed universities in the North, specifically Vassar, Wellesley, Bryn Mawr, Syracuse, and Northwestern. J.A., a University of Mississippi trustee since 1872, brought Pauline's impressive cre-dentials to the attention of the II&C trustees, who quickly offered her a position. In 1885, Pauline abandoned her dream of a journalism career and returned to Columbus to head the II&C's English and Literature Department.[10]

As a member of the college's first faculty, Orr faced extraordinary chal-lenges. Former student Blanche Colton Williams recalled: "When the college for women was founded, the state was only just reasserting herself after the [C]ivil [W]ar. English, as a subject of the curriculum, was only just beginning to be taught, even in the foremost colleges of America. The girls who came to the II&C in those earlier days, girls who were born in the late eighteen-sixties and early eighteen-seventies, were a conglomerate mixture. From ante bellum homes and backwoods cabins, the girls thronged to the new college for women." The dormitories could not accommodate the nearly four hundred new stu-dents. At the time, politicians proudly proclaimed that this "experiment" in women's education placed Mississippi "in the lead." But Rosa Peebles, a student in those early years, who later directed Vassar College's English Department, remembered that two faculty, Pauline Orr and Mary Calloway, a mathematics professor and former head of a female academy, offered an antidote to this "large oratory." Calloway and Orr, whose tastefully buttoned-up appearance, dark hair, and intense dark eyes made her an impressive figure in spite of her youth, told the students that there were few "real colleges" in the South and "none for women." For the II&C to become a bona fide academic institution, they insisted, its students had to work "not as young women in so-called colleges had been accustomed to work, but as women in Europe were working, as women in the eastern part of our country were working. It would be no easy task. Every force was against such an accomplishment."[11]

From her own experiences, Orr knew that women could perform difficult academic work, and she used her elite training to challenge her students' intellectual faculties and improve their self-expression. In her classes, Williams recalled, "We ached over Anglo-Saxon verbs and we bled over Chaucer's spelling, and we wondered . . . [w]hy should Lounsbury's History of Language be absorbed by us who would perhaps teach grammar students only? . . . [B]y the close of Senior year we increased in understanding. . . . By and by we understood more fully yet [that Pauline Orr] had given us a key wherewith to open one door of the House of Life,—once within, all other doors turned on magic hinges. . . . I am thankful to her for many things, but most of all for the courage to *think,* never be afraid of the truth."[12] This approach toward women's education reflected Orr's liberal feminist philosophies, especially her conviction that women should be able to pursue the same avenues of achievement and occupations as men and not be treated as less than or inferior to men. These convictions were visible as a common thread running through her career as she developed her role as a teacher of young Mississippi women, engaged in frequent battles on behalf of women's equality inside and beyond the academy, and fought to write feminist principles into the mission of the college.

Such ideals demanded high standards, but a significant percentage of entering students, many as young as fifteen, needed preparatory courses before beginning the required liberal arts coursework. Students and parents complained that the academic standards were unrealistic. From Orr's point of view, the college's three-tiered curriculum, which offered programs in industrial training (one year), in teaching (two years), and for a bachelor of arts degree (four years), stood in the way of her goals as a teacher. She and several colleagues considered the industrial and teaching tracks a threat to the bachelor of arts program, and women's higher education in general, and a rivalry emerged among the advocates of different programs. Orr summed up the controversy many years later: "It wasn't easy. There were those who said girls didn't belong in college. And there were those who thought we should go easy on the girls."[13]

A second obstacle was the failure of legislators to respect and appreciate the college and its faculty. The II&C's first president, Richard Watson Jones, a University of Mississippi chemistry professor, respected the all-female faculty and particularly admired Orr's "vigorous intellect" and her desire to offer advanced courses as students became capable of performing more difficult work.[14] But few legislators shared Jones's attitude. In February 1888, the House debated a bill to cut the II&C's funding and the faculty's salaries in spite of existing contracts. Infuriated, Orr and her colleagues submitted a formal protest to the legislature "in Behalf of the Womanhood of the State," accusing the men of breaking their promises to the women and the public at large.

As they stated their case, it became clear that faculty leaders, especially Pauline Orr, considered the principle of women's equality to be central to the success, indeed the mission, of the college. One purpose of the II&C, they insisted, was to counter "the prevailing superficiality in the so-called education of girls" by developing and maintaining high standards under the guidance of fairly compensated specialists and scholars. "Is it fair, is it just," they asked, "that the men who make the laws, although acknowledging an equality in the character and the influence of the work of men and women, should insist upon an inequality in the reward—that inequality in favor of their own sex?"[15] Students who wanted to be teachers, they argued, would not feel compelled to study long and hard "while you assure them that the State, and consequently society, will not recognize and reward them as their skill and knowledge justify. . . . Will you say to [II&C students]: 'Study conscientiously, laboriously, consecutively for years, . . . but remember that by the accident of sex you are debarred from ever receiving the just recompense. . . . Your work, because you are a woman, is to be branded with the mark of inferiority, and sold for what would be little more than half its market price, if offered by a man.'" In the wake of this bitter controversy, Jones resigned, but Orr continued to press the II&C's new president and the legislature to support the principle of "equal pay for equal work."[16]

The salary controversy remained unresolved, and discrimination against women at the II&C continued to be an issue. Under the hiring policy of the trustees, which stated that "no man shall be employed for service a woman can render," only women received faculty appointments and only men were hired to serve as president.[17] Many in the community wanted women on the Board of Trustees and some wanted a female president. With Jones's departure, the clamor to give women more power at the college grew louder. In September 1888, the trustees responded by revising their policy, making it clear that the president's position would be open only to men. They hired Charles Hartwell Cocke who immediately reduced the liberal arts requirements for all programs. These actions indicated to Orr and the high-standards faction that Cocke rejected their efforts to use the college to improve women's status. Indeed, it seemed to some that he wanted to institutionalize a modern version of female subjugation and exploitation to keep Mississippi's white women in a second-class position.[18]

In March 1890, Cocke's vision and authority were challenged when five alumnae from the first graduating class and fifty-four students sent petitions through the governor to the trustees protesting changes in the bachelor of arts program and calling for Cocke's removal. According to the petitions, he mistreated faculty members and was incompetent and unqualified because he failed to receive a degree after attending the University of Virginia for five years. Orr and Calloway led a faction of the faculty in support of the student movement and submitted their own list of Cocke's faults and inadequacies.[19] After the governor received two hundred letters from students threatening to leave the college if Cocke remained, the trustees asked for his resignation. The trustees asked Mary Calloway to serve as acting II&C president until a new man was hired. Then he, too, left under a cloud at midyear, and Calloway was again given temporary leadership of the school. While some critics charged that there was "something rotten" about a college that resisted the rule of men, II&C students showed their appreciation by establishing the Calloway-Orr Society to honor "truly educated, noble womanhood."[20]

Orr's students were not the only ones who applauded the young and brilliant professor's conviction to establish a model women's college that challenged gender prejudices. Early in her career, Orr became a recognized leader in the women's higher education movement in the South. In an 1891 speech on "The Education of the Modern Woman," delivered before the Mississippi Teachers' Association, Orr proclaimed that "education, with all the possibilities it implies, is the heritage of the daughters of a free and enlightened state. This is their new birthright." She stated that higher education for girls, which opened to them the doors of science, art, literature, and "all those industrial pursuits that a woman's constitution fits her to engage in," had been sanctioned with the "seal of the state." But the priorities needed to be clear. The college's primary goal, she believed, was "intellectual," to give young women the "power of thought" and "command of [their] resources." The second goal was "the industrial, fitting [a girl] for the practice of some bread winning pursuit." This, Orr argued, was simply a "recognition of practical necessities," for the value of such training "will depend largely upon those individual circumstances and surroundings *which can be confidently predicted in the case of no girl whatever.*" Young women, she argued, should be taught to fulfill a range of personal and professional goals, to be resourceful and independent as a hedge against the uncertainty and vulnerability that characterized women's lives. Her remarks impressed South Carolina's white Populists, who reprinted her address to fuel the movement for a white woman's college in their state.[21]

Orr's views concerning the fragility of women's security and her promotion of education as a preemptive strike against female dependence reflected insights from her personal life, especially her close relationship with a former student and II&C colleague Miriam "Minnie" Greene Paslay. A brilliant student of Latin, Paslay was orphaned during her college years. She worked all the harder to earn one of the first bachelor of arts degrees, and after some graduate training, was hired to teach in the Classics Department in 1891. Cornelia Orr offered Paslay room and board in her home, an arrangement Pauline initially resisted, but in time the women grew quite close. A striking red-haired beauty with a keen sense of humor and love of fashion, Paslay softened Orr's overserious temperament. Their relationship evolved into a permanent partnership as each grew to depend on the other for companionship and support, especially during Orr's "dark" periods. Both women felt the limits of their education and motivated each other to pursue advanced training and improve the quality of their academic work. With Miriam as an example of a young southern woman who had to make her own way in the world, Orr honed her arguments for a type of higher education that offered women security and independence.

Paslay's presence also seemed to inspire Orr to emancipate herself, to separate from her parents and live a more independent life. In 1892, a year after Paslay joined the faculty, the two women secured permission to take unpaid sabbaticals and sailed for Europe. Pauline had been incapacitated by long episodes of severe migraine headaches the year before and hired Rosa Peebles to take charge of her classes. Peebles became a regular member of the English Department faculty, strengthening the faction loyal to Orr and her ideals, and made it easier for Orr to leave her duties at the II&C. The majority of the trip was spent in Hanover, Germany, mastering the language and studying the culture.

The women returned to Europe several times between 1893 and 1905 to study historical and comparative linguistics, literature, and ancient cultures. Each trip expanded the scope of their experiences. They took great pleasure testing their physical stamina by hiking for miles in the Alps without a guide. Paslay, a devoted admirer of temperance activist Frances Willard, drank her first beer in Germany. Fin de siècle nightlife appealed to both women and they became habitués of biergärtens and cafés, attended the theater on a weekly basis, and increasingly disassociated themselves from traditional images of the southern belle, excepting Paslay's taste in fashion. The more time they spent abroad, the more benighted Mississippi seemed.[22]

With each trip, they brought something of Europe back to the II&C. Orr hung artwork collected during their travels on her classroom walls, and a student-run alcohol-free biergärten appeared on campus. She introduced an advanced comparative literature course on Old and Middle English works and gave dramatic readings of Chaucer's *Canterbury Tales* and Robert Browning's poetry. Inspired by Browning, her favorite poet, Orr led a class outdoors to smell the blooming hawthorn. She revealed a warm and candid side in weekly informal "heart to heart" talks she hosted for the freshmen. Paslay also altered her approach. Under her instruction, students in the Classical Club performed satirical pageants that poked fun at the inadequacies of "Zeus," a domineering college president, and the narrow-minded people of "Assinnippi."[23]

Their work at the college increasingly challenged traditional views of women's roles and gender discrimination. Both delivered glowing lectures on Frances Willard and Anna Howard Shaw, a leader in the woman suffrage movement, and Orr became bolder in her protests against discrimination. In December 1897 she complained to the trustees about the reinstatement of the "annual review" of II&C faculty, a yearly contract system used in high schools but not the state's men's colleges.[24] Changing the contract system would have given II&C's president, Robert Frazer, more leverage over the female faculty, but he resigned at midyear in the midst of intense hostilities. The legislature sent a committee to Columbus to investigate, and Orr became the center of the inquiry.

Sworn testimonies from trustees, faculty, staff, students, parents, and town residents revealed that the root of the "trouble" was the independence and influence of the female faculty. Frazer and others accused the faction of the faculty led by Orr and Paslay of placing the institution on "too high a plane," holding the students to "too high" a standard, favoring the more dedicated students, and making it overly difficult for some students to graduate. Frazer testified that if he had more power, he would rectify the "abuses" and "promote students on a lower grade." He complained that only the trustees, many of whom were related to faculty members, had the authority to force the women to alter their methods.[25] This criticism prompted one trustee to respond, "I have only stood in defense of the poor girls of Mississippi, who desire thorough education as much as men, and they are as much entitled to it. . . . This ought to be accomplished, and the school ought to be so as to accomplish it."[26] Although many defended Orr, her "ambitious" nature, critics suggested, made her suspect, perhaps even a bad influence on young women.

Unwilling to sit idly by while Frazer and the legislators attacked their college and its most revered professors, II&C students organized and published a statement supporting the faculty in a Columbus paper.[27] Suspicious legislators grilled the young women to prove that Orr and her associates encouraged the students' actions, but the inquisition turned into a rally for the II&C and the embattled faculty. The legislators, as this exchange reveals, were no match for the students.

> [Legislator:] You can say this was absolutely a voluntary movement on the part of the students, and it was their composition, and the faculty had nothing to do with it?
>
> [Miss Carter (a student):] Yes, sir; I could stake my life on that.
>
> [Legislator:] We hope that it will be a long time before the State of Mississippi is deprived of your life.
>
> [Miss Carter:] I hope that it will be a long time before it is deprived of this college. (Applause.)[28]

The testimonies revealed that the college had given the young women a sense of entitlement and power, attitudes that made some men in positions of authority uncomfortable. When asked if the college "subserv[ed] the purpose for which the state established it," Frazer ominously replied, "I think the school is doing more for the State than the State ever expected it to do," and suggested that the practice of hiring only women to serve on the faculty be abolished.[29]

The legislators' analysis invariably returned to the issue of the president's inability to impose his will and standards upon Orr and her supporters. The "trouble," one critic observed, was that, in the absence of a "manly man" president, "you have particularly ambitious women there who are in earnest in their studies, and who are anxious to put forward and develop their pupils in their own departments without regard to the others." To better control this cadre of "ambitious" females, the investigators recommended that a "proper portion of men" serve on the faculty. Some committeemen wanted department heads in particular to be male. In the end, the legislature affirmed the policy that "no one but a man should be president of the institution" and changed the 1884 Enabling Act to allow the president to hire and fire faculty, and all the trustees resigned. Orr and Paslay responded to the unrest by spending the summer taking courses at Cornell University.[30]

The next year, legislators conducted another investigation. Although Orr survived the ordeal, she was disgusted and angry over the second "fling" at the faculty, which she called a "sham." The pressure began to affect her, as she wrote in her diary: "just a little foolish depression . . . over the escalation of mediocre things."[31]

With Frazer gone and a new president, Andrew Armstrong Kincannon, in charge, Orr's situation improved. Kincannon respected Orr and Paslay and approved of their ambitions. In the summer of 1899, they attended classes at Harvard University, and in the summer of 1903, they embarked for Europe, where they spent two years studying at the University of Zurich and the University of Munich. In summers they studied art and architecture in Italy. Upon her return, Orr wrote a stunning lecture on Robert Browning and presented it to the University of Mississippi's all-male English Department. In response to a letter from the university's chancellor praising Orr's abilities, president Kincannon wrote, "In my opinion, Miss Orr is easily the most gifted woman engaged in educational work in the South, and is easily the equal of any of the great women of America." Recognition of her scholarship and speaking abilities spread quickly, due in part to her active role in the Mississippi Federation of Women's Clubs. She presented the Browning paper to literary and women's clubs and returned to lecture on the "education of women to Power Society." Her talents earned her a prestigious position on the national General Federation of Women's Club's Literature Committee. In 1909, Orr was elected president of the Southern Association of College Women, an organization she labored to establish, and received national recognition as the featured speaker at the National Association of Collegiate Alumnae's annual convention.[32]

The situation at the II&C remained tense, however. Three of Orr's close friends on the faculty, including Rosa Peebles and Peebles's life partner, Edith Fahnestock, were asked to resign due to "insubordinate" behavior. Peebles and Fahnestock left Mississippi and enrolled in graduate school at Columbia University. Both had positions at Vassar College by 1909. The third colleague, Eula Deaton, also a former student of Orr's, secured a position at the University of Chicago. Orr and Paslay were already feeling isolated when the new II&C president, Henry Lewis Whitfield, indicated his intentions to expand the domestic science program and cut the Latin and literature requirements. In October 1910, Paslay received a letter from a student complaining about Whitfield's negative attitude toward the Latin curriculum and his generally sexist approach. "I still love my Latin," she wrote. "Mr. Whitfield, however, tries to convince me that Latin will never have any connection with my life. If I love Latin, why can't I make it part of my Life? He has a peculiar idea of me, though. He tells me often that I'll never do anything but get married. He says that I'm that sort." When Whitfield dropped Latin from the home economics degree requirements in 1912, Orr, Paslay, and educators across the state protested the decision but with no effect. Following Peebles's and Fahnestock's example, Orr and Paslay went on leave to attend graduate school at Columbia University and received master of arts degrees in 1913.[33]

When Orr resigned from the faculty in May 1913, the press stated that she left for "personal reasons," but those in the II&C's inner circles knew that Orr resigned to protest Whitfield's dilution of the curriculum as well as to devote herself to woman suffrage. One month earlier, as a principal speaker at the Mississippi Woman Suffrage Association's (MWSA) annual meeting, Orr pledged to bring the suffrage question before the state legislature and accepted appointment to the MWSA's Legislative Committee, where she was placed in charge of "educating" the public. Sensing that Orr's embrace of woman suffrage work was also meant as a strike against him, Whitfield waited several months before issuing a statement thanking her for twenty-eight years of service to the college and the state. In sharp contrast, pages of testimonials to Orr's influence on students and the college were published in the *Spectator,* a student literary magazine she helped establish. The Alumnae Association publicly expressed its "loving gratitude [for] . . . Miss Orr's power to illuminate . . . [and] give to the day's work a sense of connection with what endures forever. . . . [T]hroughout our maturer lives, . . . we have found our personal duties and relations to others clarified and ennobled by the lessons of Miss Orr's classroom, and by what we felt to be the moving principles of her life." In his tribute, R. W. Jones, the college's founding president, proclaimed that in the history of education in Mississippi, "Her name should be written among the stars."[34]

This outpouring of affection for Orr disturbed Whitfield, in part because it indicated that Orr's commitment to woman suffrage had not diminished her popularity. Instead, she had made the cause more acceptable. MWSA president Annie Dent wrote Orr: "You have already accomplished a great work in awakening so many of the girls of Mississippi to a consciousness of their citizenship." Now was the time, suffrage leaders insisted, for Orr to take advantage of the "mental enfranchisement" of the young II&C women. Nellie Nugent Somerville, a seasoned activist, asked Orr to use her influence to "get a few, three or five of [your former students], to form a committee to put this work before graduates and enlist them? If you can get the committee & hand them over to me I could carry the real work. But your direct personal influence would do more than I can. . . . I am for going after these young women." Orr invited graduates of the II&C's bachelor of arts program to join her in the campaign, and several became devoted suffrage activists.[35]

True to her promise, Orr testified before the state House of Representatives in January 1914 in support of a state constitutional amendment to enfranchise women. In an increasingly modern, uncertain, and industrialized world, Orr told the legislators, women needed to have their interests represented and protected, and this was impossible without the right to vote. Although the House rejected the measure, Orr's arguments resonated, particularly with young II&C graduates, and a new enthusiasm invigorated the Mississippi campaign. Orr was elected vice president when the MWSA held its annual meeting in May.[36]

In the midst of this activity, a scandal erupted that sent a shock wave through the legislature and the II&C and irrevocably influenced the lives of Pauline Orr and Miriam Paslay. Shortly after Orr's speech before the House, Mississippi's legislators received an obscene and hostile pamphlet that charged Henry Whitfield with a variety of abuses. Although the pamphlet was signed "S[tate]. T[ax]. Payer," the author or authors were unknown. The legislators declined to publish the crude piece in the *Senate Journal,* but delicately hinted at its charges that Whitfield's "demeanor towards the girls had been improper" and that II&C students wore "indiscreet dress." Another investigative committee traveled to Columbus, this time to interrogate Whitfield and fifty other witnesses "under oath, and behind closed doors." The official report exonerated Whitfield, stating that his "interest in the girls was that of a father or a brother," but the matter did not end there as legislators sought to determine the source of the slander.[37] Senator E. T. Sykes of Columbus speculated that the authors were "a few dissatisfied ex-members of the faculty and a few mislead alumnae" inspired by "renewed hope arising out of the prevailing craze of 'Woman Suffrage,' to secure a Board of female trustees of the II&C in expectancy by them of the logical sequence of a 'Woman President.' "[38] Sykes's thinly veiled statements essentially accused Orr, Paslay, and their followers of writing the obscene tract.

Deeply humiliated, Whitfield turned his anger on Orr and Paslay. He circulated rumors that the women were "S. T. Payer" and enlisted Governor Earl Brewer, whose daughter Minnie had attended the II&C and was a suffragist, to help prove their involvement. A U.S. Post Office investigator, called in by Brewer, was given instructions to focus on Orr and her associates. His insinuating questions smeared her reputation and challenged the loyalties of the faculty. Four faculty members, including Paslay, refused to sign an exaggerated testimonial of Whitfield's abilities, which he wrote and insisted they sign. In June 1914, all four learned they would not be rehired to teach in the fall. When Paslay pressed Whitfield to explain his actions, he accused her of holding "secret meetings" of the Classical Club, making derogatory statements about him, and prejudicing students against the Home Science Course.[39] Paslay demanded that he bring the matter into the open for the sake of "simple justice," but he would not make formal charges, he told her, unless forced to do so.[40] The II&C alumnae, led by young suffragists, launched a letter-writing campaign, raised money for an attorney, and hired a detective in hopes of suing Whitfield for slander. According to their sources, he wanted to purge the II&C of all faculty who "bore the stamp of Miss Orr." They publicly accused Whitfield and Brewer of violating "the rights of defenseless women" and conducting a cowardly campaign of "slander by implication."[41]

In September, pressured by negative publicity, Whitfield and Brewer began negotiating with Paslay's brother. He reported that Whitfield told the governor that Orr was "extremely unfriendly" to the II&C's administration and that "it would be a mistake to have Miss Miriam back in place if she holds on to Miss Orr." Paslay could be rehired, Whitfield indicated, if "she just let go of Miss Orr" and pledged her loyalty to him. Paslay refused to sever her twenty-two-years relationship with Orr but agreed not to "irritate conditions" and signed a letter drafted by Whitfield stating that the rift had arisen from a misunderstanding on her part. Without Paslay's permission, Whitfield published the "humble pie" letter in newspapers and then refused to reinstate Paslay immediately as promised. Furious, Orr hired a lawyer and investigated the possibility of suing Whitfield. But Paslay, concerned about Orr's health, preferred to let the matter drop. She secured a temporary teaching position in North Carolina, and in June 1915 she was rehired at the II&C.[42]

It is difficult to gauge the impact of the scandal on the woman suffrage movement in Mississippi. As the MWSA's correspondence secretary, Nellie Nugent Somerville dealt with the flurry of mail generated by the scandal and offered to write the newspapers in support of Orr, but her interest in using Orr as a high profile leader waned. The Mississippi Federation of Women's Clubs (MFWC) showed its support by inviting Orr to address their 1914 annual convention but insisted that she not deliver an openly prosuffrage speech.[43] Many younger women, especially II&C alumnae, considered Orr and Paslay martyrs and admired them for their commitment. In October, Orr's woman suffrage speeches drew large audiences at the State Fair.[44] But the year's events had taken a heavy toll, and in winter Orr suffered from another bout of headaches and feelings of "uselessness" and "helplessness." She recovered sufficiently by April 1915 to share the speaker's platform at the MWSA's annual meeting with Anna Howard Shaw, leader of National American Woman Suffrage Association (NAWSA), and delivered a powerful speech on "Mississippi Women and the Ballot." At that meeting, Orr was elected president of the MWSA.

The fight for woman suffrage in Mississippi was especially tough due to legislators' aversion to federal action that might threaten states' rights and state control of politics. To blunt this opposition, Nellie Nugent Somerville issued a statement at the 1915 MWSA meeting that the suffragists "did not 'oppose other methods' but preferred 'to obtain the ballot at the hands of Mississippi men.' "[45] Orr generally dealt with the issue by de-emphasizing the "method" of obtaining woman suffrage (state vs. federal) and supporting Shaw, whom she greatly admired, and her policy of promoting woman suffrage on all fronts. Orr's arguments for woman suffrage focused on women's economic independence and equality. As "breadwinners" in a modern democracy, she stated, women needed the vote to deal with the challenges of an increasingly industrialized and uncertain economy. The intelligence of the II&C girls, she said, convinced her of the fitness of Mississippi women to vote. If one believed in higher education for women, Orr argued, one had to believe in woman suffrage.

As MWSA president, Orr embarked on a statewide speaking tour for woman suffrage, accompanied by a former student and the organization's new corresponding secretary, Ruth Stockett. Local women's clubs sponsored her suffrage talks, but the state MFWC leaders avoided the controversial issue and refused to endorse the cause. While touring, Orr's status as an educated white woman from a prominent family did not spare her from ridicule or abuse any more than it had protected her from scandal. In Meridian, the women's campaign materials and several valuable items were stolen. Orr told reporters that more than likely opponents of the equal suffrage movement were responsible, but such scare tactics, she assured them, would not be effective.[46]

Orr was again elected president of the MWSA in spring 1916. That year, at the request of NAWSA, she organized May Day suffrage parades. In Columbus, the parade was particularly large and exuberant. Three women on horseback led fifty students dressed in white carrying suffrage banners through the streets. "Judge" Orr proudly shared the platform with his daughter and delivered a pro-suffrage speech. In December 1916, the MFWC leaders relented and invited her to present a "distinctly suffragist's" talk on "Democracy" at the annual convention, where she also introduced a resolution endorsing woman suffrage, and many MFWC officers voiced their support. A slight majority defeated the measure, but no longer was the cause "unpopular." In Columbus, Pauline noted, the president of the local equal suffrage league was elected president of the Women's Civic League, the largest women's organization in the town.

In addition to organizing, Orr played a crucial role as a speaker at large and important venues. In June 1916 she spoke at a convention in St. Louis where NAWSA suffragists were battling to persuade the Democratic party to place a prosuffrage plank in their platform. "[A]n aristocracy of sex," Orr proclaimed from the podium, "is as undemocratic and unjust in principle as an aristocracy of rank and wealth." Loud cheers came from the crowded gallery filled with women, but their hopes were dampened when antisuffrage Texas Democrats proposed a measure to remove the issue from the platform altogether. Orr and the MWSA contingent were ecstatic when the Mississippi delegates all voted against it. The Democrats finally compromised by endorsing a plank supporting the passage of woman suffrage by the states. Back in Mississippi, Pauline Orr thanked the Mississippi delegates for fending off the Texas antisuffragists and "declared that the suffrage resolution inserted in the Democratic platform will set the cause of suffrage in the South forward as nothing else has done in the history of the movement." Carrie Chapman Catt, however, had been greatly disappointed by the platform resolution and considered it a victory for the states' rights faction even though NAWSA had not opposed the plank. From Orr's perspective, the plank was a victory because it accepted the principle of woman suffrage and did not patently reject the possibility of a federal amendment. In July, NAWSA sponsored a large meeting of southern suffragists in Birmingham and again called on Orr to deliver a major address. [47]

Because of Catt's emphasis on federal action, NAWSA encouraged state woman suffrage initiatives in only a few states where passage seemed likely. Mississippi and all of the southern states were considered poor risks, so under Orr's leadership, the MWSA did not submit any state woman suffrage initiatives in 1916. But, when a state senator introduced a resolution for a state constitutional amendment to enfranchise women, the organization was forced to support the doomed effort. [48] Under these circumstances, Orr worked for ancillary feminist causes, such as a state constitutional amendment to allow women to serve on boards of educational and charitable institutions and as state and county superintendents. Nearly every white woman's organization in the state backed the amendment. Orr treated the issue as a test of antisuffragists' arguments that Mississippi women did not need the vote because it would "always be the highest privilege and pleasure of the men to act on the expressed wishes of the women and to freely accord them anything they demanded." When legislators rejected the measure, Orr told the press that the men had failed to keep their chivalrous promises, which was exactly why their sisters, wives, and mothers needed the ballot. [49]

Perhaps what is most intriguing about Orr's leadership style was her rare use of racist rhetoric in spite of her distinctly racist attitudes toward African Americans, immigrants, and ethnic minorities in general. In Mississippi, black women outnumbered white women, so the state's white suffrage activists were especially vulnerable to white supremacist and racist antisuffrage arguments that the federal amendment would enfranchise thousands of black women. Orr essentially ignored the issue of black women voters, and her opinions concerning the injustice of racial discrimination do not appear in the preserved records. Orr articulated a philosophy that has been called "the feminism of personal development." She promoted women's higher education as an avenue toward greater opportunities and self-determination. The vote, she argued, was a necessary part of achieving those goals. Orr also emphasized the dangers of gender discrimination in an increasingly industrialized society and promoted education and the ballot as weapons against further economic exploitation of women. Her message struck a responsive chord among southern white women dependent upon the precarious and uneven economy of the New South.[50]

In April 1917, after serving as MWSA president for two years, Orr announced that she would not run for another term. Several former students whom she groomed for leadership continued to organize and were elected officers in the MWSA. As Orr left office, the Mississippi suffragists adopted a resolution specifically requesting that Congress submit a federal woman suffrage amendment to the states. An article in the NAWSA's *Woman's Journal* credited Orr with increasing the acceptance of woman suffrage in Mississippi and advancing the cause through her "strong hold upon the love and admiration of college and club women" and as "the leading educational force among the women of Mississippi."[51] She had spoken in towns and cities across the South, organized many new local woman suffrage societies, and created an organizational system based on congressional districts with an eye toward passing a federal woman suffrage amendment. In a personal note to Orr, the revered suffrage leader Alice Stone Blackwell wrote, "You are a light shining in darkness."[52]

Orr continued to address organizations on behalf of woman suffrage, but personal responsibilities made this difficult. Her parents were elderly and her mother's health was declining. In the summer of 1917, Miriam also became ill and Pauline accompanied her to New York for medical treatment. Orr felt guilty about neglecting her mother and confided to her sister, "I feel so terrible that I did not do more for Mamma last winter. I had that suffrage work on me continually, & wasn't equal to the strain of it. I got out of it thinking next winter I could relieve Mother in so many ways & be more to the home!"[53] In September, within a few weeks of their return to Columbus, Cornelia Orr died.

Cornelia Orr's death seemed to make it possible for Pauline and Miriam to let go of Mississippi. In a 1917 letter from New York City, Orr admitted to her sister, "With an easy mind, one could enjoy it so much. As it is I would rather stay here than anywhere else."[54] Both women had felt like "aliens" and "strangers" in Columbus for some time. By 1919, Paslay had published a major article on ancient Greek culture and was confident about her prospects elsewhere.[55] In the summer of 1920, as they vacationed in the West, the battle for the Nineteenth Amendment reached its climax, but Pauline made no mention of the victory in her diary. Upon returning home, they packed and left for New York to set up permanent housekeeping in a large brownstone at 252 West 74th Street.

Orr and Paslay's new household also included former II&C student Mary "Max" Hathorn, a physician, and Orr's nephew Jerome Harris, Assistant Rector at St. Ignatius Episcopal Church. Miriam secured a teaching post at the Alcuin Preparatory School for Girls.[56] Pauline followed her mother's example by managing and investing their resources and taking in boarders to supplement their income. Her father, now nearly blind, joined them in 1921 and basked in his celebrity as the oldest living former Confederate congressman. Within a year, at age ninety-three, J. A. Orr died in a Manhattan hospital.

Their New York City home became a way station for former II&C students and colleagues who wanted to pursue advanced degrees, establish professions, and try out their literary talents in the big city. Several devoted former students became successful writers, professors, and academic administrators at leading women's colleges and coed universities. Rosa Peebles, chair of the Department of English at Vassar College, developed some of the first and most innovative comparative literature courses in the country. Blanche Colton Williams chaired the English Department at Hunter College in New York, published biographies of George Eliot and Clara Barton, and established the O. Henry Story Awards. Another former student, Frances Jones Gaither, author of *Follow the Drinking Gourd,* currently receives attention from feminist literary scholars for her independent female characters and her willingness to address issues of racial injustice in her fictional works. One of the young II&C suffrage campaigners, Helen Carloss (1913), who defended Orr and Paslay during the "S. T. Payer" scandal, earned a law degree, served on the federal Court of Appeals and became U.S. assistant attorney general.[57] Many former students found Orr's and Paslay's feminist lifestyles and "high standards" to be powerful examples long after they left Mississippi, and frequently wrote their aging former professors to thank them for the influence they had on their lives.

When Miriam died in April 1932, the tight community of II&C alumnae mourned.[58] In expressing their deepest sympathies to Orr, they recognized how crucial the women's relationship, their personal and professional life partnership, had been to the development of women's higher education in Mississippi during a time when few believed women capable of learning what men learned. In fact, the young women at the II&C were taught something different from that which their brothers at universities learned. Orr's students were instructed, through example and rigorous training, to reject ideas about women's inherent inferiority to men and to fight for equal treatment regardless of sex. They also learned the power of great friendships and devoted "marriages" between women, how these could sustain, empower, and leave enduring legacies of strength and ideological commitments.

For decades, alumnae revered Orr as a southern feminist who steadfastly believed in women's abilities to alter the status quo. Shortly before her death in 1955, at the age of ninety-four, the alumnae renovated the campus chapel and honored Pauline Orr and her legacy in Mississippi by rededicating the building in her name.

NOTES

1. *Memphis Commercial Appeal,* 18 May 1913.

2. *Who's Who in Mississippi* (Jackson, Miss.: Tucker Printing House, 1914); "Reminiscences of J. A. Orr," *Biographical and Historical Memoirs of Mississippi,* typescript, Lindsey-Orr Papers, Mississippi Department of Archives and History (henceforth MDAH), Jackson; "Biography of J. A. Orr," *Memoirs of Mississippi,* Lindsey-Orr Papers.

3. "Statement of J. A. Orr," 25 August 1888, Jehu Orr Papers, Southern Historical Collection (henceforth SHC), University of North Carolina, Chapel Hill.

4. Blanche Colton Williams, draft of biographical essay on Pauline Orr, Lindsey-Orr Papers.

5. *East Mississippi Times,* 15 January 1876; clippings from the *Independent,* n.d., folder 52, Jehu Orr Papers.

6. "Pioneer Opened Doors in Women's Education," *Bulletin of Mississippi University for Women, Alumnae News* (spring 1979): 47.

7. *Circular and Catalogue of the Packer Collegiate Institute, 17 June 1879* (Brooklyn: Martin and Bennett, 1879), 10, 17, 19–21; Mary Lowe Dickinson, "A Half Century of Progress," *Arena* (February 1896): 361–71; "The National Council of Women of the United States," *Arena* (February 1897): 478–93.

8. Pauline Van de Graaf Orr diary, 1881–82, Jehu Orr Papers.

9. *Clinton (Miss.) Sword and Shield,* 21 November 1885; "Exhibit of the Deposition of Mrs. [Annie C.] Peyton," 29 September 1887, *Mississippi House Journal,* 1898, 554–55; *Senate Journal,* 1880, 279, 352; Bridget Smith Pieschel and Stephen Robert Pieschel, *Loyal Daughters: One Hundred Years at Mississippi University for Women, 1884–1984* (Jackson: University Press of Mississippi, 1984), 5; Donald B. Marti, *Women of the Grange: Mutuality and Sisterhood in Rural America, 1866–1920* (New York: Greenwood Press, 1991), 96; D. Sven Nordin, *Rich Harvest: A History of the Grange, 1867–1900* (Jackson: University Press of Mississippi, 1974), 65–66. See also Trey Berry, "A History of Women's Higher Education in Mississippi, 1819–1882," *Journal of Mississippi History* 53 (1991): 303–19; Christie Anne Farnham, *The Education of the Southern Belle: Higher Education and Student Socialization in the Antebellum South* (New York: New York University Press, 1994); Suzanne Lebsock, "Radical Reconstruction and the Property Rights of Southern Women," *Journal of Southern History* (May 1977): 195–216.

10. Prof. D. G. Eaton to the Trustees of the State Industrial School of Mississippi, 1 June 1985; Mary L. Dickinson to Pauline Orr, 13 September [1885?]; Stanley Bond to Dickinson, 30 May 1885, box 1, Lindsey-Orr Papers.

11. Williams, draft of essay; Rosa Peebles, rough draft of bibliographic essay on Pauline Van de Graaf Orr, n.d., copy in Lindsey-Orr Papers.

12. Williams, draft of essay.

13. "Pioneer Opened Doors," 47.

14. R. W. Jones to Orr, 26 June 1888, Lindsey-Orr Papers.

15. "A Protest in Behalf of the Womanhood of the State, By the Faculty of the Industrial Institute and College," *Mississippi House Journal,* 1888, 419–24.

16. Ibid.; "Statement of Incidental Account, Etc.," testimony of Mr. Nielson, *Mississippi House Journal,* 1898, 635; R. W. Jones to Pauline Orr, 10 April 1889, Lindsey-Orr Papers.

17. "Statement of Incidental Account, Etc.," testimony of Nielson, 565.

18. Pieschel and Pieschel, 25.

19. Ibid., 26.

20. Ibid., 37. For more on the "Cocke fight," see "Miss Calloway and the *Index,*" *Columbus (Miss.) Index* [26 March 1890?]; *Jackson Clarion-Ledger,* 27 March 1890; clippings from *Daily Age-Herald,* 12 June 1890, Senator E. T. Sykes scrapbook, Special Collections, John Clayton Fant Memorial Library, Mississippi University for Women, Columbus; "Columbus Women's Protest," *Columbus Dispatch,* [20 March 1890?], Special Collections.

21. Clipping from *Anderson (S.C.) Peoples' Advocate,* March 1892, Jehu Orr Papers.

22. Congressman John Sharp Williams to "any Ambassador, Minister or Consul of the United States," 8 July 1903; Orr diary, Lindsey-Orr Papers.

23. Miriam Paslay, draft of Classical Club pageant script, n.d., Lindsey-Orr Papers.

24. R. W. Jones to "Miss Pauline," 24 December 1897, Lindsey-Orr Papers.

25. "Statement of Incidental Account, Etc.," testimony of Robert Frazer, *Mississippi House Journal,* 1898, 561.

26. "Statement," testimony of M. M. Evans, member of the Board of Trustees, *Mississippi House Journal,* 1898, 575.

27. "The Student Voice of the II&C," *Columbus (Miss.) Commercial,* 13 January 1898; "Statement," testimonies of Miss Torrey, Miss Selina Martyn, Miss Carter, and Miss Ruby Ferris, *Mississippi House Journal,* 1898, 607–14.

28. "The Student Voice of the II&C"; "Statement," testimonies of Miss Torrey et al., 609.

29. "Statement," testimony of Frazer, 565.

30. "Report of Special Joint Committee to Investigate the Industrial Institute and College at Columbus," 29 January 1898, *Mississippi Senate Journal,* 1898, 187–90; D. L. Sweatman to Pauline Orr, 9 March 1898, Lindsey-Orr Papers.

31. Orr diary, 23 March 1899, Lindsey-Orr Papers.

32. Hume to Judge J. A. Orr, 11 December 1906, Lindsey-Orr Papers.

33. II&C *Catalogue,* 1909–10; Pieschel and Pieschel, 65–66.

34. Spectator, 7; rough notes from a testimonial dinner, n.d., Lindsey-Orr Papers.

35. Annie Dent to Pauline Orr, 28 July 1913; Nellie Somerville to Pauline Orr, 5 June [1913]; Jane Addams to Miss Eula Deaton, 16 October 1913, Lindsey-Orr Papers.

36. A. Elizabeth Taylor, "The Woman Suffrage Movement in Mississippi, 1890–1920," *Journal of Mississippi History* (February 1968): 19; Nellie Nugent Somerville ledger, 1914, Nellie Nugent Somerville Papers, Somerville-Howorth Family Papers, Arthur and Elizabeth Schlesinger Library, Radcliffe Institute for Advanced Study, Cambridge, Mass.

37. *Mississippi Senate Journal,* 1914, 267–68.

38. Quoted in Pieschel and Pieschel, 66.

39. B. Powell to Paslay, n.d.; Paslay to Whitfield, 16 June 1914; B. Powell to Paslay, n.d.; Nettie May Herrington to Paslay, 2 June 1915, Lindsey-Orr Papers.

40. Rough drafts of letters from Paslay to Whitfield, 16 June 1914, Lindsey-Orr Papers.

41. "Dear Girls" from Eula Deaton, Rosa Peebles, Ruth Stockett, Blanche Williams, Helen Brownlee Baldwin, Pauline Whitten, Lucille Crighton, Helen Carloss, 4 July 1914; clippings, n.d., Lindsey-Orr Papers.

42. J. S. Hudson to "Dr. Paisley," 1 September 1914; William Watkins to Pauline Orr, 25 September 1914, Lindsey-Orr Papers.

43. Emily Hyer Price to Pauline Orr, 30 September 1914, Lindsey-Orr Papers.

44. Taylor, 21.

45. Marjorie Spruill Wheeler, *New Women of the New South: The Leaders of the Woman Suffrage Movement in the Southern States* (New York: Oxford University Press, 1993), 151.

46. Clippings, n.d., Lindsey-Orr Papers.

47. *New York Times,* 17 June 1916; *Woman's Journal,* 1 July 1916; *Birmingham News,* 2 July 1916.

48. Taylor, 24–25.

49. Clippings, n.d., Lindsey-Orr Papers.

50. "Woman Suffrage and the Negro Vote," NAWSA flyer, 25 June 1915, Pattie Ruffner Jacobs Papers, Department of Archives and Manuscripts, Birmingham Public Library, Birmingham, Ala.; Wheeler, ed., *Votes for Women! The Woman Suffrage Movement in Tennessee, the South, and the Nation* (Knoxville: University of Tennessee Press, 1995), 37; Suzanne M. Marilley, *Woman Suffrage and the Origins of Liberal Feminism in the United States, 1820–1920* (Cambridge: Harvard University Press, 1996), 188.

51. *Woman's Journal,* 14 April 1917; Sara Hunter Graham, *Woman Suffrage and the New Democracy* (New Haven: Yale University Press, 1996), 100–101.

52. Quoted in *Memphis Commercial Appeal,* 15 April 1917.

53. Pauline Orr to Corinne Harris, 4 August 1917, Jehu Orr Papers.

54. Pauline Orr to Corinne Harris, 9 August 1917, Jehu Orr Papers.

55. Miriam Greene Paslay, "Does the Style of the *Civil War,* Justify the Doubt as to Its Authenticity?" *Classical Journal,* February 1918, 343–53; "Greece," unpublished pageant performed 1 February 1919 at the College Chapel.

56. Obituary of Miriam Paslay, *New York Times,* 27 April 1932.

57. Pieschel and Pieschel, 57.

58. Clara Paslay Clayton to Pauline Orr, 27 July 1932, Lindsey-Orr Papers. Historians have often referred to devoted and intimate life partnerships between nineteenth-century women as "Boston marriages." Orr and Paslay's Mississippi "marriage" was certainly rooted in the nineteenth century, but it survived and flourished well into the twentieth century when such relationships would begin to be questioned as "unnatural" and characterized, accurately or not, as lesbian, a label that denotes sexual acts and preferences but does not necessarily include the kind of lifelong commitment that characterized Orr and Paslay's relationship. Rather than defining and labeling the sexualities of these individuals, a prospect fraught with possibilities of error, I prefer to characterize their relationship as a "marriage," and a very good and lasting one at that.

Part Two

Becoming Professionals

By the late nineteenth century, developments were underway that made it possible for some of Mississippi's women to pursue a higher education and to enter the public arena. Barriers, however, remained that denied women participation on an equal basis with men. Segregation prevented black women's entry into almost all professions except for teaching in segregated schools. Tougaloo College, originally founded by the American Missionary Society as a coeducational school for African Americans, began offering a collegiate curriculum in 1897. Rust College, created by the Freedmen's Aid Society of the Methodist Episcopal Church in 1866, was also coeducational. Alcorn State University, the state's land grant institution for blacks, began admitting women in 1895.

In the antebellum era and post–Civil War years, several Protestant denominations created colleges for white women. The Methodists established Whitworth College in 1858 and Grenada College in 1882, and the Baptists founded Blue Mountain College in 1873. The Presbyterians created Belhaven College in 1883 and Mississippi Synodical College in 1891. The state-supported University of Mississippi opened its doors to white women in 1882, but few entered.

In terms of women's education, Mississippi history embodies two important firsts. Mississippi College, which later affiliated with the Baptist Church, offered the first baccalaureate to a female in the United States in 1831, a full decade before Oberlin College (which claims credit for that distinction) awarded its first collegiate degrees to women. More significant, the state legislature in 1884 authorized the creation of the first state-supported college for women in the country: the Institute of Industry and Commerce for the Education of White Girls (II&C), later renamed Mississippi State College for Women (MSCW). The significance of this institution in Mississippi during this period can hardly be overstated. Graduates fanned out to virtually every community in the state as teachers and civic leaders. In the 1920s, MSCW graduates were credited with electing Henry

Whitfield, former president of the school, as governor. The college provided an education to a number of women in the sciences, the liberal arts, pedagogy, and commerce, which enabled them to establish careers or enter occupations opening for women in the New South. Even so, those talented women who sought advanced or graduate education of a superior quality were compelled to leave the state, most often drawn to New York, where they achieved the highest rank among scientists, academics, and artists. Such was the experience of several of the early II&C faculty and its students, among them Blanche Colton Williams and Elizabeth Lee Hazen.

Other women left the state under different circumstances, some never to return, but nonetheless reflecting luster upon their Mississippi origins. World War I drew Burnita Shelton Matthews to Washington to enter government work, and there she found an inviting opportunity to study law and became a successful lawyer and a federal judge. Kate Freeman Clark, an artist, found her niche among art colonies in the East that had no equal in her state.

Most Mississippians, both male and female, black and white, did not have access to a local high school until the 1920s. African American women's possibilities remained confined mostly to agricultural and domestic work. Textile factories, especially, in the northeastern part of the state provided employment during the 1920s and 1930s for farm and small-town women who sought jobs to provide cash to their families. In 1937, many of these women participated in strikes led by the Congress of Industrial Organizations and replicated struggles of factory women in New England a century earlier.

For certain women, especially those in the smaller towns of the state, the women's club movement that began in the late nineteenth century and came into full flowering in the early twentieth century offered an "education without walls." Many groups that began as reading or literary clubs became civic improvement leagues and adopted reform agendas that stressed moral reforms, such as temperance, and the advancement of women's rights through suffrage. The League of Women Voters made its way into a number of towns in the early 1920s, and in 1924 the National Federation of Business and Professional Women's Clubs (BPW) organized in Mississippi. The emerging organizations all urged the new "woman citizens" to take a vital interest in voting and in the removal of legal disabilities remaining against women. The groups, however, did not always speak with one voice, as the frustrated journalist Minnie Brewer learned. Disagreement about the efficacy of the Equal Rights Amendment remained through the twentieth century.

Women's organizations became the proving ground for a number of women who entered politics, and by 1923 women were in the Mississippi state senate and the House of Representatives and remained from then on, even if their numbers were small. Nellie Nugent Somerville, Ellen S. Woodward, and Lucy Somerville Howorth were among the best known of the early legislators. The careers of Woodward, Howorth, and Burnita Matthews point to the fact that many Mississippi women who have achieved position and acclaim in the law have done so through work outside the state, usually in Washington, D.C. Just as the crisis of a world war drew Matthews to Washington, the onset of the New Deal in 1933 resulted in presidential appointments for both Woodward and Howorth in the new administration. Although not the subject of essays in this collection, the work of Woodward and Howorth during the New Deal had a significant impact upon the women of Mississippi. As head of women's relief work under successive New Deal work programs from 1833 to 1838, Woodward enabled many women in her home state to support themselves or their families during the Depression; Howorth spoke for the appointment of more women to federal policy-making positions through her national leadership of the BPW and the American Association of University Women.

Eudora Welty began writing in the 1930s. Deeply connected to her family and Jackson friends while also drawn to artists and intellectuals beyond Mississippi, Welty captured the lives of ordinary people in her native state. In her writing, she defied the idea of the writer as the alienated artist at odds with her world. As a lover of humanity, she transformed the stories of old women, young children, black jazz performers, and desperate sharecroppers into tales of dignity and intrigue. At her death in 2001, all of the state mourned her passing.

The subjects of the chapters in part 2 were all white. Some appear to have given little thought to the plight of black women in the state, or at best, paid only lip service to the economic and political ramifications of the latent racism within their own organizations and communities. Whenever they did speak out they found themselves in the minority and virtually voiceless in efforts to improve the lives of both poorer white women and blacks. It was not until after World War II that the powerful words and actions of primarily black women activists would ensure civil rights for all Mississippians.

Kate Freeman Clark

(1875–1957)

An Artist and a Lady

KATHLEEN MCCLAIN JENKINS

She aspired from an early age to be an artist, or an authoress, anything but a commonplace girl. Kate Freeman Clark was a delicate child, of fragile health and dutiful nature, protected and pampered by her mother's upper-class family, whose roots ran deep in Mississippi history and strongly shaped the course of Kate's life. The Walthalls had numbered among the earliest white settlers in the Holly Springs area. Her grandmother's younger brother, Edward Cary Walthall (1831–98), achieved prominence as a North Mississippi attorney and in his service to the Confederate Army. After the Civil War, Walthall practiced law with the politician and future supreme court justice L. Q. C. Lamar (1825–93), who had authored the state's articles of secession in 1861. The two established attorneys took in a younger assistant, Edward Donaldson Clark (d. 1885), who later married Walthall's niece, Cary Ann Freeman (1849–1922).[1] Their only child was born 7 September 1875. They named her Kate Freeman Clark after her grandmother Kate Walthall Freeman (1828–1919) and called her Little Kate to distinguish her from Mama Kate.[2]

Edward Clark established his own law practice in Vicksburg, settled his family into a comfortable home on Cherry Street, and purchased a cotton plantation along Deer Creek in the lower Mississippi Delta later incorporated into a town named for his bride, Cary. Mindful of Little Kate's delicate constitution, Cary Clark removed their young daughter during the summer from the disease-ridden heat of the Delta and traveled north to Holly Springs, where the air was considered cleaner and healthier.[3] During their absences, Edward Clark would write his daughter long, affectionate letters full of paternal instruction and news.[4]

Kate's large dark eyes and soft brown ringlets helped secure her role as princess of the extended Walthall clan, a role she enjoyed. Her mother recognized an artistic sensitivity in the girl from a very early age, claiming that even in infancy Kate delighted in spools of colored silk strung from her bassinet and could point to the colors by name when asked. In the fashion of the late nineteenth century, Kate kept large scrapbooks into which she would paste newspaper or magazine images of famous people, as well as advertisements with pretty pictures.[5] "My greatest delight," she later recalled, "was dabbling in watercolors or playing with a pencil—& I would be flat on the floor & draw in an English drawing book sent me by my Uncle Russell, by the hour while my mother read to me."[6]

A thousand miles away, the election of Democrat Grover Cleveland to the presidency in 1884 with the support of southern Democrats initiated a chain of events that placed L. Q. C. Lamar in Cleveland's Cabinet as Secretary of the Interior, Edward Clark as Lamar's first assistant, and Edward Cary Walthall into Lamar's unexpired U.S. Senate term.[7] Within days of his Senate confirmation, before his wife and daughter could join him in Washington, Edward Clark contracted pneumonia and died.[8] From Vicksburg, the widowed Cary Freeman Clark packed up her belongings and her daughter and returned to the Walthall home place in Holly Springs.[9] Nine-year-old Kate suffered the greatest dislocation of all, losing at once both her idyllic childhood home and her beloved father. Cary Clark, however, soon began making alternative plans to leave the state. In fact, for the rest of her life she used excuses such as promoting her daughter's artistic talent and protecting Kate's delicate health to justify her own absence from the family home place, much to the dismay of her two brothers. They expected their sister to shoulder the primary responsibility of caring for their aging mother, but Mama Kate refused to give up the Walthall house in Holly Springs, where she had resided since being widowed in 1857, and Cary refused to stay home.

In 1892 Kate Freeman Clark and her mother departed Holly Springs, first for Kate to attend school in Memphis, then later in the year, on to New York. That fall they moved into a boarding house on West 69th Street in New York City so Kate could attend the Gardner Institute, a finishing school for young ladies.[10] Kate and her mother supported themselves with income from the Walthall family and an annuity from the lease of Clark's plantation to his sister and brother, Pearl and Stonewall Jackson Clark.[11]

For the better part of the next thirty years, Kate Freeman Clark and her mother wintered in New York and left behind the oppressive city heat every summer for various resort areas out in the country. Kate's health continued to

KATE FREEMAN CLARK

circa 1900. Portrait by William Merritt Chase.

Courtesy of the Kate Freeman Clark Gallery,

Holly Springs, Mississippi.

be a great concern to her family, and her perceived need for "country air and out-door occupation" always influenced their summer plans.

At age seventeen Kate met a handsome young West Point cadet, Hamilton Foley, who was also staying at the Villa, Highland Falls on Hudson, New York. He was only one among numerous boys who sent her flowers and candies and with whom she danced at hops and met for picnics. His courtship of Kate began with daisies, frequently left on her breakfast plate. The two continued to correspond over the next decade, but the Spanish-American War took Foley to the Philippines with disastrous consequences for his military career and his relationship with Clark. In 1905 he was court-martialed in Manila for embezzling the pay due the men of his company.[12] There is no evidence of any further contact between them, or of any other serious beau for Kate.

Meanwhile, after Kate's graduation from the Gardner Institute in 1894, she and her mother had remained in New York for her to enroll in the Art Students League. The school offered one of the country's finest courses of artistic study in traditional studio techniques as well as an active social life of grand balls, student dances, and exhibition openings. The League faculty included a number of prominent American Impressionist painters who had followed the nineteenth-century movement away from tightly controlled classicism toward a more painterly approach. Impressionism typically conveyed an immediate sense impression of nature with special attention paid to faithfully representing the quality of light.[13] Kate Clark began in the drawing class instructed by John H. Twachtman (1853–1902), founding member of the Ten, a highly influential group of American painters. She then progressed to the watercolor class taught by renowned portraitist Irving R. Wiles (1861–1948). Painting in watercolors enjoyed a long history as a traditional means of creative expression for women, perhaps because it did not soil the hands. Clark naturally began her art studies preferring watercolors to oils. Then she met the League's master teacher, William Merritt Chase (1849–1916), who specialized in the dark, moody style of portraiture and still life painting he had perfected during his student years in Munich. Chase particularly impressed his students by handling a palette laden with oils while wearing an immaculate white flannel suit.[14]

Kate and Cary Clark spent the summer months of 1895 among the grassy pink dunes of Long Island, where resort settlements were springing up along the railroad connections to New York. There the Clarks encountered "a set of most charming people," and Kate wrote that "sometimes we play games indoors, at others sit on the porch, talk & sing songs or walk down to the Sound. We have a nice croquet ground."[15] The primary reason for their vacation choice was the French-style plein air summer art class operated that year under the azure skies of the Atlantic coastline by Irving Wiles at Peconic Bay, where students had the freedom to wander the beaches or fields sketching at will out in the open air. Like the students in his winter classes at the League, Wiles's summer pupils were predominantly stylish female members of the upper class.[16]

The next fall when Kate and Cary Clark returned to New York, Kate was able to enroll in Chase's life class for the first time. Over the next few years, she followed her mentor back and forth between the Art Students League and the newly created Chase School of Art (later the New York School). With his impeccable manners and elegant demeanor, William Merritt Chase provided a reassuring mentor for the aristocratic young ladies who flocked to his classes and posed as classroom models for Chase and for one another. He created a studio environment that did not threaten their sense of social propriety yet challenged them to meet the high artistic standards of his own traditional academic training.[17] Before the onset of twentieth-century individualism, painting students struggled to learn how to render realistic imagery by studying under an established artist. Because of his reputation for painting excellence, Chase's classes attracted pupils intent on careers as professional artists, but they also drew a high proportion of young socialites seeking stimulating occupation during the winter season. Kate Freeman Clark was a bit of both.

The Clarks in 1896 began six consecutive years of migrating with Chase to his newly formed summer art colony in the Shinnecock Hills of Long Island.[18] Chase's seasonal move from New York City to the open landscape allowed him to practice and teach the plein air Impressionist painting techniques he had observed at Durand-Ruel's 1886 landmark New York exhibit of modern French art.[19] These employed brilliant, clear colors to execute paintings filled with light entirely in the open air rather than relying on the traditional process of site sketches leading to a canvas finished back in the studio. The growing Long Island summer population provided plentiful students for Chase's school as well as an ample supply of sun-dappled models for his paintings and pastel drawings.

Chase's Shinnecock students followed a weekly regimen: On Tuesdays they gathered outdoors to observe his demonstration paintings under the billowing white clouds on the rolling dunes or among the sprawling cottages, the young ladies protected from the bright summer sun by large hats and parasols. Then for the remainder of the week they were free to wander the island in search of suitable painting subjects. Sometimes they executed small quick sketches in oil on wooden cigar box lids, and sometimes they created larger paintings on canvas. Kate's mother accompanied her on these and many other, purely social, outings. On Mondays, Chase's pupils would haul their assorted works into a

special part of his studio for a full critique session that progressed from beginners to the most advanced.[20]

Clark showed true talent as an artist. Her master acknowledged as much in
his class critiques and by selecting two of her works for his personal collection.
In fact, some of her still lifes, such as *Copper Pot, Tin Plate with Fruit,* are virtually indistinguishable from Chase's. Years after her death, a thorough cleaning of
one of the small paintings in her collection surprisingly revealed Chase's signature rather than her own.[21] Kate Clark's growing body of work clearly reflected
William Merritt Chase's two different styles of painting, the dark studio works
and the bright Impressionist landscapes. Only the details of the faces in her figure paintings such as *Golden Locks* betrayed a lingering lack of confidence that
marked her work as that of a perpetual student who never quite progressed to
the master's level.[22]

Rather than returning to New York after their first summer at Shinnecock,
Kate and her mother spent the next two winters in Washington, D.C., near her
mother's uncle, Senator Edward Cary Walthall, and his wife, Mary. Kate had
"a lovely time" in Washington.[23] She dressed to the nines in her white crepes
and yellow satins with violets and high combs in her hair to make senatorial
social calls with her Aunt Mary, and she was quite pleased to receive "many
compliments on dress & self."[24]

If Kate privately bemoaned their nomadic existence, likening their residence
in different cities and boarding houses to the pieces of a patchwork quilt, she
also remained confident that "if in the quilt of my life a certain material should
predominate, it would represent Art. That is the one unbroken thread that follows me everywhere."[25] She had developed a strong loyalty to the faculty at
the Art Students League, however, and she resisted enrolling in Washington art
classes until driven to it by the "continual gadding" of her mother.[26]

The emotional price of living under a forceful mother, constantly moving
about, continually having to make new friends and attachments, trying to maintain family connections cast over thousands of miles, and losing her father and
her childhood home all contributed to a temperament in Kate Clark that tended
toward depression. She characterized their first Washington Christmas as "a
quiet one, but I did not have the blues, because I fixed my thoughts on the
present and did not allow them to dwell on the past or the might be's."[27]

At the end of their second season in Washington, in April 1898, Cary Clark's
beloved uncle Edward Cary Walthall died. After his funeral services were held
in the Senate Chamber, Kate and her mother returned with the body to Mississippi. The interment that followed at Hill Crest cemetery in Holly Springs
demonstrated the broad public devotion still attached to the Walthall name, as

a reverent crowd of Confederate veterans estimated at five thousand gathered to lay the major general to rest.[28]

Kate Clark and her mother then resumed their annual cycle of spending winters in New York and summers at Shinnecock or at various other art colonies springing up at the turn of the century. But Kate was hampered by her lack of private studio space. Cary Clark thought it improper for a young lady to rent a studio on her own and so refused to allow it. Because there was no extra room in their boarding houses in New York, Kate's painting opportunities were almost entirely restricted to classroom settings, especially when Mama Kate was in residence. Cary Clark's remaining brother died in 1904, leaving the responsibility for Mama Kate's care solely on Kate and her mother. They brought her to New York to live with them full-time.

Other points of gender-related conflict arose around the questions of how Kate should sign her paintings and whether it would be proper for her to sell them. Kate feared the traditional critical prejudice against women painters, so whenever she planned to exhibit her work, she would sign it "Freeman Clark" in order to mask her gender. On the one hand, she wanted to live up to the social standards her family had set for her as an upper-class lady who should never personally engage in trade.[29] On the other, she worked hard toward the professional goals set for artistically talented students that required the exhibition and sale of paintings as a natural part of advancing an artistic career.

Clark tried to steer a middle course, exhibiting her major paintings but not pushing their sale. She established a respectable exhibition record between 1904 and 1920 that encompassed many of the nation's most prestigious venues, showing *The Lower Field* at the National Academy of Design (1904); *Columns and Cosmos* at the National Academy of Design (1905); *Laurel* at the National Academy of Design (1911) and the Pennsylvania Academy of Fine Arts (1915); *Oh! Happy Days of Innocence and Ease* at the Corcoran (1907) and the National Academy of Design (1908); *Neighbors* at the National Academy of Design (1906) and the Corcoran Gallery (1908); and *Silver and Gold* at the National Academy of Design (1917).[30] As the years passed, Clark accumulated a growing collection of her own works, usually packed away in the cellar of whatever house in which she and her mother happened to be residing.

Approaching middle age forced Kate Freeman Clark to balance her own blossoming career with the growing needs of her elderly grandmother and aging mother. Although the houses where they boarded maintained servant staffs that handled the cooking and cleaning, personal care for the family matriarch fell to her daughter and granddaughter. Out of frustration and her sense of family responsibility, by 1914 Kate stopped painting altogether. She quit her classes at the Art Students League because of concern for her mother's safety, noting in her diary that "she would not let me go alone & I was too afraid to have her cross those dreadful streets with her defective vision."[31]

Still, in 1915, Braus Gallery in New York mounted a solo exhibit of her paintings. That same year, her *Climbers* was one of sixty paintings accepted out of more than nine hundred pieces submitted to the juried show at the Panama-Pacific Exposition held in San Francisco to celebrate the opening of the Panama Canal. William Merritt Chase's prominent position on the jury probably played a part in the selection of Kate Clark's work, as did the overall celebration of Impressionist painting, both French and American, at the fair. In fact, the organizers of the fair's Palace of Fine Arts devoted an entire gallery to thirty-two paintings by Chase.[32]

Then suddenly Chase was gone. He had become seriously ill with what was probably liver cancer, and he died at his New York home in October 1916. Chase's death shocked his students and colleagues, for he had kept quiet the nature and severity of his illness.[33] The loss of the father figure who had nurtured her artistic hopes for more than two decades hit Kate Clark very hard. She desperately wanted to attend the auction that sold off the contents of Chase's New York studio so she would have something meaningful to remember him by, but she was not able to leave her grandmother's side in time to get there. In particular, she wanted an old black kettle that Chase had used as a prop for still life paintings. It sold to someone else for seven dollars. In anguish, she described the sale as "like a party of Harpies preying on his body & picking the bones."[34]

Because Mama Kate's condition seemed too fragile to endure summer moves to the countryside, Kate and Cary Clark reluctantly remained in the city year-round with her during the first years of World War I. In addition to suffering record-breaking heat over the summers, they faced coal and gas deprivations during bitterly cold winters. Kate passed the time during the winter months knitting sleeveless jackets, mittens, and scarves. The three generations of women learned to make adjustments when members of the boarding house staff departed for higher paying wartime jobs elsewhere. This left them to fend for themselves in tasks they were unaccustomed to performing, such as changing their bed linen and emptying their own slops.[35] As their living conditions in the city deteriorated, Kate Clark wrote, "Life is most uncomfortable here. Would give anything in the world if we were at home."[36] A month later she added, "Oh for the old home under *any circumstances*. I am urging mother to go back, but she is harder to move than a mountain."[37] Kate and her mother sometimes enticed Mama Kate out for bus trips from Washington Square to Ft. George, but she resisted leaving the house. Kate described them all as looking "positively shabby" from the inability to get away from her care even to shop for clothes. [38]

Perhaps prodded by Chase's death and feeling guilty about giving up her art, Kate Freeman Clark decided to find a way to begin painting again, although even at age forty-two she worried about obtaining her mother's approval. In November 1917 she embarked upon her "second career" at the Art Students League, but she characterized it as "entirely different from former days." [39] The changes in the American art world, epitomized by the 1913 Armory Show that introduced into this country the most radical of European art trends, had created a broad chasm between her present and her past experiences at the League. "There seems to be little instruction," she concluded, "really everyone following his own bent & considering their judgement as good as anyone elses." [40]

In April 1918, the City Club of New York hosted a two-week exhibition that focused solely on the paintings of Kate Freeman Clark. Like her previous maternal pushes, Cary Clark's initiative provided the contact that led to the show of sixteen paintings including the *Climbers* from the Panama-Pacific Exposition. The next year, after months of declining health, Mama Kate Walthall Freeman died at age 101. Once again, Kate and Cary Clark traveled to Mississippi briefly for the funeral and then returned to New York, even though, as Mama Kate's primary heirs, the Walthall family home in Holly Springs had passed to their ownership. [41]

Cary Freeman Clark died in August 1922, and for the first time ever, Kate was left alone. Without her mother's bullying, and without others to plan her life around, Kate Freeman Clark found herself adrift. Her attempt to revive her painting career had stalled. Times had changed. Tastes had changed. The art world had changed. In despair and confusion she agonized over whether to stay in New York or to give it up for the Walthall home place that was now her own. Old family friends urged her to retreat to the comfort and security of Holly Springs, but her artist friends and former teachers were equally adamant in their contradictory advice. They sincerely believed that the best thing for Kate to do would be to remain in New York, to enjoy her freedom from family responsibilities at long last, and to throw herself back into painting. But even they considered her "not very strong" and urged her to take care of herself. [42]

The siren song of home pulled her South. Kate Freeman Clark settled down in a permanent place in 1923 for the first time in more than thirty years. She left her paintings behind, packed in bales for storage at New York's Lincoln Warehouse, and she directed her attorney to oversee the renovation of the old

Walthall house, which had fallen into disrepair. The Holly Springs locals received this news with eager anticipation.[43] But the folks back home were not entirely insensitive to Kate's other aspirations. One woman wrote, "I can but hope that your beloved art, which you have neglected of late years to minister to your two dear ones, will again give you some comfort and interest."[44]

The fact that Kate Freeman Clark included a new studio in the renovations of the old Walthall house attests to her plan to take up painting again back home. She hoped that a close-knit community of family friends might satisfy her yearning for security and provide a place where she could recover herself as an artist, but instead the routines of small town life and the clutter of ordinary days interfered. The weight of her family history interfered. Not least, the loneliness of her separation from her artistic friends and the stimulation of the New York art world interfered. Although Clark received invitations to show her work in exhibitions sponsored by various amateur and semiprofessional art clubs that were springing up across the South in the 1920s and 1930s, she always declined.[45] None of them could begin to match the artistic standards set by her years in New York. Perhaps the very act of painting came to seem pointless to her.

Kate's old New York friends sent her a barrage of encouraging letters. They knew her well and tried numerous psychological prods to get a paintbrush back into her hand. One even attempted to use the power of maternal persuasion from the grave, writing, "Your mother would not want you to give up your work, I'm sure."[46] In response to Kate's apparent enjoyment of her house and her pets, May Lyman, her best friend from the years of seasonal migrations, voiced her fears that "it is all going to enwrap you so you will not paint. Don't let it, Kate. Don't embroider. Let things go unembroidered."[47] Kate Freeman Clark's former teacher Irving Wiles added his concern that she was "making a great mistake not to paint" and laced the message with his own dose of guilt about "how many would be happy if they had your talent and experience and the opportunity."[48] The issue of "opportunity" was a telling one. The modern changes in times, tastes, and the art world had crippled the ability of traditional painters to make a living from their work, and few struggling artists could fall back on such an attractive safety net.

From a financial perspective, Kate Clark should have had no excuses, for she could well afford to hire servants to attend her every need, including a maid, cook, gardener, and chauffeur. Yet once ensconced back home, it became easier for her to slip into her grandmother Mama Kate's established social niche in Holly Springs as a southern lady than to carve out a new one for Kate Freeman Clark, the artist. Instead of painting, she held tea parties and composed patriotic and school songs. Instead of painting, she joined the Audubon Society and the Holly Springs Garden Club. Instead of painting, she celebrated her Walthall family heritage with membership in both the Colonial Dames of America and the Daughters of the American Revolution. Instead of painting, she opened the doors of her family's antebellum home to paying guests during spring pilgrimage tours.[49]

Certainly Kate Freeman Clark enjoyed a life of relative ease that contrasted with the financial straits of her former colleagues in the North, which only worsened with the onset of the Great Depression and deteriorated further after the beginning of World War II.[50] In 1943, Wiles's daughter wrote Kate, "I who did not know how to boil water have had to try and learn cooking, plumbing, furnace-tending, marketing, gardening and a hundred other things which I dislike and do very badly."[51] The sophisticated and genteel culture that Kate Freeman Clark remembered from her young adulthood in New York no longer existed. The letters from her frustrated and jaded friends proved as much. As Kate Clark approached her seventieth birthday in 1945, her old friend May Lyman wrote to her, "I do not go to picture exhibitions anymore. What you are apt to see isn't worth a trip on the crowded train."[52] Kate's devoted friend's death the following year broke one of the last tangible links to her former life as an artist. Kate kept those years alive in her memories, though. Since childhood she had kept a series of diaries to record her travels and her impressions of art and society. On occasion, she shared some of those remembrances in programs with the club women of Holly Springs. Her presentations to the Thursday club, a women's cultural organization, often focused on William Merritt Chase and her years of art study in the North.[53]

Kate Freeman Clark lived out the rest of her days at the old Walthall home place on College Avenue in Holly Springs. She died in 1957 at age 81, and like all the other Walthalls before her, was laid to rest in Hill Crest Cemetery. Her will detailed her hopes for a museum surrounded by gardens to be constructed next to her family home, one that would house her paintings and celebrate her family's history.[54] The eventual settlement of the estate left a bequest to the city of Holly Springs that included the Walthall cottage, all the paintings that she had stored in New York, and funds to be used for construction of the Kate Freeman Clark Art Gallery. Luckily, the New York tax authorities chose not to examine closely the dirty bales of pictures removed from the Lincoln Warehouse, and they judged the entire contents as valued for tax purposes at one dollar. The museum organizers who unpacked the bales back in Holly Springs discovered that few pictures had been titled or dated and that some had suffered severe deterioration, but they cleaned and framed enough paintings to mount an impressive exhibition when the small brick gallery opened in 1963. Unfortunately the modern art world of the 1960s showed little enthusiasm for the painting styles of William Merritt Chase or his students, and declines in the local economy prevented keeping the gallery open to the public on a full-time basis.[55]

Tastes, times, and the art world, however, have continued to change. As a result of new interest in American painting, especially American Impressionism, museums and galleries have mounted a number of exhibitions featuring the works of William Merritt Chase, his contemporaries, and his students, and their pictures have become intensely sought after by collectors. A similar development has focused increased public attention on the contributions of American women artists, though Clark's choice to mask her gender in signing her work has led to an omission of her paintings from some of the more recent exhibitions devoted exclusively to women artists.[56] Nonetheless, these movements have raised the reputation of Kate Freeman Clark and led to a broader awareness of her work. Major American museums have displayed and cited her personal papers and photographs in exhibits and catalogs because of the light they shed on student experiences at the Art Students League and the Shinnecock art colony.[57] Scholars of Mississippi history have studied and published excerpts from her collection of Walthall family papers because of the family's historical and political importance in the state.[58] Finally, the display of Kate Freeman Clark's paintings and drawings has not been limited to her hometown gallery. With increasing frequency her works have found prominence in exhibitions from Mississippi to U.S. embassies overseas.[59]

The story of Kate Freeman Clark is that of a poor little rich girl, for she seemed in some ways blessed with a fairy-tale life, but one tempered by human tragedy and struggle. She was born into the upper echelons of Mississippi society and progressed to similar status in Washington and New York. She partook of the country's best art education in the cities and in the new summer art colonies. She found confirmation of her artistic talent from the greatest painter and the most prestigious exhibition venues of her day. But her father, her best suitor, and her adored mentor each in their turn disappeared unexpectedly from her life. Her strong-willed mother fiercely protected and pushed her, almost to the point of destroying her ability to function on her own. Ironically, it was her little southern lady grandmother who doggedly held to the Walthall heritage in Holly Springs and maintained the connection that eventually enabled Kate Clark's return to Mississippi. Kate Freeman Clark loved her family and her art, and when she had lost both, she followed the example set by her widowed mother and grandmother before her. She went home.

NOTES

1. Edwin C. Bearss, "Edward Cary Walthall," in *The Confederate General,* ed. William C. Davis (Washington, D.C.: National Historical Society, 1999), 105–7; Walthall family genealogical chart, Walthall Family Papers, Marshall County Historical Museum (henceforth MCHM), Holly Springs, Miss.

2. W. F. Adams to Cary Ann Freeman Clark, April 1885, Walthall Family Papers; Kate Freeman Clark, diary, 17 August 1897, Kate Freeman Clark Papers, MCHM.

3. Edward Donaldson Clark to Cary Ann Freeman, 15 March 1869, Walthall Family Papers.

4. Edward Donaldson Clark to Kate Freeman Clark, August 1882, Clark Papers.

5. Scrapbook, Clark Papers.

6. Clark, diary, 41–42.

7. "Lucius Quintus Cincinnatus Lamar," *Biographical Dictionary of the United States Congress, 1774–1989* (Washington, D.C.: U. S. Government Printing Office, 1989), 1336; "Edward Cary Walthall," *Biographical Dictionary,* 2003.

8. Edward Russell Freeman to Cary Freeman Clark, 18 March 1885, Walthall Family Papers.

9. Julianna Buck to Cary Freeman Clark, 23 March 1885, Walthall Family Papers.

10. Edward Russell Freeman to Kate Walthall Freeman, 10 January 1892, 19 September 1894, Walthall Family Papers; Clark, diary, 2 July 1893.

11. Marshall County Chancery Court case no. 288, Clark Papers.

12. Edward Russell Freeman to Kate Walthall Freeman, 13 May 1900, Walthall Family Papers; Clark, diary, 6 August 1893; untitled newspaper clipping, 18 June 1905, Clark Papers.

13. Donelson F. Hoopes, *The American Impressionists* (New York: Watson-Guptill, 1972), 9.

14. Clark, diary, 8 March 1895; Marchel E. Landgren, *Years of Art* (New York: R. M. McBride, 1940), 64, 69; Clara Erskine Clement, *Women in the Fine Arts, from the Seventh Century* B.C. *to the Twentieth Century* A.D. (Boston: Houghton, Mifflin, 1905), 1–11; Ronald G. Pisano, *William Merritt Chase* (New York: Watson-Guptill, 1979), 32.

15. Pisano, *The Students of William Merritt Chase* (Huntington and Southampton, N.Y.: Heckscher Museum and Parrish Art Museum, 1973), 5; Clark, diary, 14 July 1895.

16. Pisano, *The Students of William Merritt Chase,* 5.

17. Barbara Dayer Gallati, *William Merritt Chase* (New York: Harry N. Abrams, 1995), 26; Duncan Phillips, "William Merritt Chase," *American Magazine of Art* 8 (1916): 49–50; Hoopes, 14.

18. Cynthia Grant Tucker, *Kate Freeman Clark: A Painter Rediscovered* (Jackson: University Press of Mississippi, 1981), 48.

19. Gallati, 71.

20. Kate Freeman Clark, "A Day at Shinnecock," 1921, Clark Papers.

21. Tucker, 76; Clark, "A Day at Shinnecock"; Clark's painting *Copper Pot, Tin Plate with Fruit* and Chase's painting *Still Life* are at the Kate Freeman Clark Art Gallery in Holly Springs, Miss.

22. Clark's painting *Golden Locks* is at the Clark Art Gallery; Kathleen McClain Jenkins, "Kate Freeman Clark: Her Family and Her Art" (master's thesis, Delta State University, 1989), 40.

23. Clark, diary, 18 January 1898.

24. Ibid., 27 January 1898.

25. Ibid., 29 October 1896.

26. Ibid.

27. Ibid., 1 January 1897.

28. E. T. Sykes, "Walthall's Brigade," *Publications of the Mississippi Historical Society,* ed. Dunbar Rowland, vol. 1, Centenary Series (Jackson: Mississippi Historical Society, 1916), 490–91.

29. Clark, diary, 23 April 1917; Mrs. R. L. Wyatt, interview by author, tape recording, Holly Springs, Miss., 26 June 1987.

30. Daniel Strain to [Kate] Freeman Clark, 11 January 1905; National Academy of Design 79th Exhibit catalog, 1904; National Academy of Design 80th Exhibit catalog, 1905; National Academy of Design Winter Exhibition catalog, 1911; Pennsylvania Academy of Fine Arts 110th Exhibition catalog, 1915; Corcoran Gallery of Art 1st Contemporary Exhibition catalog, 1907; John W. Beatty to [Kate] Freeman Clark, 30 April 1908; National Academy of Design Winter Exhibit catalog, 1906; Corcoran Gallery of Art 2nd Contemporary Exhibition catalog, 1908; National Academy of Design 92nd American Exhibition catalog, 1917, Clark Papers; Peter Hastings Falk, ed., *Who Was Who in American Art* (Madison, Conn.: Sound View Press, 1985), 116.

31. Edward Walthall Freeman to Kate Walthall Freeman, 20 April 1904, Walthall Family Papers; Clark, diary, 7 September 1917.

32. Braus Inc. to Kate Freeman Clark, 13 May 1915, Clark Papers; Annie L. Pierson, "Historical Research Project—Marshall County," Kate Freeman Clark subject file, Mississippi Department of Archives and History (henceforth MDAH), Jackson; Keith L. Bryant Jr., *William Merritt Chase: A Genteel Bohemian* (Columbia and London: University of Missouri Press, 1991), 230.

33. Gallati, 129.

34. Clark, diary, 15 May 1917.

35. May Lyman to Kate Freeman Clark, 3 July 1918, Clark Papers; Clark, diary, 31 July 1917, 1 January 1918, 12 September 1918.

36. Clark, diary, 7 August 1918.

37. Ibid., 12 September 1918.

38. Ibid., 29 September 1917.

39. Ibid., 7 September 1917, 12 November 1917, 25 December 1917.

40. Ibid., 25 December 1917.

41. Freeberg Allen to Kate Freeman Clark, 3 March 1918; Clark, diary, April 1918, 7 September 1917, 29 September 1917; Kate Walthall Freeman, last will and testament, 28 June 1904, filed 15 April 1919, Marshall County Courthouse, Holly Springs, Miss.

42. Pearl Strickland to Kate Freeman Clark, 11 August 1922; May Lyman to Kate Freeman Clark, 12 August 1922, Clark Papers.

43. Harris Gholson to Kate Freeman Clark, n.d., Kate Freeman Clark subject file, MDAH; Archibald Watson to Harris Gholson, 8 June 1923; Helen Craft Fort to Kate Freeman Clark, 8 October 1922, Clark Papers.

44. Albert Anderson to Kate Freeman Clark, n.d., Clark Papers.

45. Florence W. McLuter to Kate Freeman Clark, 18 August 1921, Clark Papers.

46. Ethel Q. Colton to Kate Freeman Clark, 7 January 1925, Clark Papers.

47. May Lyman to Kate Freeman Clark, 27 February 1925, Clark Papers.

48. Irving R. Wiles to Kate Freeman Clark, 8 June 1926, Clark Papers.

49. L. Glenn Fant, interview by author, tape recording, Holly Springs, Miss., 26 June 1987; Wyatt, interview.

50. Mary Wiles to Kate Freeman Clark, 14 May 1933, Clark Papers.

51. Gladys Wiles to Kate Freeman Clark, 8 May 1943, Clark Papers.

52. May Lyman to Kate Freeman Clark, 30 March 1945, Clark Papers.

53. Louise Lyman Adams to Kate Freeman Clark, 19 October 1946, Clark Papers; Clark, diary, 19 January 1935, 27 March 1936; Clark, "A Day at Shinnecock."

54. Clark, last will and testament.

55. Fant, interview; Wyatt, interview.

56. Bryant, 258–59.

57. D. Scott Atkinson and Nicolai Cikovsky Jr., *William Merritt Chase: Summers at Shinnecock, 1891–1902* (Washington, D.C.: National Gallery of Art, 1987), 18.

58. George C. Osborn, ed., "Letters of Senator Edward Cary Walthall to Robert W. Banks," *Journal of Mississippi History* 11 (1949): 185–203; James H. Stone, ed., "L. Q. C. Lamar's Letters to Edward Donaldson Clark, 1868–1885, Part 1, 1868–1873," *Journal of Mississippi History* 35 (1973): 65–74; Stone, ed., "L. Q. C. Lamar's Letters to Edward Donaldson Clark, 1868–1885, Part 2, 1874–1878," *Journal of Mississippi History* 37 (1975): 189–201; Stone, ed., "L.Q.C. Lamar's Letters to Edward Donaldson Clark, 1868–1885, Part 3, 1879–1885," *Journal of Mississippi History* 43 (1981): 135–64.

59. Patti Carr Black, *Of Home and Family: Art in Nineteenth Century Mississippi* (Jackson: Mississippi Museum of Art, 1999); Kathleen McClain Jenkins, *Summers of '96—Shinnecock Revisited: The Inspiration of Kate Freeman Clark by William Merritt Chase* (Laurel, Miss.: Lauren Rogers Museum of Art, 1996); Elise Brevard Smith, *Marie Hull and Her Contemporaries Theora Hamblett and Kate Freeman Clark* (Jackson: Mississippi Museum of Art, 1988); Ed Blake, "Time Unveils Obscure Mississippi Artist," *Cleveland (Miss.) Bolivar Commercial,* 23 December 1987, 13.

Blanche Colton Williams

(1879–1944)

Mentor of Southern Women's Literature

BRIDGET SMITH PIESCHEL

Immediately after her death in 1944, Blanche Colton Williams, noted educator, editor, and writer, was widely eulogized and mourned by the literary and educational community. Now, nearly sixty years later, she is all but forgotten. Even in her native Mississippi, the state whose best qualities she did much to support, she is remembered only by an occasional archivist or by a fond niece or nephew grown old. Why has her reputation diminished and all but disappeared?

During her lifetime, no one did more than Blanche Colton Williams for the "literary medium that supercedes all others in America—the Short Story."[1] Her creative writing courses at Columbia turned out promising young writers by the dozens, and her *Handbook on Short Story Writing* was said to be "the first practical aid to groping young writers that was put on the market in this country."[2] In 1919 she accepted the chair of the O. Henry Memorial Awards Committee and remained at its head until 1932, retiring, she said, to enjoy "the privilege of doing more of [her] own writing."[3] As chair of this committee, she gained the admiration and respect of her editorial colleagues for her sharp eye for a superior story and for her energy in her commitment to her task, which involved reading and examining, by her own admission, more than sixty thousand submissions.[4]

Perhaps her greatest contribution as editor, though, was her promotion of those struggling writers who, but for her keen judgment, might have been forgotten. A glance at the table of contents of the O. Henry Award volumes from 1919 to 1932 or at her other edited collections, such as *Our Short Story Writers,* reveals another very important point. In all of her collections and discussions of short story writers, the percentage of women writers treated is between 35 and 50 percent of the total, a remarkable percentage in a society where the published

BLANCHE COLTON WILLIAMS

1942. Blanche Colton Williams file, Special Collections,
Mississippi University for Women.

woman was only one in twelve.[5] Williams was eager to promote young writers of her own gender, those talented women who in the 1920s and 1930s were fighting great battles to preserve their literary integrity and their creative selves. In her *Handbooks* that explain the technicalities of short story writing, illustrations drawn from the works of women writers are numerous, revealing Williams's admiration of writers such as Mary E. Wilkins Freeman, Susan Glaspell, Edna Ferber, and many others.

In 1937 Williams wrote to her namesake, a niece who had literary ambitions and who had indicated a desire to write about her famous aunt, "Do not forget that before you really begin on your subject, one's ancestors are to be considered. For it is out of one's ancestors that we become what we are."[6] Blanche meant her literal ancestors, those family members from whom she had inherited her intelligence, creativity, and love of literature. But she also was referring to her literary ancestors, especially those female forebears whose writing had taught and inspired her as a young writer and still younger reader.

Williams was born at just the right time in just the right place to achieve her potential as a scholar and educator. The time was February 1879, and the place was rural Attala County in economically devastated Mississippi, populated mainly by farmers barely scraping a living from the red clay. It was a time when "Mississippians were literally back where they had been when their grandfathers first settled in the wilderness. But now the wilderness was different. It was already scarred by the exploitation of antebellum moneymaking and the destructiveness of fighting a war. . . . The end of the war found Mississippi public school education just as it was in 1860, in a state of confusion."[7]

It was a time and place when a college education for a poor woman was considered as ridiculous and useless as a frock coat for a mule. But Mississippi lawmakers recognized that girls like Blanche, smart but poor, were going to have to have a way to earn a living. This economic reality prompted the Mississippi legislature, in 1884, to vote appropriations for a women's college. Blanche didn't know it then, but that college would give her the chance southern women of her class previously were deprived—to rise in the world by means of her own brains and merit. Legislator Wiley Nash, in his first speech to his peers, called the institute a "Godsend, a blessing to the poor girls of the State . . . [where] the poor farmers of Mississippi can send their daughters . . . [for] a good practical education."[8]

Attala County was still reeling from the catastrophe of the Civil War. Its inhabitants counted themselves lucky to have a piece of land, a roof over their heads, and a graveyard for their kin. Residents of Attala County, white and black, still feared conjure women, spent a hoarded coin to hear a gypsy fortune, and daubed sticky mud in the cracks of their rough log and plank houses to keep out the cold in winter and the mosquitoes in the summer. In many ways this part of Mississippi was still a frontier far removed from the relative wealth and shabby gentility of the Delta and the Tombigbee River bottom. Here people were poor and poorer.[9]

Millard Filmore Williams and Ella Colton Williams, Blanche's parents, were considered a little peculiar. Millard (or Peter, as he was known to his family) was a schoolteacher who farmed incompetently to supplement their income. Ella was a smart and beautiful woman who had married down and then shown herself willing to lower herself to fieldwork so that her delicate husband would not do further damage to his health. Peter Williams was a born teacher who loved learning and had an open mind about issues that few Attala County residents would have even discussed. He said Blanche was "as good as a boy," that Lincoln had been an admirable man, that slavery was wrong. But he was also a romantic idealist who let his loving wife chop cotton while he protected his health and read.[10] The result of Blanche's parents' influence was that she achieved that rare combination, the best of both: her father's love of learning and democratic ideals, her mother's determination, common sense, and tolerance.

Pauline Orr, Mistress of English at the Industrial Institute and College (II&C) when Blanche came there as a fifteen-year-old student in 1894, recognized her brilliance immediately. Blanche was just old enough to be eligible to attend. Each county in Mississippi could send a fixed quota of "educable white girls" who had to be at least fifteen, "in good health," and possess a "certificate of good moral character."[11] Blanche was in the minority in that she did not have to begin her college work as a "preparatory student." In 1894, of the 314 students enrolled at the college, 194 were taking remedial work as "preps."[12] But Blanche's parents and the two other teachers she had studied under had given her a valuable gift, the scholarly background she needed to attempt II&C's rigorous collegiate curriculum.

Photographs of her as a student reveal a short, rather stocky girl with a square, solemn face. Her eyes were beautiful, round, light colored, and changeable. People who first met her were inclined to remark on her "blue" eyes, but her close friends described them as clear light gray. Her hair was thick, light brown, with a reddish cast. In her later years, after she gained some self-confidence, she was considered very charming and vivacious. As a girl, however, she was shy and serious, focused on her studies. Many years later, Orr, writing about her famous former pupil, said even as a girl Blanche was a "genius." Orr concluded: "What a woman she . . . turned out to be . . . a teacher, a writer, a friend."[13]

There were only fifteen girls in Blanche's freshman class, and it is obvious, in looking at the grade records, that Blanche was one of the most capable. One poor girl that year ended the term with only a 31 in mathematics and a 56 in English. Her name does not appear the following year. But Blanche's marks were nearly perfect in mathematics, English, history, and Latin, and she chose as her industrial art, phonography, which was an early form of shorthand. Every student at the II&C was required to complete a certificate in a vocational course so that the Mississippi legislature could be certain that their public women's college was turning out women who could support themselves. Blanche was not planning to pursue a secretarial career, but shorthand must have proved useful in note taking all her life. Her senior year, however, perhaps as proficient as she wanted to be in phonography, she studied telegraphy along with her French, chemistry, English, and philosophy. She also took anatomy that year, instructed by Dr. May F. Jones, just recently employed as the college physician. [14]

Blanche's unpublished memoir, "Kingdom of a Child," opens in March 1881, when she was barely two years old. She was a precocious child coming to terms with a beautiful and dangerous world. She heard her father talking about a man who killed President Garfield; she moved from one house to a smaller one but enjoyed the fact that then she was close to her paternal relatives who doted on her. She knew her father had been sick, but not that he was dying of tuberculosis. She was excited about the birth of her little brother, although she had not ever been the sort of child to be bored with her own company. She knew her mother worked hard, but not that she sometimes worried about where their next meal was coming from. [15]

Williams came from a family of resourceful women. Though paradoxically she said that "Kingdom of a Child" was "particularly" the story of "Peter Winn," her fictional name for her father, [16] the book mainly is the story of herself, her mother, and her grandmother. The book tells the story of their resourcefulness during the absence of Peter Winn when he left the damp Mississippi climate in 1886 to recover from tuberculosis and pan for gold in Colorado. And though young Bracebridge's (Williams's fictional name for herself) father was her schoolmaster and taught her the rudiments of learning, he seemed to fear her precocity. After a brief period of going to the school with him, Brace was left at home to "keep Mama company." [17] " 'She's learning too fast,' " her father tells her mother. But, significantly, "Brace doesn't hear him." [18] When Brace and her mother were alone together, she did not think her daughter was learning too rapidly. In fact, she had the child literally memorize the tattered reader she still possessed from her own short career as a teacher. By also having Brace memorize definitions, she teaches her precision in language, an attribute the adult

Blanche considered supremely important. " 'You are not always exact, Brace,' "
her mother says, " 'and you must learn to be so.' "[19] She encouraged Brace to read
the few novels she had and even the newspapers with which their rural cabin was
papered, but most important, she instinctively promoted her child's creativity.
When she noticed Brace molding figures out of clay dug to chink the spaces
between the logs of their cabin, she laboriously carried more from the pile so
that Brace could continue her artistic play.[20] It is Brace's mother who awakened
what Eudora Welty called "the inward voice . . . the feeling that resides in the
printed novel."[21]

Brace learned from her mother that women could be independent and happy
in their work: "Mama was happier, Brace thought. She was 'earning a living'
for her children, not having to depend upon her father or upon Papa's family."
The child realized that her mother supported Brace's inevitable excursion into
the "world of men." " 'It is a good earth,' echoed Brace. But she knew it was a
kingdom where every boy and girl must somehow learn to make a living. . . .
Though Mama knew a boy's kingdom should be other than that of a girl's, she
knew that for Brace what must be must be."[22] Certainly her mother was extremely important to the formation of the independent writer and scholar the
child Brace/Blanche would become. Williams knew that to understand herself
as a writer she could look at her mother. She asked the young women graduates
of the class of 1934 at Mississippi State College for Women (MSCW, the name
that replaced Industrial Institute and College), "What is your heritage, and what
will you do with it?"[23] Her replacement of her given second name (Gertrude)
for her mother's maiden name (Colton) as she began her publishing career is
an acknowledgment of her mother's invaluable influence.

Williams's literary heritage, the inheritance provided by a host of women
writers and scholars, was for her a significant part of her own creative talent.
She believed any woman writer should acknowledge this about herself and her
sister writers. She never forgot the excitement she felt as a child while reading
her mother's tattered copy of Augusta Evans Wilson's *St. Elmo*. She was inspired
by the biblical eloquence of Wilson's ornate style: "She did not forget the name
of the author, which Mama told her, for all the front fly-leaves . . . were lost—
Augusta Evans Wilson. That sounded good too."[24]

Blanche remained loyal to her childhood inspiration. In "Kingdom" she
wrote, "A long time after, Brace heard a critic declare this author was a sen-
timentalist of the worst type of the Victorian age in America. He could have no
idea what Brace had got from that one tattered volume, there in the cabin."[25]
Williams's unwillingness to discredit this author merely because a critic had
accused Wilson of sentimentality (a common criticism of nineteenth-century

women writers) illustrates her ability to examine literature with an eye un-affected by prevailing opinion and to see value where others chose to ignore it. In addition to praising nearly forgotten women writers, Williams was not afraid to rearrange the rankings of importance of those women writers who were included in the literary canon of her day. While she was in London in 1934 researching her biography of George Eliot, she said in an interview in the *London Daily Mail* that she considered Eliot superior to both Thackeray and Dickens and preferred *Middlemarch* to *Vanity Fair* or *David Copperfield*.[26] Her attraction to Eliot was longstanding, and she considered this novelist another strong influence on her choice of career. In her preface to the Eliot biography, she described her discovery of this writer while she was still a young student at the II&C: "In the college dining-room four hundred of us waited after din-ner . . . for the first tap of the bell at which we rose to form in line and march out. While we waited, we read Thackeray, Bulwer-Lytton, Scott and Dickens. I came to George Eliot. By chance I discovered *The Mill on the Floss.* After closing the book on the final plangent iambic lines, I said, 'She knows, she knows coun-try life, country girls and boys, how brothers and sisters feel about each other.' Not hitherto had I found anything like that saga for simplicity, humor, pathos, tragedy."[27] For Williams, Eliot came to represent that with which she sought to identify, the ideal of the sensitive, observant, and dedicated writer who did not forget her country upbringing or the women who helped shape her. In fact, Williams is careful in her biography of Eliot to mention an early teacher of the young Mary Ann Evans: "Rebecca Franklin, dissenter, educator, determinant of Mary Ann's career" who demanded "purity, propriety and precision" from all her young pupils. And Williams also praises a girlhood series of letters between Mary Ann and a friend, Maria Lewis, in which they were consciously practicing to be "literary," as "records of an incipiently magnificent mind" though other critics have labeled Eliot's letters "pedantic or unpleasantly priggish."[28] Eliot's artistic success was thus a very real inspiration to Blanche Colton Williams as she discovered the similarities in their rural upbringings, their shared admira-tion for special women in their lives, and their strong dedication to work, which Williams says Eliot valued above " 'repose and amusement' " as necessities for her happiness.[29]

Blanche's four years at the II&C were turbulent. The state was in a severe financial depression, and because of the economic situation enrollment had dropped to 241 by 1898. The college president, Robert Frazer, stayed at odds with the all-female faculty led by Pauline Orr and her staunch friends and for-mer students, Latin teacher Minnie Paslay and English instructors Rosa Peebles and Eula Deaton, all of whom had been members of the first graduating class in

1889. These were women Blanche would come to know and love as close friends all of her life, and her political and educational ideals were shaped by them. Her learning did not come as a result of library study; in 1895, President Frazer complained to the trustees that the library contained only "Chambers' Encyclopedia, the Encyclopedia Britannica . . . a few other works of reference . . . several hundred volumes of miscellaneous literature, . . . some government pamphlets and some war records."[30] Blanche must have relied heavily on Miss Orr for extra reading material.

Williams graduated with a bachelor of arts degree in 1898, determined to teach and to write. After gaining some teaching experience in English composition and elementary science at Stanton College in Natchez, Mississippi, and at Grenada College in Grenada, Mississippi, she left the state for New York in 1907, earning a master's degree at Columbia in 1908 and a doctorate in 1910, the same year she was hired as an instructor in English at Hunter College. She had been the recipient of a five hundred dollar award from the II&C Alumnae Association, which she always said was an invaluable financial boost that enabled her to pursue graduate work at Columbia. Her comment is not surprising when we consider that the average salary for a white female teacher in Mississippi during this time was $32 per month.[31]

Williams had been head of the English Department at Grenada College when she received the phone call about the alumnae scholarship, but she had already been looking outside of Mississippi. In 1906, she had made her first trip to Europe: "I landed at Naples and did the grand tour through Italy, part of Germany and Holland, Switzerland, Belgium, France, England and Scotland. When I came back, I saw that I must, somehow, find a place in which I could go forward."[32] For her, that place was going to be New York, and she would quickly become a star at Columbia. Although she had published a short piece in *Lippincott's Magazine* while still teaching in Mississippi, her first book-length publication was her dissertation, *Gnomic Poetry in Anglo Saxon.*

Her new life in New York, compared to the quiet routine of teaching in Natchez and Grenada, must have taken a substantial adjustment. In New York, she was directly exposed to some of the most famous thinkers of the century. In 1907, deep into her graduate study, she heard William James lecture on pragmatism. Early in 1910, the year she finished her doctorate, modernist Ezra Pound spoke at Columbia. She never thought much of him, however. She educated herself in the moderns, but her favorite poet was Keats.

Her first summer in New York, she worked as a file clerk in a magazine's office. The magazine published short stories and had a very organized system of multiple readers and notes on manuscript submissions. Of that experience, she said, "The editor talked a lot about stories being 'not for our beat.' . . . There was much discussion about conflict and drama—and lack of it! Before the summer was over and it was time for me to resume my studies at [Columbia], my interest had been so aroused in the technical end of the short-fiction field that I began to make notes for a book which I hoped to do on the subject."[33] This book would be her *Handbook on Short Story Writing,* first published in 1917. In it she stressed not only good writing, but also the practicality of writing what editors wanted to publish. She was pragmatic about the reality of publishing: professional writers, in order to be able to support themselves, had to be aware of what would sell.

She welcomed Miss Orr and Miss Paslay that fall; they were taking graduate courses at Columbia, as were two other II&C graduates, Emma Laney (1905) and Nannie Rice (1906). Emma and Nannie did not have a pleasant first impression of Blanche. Nannie wrote her father back in Mississippi that she and Emma "conducted Miss Orr and Miss Paslay around to show them how and where to register. . . . Miss Blanche Williams and Miss Timberlake of Mississippi have us eating at their table. . . . Miss Williams is an alumnae scholarship woman. She toots her own horn too much to be agreeable and has the unhappy knack of saying the wrong thing. Emma says she is chagrined because we do not toady to her celebrity and because we are too independent of her services, and I know she is right."[34] Their negative first impression soon dissipated. In a few years they were admirers and finally warm friends of Blanche's. Years later, after hearing Blanche's address to the 1934 graduating class, Emma wrote Nannie about how well the speech had been received and said, "I believe that she is one of the most genuine people I've ever known."[35]

Blanche was accustomed to activism; she, like many of Pauline Orr's former students, was a member of the Mississippi Woman Suffrage Association. Each year in the city there were increasingly larger marches for woman suffrage. In 1915, twenty-five thousand people demonstrated for the vote. The mid-teens in New York were anxious times. Newspaper columnists warned of possible German sabotage of trains, and anyone of German origin was suspect. The garment workers union, the Street and Electric Railway Workers Employees, and the Actors Equity Association each went on strike, which meant violence in the streets. Blanche's sympathies were with the working class, and it was during the teens that "working class woman suffragism in New York can be said to have finally come into its own."[36] Blanche and her close friends did not move in the same circle as such activists as Harriot Stanton Blatch, who had become the champion of the New York woman suffrage movement in the first decade of the twentieth century. Women teachers who also supported woman suffrage did not fit into the category of either working-class suffragists, who were more likely to be concerned about practical matters like a living wage, or the elite-class suffragists like Blatch, who had the time, intellectual training, and money to devote their energies to worthy causes.[37] As a university graduate, Williams should have been a member of the privileged class. Blanche, however, had not come from a wealthy family and had attended a free public college and had always expected to work to support herself. In addition, a high percentage of the women with whom she had studied did not choose marriage, leaving themselves alone responsible for their financial survival. Perhaps she identified more closely with these working women than with the white northern suffragists. All of her working life Blanche remained close to the early faculty members at the II&C, the alumnae of that same school, to her fellow American Association of University Women (AAUW) members, to her former students, and to colleagues with similar scholarly interests. She shared most of her political interests and activities, and the correspondence detailing those interests, with women from these groups.

Williams also became active in New York educational circles. By 1917 she was "someone to know" in the literary world. That year II&C alumna Emma Laney wrote Nannie Rice, who was doing graduate work at Vassar, giving insight into how Blanche's reputation had grown: "A bit of news before I say good-by. In Little Rock last weekend I happened to meet one Lieut. Taylor, who has been instructing at Columbia and who spoke most intimately of Blanche Williams and Minor [Minor White Latham (1901)]. Of the former, he said enthusiastically, 'She has made good tremendously. Why just before I left New York, I went to a tea of hers at which were Fannie Hurst and Miss Ida Tarbell.'"[38]

As a member of the Society of Arts and Sciences in New York, Blanche began chairing in 1919 the committee that began the O. Henry Short Story Awards. That year Blanche welcomed her former mentor and English teacher, Pauline Orr, to New York permanently. Blanche, while comfortable in her West 108th Street, Manhattan apartment, began to spend many stimulating hours at the brownstone Miss Orr bought on West 74th Street. Living there also were Miss Orr's partner, Minnie Paslay, former II&C Mistress of Latin, who soon found a position as a classics teacher, and physician and II&C alumna Dr. Mary Maxwell "Maxie" or "Max" Hathorn, who also had her medical office in Miss Orr's house. Pauline's nephew, Jerome Harris, moved in a short while later, after becoming Assistant Rector of St. Ignatius Episcopal Church down the street. Myra Lindsey (II&C, 1912) remembered: "The house on 74th Street was a gathering place for [white] Mississippians and [white] Southerners in general and for many New Yorkers, friends old and new. Among these were editors, writers, musicians and many clergymen who came to Miss Orr's on Sunday afternoons for tea and talk. My sisters and I went every week and remember those gatherings with our minds and hearts."[39] Myra, with recommendations from Pauline and Blanche, soon was hired as an editor by *Good Housekeeping*.

At Orr's home, Blanche could be a Mississippi girl again, listening and talking to her former teacher, while proudly bringing her Columbia and Hunter College colleagues to Orr's "salon," enjoying their surprise at the quality of intellect that came and went (and lived) at West 74th Street. Head of her department by 1926, Blanche spent her summers traveling, mainly to England, and one interview quoted her as saying she had been a " 'reader in the British Museum for twenty-seven years.' "[40] While on sabbatical in 1931, she toured North Africa, Sicily, and Greece. That same year she took the time to recommend Emma Laney for a summer teaching position at Hunter College.

At the height of her career, Blanche was invited to speak to the 1934 graduating class of MSCW. In the speech, titled "Heritage," she reminded the young women of the value of their education, which allowed them to shift "constantly between present and past," and which provided them with "a well-ordered array of vicarious experience." Though not all of the women she mentioned as models were writers, they all represented that originality and firmness of purpose that Williams herself so prized. She asked the graduates: "How would you like to be deprived of your long roll of names—names for you significant of human experience? Cleopatra, Judith, Boadicia, and Molly Pitcher; Jenny Lind, Sarah Bernhardt, and Eleanor Duse; Margaret Fuller, Florence Nightingale and Edith Cavell."

Elsewhere in the address she reminds the women of the examples set by Sappho, Frances Jones Gaither (a Mississippi novelist and II&C alumna), Lizette Woodworth Reese, "the passionate Brontës," "indomitable George Eliot," and Augusta Evans Wilson. She made her listeners aware that their "heritage" had two strands, that strong women as well as men had laid a foundation on which they could build. She hoped to make them more knowledgeable about these models in order to give them fresh confidence in their abilities and prospects for success in depression-ridden Mississippi and the nation.[41]

Although Williams realized the importance of a female inheritance to women, she knew that an artist was not an imitator. "Your heritage is nothing if it is not one on which you build," she cautioned.[42] A strong sense of self and awareness of oneself as a woman in the world were two things Williams prized. She knew that awareness of oneself as a separate and autonomous being would lead to a sharpened awareness of the world and an eye for detailed observation. She describes in "Kingdom of a Child" the moment she became aware of her special separateness when she had an epiphany, which followed her awed contemplation of a huge tree: " 'Who am I?' she whispered to herself. A wave of something far away floated in upon her. 'You are you.' She said, 'I am I.' . . . That was as far as she got then in realizing individuality, but from that time she was separate, an individual, yet more curious about life, the earth."[43] Young Brace's self-awareness causes her to examine closely her own world and the people who surround her, broadening her perception, preparing her for her creative future. "She had, Brace thinks, been in a little world of which she was the center; now she felt dashed out to the edge of a circle, always widening."[44] She no longer felt that she was an appendage of her father or her mother or that their way was the only way to live.

Williams felt that this sense of individuality was particularly important to the woman as artist. This was vividly illustrated in her exhortation to those 1934 graduates seeking artistic careers: "Above all," she said, "think, think every day, 'I am I; I am alive.' . . . Follow truth as you see it for truth is a variable entity and is not the same for all."[45] Underneath her words was a plea that these talented and promising young women not assume, like so many others of their generation, that their selfhood lay only in the possibility of husbands and children.

There were other important characteristics the woman artist should develop, according to Williams. Two desirable qualities formed a mutually beneficial partnership and a productive tension: originality and hard work. But originality, for her, was the preferred of the two. It provided the gem that later hard work could polish and transform. Being original meant constantly questioning the rules governing one's world. In "Kingdom," the child Brace questioned everything. Even the fervor of Protestant dogma was not immune to her examination: "They sang, 'I am washed in the blood of the lamb.' . . . Brace began thinking about the words and wondered how anybody washed in red blood could be 'whiter than snow.' She gathered [that] there was a symbolic meaning in the words, but thought it a poor symbol. She didn't believe God had anything to do with the writing of those words."[46]

Later, during a different service, while singing "Jesus I My Cross Have Taken," Brace "wondered why anybody would take a cross to follow somebody else."[47] Brace even balked at using a dictionary because she was sure she knew as much as "that definition man."[48] Brace plans to make her own path to the castle, to use one of Williams's favorite metaphors on originality, even if she must cut her way through brush and bramble to get there. Characteristics of the young Brace reflect in Williams's speech on the necessity of courageous originality: "Do not hesitate to be original; to strike out in whatever way seems to you wisest for yourself."[49]

Williams assumed that success for a woman writer required a singleness of purpose, a willingness to see the life of a writer as whole in itself and not simply as a lesser part of a "complete" woman's life. She saw traditional marriage and even certain types of careers as barriers to that single-mindedness so important to the writer. This is not to say that she condemned marriage or certain demanding careers. She felt these ways of living were not the best for artistic creation and that in her day aspiring young women writers would have to compromise their goals if they chose to marry. In *Studying the Short Story,* Williams muses on the reasons why some writers produce dozens of fine stories and others only one or two "shining examples." After mentioning ten writers who fall into the second category, eight of whom are women, she discusses in particular Rose Sidney and Harriet Welles, both of whom published only a very few, but especially fine, stories: "Rose Sidney travels from post to post with her husband, Colonel in the U.S.A., as Harriet Welles follows round the world the flagship of her Admiral husband. One young woman mentioned above has stopped writing, momentarily, to rear a family she believes of more importance than her brain children. She is the antithesis of another who gave up her daughter when the stronger urge to write meant separation from that daughter."[50] Williams is careful in the preceding passage not to condemn the choices of either young woman, but she makes her point. Williams sees a decision against marriage as an almost certain way to avoid making these choices.

The marriage that required "following" a husband all over the world or just to another part of the country was, to Williams, especially damaging to the delicate inspirational environment necessary for creative impulse. Loath as she was to write anything even mildly censorious of Mary E. Wilkins Freeman, whom she greatly admired, she commented on the altering effect of Freeman's marriage at age forty: "On January first of that year she was married to Dr. Charles Freeman, of Metuchen, New Jersey. The years since then have meant for her literary work a loss of intensity in exchange for a corresponding breadth. Uprooting her plant from New England has slightly changed its flower; it blows more freely, though it lacks the distinctive perfume of its native soil."[51]

This observation seems to imply that the new literary qualities gained from Freeman's marriage and relocation fully compensated the writer for the loss of her regional flavor, but Williams's later discussion of Freeman's work reveals that she did not believe this judgment to be true. In her essay on Freeman, Williams says that she considers the New England writer's greatest asset her fine portrayal of her region's rural life. Williams concludes: "Her best work will stand, a collection of stories of village and country life, reflecting a phase of society in an era that is passing."[52] This "best work" was written before Freeman's marriage; the later material Williams judged entertaining, but ephemeral.

Williams herself never married, saying that it was a deliberate choice, not mere chance. Little Brace in "Kingdom of a Child" wanted to make a "great deal of money" and thus told her surprised mother, "I'll never, never be married," after Brace began to realize what drudgery and near poverty her mother endured while raising her family.[53] Brace's grandmother was unhappily married to an Irishman who drank heavily. " 'I've wept tears enough to drown myself,' she told little Brace who solemnly began to understand why no one mentioned Grandpa Winn, dead twelve years."[54] Marriage, she decided, is not for every woman. As she neared her sixtieth birthday, Williams wrote about her single life to a favorite niece: "When I turned down marriage for a career in the early 1900's I knew the die was cast. Say what one will, we spinsters miss a great deal, though even as I write I think I have the best life for me."[55] Her brief pang of regret, for she genuinely loved children and wrote her nieces and nephews every week, dissipated "even as she writes" as she was reminded again of the joy she had in her teaching and her scholarship.

Williams also knew that a more subtle danger lay in the choice of careers for the woman who wanted to write for publication. There was danger that the career, the necessity to earn money to support oneself, would become so time-consuming that the writing would become secondary, even nonexistent. Blanche's popularity and success, and her energetic assertiveness, which became dramatic flamboyance in her fifties, convinced her (and everyone else) that she had decades of productive writing ahead of her, if she just planned her life accordingly. When she celebrated her twenty-fifth anniversary as chair of the English Department at Hunter College, she was looking forward "to a great renaissance in letters" in America, although she had very nearly decided that she wasn't sure one "could teach anyone anything." A feature story about her in 1935 in the *New York World Telegram* gives an intriguing personal glimpse into the woman Blanche had become.[56] The reporter described a woman who is "statuesque, looking more like an opera singer than an educator," a "saltily philosophic person with a genial laugh" who "smoked cigarets [sic] in a long pink crystal holder" as they talked in her office, "a lovely room far above the children at play on 113th St."[57] Williams talked about her relief that, in 1935, it was not considered scandalous for women to smoke and said that she was so "shocked" at the restrictions during the prohibition decade that "she made it a 'point of honor' to keep liquor in her home throughout the years of drought."[58] She, however, also expressed her concern with what she saw as her current students' "recklessness, a tendency to insurrection, a desire to overthrow old things . . . [that they] no longer prepare for life, [but] prepare to make money."[59] In other interviews Williams seemed to echo Virginia Woolf in her recognition of the paradox that money, time, and privacy were essential for the woman writer yet it was virtually impossible for a woman to earn money and still have time to write. For Williams, one answer, the answer she chose for herself, lay in early retirement at age fifty-nine. She knew that she must have the courage to begin again if she were to become the writer she hoped she could be. In an interview just after her retirement she explained: "I have long thought that educators, particularly women, have a tendency to stay in educational work too long. What happens is that person thinks she will retire at the age of fifty-five or sixty. But at age fifty-five she is feeling so fine she decides she isn't old enough to retire. And so she stays on and the years go by and before long she is seventy and knows she cannot take up a new work. But in the years between fifty and sixty one can take up a new work that has been set aside for lack of time."[60] In an interview for a Mississippi paper she admitted confidently, "I'd really enjoy doing a dozen novels and biographies if I could fit them in."[61]

Sadly, Williams had delayed too long for all of her "new work." At age fifty-nine she was at the end of that productive decade she had described in the interview. It was not ability or drive she lacked; it was time. She died after a painful illness at age sixty-four. The international success of her first biography (1936) had encouraged her to pursue other biographical research. In her remaining five years, she published, among other scholarly pieces, two more formidable biographies, one of Clara Barton and one of John Keats, both well received critically. In 1943, Blanche sent old and nearly blind Pauline Orr a first day of print signed copy of the Keats biography, *Forever Young*, with a note saying that she hoped to publish many more like that one.[62] At the time of her death, she had completed research and was working on a biography of Harriet Martineau. But the fiction she longed to write did not come, except for the brief fictionalized memoir of her childhood she wrote in the last year of her life.

She wondered if her lack of inspiration could have been related to her decision to live in New York after she finished her graduate work. In an interview for *Holland's Magazine* she said with some regret, "New York has given me much that I could not have gotten [in Mississippi]. Yet . . . I just wonder if I might not have developed my own talents more had I stayed in Mississippi and not flown up here where I have become so entangled in a very complicated life."[63] Her "complicated life" left behind in 1943, she traveled to Mississippi to visit her family, to write, and to teach a short series of lectures at MSCW. She never returned to New York. In the spring of 1944, suffering from cancer, she went home to Attala County to stay with family members until her death that August.

The world of the woman writer and scholar has changed a great deal in the nearly sixty years since the death of Blanche Colton Williams, and her efforts brought about some of those changes. Williams felt a strong responsibility for other women writers and wanted her life to be an example to imitate where she had succeeded or to shun where she had failed. She did her best to fulfill for herself the future she imagined for one group of young women looking to her for guidance and inspiration. She said to them, "Through your lives or your money, you may . . . help women everywhere find their heritage; and if you do, then in the language of good King Duncan, 'signs of nobleness, like stars, shall shine on all deservers.' "[64]

Today Hunter College senior English majors compete every spring for the Blanche Colton Williams graduate fellowship to help them pay for their first year of graduate school. Mississippi University for Women's Library's Special Collections Room houses her prized George Eliot first editions and signed first editions of Williams's own books. While she didn't forget her Mississippi roots, she, like many white southern women of her generation, went north to realize her professional potential. The weighty biographies on which she based her intellectual reputation have been eclipsed by new generations of biographical revisionists. But her groundbreaking work on structure and analysis of the short story and her participation in the founding and direction of the O. Henry Prizes for short fiction earned her an important place in the teaching, writing, and promotion of modern fiction.

NOTES

1. Grace Leake, "Southern Personalities: Blanche Colton Williams, Molder of Literature," *Holland's, The Magazine of the South,* July 1933, 7.

2. Ibid.

3. Ibid., 15.

4. Ibid.

5. Tillie Olsen, "One out of Twelve: Women Who Are Writers in This Century," *Silences,* ed. Olsen (New York: Delacourte Press, 1978), 22–46.

6. Blanche Fields, tribute speech honoring Blanche Colton Williams, 1944, Blanche Colton Williams Folder, Special Collections, J. C. Fant Library, Mississippi University for Women (henceforth MUW), Columbus.

7. John K. Bettersworth, *A History of Mississippi,* vol. 1, ed. Richard A. McLemore (Jackson: University Press of Mississippi, 1973), 622.

8. Wiley Nash quoted in *Loyal Daughters: One Hundred Years at Mississippi University for Women, 1884–1984,* by Bridget Smith and Stephen Robert Pieschel (Jackson: University Press of Mississippi, 1984), 6.

9. Blanche Colton Williams, "Kingdom of a Child," 1944, Special Collections, J. C. Fant Library. These details are taken from the descriptions throughout this manuscript.

10. Williams, "Kingdom," note to publisher, and chap. 1.

11. Sarah Neilson, "The History of Mississippi State College for Women," 1954, Special Collections, J. C. Fant Library, 13.

12. Ibid., 14–15.

13. Fields, 6.

14. Grade reports, 1894–1898, Office of the Registrar, Welty Hall, MUW.

15. Williams, "Kingdom," 1–50 passim.

16. Ibid., note to publisher.

17. Ibid., 27.

18. Ibid.

19. Ibid., 122.

20. Ibid., 23–24.

21. Eudora Welty, "Listening in the Dark," *New York Times Review of Books*, 9 October 1983, 3.

22. Williams, "Kingdom," 7, 184.

23. Williams, "Heritage," speech to the MSCW graduating class of 1934, Special Collections, J. C. Fant Library.

24. Williams, "Kingdom," 83.

25. Ibid., 83–84.

26. "U.S. Woman's Life of George Eliot," *London Daily Mail,* 27 November 1934, 22.

27. Williams, *George Eliot: A Biography* (New York: Macmillan, 1936), vii.

28. Ibid., 23.

29. Ibid., viii.

30. Neilson, 39.

31. James P. Coleman, "The Mississippi Constitution of 1890 and the Final Decade of the Nineteenth Century," in *A History of Mississippi,* ed. Richard A. McLemore, vol. 2 (Jackson: College and University Press of Mississippi, 1973), 4.

32. "Former Mississippi Teacher Heads English Department in Largest Girls' College," [New York City?] newspaper article fragment, [late 1920s?], in Blanche Colton Williams Scrapbook, Special Collections, J. C. Fant Library.

33. Leake, 7.

34. Nannie Rice to Arthur H. Rice, 2 October 1910, Nannie Herndon Rice Collection, Special Collections, Mitchell Memorial Library, Mississippi State University, Starkville.

35. Emma Laney to Nannie Rice, 24 June 1934, Nannie Herndon Rice Collection.

36. Ellen Carol Dubois, "Harriot Stanton Blatch and the Winning of Woman Suffrage," *Woman's America: Refocusing the Past,* 5th ed., ed. Linda K. Kerber and Jane Sherron De Hart (New York: Oxford University Press, 2000), 334.

37. Dubois, "Working Women, Class Relations, and Suffrage Militance: Harriot Stanton Blatch and the New York Woman Suffrage Movement, 1894–1909," *Journal of American History* 74, no. 1 (June 1987): 36.

38. Emma Laney to Nannie Rice, 16 May [1917?], Nannie Herndon Rice Collection.

39. Letter of tribute to Pauline Orr on dedication of Orr Chapel, MUW, 1954, box 3, Lindsey-Orr Papers, Mississippi Department of Archives and History, Jackson.

40. Evelyn Allen Hammett, "Biographical Sketch of Blanche Colton Williams," *Delta State Teachers College* 23 (September 1947): 6.

41. Williams, "Heritage."

42. Ibid.

43. Williams, "Kingdom," 115.

44. Ibid.

45. Williams, "Heritage."

46. Williams, "Kingdom," 111.

47. Ibid., 113.

48. Ibid., 122.

49. Williams, "Heritage."

50. Williams, *Studying the Short Story* (New York: Doubleday, Page, 1926), 10.

51. Williams, *Our Short Story Writers* (New York: Dodd, Mead, 1920), 162.

52. Ibid., 180.

53. Williams, "Kingdom," 74.

54. Ibid., 93.

55. Fields, 8–9.

56. Sutherland Denlinger, " 'We No Longer Prepare to Live, But to Make Money,' Says Dr. Williams, 25 Years with Hunter College," *New York World Telegram,* 2 March 1935, Blanche Colton Williams Scrapbook.

57. Ibid.

58. Ibid.

59. Ibid.

60. "Blanche Colton Williams," *Household Magazine,* February 1941, 17.

61. "Noted State Woman in New Career," *Jackson (Miss.) Daily News,* 21 May 1939, 16.

62. Williams, *Clara Barton: Daughter of Destiny* (Philadelphia: J. B. Lippincott, 1941); *Forever Young: A Life of John Keats* (New York: G. P. Putnam Sons, 1943); note to Orr found in copy of *Forever Young,* Special Collections, J. C. Fant Library.

63. Leake, 7.

64. Williams, "Heritage."

Elizabeth Lee Hazen

(1885–1975)

A Mississippi Microbiologist's Quest for a Cure

DAVID D. CARSON

A young woman infected with the human immunodeficiency virus (HIV) is visiting her doctor for what seems like the hundredth time. Over the past few months, her CD4+T cell count, the measure of her immune system's infection-fighting power, has dipped dangerously low. On this visit, the recesses of her mouth and throat are coated with a thick layer of white cells. Red patches on her palate and in her throat make swallowing painful and difficult. After taking a scraping of the white coating and examining it under a microscope, her physician verifies the presence of yeast cells, *Candida albicans,* and records a diagnosis of oral candidiasis—better known as thrush. A common complaint of AIDS patients, thrush is one sign of an inadequate or compromised immune system.[1]

Far from being exclusively a problem in AIDS patient care, candidiasis is a broad term covering several common diseases, all of which are manifestations of yeast infection by strains of the *Candida* microorganism. For example, thrush is an oral yeast infection frequently seen in infants. Vaginitis, also called moniliasis, is the bane of every woman or teenage girl who encounters the irritating and embarrassing vaginal itching and cheesy discharge caused by yeast infection. *Candida* also causes ringworm and athlete's foot. Diabetics may be plagued with a variety of all these different forms of yeast infection. Although candidiasis is rarely life threatening, on occasion, the infection can prove fatal if it moves to internal organs, a particular risk during surgery.[2]

Yeast is not typically a disease-causing microbe, but rather a normal part of the microscopic flora and fauna present on the surface of every human body. Our bodies' other natural microscopic inhabitants, bacteria cells, along with a

ELIZABETH LEE HAZEN AND RACHEL BROWN
1955. Courtesy of Wadsworth Center,
New York State Department of Health.

healthy immune system, help keep in check the level of yeast cells on our skin and in body cavities. But when our immune system breaks down or the use of strong antibiotics destroys too many of the beneficial bacteria that help keep microbes like *Candida albicans* under control, the delicate ecological balance between bacteria and yeast is subtly altered. Quick to take advantage of the opportunity to proliferate in the absence of their normal competitors, fungal cells multiply rapidly, resulting in candidiasis—a yeast infection. Such an overgrowth of naturally occurring microbes is called an opportunistic infection.

When bacteria take advantage of the opportunity to grow out of control, a whole battery of bacterial antibiotics is available to combat the resulting diseases. On the other hand, when opportunistic yeast infections occur, a much smaller arsenal of antifungal medications is at our doctors' disposal. Without the efforts of one microbiologist from Mississippi, Elizabeth Lee Hazen, victims of yeast infections might still be defenseless against those merciless microbes.

Elizabeth Lee Hazen was born on 24 August 1885 in Rich, Mississippi. Lee, as she was known to her friends and family, was the middle of three children born to William Edgar Hazen and Maggie Harper Hazen. The Hazen family farmed the fertile cotton land of the Mississippi Delta sixty miles south of Memphis, Tennessee. By 1888, the three children were orphaned and distributed to separate family members. A year later, their uncle Robert Henry Hazen and his wife, Laura, reunited the siblings and moved them to Lula, Mississippi, to become part of their family. Robert's three daughters were nearly identical in age to his brother's children, and Lee soon came to think of them as her "sister-cousins." Her brother died at age four, leaving Hazen especially close to her sister, Annis.[3]

Hazen received the same opportunity for an education as her cousins, entering the one-room school in Lula in 1891. Robert Hazen had not gone to college, but education was clearly important to him and his family, as evidenced by his role as a trustee of the Lula school. The Hazens, in fact, boarded one of the teachers for a time. Lee Hazen gave the valedictory address in 1904 at her graduation from the tiny Lula School.

Hazen needed private tutoring in Memphis for a year following graduation plus an additional year of preparatory training at the Mississippi Industrial Institute and College (II&C) before she could enter college.[4] Finally, in 1907, she officially enrolled in the II&C, now known as Mississippi University for Women (MUW). There she excelled in the sciences, studying animal and plant physiology, zoology and botany, anatomy, and physics. She was active on campus, participating fully in extracurricular student life, including the Baptist Missionary Society and the *Spectator,* the campus newspaper. Her classmates recognized her quick wit and intelligence and lauded her scientific mind.[5]

Hazen completed a four-year bachelor of science degree in three years, graduating in May 1910. Following graduation, she taught biology and physics to high school students in Jackson, Mississippi. She continued her education by studying biology and physics during summer sessions at the University of Tennessee and University of Virginia. Six years after graduating from the II&C, Hazen traveled to New York City to pursue formal graduate work at Columbia University. Hazen's passion for learning and teaching appears to have motivated her throughout her life. She worked hard to compensate for the inadequacies of her rural education, and despite many obstacles, Hazen earned a master of arts degree in 1917.[6] Further studies at Columbia were cut short by World War I, when Hazen volunteered her bacteriological expertise to the U.S. War Department. She worked in army laboratories at Camp Sheridan in Alabama and at Camp Mills in New York and for a while was the assistant director of the Clinical and Bacteriological Laboratory at Cook Hospital in Fairmont, West Virginia.

Hazen returned to Columbia in 1923 to continue her graduate work in bacteriology and immunology and in 1927 received a doctorate for her work on general and local immunity to ricin, a toxic substance derived from the castor bean.[7] At age forty-two, Hazen was among the first women to receive a doctorate in biomedicine from Columbia, an institution that had granted only two Ph.D.s in the field of microbiology to women before 1920.[8] She continued her research at the university until the following year when she became the resident bacteriologist at New York's Presbyterian Hospital. After another year, she returned to familiar surroundings at Columbia to teach in the Department of Bacteriology and Immunology of the College of Physicians and Surgeons.[9]

In 1931, Augustus Wadsworth of the Division of Laboratories and Research at the New York State Department of Health hired her away from Columbia. Wadsworth was known for appointing women to responsible positions. At the time, New York state led all others in employing women scientists, possibly because female social activists had been pushing for health reforms and disease detection, especially in crowded urban centers, since the 1890s.[10] Wadsworth put Hazen in charge of the Bacterial Diagnosis Laboratory in New York City. Delighted to remain in New York, Hazen found an apartment only a few blocks away from Columbia, from which she could walk to attend evening lectures in organic chemistry. She maintained that apartment for the rest of her working life.[11]

In the 1930s and 1940s, Hazen analyzed vaccines and serums for a variety of viral and bacterial infectious diseases. She traced outbreaks of anthrax and tularemia to their sources. She was the first scientist in North America to determine the exact toxin leading to deaths from imported canned fish.[12]

At the height of World War II, Wadsworth recognized the need to investigate the opportunistic fungal diseases that were becoming increasingly common in the wake of the widespread use of broad-spectrum antibiotics like penicillin.[13] The problem of prolific, opportunistic, pathogenic fungi began, ironically, with Alexander Fleming's discovery of a very useful fungus called *Penicillum notatum* in 1928. During World War II, Howard Florey and Ernest Chain continued Fleming's work, purifying the antibacterial substance penicillin from Fleming's famous fungus and proving that it could be used medicinally to fight bacterial infections in humans. Around the same time, Selman Waksman and his associates isolated another antibiotic, streptomycin, from the soil microbe *Streptomyces griseus* and showed its usefulness in fighting a wide range of diseases caused by bacteria. The widespread use of penicillin and streptomycin saved many lives in field hospitals and at home during the war. Unfortunately, the excessive use of both "miracle drugs" opened the door for relatively uncommon fungal infections.[14]

Wadsworth sent Hazen back to Columbia in 1944, this time to the Department of Dermatology, where doctors specialized in the treatment of skin ailments, to learn from mycologist Rhoda Benham, the expert in the treatment of fungal diseases. Although Hazen had no formal training in mycology, her broad education in the sciences and her quick intelligence were an ample foundation for Benham to build upon. Under Benham's supervision, Hazen helped to collect and prepare fungal specimens from patients for later identification and culture in the laboratory. At Benham's encouragement, Hazen began her own collection of stock cultures and microscope slides for her eventual use back at the Department of Public Health. Hazen's expertise was growing, and her specimens made a major contribution to the burgeoning field of mycology, especially for training other public health workers encountering fungal diseases.[15]

After undertaking an examination of a fast-growing epidemic of ringworm in children's scalps and making important discoveries about the conditions that led to the rapid development of the fungus that caused it, Hazen was struck by the absence of fungicides comparable to the antibiotics that were so successful in fighting bacterial disease. She was especially concerned that existing fungicides were too toxic, particularly for children and women. "Her research feet were itching" (like a case of athlete's foot), said fellow microbiologist Margarita Silva-Hunter. Hazen became fascinated by disease-causing fungi and began to search for an effective antifungal treatment.

With the antibacterial work of Florey, Chain, and Waksman in mind, Hazen struck out on her own search for antifungal drugs. Since streptomycin had been isolated from organisms found in the soil, Hazen thought this was a good place to begin her search for microbes that might be capable of producing antifungal agents. She gathered soil, compost, peat, and manure samples wherever she traveled and entreated her colleagues to do likewise. Once back in the lab, she analyzed each soil sample to determine whether it harbored any organisms that might produce a useful fungicide.[16]

In the laboratory, Hazen coaxed the microbes hiding in each soil sample to multiply, hoping to promote the growth of actinomycetes, a particular class of moldlike microbes containing many antibiotic-producing species. Hazen isolated many different kinds of actinomycetes from each soil sample and tested each one against two important fungal strains: the familiar *Candida albicans,* which is behind approximately 95 percent of all fungal diseases on the human body, and *Cryptococcus neoformans,* which can cause an extremely dangerous infection of the brain and central nervous system.

Hazen's approach could only identify organisms capable of manufacturing a potential antifungal agent. That was a long way from isolating, characterizing, and testing a fungus-killing drug in living animals. She needed the help of a chemist. Hazen teamed up with Rachel Brown, a graduate of Mount Holyoke College who was working in the Albany laboratories of the New York State Department of Health. Thus a productive scientific partnership and lifelong friendship developed between the "impatient, intensely active" Hazen and the "solidly dependable, seemingly imperturbable" Brown.

Hazen grew those specimens that showed potential for fighting against one or both of the test fungal strains in a nutrient broth. Then she mailed the liquid culture from New York City to Albany for Brown to determine whether the promising antifungal compound resided in the broth, the organism, or in both. Brown meticulously extracted each part of the sample, keeping careful notes on what chemicals and methods she tried and why, then mailed samples from each part back to Hazen for further testing. Hazen applied each sample Brown had sent her to both strains of fungus, *Candida* and *Cryptococcus,* using increasingly diluted amounts. In this way, the women were able to determine not only what substance possessed antifungal properties but also the relative potency of each. They also tested the potential fungicides on mice and other animals to see whether or not the compounds were toxic.[17]

At last, one of Hazen and Brown's cultures proved to be both antifungal and nontoxic to mice. It was a previously unknown microorganism from a soil sample that Hazen had collected in 1948 on the dairy farm of her friends, the Nourses, while vacationing at their home in Warrenton, Virginia. To honor them, Hazen named the new actinomycete she had discovered *Streptomyces noursei.*[18]

Streptomyces noursei yielded not one but two different extracts under Brown's purification procedure. The first contained an antimicrobial chemical that inhibited the growth of only *Cryptococcus* but not of *Candida*. Furthermore, it was extremely toxic to mice and seemed, therefore, to hold little promise as a medicine for humans. Brown, nevertheless, continued to work on this compound and identified it as cycloheximide, which had been previously extracted from the same microorganism that produces the antibiotic streptomycin. In fact, cycloheximide was already in use, not in doctors' offices but rather as an agricultural fungicide used to keep mushrooms and other fungi off golf course greens. Today, cycloheximide has moved from the golf course into the laboratory, where it continues to be an important tool for researchers investigating basic molecular biology.[19]

The second product extracted from Hazen's discovery was active against both *Candida* and *Cryptococcus* as well as fourteen other species of fungi. Brown was able to obtain a fine yellow powder and then some small crystals that were very mildly toxic to mice and even less toxic to rats and guinea pigs. Hazen and Brown named their discovery nystatin to honor the New York State Department of Health, Division of Laboratories and Research.[20]

In 1950, Gilbert Dalldorf, who had succeeded Augustus Wadsworth as head of the Division of Laboratories and Research, scheduled Hazen and Brown to present their findings in a presentation at the upcoming regional meeting of the National Academy of Sciences. True to her reserved character, Hazen declined to deliver the paper, letting Brown take center stage. It would set a precedent for all of their collaborative presentations.[21]

Soon, word of their work reached a larger audience. The interdisciplinary journal *Science* published an abstract of their initial results, then the *New York Times* took notice of the women's accomplishments and the potential that this new drug held for medical use. Once their discovery became widely known, pharmaceutical companies began aggressively to pursue the rights for its manufacture.[22]

Dalldorf recognized the necessity of obtaining a patent to protect their discovery, not so much to direct profits into their pockets, but rather to be able to control crucial decisions that would affect the use of the drug and the quality of its production. In 1951, Dalldorf sought the help of the Research Corporation, which specialized in just such activities.[23]

Research Corporation played a major role in the development of nystatin into a drug by guiding Dalldorf, Hazen, and Brown through the lengthy and convoluted process of obtaining a patent and by mediating the licensing of production to E. R. Squibb and Sons, Inc. In 1951 Squibb began producing the drug, which they gave the trade name Mycostatin, in the quantities necessary to perform clinical trials. Data from these trials helped to secure the patent for nystatin by proving the utility of Hazen and Brown's "invention." The data further helped the Federal Drug Administration (FDA) to evaluate the product's safety and efficacy for human consumption. Final approval from the FDA to market Mycostatin in tablet form came in 1954. Eventually Squibb produced Mycostatin in the form of creams, ointments, topical powders, and vaginal tablets.[24]

By the time Hazen and Brown received the final patent for nystatin in 1957, Squibb had already been marketing Mycostatin, which they hailed as "the first broadly effective antifungal antibiotic available to the medical profession," for nearly two years. Such quick drug development and approval from its initial discovery in 1948 to its marketing for medical use in 1954—a short six years—is remarkable by today's standards. Even more unusual is the open collaboration between Squibb, which risked the significant amount of capital it had invested in development of the new drug, and the discoverers, whose legal right to a share in profits from Mycostatin had not yet been secured by patent.[25]

Nystatin, the first antifungal medication to be discovered, is still one of the drugs most frequently prescribed to combat initial occurrences of yeast infection, particularly vaginitis. A relatively new class of antifungal drugs belonging to the imidazole family has become popular for its ability to produce faster results, but comes with a number of potentially serious side effects. Nystatin has the advantage of being highly effective, causing virtually no adverse effects, and being relatively inexpensive. Nystatin is still the preferred treatment for children and infants with thrush. Furthermore, it is rare to find strains of yeast that have developed a resistance to nystatin.[26] For all these reasons, Elizabeth Lee Hazen's discovery of the microbe that produces nystatin and her elucidation of its medical benefits were a godsend to physicians and their patients everywhere.

In a characteristic spirit of humility and public service, Hazen and Brown relinquished all royalties due them from their patent and dedicated the money to furthering scientific research. They apportioned one-half of all royalties to the nonprofit Research Corporation for its grant program to promote basic research and to assist academic and public institutions in bringing other inventions and discoveries to the public. They placed the other half in a special Brown-Hazen Fund dedicated to supporting biomedical research and to fighting fungal disease. Hazen and Brown took an active role in administering this fund. Over the life of the patent from 1955–76, the two funds shared over $13.4 million in royalties. For several of those years, the Brown-Hazen Fund provided more nonfederal support for medical mycology than any other source.[27]

After her success with nystatin, Hazen continued to search for other antifungal agents, discovering two more antimicrobials, phalamycin and capacidin.[28] Although toxic to humans, and therefore of little medicinal value, these compounds proved to be of interest to other scientists studying basic microbiology.

Hazen continued in her role as teacher and mentor to the young scientists and technicians entering the department by instructing newcomers in mycological techniques and offering input on various research projects. She authored or coauthored more than fifty scientific articles, and in 1955 she published an important guide with a colleague, medical illustrator Frank Curtis Reed, entitled *Laboratory Identification of Pathogenic Fungi Simplified.*[29]

After her retirement in 1958, Hazen continued to act as a consultant to the New York Department of Public Health and to work on revisions for the second edition of her book. Columbia, where she maintained active ties as a guest lecturer in the University's Medical Mycology Laboratory and as a provider of "bench-side instruction" to students, honored her with the title of emeritus research professor. She also devoted more of her time to administering the Brown-Hazen Fund, which she did until 1973.[30]

Elizabeth Hazen's legacy as a scientist extended well beyond her discoveries in the laboratory. Seeking to encourage young women to enter fields in science and medicine, the Brown-Hazen Fund endowed scholarships at both Mount Holyoke and Mississippi University for Women. In 1975, Hazen personally bequeathed one-half of her interest in the Hazen family property in Mississippi to the Hazen fund at MUW, bringing the total scholarship endowment to $300,000. In 1977, Hazen's associates Gilbert Dalldorf and Rachel Brown dedicated the Elizabeth Lee Hazen Microbiology Laboratory at MUW, which was furnished through a $50,000 Brown-Hazen grant, in her honor. A colleague at the Research Corporation wrote, "Few have been able to pay their professional debts so generously and magnificently" as this remarkable pioneering scientist from Mississippi who never forgot her origins.[31]

Elizabeth Lee Hazen also led a happy life outside her laboratory. She attended as many Broadway productions as she could and liked to shop on Manhattan's Fifth Avenue. She had numerous friends whom she loved to entertain at her apartment, where she was known as a gourmet. She never seemed to lose her southern manner, although her views on public affairs and race were not those of her Mississippi kin. A next-door neighbor in New York described Hazen as "a true Southerner," but added that she was "one of a few in her era who saw the evils of racial discrimination and was outspoken even in the South."[32]

Hazen was active nearly to the end of her life. Despite her own failing health, she traveled frequently from New York to Seattle to care for her blind sister, who was in a nursing home there. When Hazen's own condition began to decline, she entered the nursing home with her sister. On 24 June 1975, only a few months after her sister's death, Elizabeth Lee Hazen died in her sleep at the age of eighty-nine. Having never married and with no surviving family, Hazen was buried in a Seattle cemetery next to her sister and brother-in-law.[33]

Hazen's lasting legacy is her scientific work, which she considered her investment in the future. Basic research on the structure and function of nystatin continued throughout the 1960s and 1970s. Although Brown had deduced its basic structure early in her work with Hazen, the exact chemical structure was not determined until 1976 when it was separated into two distinct compounds.

Both forms of nystatin are large organic molecules, a chemical structure responsible for its distinctiveness as an antifungal agent. First, nystatin is rather insoluble, so the drug does not stay dissolved very easily in the water-based fluids of the human digestive tract or circulatory system. Therefore, the drug is virtually nontoxic and without side effects because almost none of it is actually absorbed into the body. This fact also explains why nystatin is rarely effective against so-called "deep" fungal infections of the bloodstream and internal organs. Secondly, nystatin's large carbon-based structure helps it to bind with the outer membranes of fungal cells. This causes gaps to form in the cell walls and causes the fungus to die. The drug does not have the same effect on the cells of animals or green plants, making it innocuous to people, pets, or crops.[34]

Hazen lived to see her discovery applied in a number of interesting ways. In 1960, French, Italian, and Argentine wine makers experimented with nystatin as a preservative. Fresh produce importers used nystatin for a time to preserve bananas being shipped from their tropical origins to temperate markets. In 1970, nystatin was approved as a feed additive for domestic poultry production to prevent fungal infections in turkey and chickens. By the mid-1970s nystatin had been used to defend American elm trees threatened by the seemingly unstoppable Dutch elm disease. Although expensive and impractical for widespread use, nystatin saved many historically significant and aesthetically important elms in the northeastern United States.[35]

A most unusual application of nystatin occurred following the devastating flood of Italy's Arno River in 1966. As the floodwaters receded, art curators in Florence faced the enormous task of salvaging and restoring an overwhelming number of paintings and frescoes damaged by flood waters. The situation was made even worse by the rapid growth of mold and mildew on the centuries-old artworks. Researchers at the University of Florence found that nystatin was the most effective tool for halting the growth of fungi without damaging the priceless paintings. The drug gave researchers the time they needed to conduct the painstaking process of restoration.[36]

An important new medical use of nystatin arose in the 1990s at the University of Texas's M. D. Anderson Cancer Center in Houston, where an injectable form of nystatin, called Nyotran, was developed. Nyotran encapsulates the insoluble nystatin in microscopic carrier droplets so that it can be dissolved by the bloodstream to treat life-threatening deep fungal infections of internal organs. In September 1998, data from Phase II clinical trials were presented at a science conference in San Diego, California. In a limited trial of seventy-five patients, patients treated with Nyotran responded positively to the new treatment, including some of those who had been infected with strains of yeast that had become resistant to other antifungal drugs. None of the patients in the trial suffered the kind of severe side effects, such as kidney toxicity, associated with other treatments for systemic fungal infections. Success of a larger Phase III clinical trial begun in 1996 involving nearly two hundred patients led to the approval of Nyotran by the FDA and its production by Abbott Laboratories in 2000.[37]

Clearly, Hazen and Brown's discovery of nystatin has had far-reaching significance. The many awards presented to the two during and after their lifetimes bear witness to the world's recognition of their accomplishments. They received the Squibb Award in Chemotherapy in 1955. Hobart College and William Smith College granted both women honorary degrees in 1968. They received the Rhoda Benham Award from the Medical Mycological Society of the Americas in 1972. In 1975, the American Institute of Chemists altered its tradition of exclusively recognizing men and amended its charter, which had previously allowed the group to reward only chemists, in order to give Brown and Hazen its Chemical Pioneer Award. In 1994, they were the second and third women inducted into the National Inventors Hall of Fame.

NOTES

The author wishes to thank Dr. Ginger Hitt, Mississippi University for Women professor emerita, for first suggesting that he undertake this project and for reading early drafts of this chapter.

1. United States Public Health Service/Infectious Disease Society of America Prevention of Opportunistic Infections Working Group, "USPHS/IDSA Guidelines for the Prevention of Opportunistic Infections in Persons Infected with Human Immunodeficiency Virus: A Summary," *Annals of Internal Medicine* 124 (1996): 348–68.

2. Josephine A. Morello et al., *Microbiology in Patient Care*, 6th ed. (Boston: McGraw-Hill, 1998), 420–24; John W. Rippon, *Medical Mycology: The Pathogenic Fungi and the Pathogenic Actinomycetes* (Philadelphia: W. B. Saunders, 1974), 175–204.

3. W. Stephenson Bacon, "Elizabeth Lee Hazen, 1885–1975," *Mycologia* 68 (September–October 1976): 961–69; Martha J. Bailey, *Women in Science* (Denver: ABC-CLIO, 1994), 158–59; Maria Chiara,

"Elizabeth Lee Hazen," in *Notable Women in the Life Sciences: A Biographical Dictionary,* ed. Benjamin F. and Barbara S. Shearer (Westport, Conn.: Greenwood Press, 1996), 164–71; Marilyn Ogilvie and Joy Harvey, eds., *Biographical Dictionary of Women in Science* (New York: Routledge, 2000), 573–74; Louis P. Rubin, "Elizabeth Lee Hazen," in *Notable American Women: The Modern Period,* ed. Barbara Sicherman and Carol Hurd Green (Cambridge: Harvard University Press, 1980), 326–28; Patricia Joan Siegal and Kay Thomas Finley, *Women in the Scientific Search: An American Bio-Bibliography, 1724–1979* (Metuchen, N.J.: Scarecrow Press, 1985), 248–49; Richard S. Baldwin, *The Fungus Hunters: Two Women Scientists and Their Discovery* (Ithaca: Cornell University Press, 1981), 36–37.

4. Baldwin, 38.

5. Ibid., 39; Chiara, 166.

6. Baldwin, 40.

7. Elizabeth Lee Hazen, "General and Local Immunity to Ricin," *Journal of Immunology* 13 (1927): 191–218.

8. Margaret W. Rossiter, *Women Scientists in America: Struggles and Strategies to 1940* (Baltimore: Johns Hopkins University Press, 1982), 242–45; Rossiter, *Women Scientists in America: Before Affirmative Action, 1940–1972* (Baltimore: Johns Hopkins University Press, 1995), 300.

9. Baldwin, 44–45.

10. Bacon, 962.

11. Baldwin, 42.

12. Ibid., 43.

13. Bacon, 963–64.

14. Baldwin, 75.

15. Ibid., 44–45.

16. Ibid., 74–75.

17. Edna Yost, *Women of Modern Science* (New York: Dodd, Mead, 1959), 75.

18. Baldwin, 78, 83.

19. Ibid., 78.

20. Ibid., 79.

21. Ibid.

22. Hazen and Rachel Brown, "Two Antifungal Agents Produced by a Soil Actinomycete," *Science* 112 (13 October 1950): 423; *New York Times,* 18 October 1950.

23. Baldwin, 95–96.

24. Ibid., 101.

25. Ibid.

26. Rippon, 532–34.

27. Ibid., 102; Bacon, 968.

28. Hazen and Brown, "Capacidin: A New Member of the Polyene Antibiotic Group," *Antibiotics and Chemotherapy* 10 (November 1960): 702–8.

29. Hazen and Frank Curtis Reed, *Laboratory Identification of Pathogenic Fungi Simplified* (Springfield, Ill.: Charles C. Thomas, 1955). The work has been used widely and is referenced today; it now is in its third edition.

30. Rubin, 328; Bacon, 969.

31. Bacon, 968; Baldwin, 134.

32. Baldwin, 111.

33. Ibid., 186; Rubin, 327; Hazen obituary, *New York Times,* 28 June 1975. The *New York Times* obituary contains numerous errors regarding Hazen's early life.

34. Ramesh Pandey and Kenneth L. Rinehart Jr., *Journal of Antibiotics* 29 (1976): 1035.

35. Ogilvie and Harvey, eds., 573; Bacon, 966.

36. Joseph Judge, "Florence Rises from the Flood," *National Geographic,* July 1967, 32–33.

37. S. W. Key, D. J. DeNoon, and S. Boyles, "Data Presented from Nyotran Phase II Clinical Study," *World Disease Weekly Press,* 12 October 1998; Key, "Phase III Clinical Study of Nystatin (LF) Announced," parts 1 and 2, *Cancer Biotechnology Weekly,* 5 February 1996, 12 February 1996.

Burnita Shelton Matthews

(1894–1988)

The Struggle for Women's Rights

KATE GREENE

When Burnita Shelton Matthews left Mississippi following her marriage to Percy Matthews in 1917, she never looked back. Percy joined the army as a pilot and left to fight in World War I shortly after the wedding, and Burnita moved to a small town in Georgia to teach music. Yet a small town in Georgia and a life of teaching music was not the destination she had in mind. Indeed, it was no more than a short stop on her journey. Like many talented and creative Mississippians before and since, Matthews left her home state and eventually the Deep South in pursuit of a calling. For Matthews, that calling was to advance the rights of women through the law. Burnita Shelton Matthews rejected the cult of domesticity that dominated her class in Mississippi society and chose to become a lawyer, a feminist, and the first woman appointed to a U.S. district court.

Born on 28 December 1894 in Copiah County, Mississippi, to Burnell Shelton and Lora Barlow Shelton, Burnita Shelton belonged to an educated, civic-minded family. Her mother was a graduate of Whitworth College, a boarding school for young women in Brookhaven, Mississippi, and her father was a planter and cattleman and elected official. Her father served, at various times, as sheriff and tax collector of Copiah County and as the clerk of the chancery court. Her older brother Allen became a lawyer, was a member of the Arkansas legislature, and later served as city attorney for Hot Springs, Arkansas.[1] Her younger brother John would later follow her to Washington, D.C., and into the practice of law.

Although she was the only daughter among five sons, Burnita Shelton was not excluded from her father's political life. He often took her along on the campaign trail and brought her to the courthouse when he worked. She listened to the trials and became fascinated with the law early in life. According to Matthews, she felt at home in the courthouse.[2] At the age of eleven, she won an oratory contest and overheard a friend of her father, a noted criminal attorney, tell him, "You ought to make a lawyer out of that little girl."[3] From that point on, she decided that that was what she wanted to become.[4]

Burnita Shelton never wavered from her desire to attend college and law school, but her father preferred that she pursue music, a more ladylike profession. After the early death of her mother, Burnita's father sent her to the Cincinnati Conservatory of Music. While studying for her teaching certificate, she wrote her relatives asking for law books to read. They sent her the dullest books they could find, hoping to discourage her. Their efforts failed.

After receiving her teaching certificate, Burnita taught music and piano in Texas for a year and then at a high school in Fayette, Mississippi, for two years. In 1916, a high school friend, Percy Matthews, returned from Chicago, where he had just received his law degree at the Chicago-Kent School of Law. In 1917, they married. Her family, particularly her father, opposed the marriage because the Matthews were Republicans and had past ties to a Copiah County antiracist and progressive activist, Print Matthews.[5] Almost immediately after the marriage, Percy Matthews enlisted in the army and went to fight in World War I as a pilot, and Burnita Shelton Matthews left for a small town outside of Atlanta, Georgia, to teach.[6]

According to Matthews, she had not been in Georgia long when she saw an advertisement for jobs with the federal government during the war.[7] She took the civil service exam required to secure a position, but before she learned of the results, she left Georgia for a job in a music store in Chicago. She had hardly arrived in Chicago when she received word that she had passed the exam. Although the time for her to report had passed, Matthews jumped on a train and presented herself to the Veteran's Administration, where she became employed as a clerk.[8]

Matthews's determination to land a job in D.C. was influenced by the fact that there were three law schools in the capital city that admitted women: National University Law School, Washington College of Law, and Howard University Law School. Indeed, shortly after her arrival in D.C., Matthews enrolled in the National University Law School's night program.

Matthews did not have to leave Mississippi to find a law school that admitted women. She could have attended the University of Mississippi Law School. Bessie Young graduated from the University of Mississippi Law School in 1915, and Linda Rives Brown graduated with honors in 1916.[9] In fact, women includ-

BURNITA SHELTON MATTHEWS

May 1972. From the *Biographical Directory of
Justices and Judges of the United States Courts.*
Courtesy of Mississippi Department
of Archives and History.

ing Lucy Somerville and Vivien Cook attended the University of Mississippi Law School throughout the 1920s.[10] It is likely that the opposition of Matthews's father to her becoming a lawyer obstructed this possibility. By marrying Percy Matthews and leaving Mississippi, Matthews was able to escape her father's influence. When Matthews wrote her father to tell him that she had enrolled in the night program, he softened his stance. Burnell Shelton seemed to understand that his daughter would not be persuaded. Instead of opposing her, he expressed displeasure to her working all day and attending law school at night. He did not think she was strong enough to do both. Indeed, he offered to pay for her school so she would not have to work. She refused his offer.[11]

While attending law school, Matthews met Julia Jennings, a law student who was a member of the National Woman's Party (NWP). The NWP, led by Alice Paul, was a militant suffrage organization that had broken with the National American Woman Suffrage Association (NAWSA). Rather than lobbying state legislatures for voting rights, the NWP organized parades and picketed the White House advocating a national amendment. Jennings invited Matthews to join the picket lines with the NWP, and she did.[12]

Matthews earned a bachelor of law degree in 1919 and both a master of law and a master in patent law in 1920.[13] She found law school a pleasant experience. According to Matthews, the professors sometimes told "little jokes" designed to "put women in their place," but she was apparently unmoved by their attitudes as well as those of male students toward the woman suffrage effort she had joined.[14] The men students, many of whom were just returning from the war, criticized the NWP as unpatriotic for "bothering the President."[15] Yet Matthews enjoyed law school and earned the respect of her peers, who elected her vice president of their class.[16]

In June 1920, Matthews passed the bar exam on her first attempt. She applied for a job with the legal department of the Veteran's Administration, where she had been working throughout her legal studies, but the VA hired few women lawyers and those few did nonlegal work.[17] So Matthews rented a one-room office across the street from the municipal courthouse and established a private legal practice.[18] Around this time, the ratification of the Nineteenth Amendment had secured national woman suffrage, and the NWP shifted its focus onto the gigantic task of eliminating remaining discriminations against women. Alice Paul asked Matthews if she would help the NWP by researching the discriminations against women that still existed in state laws. Matthews began spending her spare time at the Supreme Court Law Library and the Library of Congress examining the state codes for discriminatory laws and drafting legislation to eliminate gender bias.[19]

Although Matthews worked with several other volunteers, the job eventually became so time-consuming that Matthews had to inform Alice Paul that she could no longer "give" her time. In response, Paul named Matthews the Legal Research Secretary over the Legal Research Department at a salary of $200 per month.[20] By May 1922, the NWP was seeking to hire three other paid researchers in an effort to complete the job by the end of the year.[21] Soon Matthews was directing the work of several other researchers and eventually was supervising the efforts of a dozen women lawyers.[22]

The NWP Legal Research Department researched all the laws that discriminated against women in each state, compiled those laws into a state digest, and drafted laws to remove those prejudices.[23] The first completed digests of the department related to Louisiana and Mississippi, states chosen because their legislatures met during 1921–22. The NWP had a party member in Louisiana, Mrs. J. D. Wilkinson, who was able to push some of the legislation Matthews drafted through that state's legislature.[24] The effort in Mississippi was much more difficult.

Soon after its success in Louisiana, the NWP decided that instead of trying to push through separate pieces of legislation to address each instance of discrimination, it would introduce a "blanket" equal rights bill that included provisions covering all areas of concern. Wisconsin had passed such a bill, and the NWP modeled their proposed legislation on it. When the Mississippi legislature met in early 1922, the NWP was ready to introduce a blanket equal rights bill.[25] Unfortunately, the NWP did not have homegrown leadership in Mississippi equal to that of Louisiana and Wisconsin. Indeed, the NWP hardly existed in Mississippi. Despite extensive recruitment efforts by Elsie Hill and Anita Pollitzer, the Mississippi branch of the NWP ostensibly had only one member, Ellen Crump, of Nitta Yuma. Crump was elderly and hard of hearing and unable to lobby for the bill. Alice Paul recognized the importance of having local connections in the South and pleaded with Matthews to lead the campaign. She pressured Matthews to go home and run the campaign for the blanket bill. Matthews refused.[26]

According to Matthews, she did not want to leave her developing law practice or the work she was doing for the NWP in Washington.[27] Matthews agreed to coordinate the effort with Crump through the mail, but eventually Paul sent NWP lobbyist Isabelle Gill to run the legislative effort in Jackson. Gill's efforts failed miserably. She faced well-placed, influential opposition from the League of Women Voters, who easily undermined the support she was able to gather. The League of Women Voters in Mississippi opposed the NWP legislation because it feared protective labor legislation for women would be undermined.[28]

Despite her refusal to lead the legislative campaign in Mississippi, early the following year, Matthews traveled to Chicago and Detroit to assist the Illinois and Michigan branches of the NWP in their legislative efforts.[29] Matthews was not in charge of these efforts, however, and seemed to have been absent from Washington for only a short time. Although Matthews made some efforts throughout the 1920s and 1930s to push equal rights legislation through the Mississippi legislature, she had no support from local NWP membership and had to rely on sympathetic legislators to introduce bills she drafted and sent to them.[30] Her work inevitably came to naught.

Mississippi was hardly the only state that concerned Matthews and the NWP. By the end of September 1922, the Legal Research Department had completed twenty-five state digests.[31] In addition, Matthews was preparing reports on specific areas of concern, such as jury service and protective labor laws, as well as articles for publication dealing with the need for more equal rights legislation. Much of her time was spent corresponding with the women who were coordinating legislative lobbying efforts in various states; seeking information from state attorneys general and secretaries of state on recent legislation, legal interpretations, and court decisions; and answering general inquiries from NWP members dealing with equal rights legislation.[32]

By 1928, much of the work on the digests was finished and Matthews found herself in a different legal role with the NWP. Although still head of the Legal Research Department, she also served as legal counsel for the NWP in a condemnation dispute. The NWP operated from a building on First Street across from the Capitol. The building, the "Old Capitol," which had housed Congress from 1815–19 and had served as a prison during the Civil War (holding southern spy Rose O'Neal Greenhow), was a perfect location for lobbying Congress, but Chief Justice William Howard Taft wanted the site for a Supreme Court building.[33] Matthews began her case outside the courtroom by seeking the help of Senator Thaddeus Caraway of Arkansas, who secured a Senate resolution stopping the condemnation proceedings. She then appealed to Chief Justice Taft himself during a visit to his home. He responded that while he disliked having to evict the women from the building, their land was the most appropriate. Congress and the president were both suitably housed, and the Supreme Court deserved the same type of accommodations.[34] He concluded the interview by stating that he intended his view to prevail. Taft then called upon Speaker of the House and fellow Ohioan, Nicholas Longworth, who assured the failure of the Caraway resolution in the House.[35]

Unable legislatively to halt the government's condemnation proceedings, Matthews superbly represented the NWP in court in its effort to maximize their

monetary compensation for the land from the government. She argued that the
property was worth at least one million dollars because of the historical value of
the building and because it was located on prime real estate. Matthews brought
forward many prominent historians, congressmen, and real estate experts to
testify to the value of the land. According to a report in the journal of the NWP,
Equal Rights, the government was unable to impeach the testimony of any of
Matthews's witnesses. [36]

When the government made its case in the proceedings, the Justice Department found that even dirty tricks could not stop Matthews and the NWP.
In order to reduce the market value of the property, the government had to
disprove the historical significance of the building. The Justice Department's
lawyers argued that the building standing on the land was not, in fact, the Old
Capitol, which had been demolished, but a newer building erected in 1869.
To support this claim the department brought in two purported experts who
claimed to have examined photographs of the Old Capitol and suggested that
the present building was not the same. When Matthews cross-examined the
two witnesses, she exposed their misrepresentation. Although the Justice Department had claimed that these men were architectural engineers, Matthews
succeeded in having one admit that he was neither an architect nor an engineer
and that the title was given to him by the Treasury Department for occasions
such as the proceedings that the NWP now faced. She also managed to have
both men admit that they were not even builders but had only assisted in re-
modeling one building each. In addition, Matthews searched the city for someone to testify from personal knowledge that the Old Capitol had not been torn
down, but only remodeled, in 1869. The night before she was to close her case,
Matthews located a paperhanger named John Mahoney who then testified that
he had tried to secure a papering job when the building had been remodeled
in 1869. [37]

Matthews also obliterated the Justice Department's argument that the bricks
of the Old Capitol had been laid in a pattern known as Flemish bond while the
building owned by the NWP was laid in a building pattern known as common
bond. Matthews argued that the photograph presented in evidence by the government was too indistinct to show the bond, and she then set out to counter
the argument by finding a better photograph. Members of the NWP canvassed
all the photographers in the city and located a Mr. Handy, who had inherited
the collection of Civil War photographer Matthew Brady. This collection contained a photograph of Mrs. Greenhow, the spy, taken against the wall of the
building, which clearly showed the building was laid in common bond. Finally,
Matthews presented the most damning evidence of all against the government's

case: a voucher by an official government committee affirming that the building was the Old Capitol, a bronze tablet on the building designating it as such.[38]

The jury awarded the National Woman's Party $299,200, at the time the largest condemnation award ever made by the United States government. In March 1929, Attorney General William D. Mitchell presented the check to Matthews and the NWP. With that money, the NWP was able to buy more property. Matthews received a great deal of business from this condemnation proceeding. She went on to represent private clients and a large apartment complex in a similar type of proceeding and later served as legal counsel for other condemnations in the area, including land acquired by the Library of Congress and some at the foot of the Capitol.[39] Land law became one of her specialties.[40]

The NWP also called on Matthews to assist in its campaign for the Equal Rights Amendment. While fighting for equal rights legislation in the states, Alice Paul and the NWP learned how long and difficult that process would be and decided to expand their campaign to the national level by seeking an equal rights amendment to the Constitution of the United States. Throughout 1921 and 1922, the NWP wrote hundreds of drafts of an equal rights amendment, seeking input from law professors, senators, and others. Early in the drafting process, the NWP hoped to write an amendment that would not invalidate protective labor legislation for women, but eventually Alice Paul decided against a long and specific amendment in favor of a short and general amendment modeled on the Susan B. Anthony (Nineteenth) amendment granting woman suffrage. In July 1923, at Seneca Falls, New York, site of the first Woman's Rights Convention seventy-five years earlier, the NWP introduced its proposed amendment. It read: "Men and women shall have equal rights throughout the United States and all places subject to its jurisdiction."[41] According to Matthews, she played a minor role in the drafting of the amendment. Once Paul developed the wording for the amendment, Matthews examined cases dealing with each phrase used in order to shed light on their possible interpretation.[42]

Matthews's most significant role regarding the Equal Rights Amendment (ERA) was as a spokesperson. She testified before congressional committees on behalf of the ERA on at least eight occasions, spoke to various women's groups, and wrote extensively in support of women's equality.[43] Two of her most significant appearances on behalf of the ERA came in 1934 and 1935 when she spoke at the Council Meeting of the General Federation of Women's Clubs (GFWC) in Hot Springs, Arkansas, and at the Second Annual Conference on Current Problems (another GFWC event) at the Palmer House in Chicago. As a result of her effort, the GFWC eventually supported the ERA. Matthews also wrote much about equal rights legislation and the ERA for the NWP's journal, *Equal Rights*.

While she was always comfortable in the courtroom, Matthews's testimonies before congressional committees were not easy experiences for her. She often faced hostile senators and representatives who patronized her or continually interrupted her. There was even a time when Matthews openly admitted to one committee that she "dreaded" testifying.[44]

Appearing before the House Committee on Immigration and Naturalization in 1933 on several bills concerning women's citizenship rights, Matthews faced questions linking race discrimination and sex discrimination. While arguing that there should be a rule that applies equally to women and men, Matthews faced this line of questioning:

> Mr. Dies: The laws all over the country provide different rules, you know, about that.
>
> Mr. Weideman: What state did you say you were from?
>
> Mrs. Matthews: Mississippi.
>
> Mr. Weideman: They have different rules down there, do they not, for different classes of citizens.
>
> Mrs. Matthews: I do not know to what you refer.
>
> Mr. Kerr: You have different social rules, but you do not have different political rules.
>
> Mrs. Matthews: Yes, we have some political differences and political rules, I think.
>
> Mr. Kerr: But principally they are social rules.
>
> Mr. Kramer: Let me ask another question. Will they permit, in Mississippi, a colored boy to attend the same school as a white boy?
>
> Mrs. Matthews: They have separate schools, but they are supposed to have the same facilities.[45]

The congressmen's argument was that women's equality was intrinsically linked with racial equality. No doubt, Matthews appreciated the dilemma of arguing for equality between men and women in a world divided by the color line. While Matthews avoided the issue while testifying before Congress, later as a judge she would deal directly with questions of race discrimination.

Matthews maintained her affiliation and activism with the NWP throughout the 1930s and 1940s, but she no longer worked for the party, opting to devote more time to her legal practice. Two women with whom she had worked at the NWP, Laura Berrien and Rebekah Greathouse, joined her in her legal practice.

For the next decade, the firm of Matthews, Berrien, and Greathouse specialized in the general civil practice of law. Each woman, however, continued to work for equal rights for women.[46]

Laura Berrien was a native of Georgia who had worked to secure legislation in her home state that allowed women to practice law. Prior to joining Matthews, she had also worked with the NWP on securing equal rights legislation in the states and served as NWP Treasurer. Berrien had also served as special attorney for the Bureau of Internal Revenue, but lost her job, a political appointment, when Franklin Roosevelt came into office.[47] Rebekah Greathouse, too, was a member of the NWP, having served as its secretary for a time. Greathouse worked as an Assistant United States Attorney during the Calvin Coolidge administration and taught law at Washington College of Law. Greathouse would later leave the firm when her husband, a chemist, accepted a position in New Orleans.

According to Matthews, "Since she always put her husband first, ahead of everything, she went with him to New Orleans."[48] Matthews's disappointment with Greathouse was evident. Matthews never abandoned Washington, D.C., or her practice, regardless of her husband's whereabouts. Like most members of the NWP, she considered career and the fight for equal rights more important than marriage or children. In fact, Burnita and Percy Matthews did not live together for any significant period of time until Percy Matthews retired from the U.S. Army in the mid-1950s.

The 1930s and 1940s were a time of great activity in Matthews's life. From 1933 to 1937, she taught the law of evidence at Washington College of Law. In addition to managing her practice, she was also very active in professional associations.[49] After admission to the bar in 1920, Matthews and three other women sought membership in the District of Columbia Bar Association. Their effort was met with great resistance. She and the other women filled out the printed applications and sent in their dues, but their materials were returned with a letter. According to Matthews, "They said that our sponsors had withdrawn their sponsorship. But that wasn't true; they hadn't. And these men that sponsored us all said that wasn't true. But, nevertheless, they got rid of us that way and said we couldn't be admitted, and we weren't for a long, long time."[50]

Matthews joined the Women's Bar Association of the District of Columbia and the Women's Lawyers Association, which in 1923 became the National Association of Women Lawyers (NAWL). She joined the American Bar Association in 1924.[51] Matthews served as president of the Women's Bar Association of the District of Columbia from 1925–26. She was also very active in the NAWL in

the 1930s. In 1934–35, Matthews was both the president of and an associate editor of the *Women Lawyers' Journal*. She also served as the chair of the NAWL's
Committee on Jurisprudence and Law Reform and Status of Women.[52]

Active in the American Bar Association, she nevertheless believed that wom-
en's associations were important and necessary. While president of the NAWL,
Matthews reminded her members that many bar associations still remained
closed to women and those open to women did not give them committee appointments or leadership positions.[53] She and others recognized that women
lawyers still faced discrimination and urged women to work together. Whether
working through the National Woman's Party or professional associations,
Matthews struggled to improve the status of women and to eliminate discrimination against them.

Matthews's professional memberships and work eventually led to her appointment to the bench. In 1948, Congress created twenty-seven new federal
judgeships, including several seats on the U.S. District Court for the District of
Columbia. Matthews informed some of her friends and clients that she was interested in a judicial appointment, and they began a letter-writing campaign
to President Harry Truman.[54] She even received a public endorsement from
the District of Columbia Bar Association, the same group that had rejected her
membership application twenty-eight years earlier. Joined by eight other senators, both senators from Mississippi, John C. Stennis and James O. Eastland,
endorsed Matthews. She also received significant support from NAWL, the National Federation of Business and Professional Women's Clubs, and members of
the GFWC.[55] Mary McLeod Bethune, black educator and founder of Bethune-
Cookman College, lobbied President Truman on Matthews's behalf. Matthews
learned of Bethune's efforts later and returned the favor with generous monetary contributions to the Bethune-Cookman College Foundation.[56]

When President Truman originally compiled a list of names to send to the
Senate, Matthews was not on the list. This information leaked to the press, and
when discovered by India Edwards, head of the Women's Division of the Democratic National Committee and a friend of Truman, she wrote several letters to
the Democratic leadership and transmitted copies to President Truman. The
next day he asked Edwards to bring Matthews in for an interview. When the
list went to the Senate that afternoon, Matthews's name was on it.[57] Matthews
received a recess appointment in 1949 to the U.S. district court and was officially
confirmed by the Senate in 1950. In Matthews's version of the story, she had a
brief interview with Truman after her appointment.[58]

Matthews's initial reception at the U.S. district court was, in a word, "icy."
While Matthews was still under Senate consideration, U.S. District Court Judge

T. Alan Goldsborough was quoted publicly, "Mrs. Matthews would be a good judge," there was "just one thing wrong: she's a woman."[59] In her first years on the bench, Matthews's fellow judges agreed among themselves to assign her all the long motions (those that require more than thirty minutes to argue). Her former law clerks later recalled that Judge Matthews was sometimes assigned motions for three months at a time.[60] True to her nature, Matthews never let these incidents bother her, and although it took several years, all the men on the court eventually came around. Even Judge Goldsborough recanted his earlier statement.[61]

Matthews's twenty-five years on the bench encompassed an entirely new phase of her life, as she was unable to work actively for women's rights. Instead, these years were almost exclusively dedicated to the law and justice. For the majority of Matthews's tenure on the bench, the U.S. District Court for the District of Columbia served as both the federal trial court and the major trial court for the district's local criminal and civil cases. Its federal jurisdiction was unusual because it included cases in which individuals sued the United States and its agencies, particularly the cabinet departments. Its local jurisdiction included felony cases, such as murder, rape, assault, and drug possession, as well as civil cases dealing with divorce, child custody, and estates. Until the passage of the Federal Court Reform Act of 1970, under which the District of Columbia court system finally assumed responsibility for local matters, Matthews presided over an extraordinary variety of cases.[62]

Her decisions included a number of celebrity cases, one of the most noteworthy of which was the 1955 case in which she blocked the deportation of crooner Dick Haymes, husband of actress Rita Hayworth, to Argentina. She refused in 1956 to order the State Department to reissue a passport to singer and communist human rights activist Paul Robeson. She presided over the 1957 bribery trial of Teamster labor leader Jimmy Hoffa.[63] Many of her colleagues avoided these cases, but Matthews never ran from controversy. In these cases, Matthews proved that a woman judge could control a courtroom, despite unrelenting press coverage and the legal antics of lawyers.

Two other controversial cases that Matthews decided were the 1957 case in which she upheld the segregation of the Boys Club of Metropolitan Police in the District of Columbia and the 1962 case in which she upheld the right of Black Muslims to conduct religious services in the local prison. In the Boys Club case, Matthews addressed the questions of racial segregation, holding that the Boys Club could remain segregated, as the equal protection clause of the Fourteenth Amendment did not apply because the Boys Club was a private organization. In the Black Muslim case, she dealt with the question of religion and upheld the claim that the Black Muslims were a religious organization, deserving the same First Amendment protection as other religious groups.[64]

In 1968, Matthews took senior status, a form of semiretirement. From this time, until her retirement in 1978, she served mostly by special assignment to the U.S. Court of Appeals for the District of Columbia. While on the appeals court, Matthews participated in her only case involving sex discrimination. *Evans v. Sheraton Park Hotel* involved an international labor union that maintained sex-segregated local unions for banquet waiters and waitress. Matthews wrote the opinion in this case, in which the court held that this practice violated Title VII of the Civil Rights Act of 1964, which prohibits employment discrimination on the basis of race, color, religion, national origin, or sex.[65]

Although Matthews felt that her position as a judge precluded her from publicly working for women's rights, she continued to find private and personal ways of advancing opportunities for women. In her years on the bench, all eight lawyers who served as Matthews's law clerks were women. Matthews knew that the other judges hired only men and that her appointment would be for many years the only opportunity for young women lawyers to clerk for a U.S. district court judge. Several of Matthews's "girls" went on to successful legal or judicial careers. Sylvia Bacon, her second clerk, became a municipal court judge and was considered for an appointment to the U.S. Supreme Court in 1971.

While on the bench, Matthews maintained her relationships with other women lawyers and helped them as she could. According to another of Matthews's clerks, Patricia Frohman, the judge saved old supplements to the U.S. Code for one of her struggling lawyer friends. When the judge found Frohman discarding supplements in the wastebasket, she said, "Patty, you put those in there and the cleaning people are liable to think you want to throw them out."[66]

Matthews was also instrumental in establishing a family court in the District of Columbia.[67] As one of five judges on the U.S. district court's committee for the creation of a family court, she helped to study laws and procedures in those states that already had family courts, much as she had studied state gender-biased laws in the 1920s. Matthews worked for three years to amass support among local civic leaders and members of Congress until, in 1956, Congress enacted the legislation that created the family court.

Seventy years after leaving Mississippi in search of a legal career, Burnita Shelton Matthews returned for the last time to her home state when she was buried in the Shelton family cemetery in Copiah County. Her headstone notes that she wished to be remembered for two things: her appointment as the first woman to a U.S. district court and as the "author of laws advancing the status of women." That simple epitaph, however, like this short chapter, cannot adequately convey the value of Burnita Shelton Matthews's life. Matthews worked hard for her achievements and she received the respect and admiration of her peers in return. She overcame many of the obstacles of her culture and then invited all women to join her in living life earnestly and with integrity.

NOTES

1. Elbert R. Hilliard, remarks at Shelton Cemetery Association Meeting, Mississippi, 21 May 1983, Burnita Shelton Matthews Collection, Mississippi Department of Archives and History (henceforth MDAH), Jackson, 2.

2. Burnita Shelton Matthews, "Burnita Shelton Matthews: Pathfinder in the Legal Aspects of Women," interview by Amelia R. Fry, Washington, D.C., 29 April 1973, Suffragists Oral History Project, Bancroft Library, University of California, Berkeley, 2.

3. Ibid., 3.

4. "Woman Appointed to Federal Trial Court," *Washington Post,* November 1949, clipping, scrapbook no. 1, Matthews Collection.

5. See William Ivy Hair, *Carnival of Fury: Robert Charles and the New Orleans Race Riot of 1900* (Baton Rouge: Louisiana State University Press, 1976), 13–14.

6. Matthews, interview, 2.

7. "Leader of the Women's Rights Movement Recalls Suffrage Fight and Appointment to Bench," *Third Branch* 17 (March 1985): 1.

8. Ibid., 6.

9. Michael De L. Landon, *The Honor and Dignity of the Profession, A History of the Mississippi State Bar: 1906–1976* (Jackson: University Press of Mississippi, 1979), 43.

10. Ellen Crump to Alice Paul, 5 January 1923, reel 20, National Woman's Party Papers (henceforth NWP Papers), Library of Congress, Washington, D.C.

11. Hilliard, 6.

12. Matthews, interview, 4.

13. Biographical sketch, Matthews Collection.

14. Matthews, interview, 13.

15. Ibid., 14.

16. Ibid.

17. Mary Agnes Brown, "New Dealer Feted: Lucy Somerville Howorth Honored by Associates in Veterans Administration," *Women Lawyer's Journal* 17 (November 1934): 33.

18. Matthews, interview, 33–34.

19. Ibid., 7.

20. Elsie Hill to Pope Yeatman, 9 May 1922, reel 14, NWP Papers.

21. Ibid.

22. Mrs. H. W. Wiley, remarks before the Arlington County Club of Clarendon, Va., 9 December 1922, reel 19, NWP Papers.

23. Matthews to Katherine Fisher, 16 June 1922, reel 15, NWP Papers.

24. Matthews, interview, 8.

25. Martha Swain, "Organized Women in Mississippi: The Clash over Legal Disabilities in the 1920s," *Southern Studies* 23 (spring 1984): 91–102.

26. Ibid., 95

27. Ibid.

28. Ibid., 96–99.

29. Paul to Matthews, 31 March 1923; Matthews to Paul, 1 April 1923; Laura Berrien to Paul, 4 April 1923, reel 21, NWP Papers.

30. Swain, 100–101.

31. Matthews to Paul, 26 September 1922, reel 17, NWP Papers.

32. See reels 10–30, NWP Papers.

33. Matthews, interview, 20.

34. Ibid.

35. Draft of an article prepared for the *D.C. Beeper,* Business and Professional Women newsletter—District of Columbia, 9 May 1984, MDAH.

36. "Senate Moves to Save Historic Headquarters," *Equal Rights,* 28 May 1928.

37. Ibid.

38. Ibid.

39. Matthews, interview, 35.

40. Ibid.

41. Ibid., 18.

42. Matthews, notes, Matthews Collection.

43. House Committee on the Judiciary, *Hearings before the Committee on the Judiciary on H.R. 75, 68th Cong., 2d sess.,* 4–5 February 1925; Senate Committee on the Judiciary, *Hearings before a Subcommittee of the Committee on the Judiciary on S.R. 64, 70th Cong.,* 1 February 1929; Senate Committee on the Judiciary, *Hearings before a Subcommittee of the Committee on the Judiciary on S.R. 52, 73rd Cong., 3d sess.,* 6 January 1931; House Committee on the Judiciary, *Hearings before the Committee on the Judiciary on H.R. 197, 72d Cong., 1st sess.,* 16 March 16 1932; Senate Committee on the Judiciary, *Hearings before a Subcommittee of the Committee on the Judiciary on S.R. 1, 75th Cong., 1st sess.,* 27 May 1933; Senate Committee on the Judiciary, *Hearings before a Subcommittee of the Committee on the Judiciary on S.R. 65, 75th Cong., 3d sess.,* 7–10 February 1938; and House Committee on the Judiciary, *Hearings before Subcommittee One of the Committee on the Judiciary on H.R. 49, 62, 85, 89, 104, and 110, 80th Cong., 2d sess.,* 10–12 March 1948.

44. Senate Committee, *Hearings on S.R. 65, 75th Cong., 3d sess.,* 7–10 February 1938.

45. House Committee on Immigration and Naturalization, *Hearings before the Committee on Immigration and Naturalization on H.R. 3673 and 77, 73d Cong., 1st sess.,* 28 March 1933.

46. Matthews, interview, 35.

47. Ibid., 36

48. Ibid.

49. Ibid., 15.

50. "Leader," 1. The returned check is in the Matthews Collection.

51. Mary Seaton, biographical sketch, Matthews Collection, 18.

52. Ibid.

53. Virginia H. Drachman, *Sisters in Law: Women Lawyers in Modern American History* (Cambridge: Harvard University Press, 1998), 237.

54. Truman received at least sixty-six endorsements from women's groups throughout the country. Official file, Harry Truman Papers, Harry S. Truman Library, Independence, Mo.

55. Matthews, interview, 40.

56. Mary McLeod Bethune to Matthews, Matthews Papers, Arthur and Elizabeth Schlesinger Library, Radcliffe Institute for Advanced Study, Cambridge, Mass.

57. India Edwards, *Pulling No Punches: Memoirs of a Woman in Politics* (New York: G. L. Putnum's Sons, 1977), 184–86. Matthews tells the story somewhat differently than Edwards in Matthews, interview, 39–41.

58. Matthews, interview, 42.

59. Mary Seaton, Betty Jones, and Patricia Frohman, interview by author, Washington, D.C., 12 August 1992, U.S. District Court, District of Columbia.

60. Ibid.

61. Ibid.

62. Matthews, interview, 43.

63. See *Haymes v. Brownwell,* 131 FSupp 784 (1955); *Robeson v. Dulles,* 235 F2d 810 (1956).

64. *Mitchell v. Boys Club of Metropolitan Police, D.C.,* 157 FSupp 101 (1957); and *Fulwood v. Clemmer,* 206 FSupp 370 (1962).

65. *Evans v. Sheraton Park Hotel,* 503 F2d 177 (1974).

66. Seaton, Jones, and Frohman, interview.

67. "Family Court Proposal to be Weighed," *Washington Daily News,* 21 April 1953; "Judges to See D.C. Heads on Family Court," *Washington Times Herald,* 21 April 1953, Matthews Collection.

Minnie Brewer

(1898–1978)

The Life and Times of a Flapper Feminist

DOROTHY SHAWHAN

When Minnie Brewer mailed her dark curls home to the Mississippi Governor's mansion in a box, the Earl Brewer family felt great consternation over her "disgrace." The year was 1914, and nice girls did not bob their hair. Inspired by a stage star, Minnie had a friend in her Hollins College dormitory crop her curls. The Hollins administration ruled that the next head bobbed would be expelled and had a faculty member take Minnie to a barber in Roanoke for repairs. The next day, Brewer's sister recalled, the barber hung a sign in his shop window bragging, "Ladies, come in and let us bob your hair. We've just cut the hair of the daughter of the Governor of Mississippi."[1] Ever one to relish stirring things up, Minnie must have enjoyed the uproar her bobbed hair, that "badge of flapperhood," caused among family and faculty.[2] At age fifteen, having lived a sheltered life, she was probably more motivated by the glamour of the stage star than by any conscious desire to make a sexual statement. In the upcoming decade, however, bobbed hair would become a symbol of promiscuous sexuality and a denial of the nineteenth-century domestic cult of true womanhood.[3] Minnie Brewer's haircut was prophetic in pointing to the liberated, risk-taking flapper she would become.

Alongside the flapper, however, existed another Minnie Brewer. The much-discussed "New Woman" of the twenties included not only flappers but a variety of feminists from several generations, "social feminists, radical, pragmatic, and even 'general' feminists."[4] Minnie Brewer, with the founding of her political newspaper, the *Woman Voter,* in Clarksdale, Mississippi, in 1922, was a feminist who believed women were capable of social action, that "the talents, skills, and virtues so valuable in the home were needed to clean up the larger households of community and nation."[5] She often used the house-cleaning analogy in her newspaper, and an account of a speech she made at the Neshoba County Fair in Martin S. "Mike" Connor's race for governor carried this headline in the *Jackson Daily News:* "Miss Minnie Brewer Urges Clean Up Man."[6] The feminist Minnie Brewer had as her goal educating the women of Mississippi in the wise use of their newly won right to vote.

Minnie Elizabeth Brewer was born 28 July 1898, in Water Valley, Mississippi, to Earl Leroy Brewer and Minnie Marian Block Brewer. She was followed by two younger sisters, Earlene and Claudia. Mrs. Brewer was described as a charming hostess, expert gardener and cook, and devoted "helpmeet," who kept her husband's home life "serene and sweet, and afar from the bitter turmoil of public life," an ideal role model for young women of the time. Minnie Brewer, however, seems to have looked more to her father for inspiration.[7] Minnie "didn't get on with her mother at all," according to a cousin, but her sister wrote that "Daddy inspired Minnie, he adored her, and urged her on."[8]

When Minnie was three, the family moved to Clarksdale when Brewer was appointed district attorney for the Eleventh Circuit District Court. He began to amass a fortune in land and cotton and bought a house at 41 John Street, an address that would remain the Brewers' permanent one for over thirty years.[9] Minnie attended school in Clarksdale until she was thirteen years old when her father was elected governor of the state of Mississippi.[10] The glitter of her father's inauguration must have been thrilling for a young girl. On 16 January 1912, thousands of Mississippians flooded into Jackson by train, wagon, horseback, and some few cars for the inauguration of the governor who had been described in the *Weekly Clarion Ledger* as "young, vigorous, and able" as well as "brilliant, eloquent and attractive, magnetic, bold and dashing."[11] The festive parade with the Brewer family in their Hudson convertible, marching bands, and military units made its way through the streets in near-freezing weather to the capitol.[12]

The outspoken and progressive Earl Brewer, who was not without political enemies, was soon embroiled in the "bitter turmoil of public life." To what extent the Brewer home life was insulated from the political cloud that hovered over the state capitol is anybody's guess, but the mansion was probably more orderly than state government. The governor often began the day by gathering the family for a morning prayer.[13] The Brewers entertained a great deal and also made the mansion available to clubs and organizations that wished to hold functions there.[14] The Brewer children seem not to have been stifled by life as

MINNIE BREWER

1915. From *The Spinster*, yearbook of
Hollins College. University Archives,
Robertson Library, Hollins University.

Mississippi's first family. Minnie's sister Claudia remembered riding her tricycle through the parlors.[15] She also remembered hearing screams from upstairs once during a dinner. When the family rushed upstairs, they found Minnie pinned underneath a wardrobe that had turned over on her when she had stood on a drawer to reach a dress. She was not hurt because the bed had broken the fall of the huge piece of furniture, but this would not be the last time young Minnie would get herself into trouble.[16]

Minnie attended school in Jackson briefly, but in the fall of 1912 at age fourteen she entered Hollins preparatory school in Virginia. In September 1915 she entered Hollins College as an "irregular" student. Her educational career continued to be irregular for the duration. She stayed one more year at Hollins, attended summer school at the University of Virginia, attended Millsaps College in Jackson, Mississippi, for one semester, and then studied journalism and political science for a year at the University of Wisconsin.[17] She never earned a degree because she took only those courses that interested her, and the sciences did not. "Why would I want to know about bugs?" she asked.[18]

Judging from the Hollins College yearbook, *The Spinster,* Minnie Brewer threw herself wholeheartedly into college life with memberships in Gamma Phi Beta sorority; D-R-A-G-O-N, Sphinx, and the Mississippi Club, all social clubs; Euepian, a literary society that staged plays and debates; and ADA, a group said to have been named for a nineteenth-century Hollins maid known for her pranks and sense of humor.[19] One year Minnie won the "Buzz in the Bee" designation as biggest gossiper.[20] A classmate remembered her as "silly little Minnie" and a girl who "giggled a lot."[21] Her sister described her more positively as "a ball of fire, always at a fast pace, entertaining, interesting, fun . . . a free spirit and original thinker."[22]

The Spinster is an intriguing title for a yearbook at a Virginia girls' school where one might expect "finishing" to imply that the central mission of the college was preparing young women for marriage within their social station. Since originally the word simply meant "one who spins," perhaps those who named the yearbook were drawing an analogy between making a book from words and pictures and spinning thread from a lump of wool. The epithet on the title page, however, is pointed: "Where singleness is bliss, 'tis folly to be wives." This play on Thomas Gray's "Where ignorance is bliss, 'tis folly to be wise" suggests that at Hollins young women focused on forging their own identities rather than on finding husbands.

When Earl Brewer's term as governor ended in 1916, he and the family returned to Clarksdale, his law practice, his plantations, and 41 John Street. Soon they moved the existing house from that address and constructed a new one that replicated the governor's mansion. They particularly liked the way the parlors and front hall could be opened up with sliding doors for ballroom dances and large parties befitting a wealthy Delta planter.[23]

With the coming of World War I, Minnie, like many young women, wanted to make a contribution to the effort that was to end all wars. She exaggerated her age and enlisted to patrol the Jersey shore for enemy ships. She frequently had to sleep among the sand dunes and was terrified of sand bugs, but whether she wanted out of her enlistment or her parents insisted she come home is not clear. In any case, Earl Brewer got her out, and "she did her duty knitting soldiers' scarves."[24]

In the summer of 1920, Minnie went on a two-month grand tour of Europe with a group from Hollins College and persuaded her parents to let Claudia go too, though she was only thirteen years old. She wanted her little sister to have this experience because she might not soon have the chance again. When the sisters returned to Clarksdale, they learned that the bottom had fallen out of the cotton market and that Earl Brewer was land-poor, without sufficient cash to run his plantations, let alone maintain his daughters in the lavish lifestyle to which they had grown accustomed.[25]

Despite her family's financial straits, Minnie apparently lived the life of a 1920s flapper. She "ran with a wild crowd, returned soldiers, short skirts, women drinking and smoking in public. She *never* smoked but did drink."[26] Young Americans in the 1920s asserted their freedom and modernity by drinking, smoking, and dancing. To traditionalists such behaviors signaled sexual promiscuity and the decline of moral values.[27] Minnie's friend Lucy Somerville Howorth put it this way: "Minnie Brewer was full of zest—she was her father's daughter."[28]

Not all was frivolity, however. The flapper had a serious side. She joined the newly formed National League of Women Voters, the organization that replaced the National American Woman Suffrage Association after the passage of the Nineteenth Amendment in 1920, and became involved in state Democratic party politics. She read seriously, including authors like Tolstoy and Fitzgerald.[29] She also got together some schoolbooks and taught the Brewers' cook, a black woman named Libby, how to read and write. This suggests a liberal bent in Minnie's feminism; during the Jim Crow era, illiteracy of blacks was used as a reason to keep them from the ballot box. Libby, who was married to another of the Brewers' servants, lived in an apartment above the garage and wrote to Claudia every week when she was at the University of Wisconsin to tell her "all the family news."[30]

Although the editorials she would later write for the *Woman Voter* put the highest value on marriage and family, Minnie herself always stopped short of the altar for reasons that are humorous but not convincing. Claudia wrote, "She always said she could not marry a doctor because they were all quacks, and she didn't believe in medicine. She could not marry a lawyer because she would argue with them and would win because she'd learned her law from her Daddy and he was the smartest and the best."[31] She admired her father to such an extent that perhaps no other man could measure up.

For a time, she had a relationship with a doctor whom she first met at the University of Virginia, but she saw him for the last time when she returned from Europe in 1920. Then distance and finances separated them.[32] She was later engaged to an architect, the trousseau was complete, but the wedding was called off. The only explanation her family got was that the relationship "wore out."[33] A man who became the international secretary of the Young Men's Christian Association (YMCA) proposed next, but when Minnie said yes, he dropped to his knees to pray for a blessing on the engagement, and that was the end. Despite having grown up in the heart of the Bible Belt, Minnie said that she "did not want anybody praying over her and especially not her husband."[34] A Mississippi man who was with Standard Oil in Java proposed, but Minnie said, "I got to thinking, if Daddy had a bad cotton year and I fell out with him, Daddy couldn't send me money to come home on."[35] So she remained blissfully single, as her school yearbook had prescribed.

When she was twenty-four, Minnie began channeling her passions into the weekly *Woman Voter*. The idea for the paper came to her as a delegate to the third annual convention of the National League of Women Voters in Baltimore in April 1922.[36] The meeting seems to have been a turning point and an occasion of consciousness-raising for Minnie. Presided over by league president Maud Wood Park, with over a thousand women in attendance, the meeting must have been impressive. Other prominent women there included suffrage leaders Carrie Chapman Catt and Emmeline Pankhurst; Assistant Attorney General Mabel Walker Willebrandt; social reformers Jane Addams and Lillian Wald; and actress Josephine Baker. The conference program promised discussions on "Education, Child Welfare, Women in Industry, Prevention of Traffic in Women, Civil and Political Status of Women, and International Friendliness." "PEACE among nations," the publication asserted, "is essential to the work that women have most at heart."[37] Organizers also held a Pan-American conference for women in conjunction with the league meeting, firmly pinning the hope for progressive social changes throughout the hemisphere on woman's right to vote.

The league's plans were ambitious. The idea of starting a political newspaper for women in Mississippi in 1922 was equally daring. The project would require a person with a pioneering spirit, boundless optimism, and perhaps the naïveté of youth. When the Mississippi House defeated the Nineteenth Amendment a year earlier, R. H. Watts of Rankin County said "he would rather die and go to hell" than vote for it, and many legislators cheered. The *Jackson Clarion-Ledger*, which had led the opposition to woman suffrage, congratulated the House for its "good, glorious, and grand work."[38] Mississippi would not ratify the amendment until 1984.

Minnie Brewer had the pioneering spirit as well as her father's encouragement, and as long as it lasted, his money. The first issue of the *Woman Voter*, 3 August 1922, was published two weeks before election day. Called the official organ of the League of Women Voters of Mississippi, the paper's sole proprietor was Minnie Brewer. From a marketing perspective, early August was an ideal time to start a political newspaper.[39] The Senate race to fill the seat vacated by the retirement of John Sharp Williams was in full swing. Candidates were U.S. Senator James K. Vardaman, who as a U.S. congressman had supported many issues important to women, but because of his "redneck" connections was unpopular with upper-class white women of the Delta; Belle Kearney, the first woman in the state to run for a major office; and Hubert Stephens, a U.S. congressman since 1911. The *Woman Voter* endorsed Kearney, who lost. The August 17 issue bemoaned the fact that the paper went to less than 10,000 people in a state where 150,000 votes were cast but promised a different day in Mississippi when the women came into their own.

The *Woman Voter* included a great deal of Vardaman coverage in the form of paid advertisements and also included balanced coverage of voting records on women's issues, which made Vardaman look good. During the run-off race between Stephens and Vardaman, Brewer failed to put a "paid advertisement" disclaimer on a Vardaman article, which brought the wrath of the league down upon her, despite the fact that Stephens won. The negative reactions to Brewer's newspaper in 1922 reflected not only the antipathy toward Vardaman in the Delta but a fear about what the woman's vote would mean in Mississippi.[40]

During this tumultuous beginning, a significant friendship developed between Minnie Brewer and Lucy Somerville, a young lawyer practicing in Cleveland, Mississippi, who was the daughter of suffrage veteran Nellie Nugent Somerville. The two were different in many ways. Lucy was focused, ambitious, and shrewd in business, whereas Minnie was impulsive, pleasure-loving, and naive about business. But the two shared a passion for politics. According to Lucy, Minnie Brewer "knew her politics." She said that Minnie had more ideas in fifteen minutes than anybody she had ever known; she loved political scheming, and though ideas poured from her head, they tended to be disorganized and she soon lost interest.[41]

Minnie's thoughts were clear enough when it came to the controversy her paper had caused. Forty-two Clarksdale women wrote an open letter to the *Memphis Commercial Appeal* condemning the *Woman Voter* as a Vardaman in-strument and denying that it was an official publication of the league.[42] Brewer, secretary of the league's state executive committee, countered by pointing out that not all the forty-two were members of the league, nor did they have a right to speak for the entire organization.[43] Minnie's failure to conform to traditional notions of female respectability made her an unattractive spokesperson, even to those who considered themselves feminists. Daisy Lamkin, an old friend of Nellie Somerville, opined, "It's a great pity to have a girl of Minnie's reputation in a state office."[44]

Cooler heads prevailed, and Brewer kept her office with the league. The league's state convention in 1922 even commended her for "enlarging the use of her paper" to include news from other women's organizations.[45] The league, however, ultimately distanced itself from the *Woman Voter*. League news was confined to a column that carried a disclaimer saying that the organization was not responsible for anything else printed in the paper, nor was the pa-per responsible for the column.[46] The paper carried news from other women's organizations too, as well as nuts and bolts articles by Lucy Somerville and her mother, Nellie, on the workings of government, articles that helped fulfill Brewer's stated vision and purpose: To "publish with simplicity instructions as to how to qualify as a citizen, how to obtain the right to vote, how to register, in fact how to go thru every minute detail to the depositing of the ballot in the box. So that the women may be as well posted on all the procedure as a man."[47]

Aspersions on Minnie's reputation did not deter Lucy Somerville from the friendship. Lucy provided legal advice to the paper, and Minnie, creating news as usual, as well as reporting it, set up a debate between Lucy Somerville and Mary Winsor, a representative of the league's rival, the National Woman's Party.[48] Both Minnie and Lucy worked long hours, but their friendship was not all business. Their letters speak of July Fourth picnics, their first airplane ride with a barnstormer over the Mississippi River, and drives in a Ford car.[49] The Ford, that symbol and vehicle of freedom and independence, often rolled through the correspondence of these young women, still in their twenties. They, like other Americans, loved Henry Ford's Tin Lizzie, the "family pet of the nation."[50]

Although Brewer had the nerve and self-confidence to start the *Woman Voter*, she often felt inadequate and doubted her reporting ability. In one column about the Mississippi Press association, she called herself an amateur.[51] She worried about the opinions of the efficient women she hired to manage the business end of the paper. She feared that they thought because she and her

assistant "haven't any business sense that we must be titantics [*sic*] for producing news."[52]

Still, Minnie and the *Woman Voter* continued, and in one editorial she claimed that hers was the only paper to be mailed to every county in the state. She
managed Belle Kearney's state senate race after Kearney broke her arm. "Old
sister Belle is a good sport and I know we could elect her," she wrote to Lucy,
who was at the time working in her mother's campaign for the state House of
Representatives.[53] The *Woman Voter* endorsed both Kearney and Somerville,
and both candidates won.

When her father's old nemesis, the corrupt and racist Theodore Bilbo, entered the governor's race in 1923, all illusions of journalistic nonpartisanship
vanished. Brewer simply asserted that denouncing a rascal was not partisan.[54]
Her editorials went after Bilbo tooth and nail. Bilbo was elected governor once
more, thanks to the men, she wrote, but now that the women can vote, they
"hold the balance of power," and they will never vote for Bilbo because of his
moral character: "He may be crazy about the women, as he intimates. But that
is just the trouble."[55] She predicted that the women would make the election
Bilbo's Waterloo and exile him to the "St. Helena Pecan Farm, Poplarville,
Mississippi."[56] When Bilbo started his own newspaper before the election, the
Mississippi Free Lance, and took shots at the *Woman Voter,* Minnie retaliated
with a subscription campaign and a slogan suggested by Lucy: "Bilbo says you
shouldn't read THE WOMAN VOTER, SUBSCRIBE TODAY."[57] Ultimately Bilbo lost
to Henry Whitfield, who had been president of Mississippi State College for
Women and for whom many of the alumnae campaigned. The woman's vote
was an important factor in his election.

In September 1923, despite being in the thick of the political campaigning,
Minnie took time off to accompany her little sister Claudia to college, suppos-
edly to Hollins College. When she reached home, however, Minnie told Mrs.
Brewer that she was taking Claudia to the University of Wisconsin, that it would
be a waste to take her to Hollins. Earl Brewer was in New York, and his wife wired
him for support, but neither was able to dissuade the ever-determined Minnie,
who was soon out the door and on a train headed for Wisconsin with Claudia.
"You see how Minnie always had her way," Claudia later wrote. "My father wrote
me from New York how disappointed he was that I was not at a conservative
Virginia girls school—but instead at 'Wisconsin the home of Lafollete, and hot
bed of socialism,' but he was sure I would keep my head!"[58]

Minnie had tapped Claudia to join her on the *Woman Voter,* and undoubt-
edly she thought the University of Wisconsin a better training ground than
the "conservative Virginia girls school." She was so impressed with the univer-

sity, in fact, that she decided to join Claudia there for the 1924 spring semester. She wanted to study "Freshman English, composition, grammar and literature, Political Science, Short Hand, Typewriting and a beginners course in Journalism."[59] These courses would help her with the newspaper as well as prepare her for the National Democratic Convention in June, to which she was a delegate.[60] Although she lacked the college entrance requirements, Minnie was admitted as a special student and studied there for a year.

While in Wisconsin, Brewer left the *Woman Voter* under the editorship of a young Jackson lawyer, Joe Howorth, but the paper survived only until April 1924. The main reason for its demise was the bottom line: Minnie was no businesswoman, and Earl Brewer's fortunes continued to fall with the cotton market. In December 1923, Brewer wrote Somerville, "You know that I would keep money pouring into it as long as there was a dollar left but there simply isn't any more. I do think my Dad has been lovely about letting me have all that he could and goodness knows that I put all that I had, consisting of a lot which was the only thing that I possessed."[61]

The experience left Minnie in the mood to spend her last dollars on a treat for herself. After she paid off the paper's debts, she "decided to have some fun in the meanwhile so I bought that Ford with what we had left. Do you blame me?"[62] Minnie put her own pleasure first in a move typical of modern consumer culture. Consumer goods as a path to personal happiness and freedom "undercuts traditions associated with a pantheon of white southern ideals," such as family duty and Protestant frugality.[63]

When Minnie and Claudia came home for Christmas in December 1924, they learned that the family's financial situation had become so serious that they could not return to Wisconsin but would have to go to work.[64] Instead of helping her sister on the *Woman Voter,* then, Claudia went to work for the *Clarksdale Daily Register* and later WJDX radio in Jackson and Fred Sullens's *Jackson Daily News.*[65] Apparently tired of the newspaper business, and befitting her sense of style, Minnie went to work at a dress shop and beauty parlor that her cousin Eloise Coleman remembered as "the first sort of thing like that for women around."[66]

Gradually, Minnie and her old friends, and even family, drifted apart. Lucy Somerville married Joe Howorth and moved to Jackson. In 1933 Minnie's parents also moved to Jackson, where her father rejuvenated his law practice. Minnie, however, stayed in Clarksdale at 41 John Street.[67]

In 1936, in the case of *Brown v. Mississippi,* Earl Brewer successfully appealed before the U.S. Supreme Court the case of three black men from Kemper County who had confessed to the murder of a white man and had been convicted in the

Mississippi courts. Their confessions, however, had been extracted from them only after brutal beatings. The National Association for the Advancement of Colored People, the Commission on Interracial Cooperation, and the Association of Southern Women for the Prevention of Lynching raised money to help finance the defense, although Brewer clearly did not take on the generally unpopular case for the money.[68]

Both Earl and Minnie Brewer (at least in her pre-Wisconsin days) shared the white-supremacy views of most white southerners of their socioeconomic class, but not the "Radical mentality." The "radical" view that engendered the post–Civil War lynching era and was embraced by leaders like Bilbo and Vardaman held that the black person freed from slavery was "retrogressing rapidly toward his natural state of savagery and bestiality." Most whites ignored black aspirations by simply asserting white superiority. Consequently, "there was no problem with race in the conscious mind of the white South in the 1920s and 1930s."[69] Race seldom came up in the *Woman Voter;* it was understood that the audience was white women. Minnie was a bit left of many of her contemporaries on the issue, however. In one editorial Brewer called for agricultural high schools for black children like the ones provided for white students. She wrote prophetically, "And each day makes it more apparent that whether we like it or not, whether they like it or not, the negro and the southern white folks are destined to work out their salvation together in this genial clime where chance has placed us."[70] When students wanted to "fight the Civil War" with Claudia at Wisconsin, Minnie taught her to say, "Yankees (not Northerners) 'accept Negroes as a race—Southerners accept Negroes as friends' (individually)."[71] Minnie was aware of the history of Mound Bayou, the all-black municipality a few miles south of Clarksdale. She knew that the town had been founded in 1887 by Isaiah Montgomery, former valet and secretary to Joseph Davis, Jefferson's brother, as well as manager of Joseph Davis's Briarfield Plantation. She knew that one of Isaiah's daughters, Mary Montgomery Booze, was a Republican National Committeewoman from Mound Bayou, but it is not known whether the two ever met and talked.[72]

By 1939 Minnie had apparently moved from the home place on John Street to a Fourth Street boarding house that she was buying.[73] A move from a residence replicating the governor's mansion to a public boarding house represents a decline in social status, but Minnie probably cared little about that. This business venture may have been a last attempt on her part to achieve economic independence and freedom. A boarding house was likely to be profitable in the 1930s given the large influx of men building the Mississippi River levee. "The Depression affected a lot of things," observed one Clarksdale resident, who went on to say that the levee men "added spice to ladies' lives," that "Minnie had a *good time* then," and that she was "her own person always."[74]

In the mind of Clarksdale, judging from the few residents who recollect, the middle-aged Minnie with dyed red hair was a "character," the kind of eccentric to be found in many small southern towns. One woman remembered her as "a little off," a neighbor as "flighty," and another, a child at the time, as "that strange woman who walked the streets." The latter's daughter added, "Any woman who did more than have babies and churn butter was considered strange then, I'm sure."[75] Being eccentric, or flighty, or strange is not usually enough to land one in the insane asylum, however, and so events of the second half of Minnie Brewer's life are shocking.

One night in April 1939 Minnie called a neighbor with a "premonition that something was wrong."[76] The neighbor called the doctor who "gave her dope" and called Earl Brewer to come. He took her to Jackson and hired nurses to take care of her. She was "very ugly in what she said" to her parents, and eventually Mrs. Brewer and the doctors made Earl consent to send her to the state hospital at Whitfield.[77] The Hinds County Chancery Court records say that "it had been suggested in writing by Earl Brewer that Minnie Brewer was a lunatic, but that friends or family either neglect or refuse to place her in the Lunatic Asylum. Therefore, it was requested that a jury of 6 discreet persons, not kin, or interested in her estate, hear the case." The Affidavit of Lunacy dated 17 April 1939 states that Earl Brewer swore on oath that "Minnie Elizabeth Brewer is a lunatic or insane," and the Order of the Court from the same date says that the "Jury had heard the evidence and in their opinion Minnie E. Brewer is a lunatic and should be placed in the Hospital for the Insane or held in the County Jail until vacancy." Six male jurors signed the form.[78]

The evidence that the jurors heard is not given in the file, nor apparently did doctors at the time give an immediate diagnosis to the family, or at least not to Claudia. Minnie's sister wrote Lucy that the doctors cited symptoms that she thought of as "natural" to her sister: "rambling letters, detailed conversation and changing subjects in the middle, classifying people by those she liked, those she disliked and those she thought were trying to do her dirt."[79] Far advanced in pregnancy at the time, Claudia went on to attribute Minnie's current condition to the change of life, a holdover from the Victorian notion that menopause could cause insanity.[80] Lucy Howorth responded that she did not think that age was the cause, that the symptoms suggested a "well recognized psychosis."[81] Later Howorth, who had majored in psychology and who had a great deal of experience with mental illness on the Board of Veterans Appeals, said she believed Minnie was manic-depressive and that often people with a tremendous drive like Minnie's were on the verge of being manic.[82]

On 17 April 1939, Minnie was confined to the Mississippi State Hospital at Whitfield, where ironically the main building had "Earl Brewer 1915" on one of the cornerstones. The Brewers closed Minnie's house in Clarksdale and found her diaries, which were left with Earl's sister and later burned in a house fire.[83] "There were many things in those diaries that should have been burned," Claudia wrote. "They were towards her later life when her memory was better than her judgement."[84] Perhaps as had countless other women, including famous individuals like Charlotte Perkins Gilman and Catherine Beecher, Minnie was seeking order and meaning through her personal writing. She had suffered the economic losses of the Great Depression and had seen the ideal of woman change from the flapper "It Girl" of the 1920s (" 'It' combined sexual charisma and carefree self-indulgence") to the Ideal Mother and Happy Homemaker of the 1930s. As "the images of acceptable womanhood changed more rapidly than at any time in the past," she felt alienated.[85]

When Earl Brewer visited Minnie at Whitfield, she was rational, he wrote, until she began talking about "her business at Clarksdale, and then she would lose all reason and go off at a tangent."[86] Nevertheless, he thought she was much better and hoped for the day when he could bring her home. That day never came. Eventually the doctors asked him to quit visiting because Minnie wanted to go home with him and became very upset when she could not. With her mother and sisters she was calm, but not with her father.[87] Evidently she was rational enough to know that he had the power to get her out.

Minnie's initial diagnosis was "Psychosis due to Syphilitic Meningo Encephalitis" although "she lacks some of the symptoms." The prognosis was "Good." Early hospital notes on her behavior often used the adjectives "pert" and "sarcastic" and express concern that she "belittles the Institution" and "writes numerous lengthy letters to prominent people" and "smuggles" them out.[88]

During the 1940s, deplorable conditions at Whitfield came to light through efforts of some of the patients, Minnie Brewer among them reportedly, though none of her letters have been found.[89] In 1946 a series of letters to public officials from a patient named Fred Cheney itemized complaints about organization of the hospital, diet, and turnover in personnel due to low pay. He wrote that "because of this faulty system of medical supervision" he had seen a number of patients committed "in fairly favorable condition mentally and physically" decline quickly into "stark, helpless, permanent cases of insanity." These patients are written up as having "failed to respond to treatment." But, of course, he argued, they did respond "logically indeed to the diet they were fed, to the lack of exercise, of fresh air and sunshine during their delayed time in the overcrowded bedlam of these buildings." Cheney wrote from "a 5x9 cell on the back side," where he was confined "indefinitely with no chance at any daily exercise whatsoever" and subsisted on a diet of yellow mush and turnip greens. He concluded that "somewhere in somebody's record books the words should be written in Capital Letters that the disgraceful conditions at Whitfield . . . amount to as deep and black a shame against the State as anything in its entire history."[90]

Corroborating Fred Cheney's account, Dr. William J. Jacquith, who joined the staff at Whitfield in 1946, said, "If I was to recount some of the things that I saw when I first came to Whitfield, you wouldn't believe me; they would be beyond human belief." Three doctors served four thousand patients, and there was not enough food. Patients' letters were smuggled out to officials and to Hodding Carter at the *Greenville Delta Democrat Times.* Carter began writing about it, and an investigation ensued.[91] Senator Fred Jones of Inverness visited Whitfield with a legislative delegation and was "appalled," describing the hospital as like a "concentration camp."[92] Reforms were enacted by special legislative session in 1947.[93]

More questions than answers usually surround cases of mental illness, and Minnie Brewer's forty-year institutionalization is no exception. Were all her symptoms attributable to syphilis or, as some symptoms suggest, was she manic-depressive or schizophrenic? Did confinement make her worse? Had she been a man, would she have been as likely to come to the same end? Had she been more successful at business, or less flamboyant, or less defiant of social conventions, would that have made a difference? Lucy Howorth thought definitely that had Minnie been a man, she would not have ended up at Whitfield. To begin with, she would have been raised to be more independent economically, and she would have had more socially acceptable outlets for her energies.[94] More women than men are labeled "mentally ill."[95] Often the insanity label was a penalty for rebels defiant of social norms, a penalty for "*being* 'female' as well as for desiring or daring *not* to be," and "many women in asylums were not insane."[96] Using "guardianships and insanity as methods of social control against unconventional women" were not common, but such family strategies did occur.[97] When asked if it were true that families would send members to Whitfield "to get them out of the way," Dr. Jacquith, who treated Minnie Brewer, said he knew personally of no such instances but knew it happened. If families "didn't want to be embarrassed with them being in the community, they sent them to the state hospital to get rid of them."[98] Certainly Minnie Brewer was unconventional, uncontrollable, and often embarrassing, but she also had significant psychological problems. Anecdotes suggested, however, that her mind was clear at least some of the time, such as the time when Whitfield doctors kept her supplied with books, and on at least one occasion called upon her to settle a dispute they were engaged in about a particular book.[99]

A Letter of Guardianship dated 29 November 1941 made Mrs. Brewer Minnie's guardian rather than Earl Brewer. On 5 February 1942, Minnie's estate, a $500 judgment against some Coahoma County men, was settled for $350, and in March, Earl Brewer died. Minnie apparently was not aware of what went on in the outside world. By Claudia's account, Minnie knew nothing of their father's death or of World War II until 1955 when she first was given the drug Thorazine. At that point she saw pictures of the war on television and, still interested in world affairs, wrote Claudia asking for details. For two years after that she and her sister corresponded, but Minnie suffered such severe muscle spasms and other side effects from the Thorazine that doctors took her off it and her letters ceased.[100] At one point, Minnie's other sister, Earlene, took her to the coast to live in her souvenir shop, but that arrangement did not last, and Minnie returned to Whitfield. Presumably she could not adjust to the public nature of a coastal shop after so many years in isolation.[101]

In 1957 Mrs. Brewer died and Earlene had moved to California. Claudia was in Maryland, and Minnie was at Whitfield with "no one to care for her or visit her," though Claudia's letters suggest that she never ceased to grieve for Minnie and that she tried through staying in touch with the hospital to make her sister's life more comfortable.[102] Hospital records indicate that Minnie received good care in these later years, but that she retreated increasingly into a fantasy world, exhibiting characteristics of "Chronic Schizophrenia." She seemed at peace in her world of unreality, her only companions the cats she named and fed on the hospital grounds.[103]

One account suggests that Minnie contracted syphilis from a soldier in World War I.[104] Many infected people live a lifetime without the disease ever advancing to the tertiary phase; only about 5 percent develop paresis or the psychoses of syphilis.[105] If she were already at the tertiary stage when she was committed, it is unlikely she would have lived forty more years. When doctors discovered that she had been sexually active and that she had syphilis, they might have jumped to the conclusion that syphilis was the cause of all her mental problems.[106] In any case, just as she connected with other major currents of her time, such as suffrage, feminism, and the Roaring Twenties, she connected tragically with one of the twentieth century's greatest scourges.

Syphilis became "a reverberating topic" at the turn of the century because it embodied "several resonant anxieties around sex and gender at a time of ever-accelerating social change."[107] Medical treatment was made difficult because of the moral stigma, and the major remedy in terms of public policy was to regulate prostitutes, not their patrons.[108] Women's activist Christabel Pankhurst, in a collection of articles from the *Suffragette* entitled *The Great Scourge,* placed responsibility for the epidemic on the promiscuity of men, warned women away from marriage, and touted the slogan "Votes for women, and chastity for men."[109] Other feminists blamed the sexual double standard as well, pointing out how women were kept ignorant of such matters and often contracted the disease from their husbands.[110] These feminists used "syphilis as a potent metaphor for male oppression and corruption," making physical and explicit all that was wrong with the patriarchal system.[111] Other women, however, thought it an oversimplification to blame either the "fallen" woman or "fallen" man for the problem, pointing out that the brunt of the epidemic was born by "mere youths, sometimes perilously ignorant."[112]

During World War I the blame seemed to shift once again to women, with the idea that the strength of our military was being "endangered by hysterical girls, mad with 'khaki fever,' throwing themselves in erotic abandon at anything in uniform." This was "a new version of an old metaphor, in the association of sexual diseases and women who failed to fit in to acceptable social categories, who crossed boundaries, who were uncontrolled." The period between the salvarsan treatment (1909) and penicillin (1943) was "the great age of syphilophobia," and "the whole inter-war generation was literally obsessed with the fear of syphilis."[113] This obsession can be attributed in part to propaganda, including the cinema, designed to prompt people to go for treatment. In the "visual propaganda," a recurring image was that of the " 'dangerous woman,' who, if not a prostitute, was 'easy' or 'loose,' seductive and threatening."[114] Minnie Brewer's attitude that all doctors were "quacks" and her appetite for the pleasures of the flesh combined with "perilous ignorance" of syphilis's dangers. Like Tennessee Williams's Blanche DuBois, she relied too heavily on the "kindness of strangers."[115] Syphilis hastened her decline.

One of the last editorials Minnie wrote for the *Woman Voter,* titled "Keeps Em Guessing," is about the mixed messages that young girls of her generation got from the world around them. At school she is taught to be gentle and ladylike, but after school she hears stories of exciting "high jinks" that require anything but decorum. At home her mother teaches "the value of being a neat housekeeper," but her "best beau whispers into her pink ears the suggestion that as his mate she would have the exquisite pleasure of watching others do those things for her." At church the minister speaks "of the life that moulds character and ennobles humanity, while at the next dance the wild hilarious jazz music fills her with longings for the flesh pots of existence." No wonder, she concludes, the "old world . . . appears incongruous to the average girl in her teens."[116]

Minnie Brewer's life may appear incongruous as well, with her early years as a flapper-feminist with a pioneering newspaper contrasted with the last half of her life. She died 1 June 1978, in the state hospital at Whitfield, after a confinement of almost forty years. Her death certificate cites the immediate cause of death as unknown but lists an underlying cause of "senility with debility" and other significant conditions as "Central nervous system syphilis treated."[117] Her short obituary in the *Clarksdale Press Register* says of her achievements only that "she was editor of The Woman Voter, a newspaper printed in Clarksdale."[118]

A way of seeing beyond the tragic incongruity of Minnie's life as well as a glimpse of Minnie's optimism are suggested by an anecdote from her good friend Lucy Howorth. Lucy remembered that Minnie was nearsighted. But when she finally got glasses she refused to wear them because, according to Minnie, "everybody had been beautiful before," but with glasses she could see all their warts and flaws. Ironically, this inability to see the flaws and dangers in this life had tragic consequences. Her contemporaries often seemed focused on her warts and flaws, but from the vantage point of history, she emerges as a complex woman whose biography necessitates multiple angles of vision.

Viewed as newspaper founder and editor, Brewer may at first seem insignificant. While the *Woman Voter* could be dismissed by some as the toy of a rich, well-connected young woman, it is through this medium that Brewer comes to the historian's notice at all. The newspaper, microfilmed by some forward-thinking person along the way, offers a primary resource for those interested in the political thinking of Mississippi white women in the years 1922–24. Brewer's reach exceeded her grasp, for her paper sparked no revolutions. Yet she was a pioneer who deserves credit. As for her success or failure, for at least half her years, she lived on her own terms and resisted the strictures of her conservative society, an achievement for a woman of her era. Viewed as a flapper, Brewer was typical of the freewheeling twenties feminist, but her life also reflects the subsequent crash of many feminist hopes in the thirties. As a victim of mental illness, Brewer typifies the fate of many women who could not for one reason or another fit into their time in history. Lucy Howorth put it this way: "Minnie has seemed to me for a long time like a very fine race horse tied to a plow. It is a great pity that one of her extraordinary ability could not somehow have become adjusted to this life. . . . Minnie Brewer is one of the tragedies of our state."[119]

NOTES

1. Claudia Brewer Strite to Vinton Prince, 30 December 1979. Copies of all cited correspondence from Strite to Prince are in Dorothy Shawhan's possession.

2. Paula S. Fass, *The Damned and the Beautiful* (New York: Oxford University Press, 1977), 21.

3. Ibid., 280.

4. Dorothy M. Brown, *Setting a Course: American Women in the 1920s* (Boston: Twayne, 1987), 32.

5. Ibid., 33; for the difficulties involved in labeling feminists, see Nancy F. Cott, "What's in a Name? The Limits of 'Social Feminism'; or Expanding the Vocabulary of Women's History," *Journal of American History* 76 (December 1989): 809–29.

6. *Jackson Daily News,* 26 June 1923, 8.

7. David G. Sansing and Carroll Waller, *A History of the Mississippi Governor's Mansion* (Jackson: University Press of Mississippi, 1977), 112; state biographical sketch, n.d., Brewer Papers, Clarksdale Public Library, Clarksdale, Miss.

8. Eloise Coleman, interview by author, Clarksdale, Miss., 25 April 1987; Claudia Brewer Strite to author, 27 January 1986.

9. Anne Fleming, "Governor Earl Brewer," pamphlet on Clarksdale, Miss., 1972, 18, Clarksdale Public Library.

10. Nannie Pitts McLemore, "The Progressive Era," in *A History of Mississippi,* ed. Richard A. McLemore (Jackson: University and College Press of Mississippi, 1973), 44, 54.

11. *Weekly Clarion Ledger,* 15 August 1907, quoted in McLemore, 42.

12. Sansing and Waller, 109–10.

13. Ibid., 110.

14. Ibid., 111.

15. Claudia Strite to Carroll Waller, 25 February 1975, quoted in Sansing and Waller, 112.

16. Ibid., 110–11.

17. Hollins College transcript, 25 January 1924, Office of Registrar, Hollins College, Roanoke, Va.; Minnie Brewer to the Registrar, 11 January 1924, Office of the Registrar, University of Wisconsin, Madison.

18. Strite to author, 27 January 1986.

19. Beth S. Harris, E-mail to author, 19 November 1999.

20. *The Spinster* (Roanoke, Va.: Hollins College, 1917), 12, 60.

21. Helen Clark House, interview by author, Cleveland, Miss., 19 May 1987.

22. Strite to author, 27 January 1986.

23. Fleming, 19; Sansing and Waller, 111.

24. Strite to Prince, 30 December 1979.

25. Strite to Prince, 19 February 1980, 26 January 1980.

26. Strite to Prince, 11 March 1980.

27. Fass, 323–24.

28. Lucy Somerville Howorth, interview by author, Cleveland, Miss., 6 February 1992.

29. Strite and Martha Williford, "Biography of Earl Leroy Brewer," 1946, Earl L. Brewer and Family Papers, Mississippi Department of Archives and History (henceforth MDAH), Jackson.

30. Strite to author, 11 July 1986.

31. Strite to Prince, 11 March 1980.

32. Ibid.

33. Ibid.

34. Ibid.

35. Ibid.

36. Strite to Prince, 30 December 1979, 19 February 1980.

37. "Call to the Conference," Papers of the League of Women Voters, WRC 748, Arthur and Elizabeth Schlesinger Library (henceforth AESL), Radcliffe Institute for Advanced Study, Cambridge, Mass.

38. Quoted in A. Elizabeth Taylor, "The Woman Suffrage Movement in Mississippi, 1890–1920," *Journal of Mississippi History* 30 (February 1968): 29–33.

39. Vinton M. Prince Jr., "Will Women Turn the Tide? Mississippi Women and the 1922 United States Senate Race," *Journal of Mississippi History* 42 (August 1980): 212–20.

40. Ibid., 219.

41. Howorth, interview by author, Cleveland, Miss., 22 November 1985.

42. *Memphis Commercial Appeal,* 4 September 1922, A-50, folder 237, Somerville-Howorth Papers, AESL.

43. *Memphis Commercial Appeal,* 7 September 1922, A-50, folder 237, Somerville-Howorth Papers, AESL.

44. Lamkin to Lucy Somerville, [November 1922], Somerville-Howorth Papers.

45. Quoted in *Woman Voter,* 16 November 1922.

46. Ibid., 30 November 1922.

47. Ibid., 3 August 1922.

48. Martha Swain, "Organized Women in Mississippi: The Clash over Legal Disabilities in the 1920s," *Southern Studies* 23 (spring 1984): 91–102.

49. Brown-Somerville correspondence, 1922–23, A-50, folder 237, Somerville-Howorth Papers.

50. Brown, 8.

51. *Woman Voter,* 25 May 1923.

52. Brewer to Somerville, 1 January 1923, Somerville-Howorth Papers.

53. Brewer to Somerville, [June 1923], Somerville-Howorth Papers.

54. Prince, "Women, Politics, and the Press: The Mississippi *Woman Voter,*" *Southern Studies* 19 (winter 1980): 365–72.

55. *Woman Voter,* 4 May 1923.

56. Ibid.

57. Somerville to "My Dear Miss Annie," 18 May 1923, A-50, folder 237, Somerville-Howorth Papers.

58. Strite to Prince, 26 January 1980.

59. Brewer to registrar, 11 January 1924, Office of the Registrar, University of Wisconsin.

60. Brewer to W. D. Hiestand, 23 January 1924, Office of the Registrar, University of Wisconsin.

61. Brewer to Somerville, 11 December 1923, Somerville-Howorth Papers.

62. Brewer to Somerville, 13 June 1923, Somerville-Howorth Papers.

63. Ted Ownby, *American Dreams in Mississippi: Consumers, Poverty, and Culture, 1830–1998* (Chapel Hill: University of North Carolina Press, 1999), 140.

64. Strite to author, 27 January 1986.

65. Ibid.

66. Coleman, interview.

67. *Clarksdale City Directory,* 1936, Clarksdale Public Library.

68. Richard C. Cortner, *A 'Scottsboro' Case in Mississippi* (Jackson: University Press of Mississippi, 1986), xii.

69. Joel Williamson, *A Rage for Order: Black/White Relations in the American South Since Emancipation* (New York: Oxford University Press, 1986), 71, 236, 252.

70. *Woman Voter,* 28 September 1923.

71. Strite to author, 11 July 1986.

72. Howorth, interview by author, Cleveland, Miss., 31 May 1986. For the history of Mound Bayou and its connection to the utopian dream at Davis Bend plantation, see Janet Sharp Hermann, *The Pursuit of a Dream* (New York: Oxford University Press, 1981).

73. *Clarksdale City Directory,* 1939.

74. Polly Clark, telephone interview by author, 16 January 1986.

75. Ibid.; Tom Trotter Ross, telephone interview by author, 29 April 1987; Glenda Garst Bavier to author, 23 April 1987.

76. Strite to Howorth, [May 1939], A-50, folder 237, Somerville-Howorth Papers.

77. Ibid.

78. Hinds County Mississippi Chancery Court, Jackson, file no. 25,873.

79. Strite to Howorth, [May 1939].

80. Ibid.; Elaine Showalter, *The Female Malady: Women, Madness, and English Culture, 1830–1980* (New York: Pantheon Books, 1985), 59.

81. Howorth to Strite, 11 May 1939, Somerville-Howorth Papers.

82. Howorth, interview by author, Cleveland, Miss., 31 March 1986.

83. Coleman, interview.

84. Strite to author, 27 January 1986.

85. Jeffrey L. Geller and Maxine Harris, *Women of the Asylum: Voices from behind the Walls, 1840–1945* (New York: Doubleday, 1994), 249–55.

86. Earl Brewer to Howorth, 15 May 1939, Somerville-Howorth Papers.

87. Strite to author, 27 January 1986.

88. "Diagnostic Summary," n.d., case no. 17,784; "Transfer Note," 27 January 1940; "Year Note," 17 April 1940, Mississippi State Hospital, Whitfield, Miss.

89. Howorth, interview, 31 March 1986.

90. Fred Cheney to Walter Sillers, 2 November 1946, Hodding and Betty Werlein Carter Papers, series I, folder 1946, Special Collections, Mitchell Memorial Library, Mississippi State University, Starkville, Miss.

91. Dr. W. L. Jacquith, interview by John Griffin Jones and Martha Monaghan, Jackson, Miss., 20 March 1979, OH 80–03, 80–04, MDAH.

92. *Greenville Delta Democrat-Times,* 24 January 1947, 1.

93. *House Journal,* Mississippi legislature, special sess., March 1947, 4–15; *Senate Journal,* March 1947, 12–14.

94. Howorth, interview, 31 March 1986.

95. Showalter, 3.

96. Phyllis Chesler, *Women and Madness* (Garden City, N.Y.: Doubleday, 1972), 31, 16; Chesler, foreword to *Women of the Asylum,* by Geller and Harris, xxv.

97. Gregg Andrews, *Insane Sisters: Or the Price Paid for Challenging a Company Town* (Columbia: University of Missouri Press, 1999), 12.

98. Jacquith, interview.

99. Coleman, interview.

100. Strite to author, 16 May 1987.

101. Coleman, interview.

102. Strite to Prince, 11 March 1980.

103. "Return Note," 25 January 1956; "Transfer Note," 13 January 1970, Mississippi State Hospital.

104. Strite to author, 16 May 1987.

105. Milton Rosenbaum, "Similarities of Psychiatric Disorders of AIDS and Syphilis: History Repeats Itself," *Bulletin of the Menninger Clinic* 58 (summer 1994): 375–81. EPSCO Host, accessed 18 June 1999.

106. Howorth, interview by author, Cleveland, Miss., 3 December 1988.

107. Lesley A. Hall, "Syphilis as a Medical Problem and Moral Metaphor, 1880–1916" (London: Wellcome Institute for the History of Medicine, 1999), 1. EPSCO Host, accessed 17 June 1999.

108. Ibid., 2.

109. E. Sylvia Pankhurst, *The Suffragette Movement: An Intimate Account of Persons and Ideals* (New York: Longmans, 1931), 521.

110. Hall, 4.

111. Ibid., 5.

112. Rebecca West quoted in Hall, 5.

113. Hall, 5; Claude Quetel, *History of Syphilis,* trans. Judith Braddock and Brian Pike (Baltimore: Johns Hopkins University Press, 1990), 192.

114. Hall, 5.

115. Tennessee Williams, *A Streetcar Named Desire* (New York: Signet, 1964), 142.

116. *Woman Voter,* 4 January 1924.

117. Certificate of Death for Minnie Brewer, State of Mississippi, 1 June 1978.

118. Obituary for Minnie Brewer, *Clarksdale Press Register,* 2 June 1978, 2.

119. Howorth to Claudia Strite, 11 May 1939, A-50, folder 237, Somerville-Howorth Papers.

Eudora Welty

(1909–2001)

En Route to A Curtain of Green

SUZANNE MARRS

In 1931, after spending two years at the University of Wisconsin and another year at the Columbia University School of Business, twenty-two-year-old Eudora Welty returned to Jackson, Mississippi, to live—called back by her father's illness and by her own inability to find work in New York City. Shortly after her return, Welty's father died, and this devastating loss changed the course of her life. At a young age she came face to face with the transient nature of human existence and the powerful bonds and responsibilities of family life.

She would spend the next thirty-five years living with her mother in Jackson, and her life there would inevitably prove more restricted than it had been in Madison and Manhattan. Only on long trips could she go to the Cotton Club or Small's Paradise in Harlem, see an African American cast perform *Macbeth* under the direction of a young Orson Welles, take advantage of the Broadway stage, or stroll through exhibitions of Georgia O'Keeffe's paintings.[1] The artistic opportunities available in New York City obviously could not be matched in a southern town. And even Welty's trips back to New York—trips taken first in an attempt to find a job, then to sell her stories—would be tinged with guilt. Welty reported that whenever her train left Jackson for New York, "my mother was already writing to me at her desk, telling me she missed me but only wanted what was best for me. She would not leave the house till she had my wire, sent from Penn Station the third day from now, that I had arrived safely. I was not to worry about her or things at home, about how she was getting along. She anxiously awaited my letter after I had tried my stories on the publishers."[2]

EUDORA WELTY

1976. Wilson F. ("Bill") Minor Papers,
Special Collections Department, Mitchell Memorial Library,
Mississippi State University.

Her mother's anxiety troubled Welty, but her need to pursue a writing career was more compelling. As Welty has noted, "The torment and the guilt—the torment of having the loved one go, the guilt of being the loved one gone—comes into my fiction as it did and does into my life. And most of all the guilt then was because it was true: I had left to arrive at some future and secret joy, at what was unknown, and what was now in New York, waiting to be discovered. My joy was connected with writing; that was as much as I knew."[3] It was back in Jackson, however, where Welty wrote away, producing many a story that she saw as a failure. And perhaps those early, never-published stories *were* failures, because Welty had not yet discovered how to incorporate her most profound emotions, her sense of loss and guilt, into fiction. "The Children," an unpublished typescript probably written in 1934 and now held by the Mississippi Department of Archives and History, hints at a tension between mother and daughter, but that relationship is not developed. Such tensions would be fully developed in Welty's mature work, but the nature of those tensions is quite different from what many feminist scholars expect to see.

According to Carolyn Heilbrun, women of Welty's generation typically felt and repressed antagonisms toward a mother who supported the patriarchal family structure. Heilbrun writes,

> What was the function of mothers toward daughters before the current women's movement, before, let us say, 1970? Whatever the drawbacks, whatever the frustrations or satisfactions of the mother's life, her mission was to prepare the daughter to take her place in the patriarchal succession, that is, to marry, to bear children (preferably sons), and to encourage her husband to succeed in the world. But for many women, mothers and daughters alike, there moved in their imaginations dreams of some other life: of personal accomplishment, of the understanding and control of hard facts and complex problems, of a place in a community where women were in sufficient numbers to render the accomplished woman neither lonely nor an anomaly. Above all, the dream of taking control of one's life without the intrusion of a mother's patriarchal wishes for her daughter, without the danger of injuring the much loved and pitied mother.

A superficial examination of Eudora Welty's relationship with her mother might tend to support Heilbrun's view, or at least suggest that Mrs. Welty sought a socially appropriate role for her daughter. For instance, on 22 June 1930, the *Jackson Daily Clarion-Ledger* reported that "the handsome home of Mr. and Mrs. C. W. Welty, Pinehurst Place, was on Thursday afternoon at three-thirty o'clock the scene of beautiful entertaining when Mrs. Welty was hostess at eight tables of bridge honoring her attractive daughter Miss Eudora Welty." But such typical Jackson entertainments were highly unusual in the Welty household.[4]

The 1930 bridge party notwithstanding, conflicts between Eudora Welty and her mother were seldom based upon the expectation that Welty play a conventional female role but paradoxically stemmed from the deep love mother and daughter felt for each other. Chestina Welty desired to shield and protect her daughter from harm. That desire could be heroic and supportive: On the eve of surgery for breast cancer, Mrs. Welty attended her young daughter's piano recital, never mentioning the danger she faced. When as an adult Eudora Welty learned of her mother's act, she felt deep admiration and gratitude. But the very quality Welty loved and admired could also become oppressive. In 1937, for instance, Welty joined her friends John, Will, and Anna Belle Robinson for a car trip over primitive roads to Mexico City. Mrs. Welty had cautioned against the trip, not because it defied convention, but because it seemed dangerous, and Welty regretted how much her mother would worry while she was gone.

Mrs. Welty's worries were well founded, as it turned out. John Robinson was driving one day when a young Indian child darted into the path of the Jacksonians' car; the four stopped to care for the injured child and were ultimately investigated by the police. Welty had to phone her mother from the police station to request extra funds. The possibility of such events prompted the tensions between mother and daughter. The desire to protect each other, not disagreement about gender roles, was the source of conflict between the two.

Indeed, far from embracing the established social order, Chestina Welty herself was a model for defying convention. She was not as soft-spoken and indirect in manner as the typical Jackson lady. When asked to contribute to a missionary society, for example, she saw no reason for evasiveness in her reply. She did not wish, she simply said, to tell people in other countries what to think. If her outspoken ways were unusual, so were her activities. A member of the Research Club, Mrs. Welty joined because she believed in the value of the research projects members actually undertook; the more usual women's luncheon clubs were anathema to her. While conventional Jackson ladies might deprecatingly refer to intellectual girls as "brains," Chestina Welty, who had put herself through Marshall College, wanted her daughter to excel in academic endeavors and sought to support Eudora's friends who were trapped in families that did not have such ambitions for young women.

Though she loved to study her Bible and was a member of Galloway Methodist Church, Chestina Welty was not a regular churchgoer, even though church attendance was socially expected. And when Chestina Welty helped to establish Jackson's first garden club and served as its president, it was a "working, digging neighborhood group"—not a club for elaborate refreshments, stylish frocks, and pleasant conversation.[5] She thus violated in very basic ways the expectations that many Jacksonians held. Neither by word nor example did Chestina Welty pressure her daughter to adhere to convention. Eudora Welty was free to set her own course in life.

And set her own course she did. Like her mother, Welty was uninterested in most women's clubs and chose not to be active in a church. She did not make the appropriate marriage and was not pressured to. She attended concerts, including the occasional jazz artist appearance in a black movie house, patronized a black record shop, and photographed many black Mississippians. In addition, though Welty was not a political activist, she (along with her mother) cherished liberal sentiments that were held by a rather small minority in the overwhelmingly conservative South. Like many upper-middle-class Mississippians, she abhorred the very popular Theodore Bilbo's election, and she was proud when her friend Hubert Creekmore's letter criticizing Senator Bilbo was published in *Time* magazine on 22 October 1934. This political deviance, established early in Welty's life, would continue. Finally, Welty's unusual choice of a literary career, undertaken with her mother's support, also set her apart. As Anne Goodwyn Jones notes, despite an established tradition of writing among southern women, the " 'independent, self-declarative life of the writer' places the woman who writes into a special class that is in certain respects outside the norms of southern society."[6]

In certain respects, an "independent, self-declarative life" placed both Eudora Welty and her mother "outside the norms of southern society," and Welty's fiction provides a suggestive portrait of that common bond. Though Welty and her mother have quite rightly been associated with the mother and daughter in "The Winds," Chestina Welty might also be linked in spirit to the female cornetist of the story, for like the cornetist, Mrs. Welty provided her daughter with a vision of the "the other way to live."[7] (Interestingly enough, Chestina Welty actually played the cornet as a girl in West Virginia.) And Welty certainly draws upon her mother's "independent, self-declarative life" in "A Curtain of Green." In this story, the deep-seated connection between mother and daughter emerges from Welty's use of gardening, not as a conventional domestic activity but as a way of defying conventionality.

After the death of her husband, Chestina Welty found solace in the creative work of gardening, not in the social display of a garden. With Eudora as her interested and committed "yard man," she worked long hours among her plants and flowers, year after year, finding her evolving garden "to be satisfying, though never perfect." In fact, she found the garden to be satisfying because it was *never* perfect, because it was always a work in progress. It also served as a source of consolation for life's difficulties. As Mrs. Welty noted in a small (and never published) essay titled "The Perfect Garden," "The loved garden is always satisfyingly responsive to moods. It flaunts its colors joyously when we are glad, its peace and fragrance are soothing to frayed nerves when we are weary from contact or perhaps conflict with the everyday world, and its recurrent beauty whispers a message of comfort and hope when our hearts are lonely or sorrowful." But Chestina Welty found more than consolation in her garden. She found a creative activity, noting that "creating a garden is much like painting a picture or writing a poem, and artists and poets often make lovely gardens. But sometimes we less articulate folks, who can neither paint pictures nor write poems, yet feel the need of expressing ourselves, find a garden a very happy medium." What might be seen by some as a conventional domestic activity was far more for Chestina Welty. Her work in the garden was not unlike Eudora Welty's work in fiction.[8]

It seems somehow appropriate that the garden, which provided such a strong bond between mother and daughter, also provided a strong bond between Eudora Welty and her literary agent, Diarmuid Russell. Eudora Welty had her own passion for gardening, especially for growing camellias. She planted a wide variety of camellias in the Pinehurst Place yard and worked hard to see that they survived, stitching up covers to protect the young bushes from freezes. She even set up a sort of mininursery in the basement and worked at grafting the plants, and she sent Russell both camellia plants and suggestions for helping them flourish in Westchester County, New York. Russell, like the Welty women, was an avid gardener, and in his correspondence with Welty he talks about the state of his garden almost as much as he does the state of Welty's fiction. For both Welty and Russell, it seems, gardening and writing were linked at some profound level.

Welty makes this link explicit in "A Curtain of Green." In the story, the gardener, like the writer, confronts the dark irrationality of human experience and attempts to deal with that irrationality. Mrs. Larkin has seen her husband killed by a falling chinaberry tree and has realized that her love could not protect him. In the depths of her grief, she then ventures deeper and deeper into gardening, becoming "over-vigorous, disreputable, and heedless" in the eyes of her neighbors. Mrs. Larkin seeks not Chestina Welty's "well designed [garden] plot," but seeks "to allow an over-flowering"; in the process, she finds that the garden provides not solace but immersion in a hostile force. She finds herself on the brink of killing Jamey, whose hopeful essence has not yet been wounded, and seeks to penetrate and participate in the mystery of nature that has killed her husband and destroyed her faith in the power of love. But at day's end, she drops the hoe she had contemplated using as a weapon, and she finds release in the after-noon rain and in the garden's "quiet arcade of identity." Momentarily, at least, she accepts both nature's mystery and its beauty. Surely, Mrs. Larkin's isolation within her community, her grief, her venturing into the garden, and her discov-ery of some consolation there draw in oblique ways upon Chestina Welty's own experience. Mrs. Larkin's love, which like Chestina Welty's seeks to but cannot protect the beloved, sprang from a key source of tension between Welty and her mother, but the story found its starting point in the depth of Mrs. Welty's love for her husband, in her abiding grief at his loss (a grief that loomed over a concerned daughter), in her intellectual and creative toughness, and in her inability to retreat into a mindlessly conventional consolation.[9]

In *One Writer's Beginnings,* Welty writes that "all serious daring starts from within," but she also shows that her inner life was nourished by a mother who was a model of serious daring.[10] Eudora Welty was extremely fortunate, as are we her readers, that she found that model first thing and at home. She also found at home a group of friends who exemplified intellectual daring in many ways and who supported her work in fiction. As Howard Gardner observes in his distinguished study of creative people ranging from Albert Einstein to Martha Graham, "creators" typically need a "special relation to one or more supportive individuals." Eventually, in Welty's case, this role would be played, as Michael Kreyling's *Author and Agent* has so persuasively shown, by Diarmuid Russell. But Welty did not meet Russell until 1940, and prior to that time, his supportive role was filled by a number of Welty's friends who lived in Jackson or who regularly returned there for visits. Friends like Aimee Shands, Leone Shotwell, Mary Frances Horne, and Joe Skinner had, like Welty, returned from Columbia University's graduate schools. And Jackson was also home to artists Karl Wolfe, William Hollingsworth, and Helen Jay Lotterhos, all of whom were Welty's friends and one of whom literally led her to a story. Indeed, as Welty tagged along on a Lotterhos sketching trip, she saw the woman who prompted her to create Phoenix Jackson and "A Worn Path." Even more important support perhaps came from Frank Lyell, Lehman Engel, Nash Burger, Hubert Creek-more, and John Robinson, who provided Welty with an easy, good-humored, imaginatively stimulating community in which to begin writing and with ad-vice, encouragement, and friendship throughout her career.[11]

Frank Lyell earned a doctorate in English from Princeton University, taught first at North Carolina State University and then at the University of Texas at Austin, traveled widely, and was an aficionado of fine food, opera, and theater throughout his life. Lehman Engel left Jackson to study music at the Cincin-nati College-Conservatory, went on to New York City, and became an important composer of concert music and of incidental music for the stage, a choral conductor, and a music director for the Broadway stage. Nash Burger took a master's degree in English from the University of Virginia, taught English at Jackson's Central High School, and went on to become an editor for the *New York Times Book Review.* Hubert Creekmore, a graduate of the University of Mississippi, studied playwriting with George Pierce Baker at Yale University, worked for the Mississippi Highway Department, wrote scripts for local theatrical productions, and eventually settled in New York City, where he was an editor, a literary agent, and an author in his own right. He published three novels and several volumes of poetry. John Robinson, with whom Welty was for many years romantically involved and who was her longtime friend, graduated from Jackson's Central High School and from the University of Mississippi, worked in New Orleans as an adjuster for an insurance company, returned from World War II to study at the University of California, published stories in *Harper's* and the *New Yorker,* went to Italy on a Fulbright grant, and eventually settled there.

This group of friends had many good times together, viewing their own world with the affection, imagination, and irony that would eventually characterize such Welty stories as "Why I Live at the P.O.," "Lily Daw and the Three Ladies," "Petrified Man," and "Old Mr. Marblehall." Lyell, Creekmore, Engel, and Welty were all in residence in Jackson for a number of summers early in the thirties. Engel reports that "each summer all of us went home to swelter. . . . There were about five such summers before I began staying on in New York with work to occupy and to pay me. But at home Frank [Lyell], Eudora, Hubert Creekmore, and I used to meet at Eudora's, and we formed what we called the Night-Blooming Cereus Club, the total membership of which sat up to see the glorious white flower with the yellow feathery center bloom." Lyell, Creekmore, Engel, and Welty named themselves in the camp spirit of their summer activities. In those days Jackson ladies would advertise the coming bloom of a cereus in the newspaper and invite anyone interested to drop by for the blooming. This group, observing the admonition "Don't take it 'cereus,' life's too mysterious" (turning on the lyric from Rudy Vallee's "Life Is Just a Bowl of Cherries"), visited one open house where a lady informed them that in the morning the flowers would look like "wrung chickens' necks." Years later, in "The Wanderers," Welty would use "the naked, luminous, complicated" cereus as an emblem of life's beauty and its brevity, and she would have an old country woman tell Virgie Rainey that "tomorrow it'll look like a wrung chicken's neck." But in the early thirties none of the Night-Blooming Cereus Club members anticipated such symbolic implications of their activities. For them the cereus was and remained an emblem of good fellowship, of the pleasure imaginative individuals could share if they embraced the world around them. In 1956, recalling the happy past and hoping that a dramatization of *The Ponder Heart* would meet with success, Engel sent Welty on opening night the closest thing he could find to a cereus bloom, and when Welty later used the cereus as an image in *Losing Battles,* she informed Engel she had done so for him.[12]

These friends lived up to their motto; they did not take their society too seriously. They mocked an emphasis upon beauty and cosmetics when Frank Lyell photographed Welty, in a Helena Rubinstein pose, about to apply pea soup, shoe polish, and household cleansers to her face. And they mocked the stock elements of literary romance when Lehman Engel photographed a disdainful Welty in a Spanish shawl being courted by a devoted Lyell in a sombrero; Welty was, Engel asserts in his autobiography, "the unwitting inventor of camp."[13]

Comic sensibilities notwithstanding, these friends were serious about the importance of the arts, even the comic ones. They loved to talk about literature and the theater—and they did more than talk. Creekmore was a published writer before Welty. He kept a long and detailed record of his submissions to a wide variety of periodicals and established a literary magazine. He and Burger were contributors to the one issue of Creekmore's own *Southern Review* (1934), though Welty was relegated to the staff. Three years later, Welty would join Creekmore, Burger, and Peter Taylor on equal terms in contributing stories to another local publication—Dale Mullen's *River* magazine in Oxford, Mississippi.

Welty's friendships fostered an already well-established love of travel. Creekmore, Welty recalled, was the hub of a group she labeled Jackson–in–New York, and this group enjoyed the hospitality of fellow Mississippians like editor Herschel Brickell and actress Ruth Ford. Welty visited New York once or twice a year after leaving Columbia, attending concerts and the theater, taking advantage of art museums and the New York Public Library.[14] And in 1937 Welty joined John Robinson and his siblings on a trip to Mexico. As a traveler, then, Welty knew far more freedom than a southern woman earlier in the twentieth century might have. Although her early unpublished stories do not deal with journeys, Welty's travels in the 1930s reinforced an emotion that had long been hers. During childhood trips to West Virginia, Welty had discovered "a fierce independence that was suddenly mine, to remain inside no matter how it scared me when I tumbled," and this association of travel and independence would eventually find its way into Welty's fiction, into stories of travelers who are free to break from established roles and create their own identities.[15]

As one might expect, the group with whom Welty socialized and traveled was positively disposed toward her career as a writer and toward the creative endeavors of women generally. Creekmore recommended that Welty submit "Death of a Traveling Salesman" and "Magic" to *Manuscript,* which readily accepted both stories for publication. Burger had written a master's thesis about Sherwood Bonner, the first serious woman writer in Mississippi, a woman who violated all sorts of conventions to pursue her career. It was no surprise that he supported Welty in her efforts at fiction. And as years went by, Welty would correspond with Robinson, Lyell, and Engel about her literary endeavors and would value their advice. These friends, in turn, found themselves sustained and supported by Welty. In 1969, Burger recalled her devotion to the arts and to artists during his adult years in Jackson: "The large Welty home on Pinehurst, which had succeeded the earlier house near Davis School, became the center of a swarm of local writers and would-be writers, journalists, painters, practitioners in all the arts and just plain friends and disciples. All were attracted by Eudora's unflagging interest, hospitality, humor and often long-tried good manners."[16]

Welty and her friends maintained both their close emotional and professional ties with each other and their identities as southerners, but in many ways they were highly critical of southern life. Engel recalled that being a Jew and being a boy who played the piano brought him the scorn of many high school classmates.[17] Creekmore would voice his objections to a destructive class system in *The Welcome* and to race prejudice in *The Chain in the Heart,* while Welty would make the oppressive power of racism an implicit part of "Powerhouse," "A Worn Path," and "Keela, the Outcast Indian Maiden."

Furthermore, in a number of stories, Welty, Creekmore, and Robinson would go on to describe the plight of poor, rural white southerners. Welty especially, because she chose to remain in Mississippi as many of her friends departed, would come to know a great deal about Mississippi poverty, black and white, and about the resources, material and spiritual, with which Mississippians combated it. After her father died, Welty felt the effects of the Great Depression firsthand, though the Welty family remained relatively affluent by Mississippi standards. The insurance policies and Lamar Life Insurance stock that Christian Webb Welty had expected to secure his family from financial worry failed to do so. During the course of the Depression, Welty and her mother took in a boarder—Miss Fannye Cook, head of the Mississippi Wildlife Museum. Edward Welty, Eudora's brother, designed and built a duplex on the large Pinehurst Place lot where the family home was already located. The duplex generated income for his mother, and Mrs. Welty briefly gave bridge lessons as a way of further enhancing the family finances. And of course daughter Eudora worked at the WJDX radio station, then for the Works Progress Administration (WPA), and later for the Mississippi Advertising Commission, writing society columns for the *Memphis Commercial Appeal* along the way. But these financial hard times were mild indeed compared to the economic suffering Welty observed elsewhere around Mississippi.

During the months she spent working for the WPA, publicizing its 1936 projects about the state, Welty encountered a poverty she had never known as an upper-class white Mississippian. Both whites and blacks in Depression-era Mississippi knew the physically and spiritually debilitating effects of poverty—though poverty in Mississippi was a longtime condition, not a recent development. Welty's photographs of this period document the tattered clothing, shabby housing, hard work, and unbroken spirits that characterized Mississippi in the thirties. Her stories like "Death of a Traveling Salesman," "The Hitch-Hikers," "Clytie," "A Worn Path," "A Piece of News," and "The Whistle" tell us of the primitive roads, ramshackle hotels, dogtrot houses, oil lamps, open hearths for cooking and heating, and desperation that were often typical of rural and small-town Mississippi life. In 1930 Mississippi had the nation's lowest ten-year average for farm income and the nation's lowest average for days spent in school; in the thirties 50 to 90 percent of children in large areas of the South suffered from an inadequate diet; and in 1930 Mississippi had fewer than ten physicians for every ten thousand citizens. James Loewen and Charles Sallis, in vividly describing the lives of Mississippi sharecroppers, give us some indication of what Welty was seeing during her WPA work.

> Most of the unpainted wooden houses . . . had only three rooms. With families of from five to fifteen people living in them, the houses were terribly crowded. Few houses had screens and almost none had indoor plumbing. Sharecroppers usually heated their homes with wood or coal stoves.
>
> The sharecropper's diet centered around flour, cornmeal, sorghum, salt pork, lard, and dry peas. Many sharecroppers tried to grow vegetables to improve their diet, but some landowners discouraged gardening because they preferred to use the land for cotton. A better-than-average sharecropper's menu included other items such as chitterlings ("chitlins"), rabbit, molasses, butter, milk, and sweet potato pie. The poorest sharecroppers, however, lived on only two meals a day—rice, cornbread, and coffee for breakfast, and peas and cornbread for dinner.[18]

Such conditions were the ones Welty came to know, to photograph, and to write about. Her story "The Whistle" in particular indicts a one-crop, cash-crop tenant farming system for destroying the lives of tenant farmers. But Welty's WPA work had taught her that the desperate plight of tenant farmers did not unrelentingly typify all of Mississippi's poor, and her photographs of Mississippi offer cause for hope. They often focus upon individual faces, upon expressions of joy despite economic oppression. The temperate climate of Mississippi and the possibility even for those living in town to plant gardens, own chickens, maybe even have a cow—these factors meliorated the effects of poverty in an essentially rural state as they could not in a northeastern urban center. So too did the smallness of Mississippi's population. As Welty writes in the introduction to *One Time, One Place:* "In New York there had been the faceless breadlines; on Farish Street in my home town of Jackson, the proprietor of the My Blue Heaven Café had written on the glass of the front door with his own finger dipped in window polish: 'AT 4:30 AM WE OPEN OUR DOORS. WE HAVE NO CERTAIN TIME TO CLOSE. THE COOK WILL BE GLAD TO SERVE U. WITH A 5 *And* 10¢ STEW.' The message was personal and particular. More than what is phenomenal, that strikes home. It happened to me everywhere I went, and I took these pictures."[19] And in stories like "Death of a Traveling Salesman" and "A Worn Path," poverty is a backdrop, a limiting but not a controlling factor, in the lives of her characters who find sources of meaning and fulfillment despite economic deprivation.

As Welty has noted, Mississippi was not the only place where she saw people afflicted by unemployment and poverty. Probably in 1935 or 1936, on one of her regular visits to New York City, she photographed rather ordinary-looking people who during traditional business hours were sitting on Union Square park benches or gathering for protests because they had no jobs to occupy their days and provide them with purpose and sustenance. These photographs seldom focus upon a single face but instead depict numerous individuals typically overshadowed by massive city buildings. Welty sensed that the impersonal, concrete-and-steel world of the city was in some sense responsible for the suffering she saw all about her, and her relatively faceless pictures of the city's unemployed suggest the anonymity they experienced. As Welty told interviewers Hunter Cole and Seetha Srinivasan in 1989, "These people of the Great Depression kept alive on the determination to get back to work and to make a living again. I photographed them in Union Square and in subways and sleeping in subway stations and huddling together to keep warm, and I felt, then, sort of placed in the editorial position as I took their pictures. Recording the mass of them did constitute a plea on their behalf to the public, their existing plight being so evident in the mass."[20]

The same city that offered the relatively affluent Welty a vital personal and cultural life, she realized, denied others both the physical and emotional means to exist. She would write about this situation in her story "Flowers for Marjorie," showing the desperation that the city, with its massive population, impersonality, and distance from the natural world bring to Howard and Marjorie, who have migrated north from Victory, Mississippi. The effects of the Great Depression, Welty recognized, spanned the nation from farm to city.

Welty's focus upon race and poverty and her decision to become a writer point toward two paradoxes that seem central to her achievement. Paradox one: Though being a writer, especially a writer who focused upon poverty and racial discrimination, set Welty apart from most upper-class white Mississippians, it did not leave her isolated or alienated in her community. For earlier women writers this might have been the case. Jones certainly believes it was, and in *Tomorrow Is Another Day: The Woman Writer in the South, 1859–1936*, she discusses the way many of these women resorted to subterfuge rather than openly defying convention. For the woman who cherished an independent habit of mind in a South that expected "dependence, submission, and deference" from its women, Jones argues, the life of a writer had special advantages. Fiction provided a "way to circumvent the barrier between private thought and public utterance, between diary and platform." Jones thus concludes that "fiction can become a strategy for speaking truths publicly."[21]

Eudora Welty's Jackson, however, did not expect the degree of "dependence, submission, and deference" that the South may once have demanded of its women. In Welty's South, as in England, a good deal of eccentricity was tolerated and even welcomed, especially within class boundaries. As many a southerner has said, "the only sin is being boring." Southern students often relished going North to school so that they might be "characters"; in the South their relatively slight eccentricities had caused no stir. William B. Hamilton, Welty's friend and a Mississippian who taught history at Duke University, referred to the South as "the last stronghold of eccentricity." At the very least, we should note that this South was not a monolith. As John Shelton Reed has observed, neither the southern city nor the small southern town was "simply one community": "The two racial groupings are only the most obvious of the many subcommunities within most southern towns, subcommunities with the ability to mind their own business and to cooperate when circumstances require. The monolithic small-town community may be a New England or a Midwestern phenomenon, but the southern reality has usually been more complicated than that."[22] Southerners, Reed notes, object not so much to differences as to the attempt to convince them that they should do differently. Reed does not directly address the freedom enjoyed by women, but he suggests that women were often able to be both socially acceptable and unconventional in behavior. This is not to say that Welty was radically unconventional or ill at ease with the code of behavior the upper-class South held dear. She valued good manners, graciousness, concern for the feelings of others, and she was quite gentle in

manner. Indeed, Welty was willing to grant her friends the freedom to differ
from her views just as they were willing to return that favor. Yet though she
would not be willing to violate the rules of hospitality and begin a controversy
at a dinner party given by friends of opposing philosophies, Welty was quite able
to speak openly and frankly in less social situations. Except for occasions during
the racially tense sixties, Mississippi provided Welty with a place from which to
write, not in an atmosphere of hostility, but in an atmosphere of acceptance
even as she challenged society's assumptions.

Paradox two: Even as she wrote about the destructive effects of poverty and
racism, Welty experienced the exhilarating power of the imagination. When
she turned seriously to writing, she drew upon her imagination to transform
the world of Mississippi into her own fictional world—one removed from the
randomness of daily experience, a world that would be shaped by and centered
upon issues she deemed crucial. As she would later write in her essay "Place in
Fiction": "The writer must accurately choose, combine, superimpose upon, blot
out, shake up, alter the outside world for one absolute purpose, the good of his
story. To do this, he is always seeing double, two pictures at once in his frame,
his and the world's, a fact that he constantly comprehends; and he works best
in a state of constant and subtle and unfooled reference between the two. It is
his clear intention—his passion, I should say—to make the reader see only one
of the pictures—the author's—under the pleasing illusion that it is the world's;
this enormity is the accomplishment of a good story."[23] As she set about creating
her own fictional worlds, Welty focused upon issues that were often disheart-
ening, but the creative process itself brought her tremendous joy. Indeed, for
Welty, the life of the imagination was always one of joy. When an interviewer
once observed that "you clearly derive more pleasure from the act of writing
than do a good many authors," Welty's response was unequivocal: "I love writing! I love it."[24] And in the 1930s, as Welty was discovering the pleasures writing
would bring to her, she was also coming to believe that a shared act of imagination, however temporary, could be a source of meaning for people like the
simpleminded Ruby Fisher and her husband Clyde in "A Piece of News," the
desperate sharecroppers Jason and Sara Morton in "The Whistle," and the mu-
sician Powerhouse and his audiences, both black and white, in "Powerhouse."
The imagination that Welty found to be her greatest joy she also found to be her
pervasive theme in *A Curtain of Green,* the book in which she collected these and
other stories written between 1936 and 1940.

What forces transformed a bright young college graduate into a major
writer? No one can adequately answer that question. But Eudora Welty's mother,

her circle of friends, and her community combined to provide an environment in which her imagination could flourish, could transcend convention and conventional beliefs, and could take its own course. The Mississippi world in which she lived and a job that took her out into it sparked that imagination. And the pleasures of the imagination led Welty to make those pleasures a central thematic issue in her first book of fiction.

NOTES

1. The biographical information here and throughout much of this chapter comes from interviews and conversations that the author had with Eudora Welty, conversations and interviews dating from 1983 until Welty's death in 2001.

2. Eudora Welty, *One Writer's Beginnings* (Cambridge, Mass.: Harvard University Press, 1984), 94.

3. Ibid.

4. Carolyn Heilbrun, *Writing a Woman's Life* (New York: W. W. Norton, 1988), 118–19; "Miss Eudora Welty Honored at Beautiful Bridge Party of Eight Congenial Tables," *Jackson Daily Clarion-Ledger,* 22 June 1930.

5. Eudora Welty, written comments on draft of an unpublished lecture by Suzanne Marrs, 19 September 1990, Marrs's personal collection.

6. Anne Goodwyn Jones, *Tomorrow Is Another Day: The Woman Writer in the South, 1859–1936* (Baton Rouge: Louisiana State University Press, 1981), 39.

7. Eudora Welty, "Moon Lake," *The Golden Apples* (New York: Harcourt, Brace, 1949), 138.

8. Chestina Welty, "The Perfect Garden," photocopy, Marrs's personal collection, 2–3, 1.

9. Eudora Welty, "A Curtain of Green," *A Curtain of Green* (New York: Doubleday, Doran, 1941), 208, 209, 214.

10. Eudora Welty, *One Writer's Beginnings,* 104.

11. Howard Gardner, *Creating Minds: An Anatomy of Creativity Seen through the Lives of Freud, Einstein, Picasso, Stravinsky, Eliot, Graham, and Ghandi* (New York: Basic Books, 1993), 369.

12. Eudora Welty, "The Wanderers," *The Golden Apples,* 235; Lehman Engel, *This Bright Day: An Autobiography* (New York: Macmillan, 1974), 40; Eudora Welty to Lehman Engel, 3 August 1956, 5 August 1970, Engel Papers, Millsaps College, Jackson, Miss.

13. Eudora Welty, *Photographs* (Jackson: University Press of Mississippi, 1989), xxi, xx; Engel, 41.

14. Eudora Welty to Suzanne Marrs, n.d., Marrs's personal collection.

15. Eudora Welty, *One Writer's Beginnings,* 60.

16. Nash K. Burger, "Eudora Welty's Jackson," *Shenandoah* 20, no. 3 (1969): 13.

17. Engel, 23.

18. Statistics from Howard Odum, *Southern Regions* (Chapel Hill: University of North Carolina Press, 1936), 20, 51–53, 103, 370; James W. Loewen and Charles Sallis, *Mississippi Conflict and Change,* rev. ed. (New York: Pantheon Books, 1980), 204.

19. Eudora Welty, *One Time, One Place* (New York: Random House, 1971), 3.

20. Hunter McKelva Cole and Seetha Srinivasan, "Eudora Welty and Photography: An Interview," in *More Conversations with Eudora Welty,* ed. Peggy W. Prenshaw (Jackson: University Press of Mississippi, 1996), 194–95.

21. Jones, 39.

22. Eudora Welty, written comments on draft of an unpublished lecture by Suzanne Marrs; John Shelton Reed, *One South: An Ethnic Approach to Regional Culture* (Baton Rouge: Louisiana State University Press, 1982), 178–79.

23. Eudora Welty, "Place in Fiction," *The Eye of the Story* (New York: Random House, 1979), 124–25.

24. Scot Haller, "Creators on Creating," in *Conversations with Eudora Welty,* ed. Prenshaw, 314.

Part Three

Extending Rights

Perhaps no other state has witnessed such radical transformations as has Mississippi in the last half of the twentieth century. The twin revolutions of feminism and the civil rights movement of the 1960s have reshaped the state's racial, social, and gender hierarchies. Today, Mississippi has more black elected officials than any other state in the country. Now, in many middle-class and lower-middle-class families, both black and white, women's education and income are higher than that of their spouses.

In the last half of the twentieth century, Mississippi moved from an agricultural to a diversified economy, with timber replacing cotton as the primary export. In pace with the rest of the nation, the state's women joined the labor force at a vigorous rate, with the percentage of women in the workplace still rising. Women have entered every arena of public and professional life, and this change has had an especially important consequence for African American women. Whereas most of Mississippi's black women labored in the cotton fields and in the homes of white women well into the 1950s, the opportunity to enter the state's factories that began in the 1960s profoundly changed the lives of many working-class black women.

With the coming of feminism in the 1960s, the supremacy of the Mississippi State College for Women (MSCW) as the arbiter of middle-class white women's culture in the state was diffused. Like most women's schools throughout the country, the "W" after the 1960s suffered from lost enrollment and diminished influence. White women in the late 1960s began entering schools of divinity, engineering, medicine, law, and pharmacy at rates that by the end of the century in some fields outranked that of males. At the same time, desegregation of the state universities and colleges that began with the University of Mississippi in 1962 meant that many African American women gained access to a wide range of occupations.

This gain, however, has taken place against a backdrop of substantial numbers of women being left behind. Mississippi is, in fact, an exaggeration of national trends, with its richest becoming richer and its poor remaining poor. Poverty, lack of medical care, and inadequate education often entrap single mothers and their children into a second-class status that deprives them of their full citizenship.

Mississippi's most interesting and creative citizens have always been its loyal dissenters. Embodying a fierce love for the state's people and places, these individuals stood on the promises of Mississippi's best instincts by fighting against the cruelties of the state's rigid hierarchies and arbitrary power. Often driven by a religious vision of the sanctity of the individual and with a strong sense of being called to make a difference, these allies of justice and dignity called forth new possibilities. As transformers of those possibilities into realities, the six women chosen for this last section helped bring about changes that most Mississippians now welcome. In initiating these changes, African American women took center stage, and it is for this reason that five of these six chapters focus on the biographies of black women.

Sadye Wier's life is representative of those of many Mississippi women, both black and white, who devoted their lives to teaching or Extension work. Such women worked undramatically but emphatically to improve the lives of those to whom they felt responsible. In Wier's particular case, she deftly traversed the jungle of contradictions that defined race and gender in a small southern town. Professor John F. Marszalek knew Wier personally. With profound appreciation, he casts his historian's eye on the complications and contradictions of Wier's life as a black woman living in a white neighborhood on the edge of the (until 1965) white university campus at which he taught.

Hazel Brannon Smith, the only white woman in this section, was chosen in part because Smith's life captures from 1954 to 1968 the metamorphosis that many white women in Mississippi experienced over a period of several decades. Without intending to put herself into a position that would call for such radical self-definition, Smith, as a newspaper publisher and journalist, was faced with difficulties that forced her to make her often-unconscious assumptions explicit. With no ambition to become a hero, she changed her actions and policies because her religious faith and her professionalism converged to take her into new terrain. Having viewed the promised land of equal justice for all, she could not turn back.

Margaret Walker Alexander was not born in Mississippi, but she chose to become a Mississippian because she knew her creativity was directly tied to the intergenerational stories of southern African Americans. She wanted to hear in the rhythm of her daily life the cadence of the voices she remembered from her childhood's stories. In writing about those stories and giving them a voicing form, she demanded dignity for the folklore and oral history of African Americans. In so doing, she bestowed us all with a sacred trust.

Historians of the civil rights movement now agree that African American women were at the heart of that struggle. Men like Martin Luther King Jr., Stokely Carmichael, and Medgar Evers often dominated the spotlight, becoming familiar faces on the evening news. But it was women like Fannie Lou Hamer, Mae Bertha Carter, and Vera Mae Pigee who did the daily work. Often by recruiting and mentoring young people, answering correspondence, and attending to daily organizational chores, these women drove the movement. We are especially happy to offer these three chapters on women who, each in her own way and style, helped to define the civil rights movement in Mississippi.

Sadye Wier

(1905–1995)

A Life of Independence and Service

JOHN F. MARSZALEK

She was a black woman who was born and spent the majority of her life in segregated Mississippi. She had the advantage of life among the black middle class, what sociologist E. Franklin Frazier would later critically call the "black bourgeoisie," the black elite who, he said, felt superior to the black masses.[1] Both her father and mother were college graduates, and later they founded a Booker T. Washington–style school in the hill country of Mississippi. She and all her brothers and sisters were college graduates and succeeded in the segregated world that defined the South the first half of the twentieth century. Like her entire family, Sadye Hunter Wier never gained fame or fortune, but her life of service in the public schools, the Mississippi State Cooperative Extension Service, and a variety of volunteer positions resulted in her having a significant influence on black Mississippi and, after the 1960s, on the integrated state. She was a living example of ability, drive, hard work, and achievement to both white and black Mississippians. In her nonthreatening yet determined manner, she provided a role model for both races and positively influenced the perceptions of black and white Mississippians regarding African American potential.

Wier's father was Samuel J. Hunter, a native of Pine Bluff, Arkansas, born there in 1865 just after the end of the Civil War. Whether his parents were slaves or not is uncertain, but they must have experienced hard times in the years of Reconstruction. When Hunter was a young boy, his mother had to give him up to the care of a Memphis dentist. This black professional provided the lad with a high school education and then matriculation in LeMoyne Owen College. Hunter graduated from that Memphis school as valedictorian in 1886.[2]

Wier's mother was Minnie Lane, born in Macon, Mississippi, in 1869 and herself an 1887 graduate of LeMoyne Owen. On 27 December 1887, Lane and Hunter were married in Macon's Second Baptist Church. Afterwards, they settled down in Memphis. Samuel Hunter became a teacher, rising to the position of principal of Booker T. Washington School in Memphis, and Minnie Hunter, while taking care of a growing family, taught school as well.

Six children eventually resulted from this union. Three sons all graduated from Fisk University in Nashville and became teachers. Three daughters, all college graduates destined for professional careers, followed. The family later took in five other children, all of whom similarly achieved success in life.[3] The financial pressure of his growing family forced Samuel Hunter to seek more remunerative work. Looking for economic opportunity as well as a way to help others, he decided to found his own school some six miles east of his wife's hometown of Macon, Mississippi, in a small crossroads community known as McLeod. There on 3 December 1905 Sadye Wilhemina Hunter was born, the fifth child in a family firmly entrenched in the Mississippi black belt and committed to the education of the black people in the region.[4]

Hunter's educational institution was called the Noxubee Industrial School and was clearly modeled after Booker T. Washington's Tuskegee Institute.[5] Like Washington, Samuel Hunter was not interested in providing black youth with a classical college education. Washington, Hunter, and others like them wanted black people to receive a practical education that would allow them to survive in the hostile southern social and economic environment of the time. Hunter's Methodist training also influenced his philosophy. He phrased it this way in the school's 1914–15 catalog: "The aim is not a college education but thoroughness in the English branches and to make good, useful Christian citizens of our boys and girls. Our object and aim is to educate the head, cultivate the heart and train the hand." He hoped, he said, to "stem the tide" of "young Negroes . . . leaving the farm by the thousands and flocking to the cities and towns."[6]

Starting a school in one of the poorest areas of the nation was not easy. Having little money of his own and receiving little black or white help in Mississippi, Hunter realized that funding would have to come from the North. Like Booker T. Washington, he regularly traveled there to tap the region's black and white financial sources.[7]

"Students are admitted at any time and almost all ages after six years are past," the catalogue read. Admission cost was fifty cents and board was $5.25 a month. Tuition was free, but everyone had to work. At first the student body was small, but over time it increased so that in the 1914–15 academic year there were 172 students from the first through the equivalent of the tenth grade.

SADYE WIER

circa 1970. Robert and Sadye Wier Papers.

Special Collections Department, Mitchell Memorial Library,

Mississippi State University.

Not coincidentally, the term, 15 October to the last Friday in April, fit neatly between the end of the cotton harvest and planting time, a period when the children of African American farmers were not so sorely needed at home. Another 140 students were "classed as BEGINNERS." The regular students studied the usual elementary school subjects, but there was always an element of "Needle Work," "Cooking and Gardening," and "Agriculture," too. In order to graduate, "the girls must pass a satisfactory examination in Domestic Science, including house-keeping. Boys [must pass an examination] in Agriculture, both theory and practice." Black men and women both had distinctly subordinate roles to play in early-twentieth-century American society, and Hunter's school tried to prepare them for their limited place—men as laborers, women as housekeepers.[8]

In 1914–15, Samuel Hunter was principal and taught industrial science. His wife taught sewing and, beginning sometime after 1910, spent many days away from home as an Anna T. Jeanes Fund Extension Teacher, in which role she helped neighboring blacks improve their houses and home life. The young Sadye Hunter quickly became part of this black self-help educational community. McLeod, Mississippi, was a tiny hamlet on a dirt road, now known as Highway 14, six miles east of Macon and eight miles from the Alabama state line. In addition to the school, there were three stores, a cotton gin, a gristmill, and a post office. Both whites and blacks lived in the area, but they had little to do with each other, the whites apparently willing to allow the small black school to exist because it did not threaten the existing segregation system. In fact, Wier later could not recall any contact with the white people of McLeod, spending all her time on the school property. When she was five years old, she began attending classes. At 3:30 P.M., when the vast majority of the students left to go to their nearby homes, she stood at the institution's gate waving goodbye.[9]

She was a precocious child during all of her educational career in McLeod. In the seventh grade, she won the school-wide competition for the $2.50 Featherston Prize, a monetary reward for scholastic performance. In April 1916 when she was only ten years old, she was already in the eighth grade. Standing at the very top of her class, she was obviously among the best students in the entire school. She excelled not only academically, but also vocationally, although her enthusiasm got her in trouble at least once. Sadye was zealously working on a quilt one day, using any fabric she could find anywhere. "And one piece happened to be the sleeve of a dress my mother was making for a lady," she later remembered. "I got a whipping for it, too," she laughed.[10]

In the fall of 1916, she began high school at what today is Mary Holmes College in West Point, Mississippi, just north of Macon. She registered in both the teacher preparation department and as a piano pupil, but she did not like it there. That same year she transferred to Fisk College in Nashville. The climate, however, proved too cold for her, and she did not have the proper clothes to withstand it. In truth, the competition at these schools was greater than that which she had experienced at her father's institution, making the academic climate chilly as well. She moved to Talladega College in Alabama, an institution with a student population of less than two hundred, and like her father's school, located in a rural area. She thought that she would feel more at home there. She was right. In the warmer South and with more personal attention, she prospered and finished her high school and college education, graduating in 1923 at the age of eighteen.[11]

The president of Talladega was a white man, Frederick A. Sumner, who had most recently been a minister in Connecticut and was now a student favorite. Hunter became close friends with his daughter and frequently went to the president's house for meals or to sleep over. During at least one Christmas break, when she could not afford a trip back to Macon, Hunter stayed with the Sumner family over Christmas Eve and had dinner there the next day.

Most of her college career was not that privileged, however. Because she had so little money, Hunter got up at 5:00 A.M. to work as a waitress in the student dining hall, and later she helped supervise the dishwashing crews. For about four months during her career at Talladega, she waited on the tables where the football players ate. It was hard work because "by the time you set down a tray of food they would have it gone in a few minutes and you would have to go back and get some more." But their food was better than that of the nonathlete students, so she ate well herself. She never developed any romantic interest in any of these young men because she was determined not to have anything "take my mind off my lessons." Her father had died in 1918, so the financial pressures on her were great. "I've always been an independent woman, to do for myself," she remembered many years later.[12]

In the summers during her college years, Hunter worked in a Memphis drugstore during the day and was the piano player in a combo of four black and five white male musicians at night. The group played in both black and white establishments, some of them dives. The band was not infrequently arrested in a police raid. Whenever there was any hint of trouble, the male band members sent Hunter home, but she still suffered arrest on a few occasions. The band played jazz and other popular music of that age, and then and later, Sadye Hunter Wier was proud of her musical ability. As an older woman, she liked to recall humorously that, in her prime, she could "rock your soul from the bosom of Abraham."[13]

She returned to the Noxubee Industrial School in 1923 to teach home economics. At that time, her brother Lawrence was nominally in charge of the family school. He had taken over that responsibility after their father's death, with the exception of the time he served in the U.S. army during World War I, when their mother took on that task.[14]

Sadye Hunter briefly helped out in Macon, but her determination to improve her status in life drove her to new challenges. Beginning in the fall of 1923, she spent a year each as an elementary or secondary teacher at schools in Okolona, Aberdeen, and Shuqualak, Mississippi. Then she went to Starkville for three years, followed by two more one-year stints in Senatobia and Grenada. In 1932, after having spent several summers visiting her sister Vera, a Mississippi Cooperative Extension Service Negro Home Demonstration Agent in Starkville, Sadye Hunter married Robert Wier, a leader in the black community in the home city of what today is Mississippi State University.[15]

Sadye Hunter's marriage to Robert Wier was a defining moment in her life. He provided opportunities for her, such as the ability to vote when most blacks could not do so. His influence with Starkville's leading whites put him in the company of a handful of blacks who voted, so Sadye gained the suffrage when she became his wife. Through his personality and attitudes, he unwittingly forced her to become an even more independent woman. But he also strengthened her elitist tendencies and enhanced her concern to be financially secure.

Robert Wier was a native of Starkville, born on 19 March 1886 to Mary Ollie Shular, an unmarried black woman. His father was one of the city's white businessmen, with whom he never had any relationship. He never gained the level of education that Sadye had but trained to be a barber, and this was the trade that he plied all his life. Over time, he became the first black man to own a business, the City Barber Shop on the main street of Starkville, the black barber whose segregated, all-white clientele included the leading white citizens of the city. Because of his position, he was a leader of the city's black middle class.

To the white community, he was a soft-spoken black man who may have gone a bit too far in owning his own business instead of working for a white man. He was, however, servicing whites, so he was little threat to the pervasive social order of that day. The aspiring black barber certainly learned that the good will of whites was essential to his survival.[16]

Sadye Hunter first met Robert Wier when she came to Starkville in 1926 to teach, but they did not develop a serious relationship until the summer of 1930 when she visited her sister. Their first date was a car ride to a movie in the segregated Rex Theater. They had such a good time that it became a weekly ritual, a movie date every Thursday night. They did not go out on weekends because every Saturday, Robert worked at the barbershop from daybreak to midnight, and Sundays he spent most of his time at the Second Baptist Church, where he was a deacon. The two often shared Sunday dinner at his house with other relatives who lived there, but these occasions were not as enjoyable as the movies. Robert was very frugal, and the food on his table was always sparse. Sadye later laughed that "sometimes when I got up from the table I would be as hungry as I was when I sat down."[17]

Robert Wier determined to make Sadye Hunter his wife, so he pursued her even while she was teaching outside Starkville. She agreed to marry him but expected the wedding to take place at the end of the academic year in the spring of 1932. He shocked her one day, during a visit, when he suggested that they get married the following Sunday. He already had the wedding license, he said, so why delay? She was shocked, but agreed. On 24 April 1932, the two became husband and wife at his home at 321 Lafayette Street in Starkville, where they were to spend the rest of their lives together. His family was in attendance, but because of the swiftness of the decision, no Hunters were there. As part of the nuptial agreement, Robert went to the superintendent of education and got his new wife a teaching job in Starkville.[18]

The bride moved into the groom's large home with its large lot in a predominantly white neighborhood. Robert Wier's close ties to the city's white leaders allowed him to make this unusual purchase without incident. Although a Methodist, she joined his Baptist church. His brother and sister, along with the sister's husband and daughter, lived with them. Later Sadye's sister Louise moved in and, over the years, the house was always full of people, as the couple opened their home to those who needed their help. Sadye Hunter Wier's life from then on was that of a professional woman with enormous traditional and business responsibilities at home and in her work.[19]

She went back to teaching at the Oktibbeha County Training School, where she had previously been employed. Her duties were enormously time-consuming. Although her field of expertise was home economics, at various times she taught English, history, and music, and she ran the school library, taking summer classes in library science at Fisk University in 1936 and 1937. In addition, she organized the minstrels, a group of students who toured on Friday evenings and entertained other blacks throughout the area. The principal insisted that, immediately upon returning to Starkville from one of these trips, Sadye had to bring to him any money she had collected in admission charges. This meant that she would often not return home until long after midnight. Robert Wier was unhappy with this arrangement because Saturday was his busiest day, and he needed his sleep Friday night.[20]

There were other tensions, too. She often had to rise before the sun to wash towels for her husband's barbershop and hang them on an outside clothesline to dry. Then she would walk to school, teach her classes, open the library during the lunch hour, teach some more classes, do her extra curricular duties, and rush home to prepare dinner. All this constant activity and the late Fridays wore her down and caused her to suffer from a perpetual cold.

Wier found that marriage was not as fulfilling as she thought it would be. Her husband, who was nineteen years older than she was, seemed interested in nothing but his work and his church. He did not want to go to any social functions or have any parties in their home. He was also so parsimonious that he thought buying window curtains from a store was an extravagance. When he left town on a trip, one of the other barbers kept his money, and Sadye had to go to that man for grocery funds. Even more distressing, Robert kept things to himself. He did not share his problems with his wife, believing that such matters were not her concern. He wanted her to stop working, take care of his home, and do what she was told. His attitude only made her more determined to maintain her independence.

At first Wier, a woman of twenty-seven, gave in to her previously married husband of forty-six. Soon, however, she began to dig in her heels. When he continued to insist that they do without social life and refused to allow a niece that was living with them to host a party for her friends, Sadye Wier rebelled. She told him that the party for her niece would take place, and, from that point on, they were going to have friends in. She began buying necessities for the house, using her own teaching money for most of the purchases. Four years into the marriage, she bought a baby grand piano to use for teaching students. The piano cost twenty-five dollars a month, at a time when her entire salary was only that amount. She never got her husband to change his attitude about money, and he continued to keep their funds separate, but he came to understand that she would not accept his domineering ways. She was determined to have her career, although she made every effort to be the traditional housekeeper, too. In the manner of most independent women in the late twentieth century, she tried to balance a wide variety of responsibilities and seemed to be running all the time.[21]

In March 1943, Wier took a position as Negro Home Demonstration Agent with the Mississippi State Cooperative Extension Service, in the process increasing her salary from $25 to $175 a month.[22] The Mississippi State Cooperative Extension Service is part of a national-state outreach system established by the Smith-Lever Act of 1914. The idea was to have agents in all the nation's counties to "aid," as the law phrased it, "in diffusing among the people of the

United States, useful and practical information on subjects relating to agriculture and home economics." The Extension agent's job, in short, was to demonstrate to rural, often very poor people how they might improve their everyday lives through more efficient, economical, healthful, industrious, and creative activities.[23]

As a Negro Home Demonstration Agent, Wier was to work with black families and show them how to make the most of what little they had. There was no attempt to buck the pervasive racial caste system; in fact, the Extension Service officially supported segregation, and any thought of attacking it would have been professional suicide and personally dangerous besides. Wier was no crusader against the separate system. Like her father and her mother, she followed the advice of Booker T. Washington, trying to help black people pull themselves up by their own bootstraps within the existing segregated society of the time.

Robert Wier's reaction to this new example of his wife's independence was complete dismay. He became so upset that, as she later phrased it, "I was afraid he was going to put me out." She refused to budge, however, and threatened to accept separation or divorce in order to get her way. Over time she convinced him of the wisdom of her decision, shrewdly pointing out that the increase in her salary would help him financially. She purchased improvements for the house, and he saw how happy she was, so his attitude softened. He really had no choice. If he wanted to stay married, he had to accept the fact that his wife would continue to be a professional woman.[24]

Wier's first Extension assignment was in Newton County, some one hundred miles from Starkville. She lived there during the week and came home on weekends. She later commuted from Union and Winston Counties, serving the latter for ten years. She eventually filled a position in Columbus, which was close enough to her home in Starkville to allow her to spend most nights at home with her family. She continued to work in Columbus for fifteen years until she retired in 1969.[25] "Each community presented a different set of circumstances and needs," she later remembered, "therefore, programs were tailored to meet local needs and desires." But there was some similarity no matter where she worked. She established Home Demonstration Clubs for women, rarely working with men because that was the job of male agents. She taught people money management and food preparation. She taught gardening and farming methods; she taught women how to take scraps of material and make usable and beautiful quilts and functional mattresses. She taught her clients how to sew and make a variety of clothes and home accessories, and she taught them how to cook more nutritiously. Most significantly, she tackled the problem of adequate housing, teaching people how to turn ramshackle buildings into functional homes. In numerous instances, she made it possible for families to have their own water wells and others to have indoor plumbing for the first time in their lives. She also took before and after photographs of many of these houses, preserving an important documentary record of her activities.[26]

She worked with the counties' 4-H Clubs. Here she placed particular emphasis on providing training that would benefit the young girls in their adult lives. She tried to expose them to the kind of practical information that would help them become personal successes no matter what profession they entered. For example, in Lowndes County during 1962, she insisted that each 4-H member have a project ready for exhibition by April, and each club enter the county talent show; there were to be two socials a year plus twelve monthly meetings dealing with such matters as food preparation, ceramics, clothing, and furniture refinishing. Each member was to appear in at least one program per year. There were also community projects for each club, designed to demonstrate the four *H*s of "Head, Heart, Health, and Hands": landscaping the school campus and bringing flowers to the local churches every Sunday, gift baskets for the needy at Christmas, and concern for "invalids or shut-ins in our community on all occasions." There were also monthly countywide council meetings of officers from the community 4-H clubs.

Sadye had to travel all over the county from Mondays through Saturdays. An itinerary for the first week of each month of 1962 called for her to work in the Columbus office on Monday, make home visits on Tuesday, conduct 4-H and Home Demonstration Club meetings on Wednesday in outlying Crawford, then hold other meetings in Union Hopewell on Thursday, and in Plum Grove on Friday. The first Saturday of every month saw her at the Home Demonstration Council meeting back in Columbus. Other weeks were just as full. Plus, there was her husband back in Starkville who still insisted that she make sure his clothes were clean and his food was prepared.[27]

An important part of Wier's Extension work included making and maintaining contacts with the white and black establishment in the counties where she was working. She became a master of interracial diplomacy, using it all her life to get things done. She reached out to important governmental, business, and education leaders. In Columbus, for fifteen years, she had a weekly live radio program on two different stations every Saturday morning, discussing what her various clubs were doing and what progress she was making in the black countryside. She was also a correspondent for the black newspaper, *St. Louis Call.* Wier mailed photographs of her work to the Extension leadership in Washington, also sending such material regularly to her state superiors. When she needed a new office in Columbus, she visited each county supervisor on her own time during the Christmas holidays, found the building herself, obtained her superior's permission to move, had the building owner do appropriate repair work, borrowed two hundred dollars from her husband for other building needs, worked with individuals at the nearby Columbus Air Force Base to provide labor, and contacted a furniture store owner for furnishings. She convinced two bakeries and an ice cream company to donate refreshments for the dedication of the new office and publicized it all in the press.[28]

Sadye Wier also did many conference demonstrations, which gave her further visibility. For example, in 1964, she did a presentation before a farmers conference at Utica Junior College, demonstrating the many uses for the commodity foods the federal government was then giving to poor people. She gave similar demonstrations at Fisk University in Nashville and Morgan State College in Baltimore. In Lowndes County, she organized exhibits at the yearly county fair. Her 4-H exhibits regularly won awards and then went on to the state fair. She also made careful use of whatever prize money was available, dividing it so that almost every entrant won something. This created wide support in the black community for her projects.[29]

She was not without her detractors, however. Like many middle-class African Americans, she saw herself as better than the average black person. She believed that those she helped ought to be appreciative of all that she did for them and was sometimes short with those who opposed her plans. She clearly saw white people as more important to her professional needs than members of her own race and was not shy about expressing this fact to her clients. She was also careful not to alienate whites through any criticism of the existing Jim Crow system. She worked to get the most for herself and her clients within the system; she did not confront segregation in the hopes of changing it. Many civil rights activists and historians, like E. Franklin Frazier, have found fault with black professionals like Robert and Sadye Wier who had close ties to the white establishment. Because they had more to lose than many other blacks, members of the black bourgeoisie often hindered the civil rights movement by their accommodationist rhetoric and self-serving antidesegregationist stances.[30]

Yet Wier's willingness to go the extra mile within the black community made "Miss Sadye," as her clients usually called her, popular among many of the African Americans with whom she worked. In Union, for example, a family that lived ten miles out of town wanted her to show them how to can meat from a calf they had just slaughtered. The dirt roads were a sea of mud just then, but Sadye was determined to take her pressure cookers to the people for the lesson. The only way to get through the mire was by mule. Starting at 4:00 A.M. one morning, she rode a mule with one cooker tied to it followed by a second animal with the other cooker tied to it. She remembered people all along the ten-mile route "watching this strange procession." "Seeing how amazed and grateful these people were . . . was well worth any agony" that her body felt, she said. Her sense of duty to those to whom she felt responsible kept her working hard on their behalf, but always within the separate but unequal system.[31]

Throughout her years in the Extension Service, Wier took full advantage of a policy that encouraged agents to return to school every five years. Between 1949 and 1965, she attended summer classes at universities around the nation: Cornell University in 1949, University of Wisconsin in 1954, George Washington University in 1959, and Colorado State University in 1965. She took a variety of courses in psychology, journalism, sociology, and human development. Her grades were always good, and she more than held her own with other agents from around the country. The one school she never attended, however, was the university in her hometown, Mississippi State University. In 1965, when Wier was preparing to attend Colorado State University, Richard Holmes, Mississippi State University's first black student and the stepson of Wier's niece, entered the school during the second summer session. But Wier's superior told her not even to consider attending Mississippi State herself. "It wouldn't help your husband's business any and neither would it help you," he said. She went to Colorado.[32]

Although she left Mississippi during those summers, Wier did not necessarily leave prejudice behind. When attending Cornell in 1949, she found that none of the beauty shops in Ithaca, New York, would cut her hair. In Washington, D.C., while she was attending George Washington University in 1959, she found that, as always, she and the other black agents were in the clear numerical minority. "Living conditions were a little rough," she remembered, and blacks were generally kept on the fringes of all activities. At the end of the session, for example, no blacks were included in the closing ceremony. It turned out, however, that no white agent knew how to play the piano. "So I sat at the piano and played the music," she remembered. "They had no choice," she said. "That's the way we became a part of the program." Sadye never protested; she simply acted.[33]

Sadye's last years in the Extension Service witnessed a major change. In 1965, the organization was legally mandated to work equally for all people in the county rather than working separately for blacks and whites. Sadye was no longer called a Negro Home Demonstration Agent; her title became Associate Extension Home Economist. Ironically, this move toward greater opportunity for African Americans signaled an end to much of the professional autonomy Wier had enjoyed on her side of the color line. When integration came, the Extension leadership attempted to place black agents under tighter white control.

They also tried to change the way they operated. Wier refused to go along. "They saw that I wasn't going to be pushed around," she remembered, and they backed off. But, she noticed, the leadership in Columbus tried to make her feel "just like you didn't have very much sense about what you were doing." She led no protests, but rather overcame obstacles in her usual way—through persistent hard work.[34]

Four years later, after twenty-six years of determined effort, Sadye retired from the Extension Service. A newspaper in the state capital noted that during her career she had been in charge of eighteen 4-H Clubs and six homemakers clubs, an impressive number, though actually an underestimation. No one will ever know how many homes she helped improve or how many lives she touched. Elitist that she was, she was a role model to several generations of black people in Mississippi.[35]

Robert Wier had retired in 1966, so for the first time in their married lives, they were able to spend all their time together. Sadye joked that her greatest desire for retirement was to learn how to fish. "I'm going to get my husband to teach me how," she told a reporter. In reality, "for me to slow down and relax was a very hard task." So "to get me in the mood," the couple took a two-week vacation in Mexico in July 1970. Generally, they simply enjoyed each other's company in their home, attending to simple matters like washing dishes together and more complex projects such as refinishing a piece of furniture. Sadye Wier took a trip to Europe with a close friend from her Extension days, Carolyn Washington, the wife of then president of Alcorn State University, but Robert Wier stayed home. By this time, he was eighty-seven years old and incapable of such exertion.[36]

In December 1974, Robert Wier died of complications from bladder cancer surgery. Sadye was so devastated that she had to be sedated for days, and she suffered from depression for several years after his death. She could not face the idea of life without her husband despite the fact that she had been so independent throughout their marriage years. Slowly, however, Wier pulled herself out of her depression, her religious faith providing the needed solace. The implementation of several postretirement careers also helped bring back her focus.[37]

For two summers during the early 1970s, Wier was the Northeast District Coordinator of the Neighborhood Youth Corps for a twenty-one-county area of Mississippi. She worked with both white and black young people, trying to help them decide on a future career and how they might best prepare for it. This meant job training or, if they already worked, coordination with their employers. The job was perfect for her; it was clearly a continuation of the kind of work she had long done in Extension and that her father and mother had first exposed her to at the Noxubee Industrial School.[38]

Drawing on her family and Extension experience again, she began working in 1974 for Prairie Opportunity, a black self-help organization in the Starkville area. Wier helped establish canneries in West Point and Macon under a federally funded grant to help needy people improve their nutrition. The job required a great deal of her skill and even more of her hard labor. Working with the Ball Jar Company (even taking a course at their Muncie, Indiana, headquarters) and at last tapping the resources of nearby Mississippi State University, she began the West Point cannery in May 1974 and the Macon operation in June 1976. Neither building was air-conditioned, and the steam from the pressure cookers in the naturally high humidity of a Mississippi summer made the task oppressive. Despite being over seventy years of age, she persisted. She convinced individuals like the white owner of a vegetable stand on the road between Macon and Starkville to give her the food that he would otherwise throw away. In return, she baked him pies. Her canneries processed thousands of jars of vegetables and meat and instructed many families on nutrition and the advantages of canning. The "widowed mother of 12 children was one of our happiest family heads that participated in this program," she wrote in her report. The West Point operation lasted from May to November 1974, but the Macon operation continued into the 1990s, although Wier's connection with it ended in the late 1970s.[39]

During this same period, Sadye and her sister Louise took in their niece Sadye Louise, the daughter of their deceased sister, Vera. Then in her forties, Sadye Louise suffered from Down's syndrome. Seeing opportunity in this new challenge, Wier, in March 1980, became one of the founders of the Association for Retarded Citizens (ARC) in Starkville, serving as its first president. Not only did she help get the organization off the ground through her administrative and public relations skills, but she also worked directly with ARC'S clients. She taught them basic skills such as food preparation so they could better survive on their own.[40]

Another of Wier's postretirement projects that she worked on until the end of her life was the Colored Odd Fellows Cemetery on Highway 82 in Starkville. Founded sometime in the nineteenth century by Lodge Number 2948 of the Grand United Order of Odd Fellows of America, an all-black organization, the cemetery's early history is unclear. Burials apparently began there at the end of the century but did not include permanent grave markers until the 1920s. In 1939, the Odd Fellows Lodge sold the property to the white-owned National Funeral Home, which continued to operate it as an African American cemetery. The property subsequently changed hands several more times, always remaining in white hands. In 1955, a new owner suddenly stopped allowing any further burials there, even by those who already owned plots, and rumors swept through Starkville's black community that the property owners planned to level graves and erect low income housing on the site. Before his death, Robert Wier organized a committee of concerned black people and began the fight to save the cemetery. In 1956, a county court issued a permanent injunction permitting burials on the site to continue, and then the land came under the ownership of the Odd Fellows Colored Cemetery Association, an organization that Robert Wier began.[41]

Under Robert's leadership, with Sadye involved but in the background, the cemetery remained in operation. Over time, however, it became overgrown. When Robert Wier died in December 1974, his grieving widow buried him there but became upset at the condition of her husband's final resting place and that of Starkville's black citizens in general. With characteristic resolve, she decided to tackle the problem herself. The day after her husband's funeral, Wier and her sister returned to the site and began clearing it out. She never stopped. In 1977, Wier spearheaded the incorporation of the Highway 82 Odd Fellows Cemetery, and in 1979 she succeeded in having it designated a National Historical Landmark. At dedication ceremonies in late October 1979, an appropriate historical marker was unveiled. Thirteen years later, the Mississippi Historical Society awarded Sadye and the cemetery association an award of merit for the restoration of this historic burial place.[42]

This effort was long and hard and required all the skills that Sadye Wier had learned in a lifetime. She had to convince the black community of the importance of the task, she had to cajole money and assistance from a variety of black and white sources, and she had to get the white establishment to offer its support. She did it all masterfully, working at it day by day, year by year.

Much of the effort was simply backbreaking labor. Some of it she did herself, going out with a hoe and shovel and doing what she could to clear vegetation and fill sunken graves. She also convinced others to join her. Early on, she encouraged Neighborhood Youth Corps members, mostly the black youngsters, to help her, and she also recruited white fraternities at Mississippi State University to adopt the cemetery for service projects. She enticed young people from Prairie Opportunity, as well as adult individuals and groups. She scraped money together from a twelve-dollar-per-year maintenance fee on grave holders and from her own funds, and she hired a summer worker to keep weeds from taking over again. Good home economist that she was, Wier always expressed gratitude to the volunteers by bringing food to the work site or having the workers over to her home for a sumptuous dinner.[43]

Over time Wier realized that she had to work to overcome racial inequality in order to complete her task. The city maintained the white Odd Fellows cemetery at the other end of town, but it ignored her black cemetery. She began working on the city fathers, using her persistence, her charm, regular supplies of her home-baked cakes on all occasions and fruitcakes at Christmas. No matter how often someone discouraged her, she kept returning, always smiling, always polite, always bearing something good to eat. She wore the political leaders down. In 1975 they provided some help, and eventually the city of Starkville took over responsibility for upkeep of the black Odd Fellows Cemetery. The final burial places of white and black citizens were now equally secure. This was a significant change from the situation she found when she began her work. At that time, as Wier put it, the city "had six black men working at the white cemetery. I showed them I could do as much as those six men."[44]

While she was spending enormous time and effort on the cemetery, Wier was involved in a variety of other civic projects, more than enough to exhaust a woman half her age. Merely a list indicates the variety and the breadth of her commitment to her community. She continued as an active member of her church, at one time serving on the committee preparing its history and another time playing the piano for a children's vacation Bible school. She traveled to Chicago and Little Rock at the invitation of ministers to instruct their congregations on food and nutrition. She served on the Starkville beautification committee, she was treasurer of the League of Women Voters, and from 1977–89 she was a trustee of the Oktibbeha County Library System. During these years, she coauthored a book about her husband and produced a cookbook of her well-known recipes. She brought together a white Mississippi State University history professor and a local black physician and civil rights leader to produce a book of his life. She was honored with a public reception in the auditorium of the Mississippi State University Bost Extension Center in 1979 and again in downtown Starkville in 1992; she was a member of a local Black Culture Committee, visited classrooms at local elementary and high schools, and spoke to students at Mississippi State University and Jackson State University.[45]

Throughout these years, Sadye maintained friendships with a variety of people of both races in the Starkville community and all over the nation. She never forgot a birthday, and at Christmas her friends received some of her famous fruitcake (heavily laced with corn whiskey). An invitation to her table was an experience in dining, and she fed more than one husband and family when the wife was out of town. (She could never imagine a husband cooking anything for himself.) For many years, she took meals to the office of Dr. Douglas Conner, her niece's husband, worried that since his wife worked as a teacher, he was not getting sufficient nutrition during the middle of his busy medical day.

As she reached her late eighties, Wier's body began to fail. She had carried excessive weight for most of her middle-aged years, and this resulted in a weakened heart. She suffered a variety of heart-related illnesses, regularly visiting Dr. Conner and making trips to the Ochsner Clinic in New Orleans. The death of her sister Louise in November 1989 delivered a blow from which Wier never recovered. Her health declined, and, although many people black and white quietly rallied to her support, just as she had helped them over the years, the loneliness proved to be an overwhelming burden. She kept battling until the end, but on 24 August 1995, she died. The world outside Starkville little noticed the death of this elderly black woman. Her poor health had, in recent years, kept her from most of her projects, and even care of the cemetery became an impossible task. She left the world as she entered it—with little fanfare and in modest means.

Sadye Wier had a profound influence on Mississippi. All her life, she reached out to others and tried to offer a helping hand wherever she saw a need. Some African Americans saw her as an elitist and an accommodationist, and some white people saw her as presumptuous, but even Wier's critics grudgingly admitted her abilities and her successes. She was a member of the generation that moved from segregation to integration. Although she played little role in bringing about the change, she helped make it successful by demonstrating to African Americans what was possible and by showing white people the capabilities of the long-suppressed and underestimated black population. She touched the lives of thousands of children and adults, and she left a written record of her life that will help later historians examine twentieth-century Mississippi, both in segregation and integration. She constantly brought blacks and whites together in harmonious relationships, and this was her greatest achievement. Although she held traditional notions about the proper roles of both women and blacks, Wier's independence and stubborn determination allowed her to be of effective service to both blacks and whites. Her epitaph might well be what she once said about herself. "I just love to help somebody else if I can."[46]

NOTES

The author wishes to thank Robert L. Jenkins, Charles D. Lowery, and Elizabeth Nybakken of Mississippi State University for their careful reading of an earlier draft of this chapter.

1. E. Franklin Frazier, *Black Bourgeoisie* (Glencoe, Ill.: The Free Press, 1957).

2. Sadye H. Wier, interview by George R. Lewis, Starkville, Miss., 1992, Robert and Sadye Wier Papers, Mitchell Memorial Library, Mississippi State University, Starkville; newspaper clipping, n.d., Wier Papers.

3. Marriage license, 27 December 1887, Noxubee County, Miss., in Hunter Scrapbook, Wier Papers; Wier, with Lewis, *Sadye H. Wier, Her Life and Work* (privately printed, 1993), 12–18.

4. Wier, interview, 1992; Wier, interview by Kitty Galbraith, Starkville, Miss., 12 November 1980, Wier Papers.

5. Louis R. Harlan, *Booker T. Washington: The Making of a Black Leader, 1856–1901* (New York: Oxford University Press, 1972); Harlan, *Booker T. Washington: The Wizard of Tuskegee 1901–1915* (New York: Oxford University Press, 1983).

6. *Catalogue of the Noxubee Industrial School . . . 1914–1915, 17th Year,* n.d.; *Hunter's Horn* 8 (1951); photo album; Charter of Incorporation of the Noxubee Industrial School for Colored Youth, 28 January 1899, Wier Papers.

7. *Catalogue;* Wier, interview, 1992; Financial Report of the Noxubee Industrial School, 1905–1906, Wier Papers.

8. *Catalogue.*

9. Wier, interview, 1980.

10. *Catalogue;* Grammar School Examinations, 3–6 April 1916; Wier, interview, 1992; *Starkville Daily News,* 3 October 1983, Wier Papers.

11. Wier with Lewis, 19–21; Wier, interview by John F. Marszalek, Starkville, Miss., 10 October 1975, Wier Papers; Wier, interview, 1980; *Mary Holmes Seminary Annual Catalogue, 1917–1918,* photocopied pages in Marty G. Price to author, 28 September 1998.

12. Wier, interview, 1980; Wier, interview, 1992.

13. Wier with Lewis, 21; Wier, speech, 14 November 1990, Wier Papers.

14. Funeral services program, St. Paul Methodist Church, Macon, Miss., 30 November 1958, Hunter Scrapbook, Wier Papers.

15. Mississippi Public Employees Retirement System, membership information, n.d., Wier Papers.

16. Wier, with Marszalek, *A Black Businessman in White Mississippi* (Jackson: University Press of Mississippi, 1977), 23–31.

17. Ibid., 32–36.

18. Ibid., 36–37; Marriage License, Oktibbeha County, 23 April 1932, Wier Papers.

19. Wier with Marszalek, 56–59; Wier with Lewis, 76–80.

20. Wier with Marszalek, 41–43; Fisk University transcripts, summer 1936, 1937, Wier Papers.

21. Wier with Marszalek, 38–41; Wier, interview, 1975.

22. Wier with Marszalek, 42–44.

23. Lee Howard Moseley, *A History of Mississippi Extension Service* (Mississippi State: Mississippi Cooperative Extension Service, in cooperation with Rho Chapter, Epsilon, 1976); Ted Ownby, *American Dreams in Mississippi: Consumers, Poverty, and Culture, 1830–1998* (Chapel Hill: University of North Carolina Press, 1999), 98–109; Lynn A. Rieff, " 'Go Ahead and Do All You Can': Southern Progressives and Alabama Home Demonstration Clubs, 1914–1940," in *Hidden Histories of Women*

in the New South, ed. Virginia Bernhard et al. (Columbia: University of Missouri Press, 1994), 134–
49; Melissa Walker, "Home Demonstration Work among African American Farm Women in East
Tennessee, 1920–1939," *Agricultural History* 70 (summer 1996): 487–502.

24. Wier with Marszalek, 43–44.

25. Ibid., 44–47; Wier with Lewis, 34–38.

26. Wier with Lewis, 39–52. Many of these photographs are preserved in the Wier Papers.

27. *Monthly Program 1962: 4-H Lowndes County,* n.p., n.d., Wier Papers.

28. *Starkville Daily News,* 3 October 1983; S. A. Robert to Sadye Wier, 22 October 1951; Wier,
interview, 1992; Wier with Lewis, 45–46 (in this book, the official is misidentified as Robert Strong);
Alice Linn to Wier, 24 March 1953; Wier to Madge Reese, 4 April 1955; "4-H Club Work through
Extension," scrapbook, n.d.; clipping in "Souvenir Cards" photo album; R. O. Monosmith to Wier,
25 March 1953, Wier Papers; Wier, "How the Happier Living Contest Has Interested the Club Girls
in Home Improvement in Winston County," n.d., Wier Papers; *Jackson Mississippi Enterprise,* 27
October 1962.

29. Digest of the Sixtieth Annual Farmers' Conference in Observance of Founders' Day, 20
February 1964, Utica Junior College, Utica, Miss.; theme "Improving Rural Living," n.d., Wier Papers; Wier with Lewis, 48–49.

30. Frazier; John Dittmer, *Local People: The Struggle for Civil Rights in Mississippi* (Urbana: University of Illinois Press, 1994).

31. Wier, "Shades of Yesterday in Mississippi Cooperative Extension Service," speech, [ca. 1973],
Wier Papers; Wier, interview, 1980.

32. "Extension Courses 1949–1965," n.d., Wier Papers; Wier, interview, 1975.

33. Wier, talk to a class of Dr. Warren Housley's, 1979, Counselor Education Department. Mississippi State University, Wier Papers.

34. Wier, interview, 1975.

35. *Jackson Daily News,* 26 December 1969.

36. Ibid.; Wier with Marszalek, 74–75; Wier, talk to Housley class; diary of European trip, 11–29
August 1973, Wier Papers.

37. Wier with Marszalek, 75–78; Wier, "How Faith Changed My Life," Wier Papers.

38. Wier with Lewis, 93–94.

39. Wier, "Final Report: Prairie Opportunity Cannery at West Point, Mississippi, May 20–
December 22, 1974"; "Certificate of Completion of Ball Food Preservation Supervisor's Course
held at Muncie, Indiana on July 12–14, 1976," Canning Program Scrapbook; "Four Months Report:
Prairie Opportunity Cannery West Point and Macon, Mississippi June 1–October 1, 1976," Wier
Papers.

40. *Starkville Daily News,* 14 October 1980; Charter of Incorporation of the Four County Association for Retarded Citizens, Inc., 25 November 1980, Wier Papers; Wier, interview, 1992. The ARC
in Starkville has since changed its name to the Association for the Rights of Citizens with Developmental Disibilities.

41. "The Colored Oddfellows Cemetery," n.d., Wier Papers.

42. Ibid; Wier with Lewis, 84–91; *Starkville Daily News,* 30 October 1979; Mississippi Historical
Society Award of Merit, 31 January 1992, Wier Papers.

43. Wier to "Dear Friends," 23 May 1980, Wier Papers.

44. *Starkville Daily News,* 18 June, 17 August, 21, 26 October, 16, 19 November 1976, 17 March 1977; Cecil L. Simmons to Wier, 20 December 1979; Wier, "In Service Meeting, Clay County Medical Center," 14 November 1990, Wier Papers.

45. *Starkville Daily News,* 3 October 1983; Wier with Lewis, 71–72; "Certificate of Apprecia-tion . . . Second Baptist Church, June 18, 1978" in "The Book, A Black Businessman," scrapbook, Wier Papers; Wier, interview, 1992; Office of the Mayor, City of Starkville "Certificate of Appreci-ation . . . for Making a Signal Contribution toward a Cleaner City, April 24, 1973," *Starkville Daily News,* n.d., in "Black Culture Committee and League of Women Voters," scrapbook, Wier Papers; "Resolution, Sadye Wier Named Trustee Emeritus of the Oktibbeha County Library Board," 25 September 1989, Wier Papers; Wier with Marszalek; Wier with Lewis; Wier, comp., *A Book of Favorite Recipes* (Shawnee Mission, Kans.: Circulation Service, n.d.); Douglas L. Conner, with Marszalek, *A Black Physician's Story, Bringing Hope in Mississippi* (Jackson: University Press of Mississippi, 1985); "A Tribute to Sadye H. Wier . . . December 16, 1979," Wier Papers; *Columbus Commercial-Dispatch,* 28 June 1992; "Projects Started in 1971 and 1972," Wier Papers; "Jackson State University Book Review Committee Presents . . . February 22, 1994," Wier Papers.

46. Wier, interview by Jimmy G. Shoalmire, Starkville, Miss., 29 August 1975, Wier Papers.

Hazel Brannon Smith

(1914–1994)

Journalist under Siege

MARK NEWMAN

Hazel Brannon Smith won a Pulitzer Prize in 1964 for "steadfast adherence to her editorial duties in the face of great pressure and opposition" for her work as editor and publisher of the *Lexington Advertiser*. The newspaper served the small community of Lexington, Mississippi, located roughly fifty miles north of Jackson in Holmes County. During Freedom Summer in 1964, Smith welcomed civil rights workers to the area, and she also participated in the county's antipoverty program. Yet Smith had once been a Dixiecrat, a supporter of Joseph McCarthy's witch-hunts, and an opponent of the welfare state. Her transformation occurred as her core commitments to Christianity, law and order, public education, and economic development increasingly conflicted with the attempt of leaders in both state government and Holmes County to preserve white supremacy and segregation. Although Smith's stand against racial discrimination won her many awards, the long-term effects of an advertising boycott organized by the Citizens' Council proved her economic undoing. Bankrupt, ill, and almost friendless, she left Holmes County in 1986 and spent her last years dependent on the care of relatives.[1]

Smith attributed her core values to the influence of her devout, Southern Baptist parents to whom she was born in 1914 in Alabama City, Alabama. Smith recollected, "As a child I was taught to love everybody and not to hate anyone. I have grown up believing that the only way we can show our love for God is to love people and do everything we can to help them. Respect and consideration for the rights of others were engrained in me for as long as I can remember." Like her parents, Smith accepted segregation as part of the natural order. She did not encounter discussions of race relations either in high school or at the

University of Alabama. Her career as a journalist, however, coincided with both the emergence of the civil rights movement and the resulting hard-line white resistance that followed in her adopted state of Mississippi.[2]

Three stages marked Smith's career. The period between her arrival in Holmes County in 1936 and ending in 1954 can be seen as the first stage of her career. During this time, her values concerning racial issues seldom created difficulties with other whites. In a transitional phase from 1954 to 1961, however, Smith's values led to conflict with the local White Citizens' Council. Under the pressure of a boycott organized by the council against her newspaper, she began to understand not just the plight of African Americans but also that of whites afraid to speak out against the council. In the third stage, which began in 1961, Smith displayed growing sympathy for the civil rights movement, although she did not publicly advocate integration. She also began to work with civil rights leaders, covertly at first and more openly later. Smith, however, was unable to support African Americans who achieved local political office in the 1970s, and consequently the African American leadership broke with her.

The first stage of her career began in 1936 when she purchased the foundering *Durant News* in Holmes County and restored it to profitability. Following this success, she purchased the county seat's *Lexington Advertiser* in 1943 and later acquired the *Jackson Northside Reporter* and the *Banner County Outlook* in Flora. At the time of her arrival in Holmes County, Smith had little interest in the plight of its African American citizens. Beautiful, popular, and intelligent, she immersed herself in the everyday concerns of the white community, reporting births, marriages, deaths, and graduations. In 1950, Smith married Walter Dyer Smith, a Pennsylvania ship's purser. She was so enamored of the South's mythic past of romance and chivalry that she modeled their home, Hazelwood, after Tara from *Gone with the Wind*.[3]

Accepted by the white elite, Smith shared the white community's commitment to segregation, limited government, and states' rights. She attacked President Harry S. Truman's domestic policies as America's "road of socialization." Smith served as a delegate to the Democratic party's national conventions in 1940 and 1944. Abroad at the time of the 1948 convention, she later wrote that she "would loved to have been" with the Dixiecrat group that walked out in Philadelphia in protest over a civil rights plank in the party platform. A staunch anticommunist, Smith demanded "an end to the coddling of Russia and the pinks and reds in our state department and practically every branch of our federal government." She also supported Senator Joseph McCarthy's witch-hunts in the 1950s.[4]

HAZEL BRANNON SMITH
circa 1957. Wilson F. ("Bill") Minor Papers,
Special Collections Department, Mitchell Memorial
Library, Mississippi State University.

In spite of being critical of crusading journalists, Smith nevertheless displayed a willingness to speak out. Her religious beliefs and concern for law and order were offended by illegal gambling, bootlegging, and the public officials who acquiesced in these activities. In mounting a campaign in the *Lexington Advertiser* against these illegalities, Smith built up an array of enemies who later capitalized on her own difficulties. She pressured Holmes County courts into a grand jury investigation of organized crime in 1946, and sixty-four indictments resulted. In the same year, Smith's concern for the rule of law led her to interview an African American widow, who gave evidence in the trial of five white men accused of killing her husband. Holmes County courts convicted none of the defendants. Smith was found in contempt of court for conducting the interview, fined fifty dollars, and given a suspended fifteen-day jail sentence. The state supreme court later overturned her conviction.[5]

Although Smith proclaimed her beliefs in equal respect for all individuals and strict adherence to the law, she did not call for black voter registration or for black juror selection. Quick to draw attention to overt violations of the law, she did not consider whether some laws might be unjust. Smith also did not recognize everyday discrimination against African Americans, nor was she aware of their discontent. The gradual transition in her political beliefs from 1954 to 1961 occurred as both she and black Mississippians were victimized for their protests against the state's massive resistance to school desegregation.

When the Supreme Court declared public school segregation unconstitutional in *Brown v. Board of Education* in May 1954, Mississippi Governor Hugh Lawson White called the decision "unreasonable" and urged all lawful means of resistance to it. In harsher tones, Mississippi U.S. Senator James Eastland condemned the Supreme Court's judges as "indoctrinated and brainwashed." Such defiance proved overwhelmingly popular among white Mississippians.[6]

Concerned with the preservation of order, Smith did not join the calls for resistance, but she also did not urge compliance with *Brown,* which she considered unconstitutional. Instead, Smith sought to reduce fears and avert conflict by arguing that two or three years would pass before the Supreme Court's decision would be enforced. Conceding that African American schools needed and deserved to be improved, she even went as far as to declare "the Supreme Court may be morally right when it says that 'separate educational facilities are inherently unequal.'" Nevertheless, Smith maintained that in practice Jim Crow served the interests of both races. Segregation, she asserted, "will be maintained because the vast majority of both white and colored citizens want it that way."[7]

Despite her segregationist views, Smith continued to argue that all races "should have the same protection of the laws and courts." Her beliefs brought her into conflict with Sheriff Richard F. Byrd. Since the early 1950s, she had tangled with Byrd over his selective enforcement of the law. In July 1954, Byrd shot a retreating black man, Henry Randle, in the leg after ordering him to leave a roadside café. Unable to persuade the sheriff to give his version of events, Smith printed the story. The victim, she wrote, had been shot while following the sheriff's order to disperse and had not committed any crime. Smith also printed a stinging front-page editorial against the sheriff: "The laws in America are for everyone—rich and poor, strong and weak, white and black. . . . Mr. Byrd as Sheriff has violated every concept of justice, decency and right in his treatment of some of the people of Holmes County. . . . He should . . . resign." Byrd filed a libel suit against Smith. In October 1954, the Holmes County Circuit Court ruled in his favor and awarded him ten thousand dollars in damages. Smith successfully appealed the ruling to the state supreme court in November 1955.[8]

She declined an invitation to join the recently formed Holmes County Citizens' Council in the summer of 1954. As she later explained, Smith feared that the council would intimidate African Americans by economic and other means, as well as "take away the freedom of all the people in this community" by stifling discussion. She also refused to support an amendment to the state constitution that permitted the closure of schools as a last resort to prevent desegregation. This measure was endorsed by Holmes County Citizens' Council activist and state representative Edwin White. White Holmes County residents and the rest of white Mississippi overwhelmingly approved the measure by popular referendum in December 1954.[9]

Eschewing the Citizens' Council's calls for massive resistance, Smith placed her faith in school equalization as a means to keep the desegregation issue out of the courts and so preserve Jim Crow. She argued that equal schools "will make a definite contribution toward preserving and continuing the fine relationship which has traditionally existed between the white and Negro citizens of our county." Such schools would improve education, as they were "the answer to ignorance, poverty and disease." Furthermore, "money spent to equalize education facilities and salaries in Mississippi will also increase the state's economy."[10]

Smith's values brought her into conflict with the Holmes County Citizens' Council. An African American female teacher, for example, complained to a white male resident in 1954 that he had damaged her yard by turning his car around in it. He shot and wounded her in her Lexington home. Smith printed the story despite efforts by the Citizens' Council to persuade her against it. No arrests in the case followed, and both the teacher and her husband lost their jobs.[11]

The Citizens' Council also pressured other dissenters. Dr. David R. Minter, a physician at the interracial Providence Cooperative Farm near Tchula, had been a defense witness in Smith's libel trial. In September 1955, the council called a meeting of seven hundred people to accuse Minter and A. Eugene Cox, the farm's manager, of promoting interracial swimming on the farm and advocating integration. Both men denied the charges. Smith, who observed the meeting, urged reconsideration of the council's demand that Minter and Cox should leave. The Citizens' Council, however, now dominated the county, and Holmes voters had recently elected two of its members, Wilburn Hooker and J. P. Love, to the state House of Representatives. Threatened with violence and confronted by an economic boycott orchestrated by the council, Cox and Minter left the county in the summer of 1956.[12]

After the incident, Smith did not condemn the Citizens' Council by name, but she warned: "People are afraid to speak their minds because of the fear of being mis-understood and put on the wrong side of the fence." Angered by Smith's continuing critical comments, the council successfully pressured many Lexington businesses not to advertise in her paper or offer her commercial printing work.[13] Her difficulties increased when the trustees of Holmes County Community Hospital fired Walter Smith from his job there as administrator in January 1956 because, as one trustee explained, his "wife has become a controversial person." Smith reported to the Southern Regional Council that she was under "terrific strain" and feared that "my nerves will not stand anything else." She, however, felt a moral obligation to remain: "I feel that if we, who love the South and want to see it progress, leave now—then all will be lost."[14]

Unable to drive Smith out of business, the Citizens' Council organized a rival weekly newspaper in November 1958, the *Holmes County Herald*. Faced with this challenge, she broke her public silence about the campaign against her. Smith claimed that she had kept quiet "to preserve the peace and harmony of Holmes County" and to avoid dignifying the allegations and lies against her. The *Herald*, she argued, had been set up to destroy her and did not have the wide support that it claimed.[15]

Maligned by the Citizens' Council and under competitive pressure from the *Herald*, Smith, who had once condoned McCarthyism, now understood in very personal terms the threat that lies and innuendo posed to her cherished values of freedom of expression. Smith in 1959 publicly condemned "witch hunts" and defended fourteen University of Mississippi professors against charges of subversion and promoting integration made by Wilburn Hooker and Edwin White. Forced to choose between peace and freedom of expression, values that she had once thought compatible, she chose the latter.[16]

She believed in states' rights, but Smith was now prepared to turn to the federal government to administer justice when a state failed to do so. In April 1959 a mob took Mack Parker, an African American awaiting trial for rape, from an unguarded jail in Poplarville, Mississippi, and lynched him. The following November, a grand jury adjourned without issuing any indictments for the murder. Smith, who had earlier condemned the lynching as a "sordid crime," wrote that "when local law enforcement officers, citizens and grand juries fail to investigate or act when known crimes have been committed then it falls to the lot of the U.S. government to do it in Federal Court."[17]

Her outspoken concern for justice won Smith the Elijah Parish Lovejoy Award for courage in journalism in July 1960 sponsored by Southern Illinois University. At the award ceremony, Smith reiterated her segregationist beliefs. She, however, found herself increasingly out of step with the political direction of her county and state.[18]

When he became governor in 1960, Ross Barnett brought the Citizens' Councils to power in Mississippi. The Holmes County Citizens' Council continued to target Smith, and the *Holmes County Herald* succeeded in taking the county contract to publish legal advertisements and public notices away from her. The *Herald* falsely claimed that Smith had won the Elijah Parish Lovejoy Award for "editorial policies supporting integration"—a distinction that they knew their readership would find objectionable. Smith endured more immediate harassment when a group of white teenagers burned a cross on her lawn in November 1960. Acting quickly, Smith chased the teenagers and managed to remove the license tag of their car. Her editorial identified the car's owner as Holmes County attorney and leading Citizens' Council member Pat Barrett. After the incident, Smith wrote to Hodding Carter II, owner of the *Delta Democrat-Times:* "I think now that I don't have to hold back at all in any thing I want to say. They've done everything they possibly could to put me out of business. They have not succeeded and they are not going too [*sic*], I am certain."[19]

She now entered her third stage of her career. From 1961, Smith attacked the Mississippi State Sovereignty Commission and displayed public sympathy for the National Association for the Advancement of Colored People (NAACP). Formed in 1956 to improve the state's image and to act as an investigatory agent of the legislature, the Sovereignty Commission had mostly confined itself to public relations activities. Under Governor Barnett's administration (1960–64), however, the commission subsidized the Citizens' Councils and gathered files on civil rights sympathizers. Smith urged Barnett in January 1961 to "throw off the yoke of the Citizens Councils" and called on the legislature to end the Sovereignty Commission's subsidy of the Citizens' Councils and abolish the commission. "Personally," she wrote, "we felt at the time that the creation of the Sovereignty Commission was akin to creating a Gestapo. . . . But we were afraid to write about it." Smith attacked the commission because it had come under Citizens' Council control, and she knew only too well the threat posed by the councils to freedom of expression. Indeed Wilburn Hooker, one of the *Herald*'s original backers, was a member of both the Sovereignty Commission and the State Executive Council of the Citizens' Councils.[20]

Smith's repeated denunciations of the Citizens' Council movement ensured the continuance of its campaign against her. To help offset Smith's loss of advertising revenue, Hodding Carter II organized a committee in July 1961 to raise funds. Chaired by Carter, it comprised fellow publishers Ralph McGill of the *Atlanta Constitution* and Mark Ethridge of the *Louisville Courier-Journal*, J. N. Heiskell, editor of the *Arkansas Gazette*, and Francis S. Harmon, former editor of the *Hattiesburg American*. By October, the committee had generated more than six thousand dollars.[21]

Smith cut her full-time workforce but maintained the circulation of her newspapers. "Although a lot of white people here were ashamed to have it [the *Advertiser*] in their box," recalled employee Willie Wiley, "they'd send their cooks into the office to buy them." Smith also benefited from national recognition, which allowed her to sell papers outside the county. Although she maintained a brave face in public, the strain of the council boycott took its toll. Carter wrote to Harmon in October 1961 that Smith was "almost at her wit's end and is very distraught."[22]

Her treatment by white extremists opened Smith's eyes to the problems that African Americans experienced every day. Understanding the economic power whites wielded to ensure conformity in the community, she no longer mistook the general placidity of black Mississippians for contentment. "When communication does not exist between the two races," wrote Smith, "we may expect the Negro community to look elsewhere for leadership—notably the National Association for the Advancement of Colored People." In secret, Smith printed the NAACP's materials and the *Mississippi Free Press*, a weekly newspaper created in 1961 by civil rights groups in Jackson.[23]

Although her editorials maintained that both races preferred segregation, Smith argued that "we must realize that we have been 'forcing' the Negro into a segregated society for the past 100 years." Conceding that segregation laws were "by their very nature . . . discriminatory," she called for their repeal. Appreciative of the dissatisfaction of African Americans, Smith wrote, "The intelligent Mississippi Negro today is no happier under a system of forced segregation than are the white people of Mississippi under the threat of forced integration of the races. Somewhere in between the two 'forced' systems lies the answer."[24]

The first crack in Mississippi's segregated education system appeared in 1962. Governor Barnett chose to defy a federal court order to admit African American student James Meredith to the University of Mississippi. "We do not wish to see the University of Mississippi integrated any more than any other white Mississippian in the state," wrote Smith, before delivering her real message that federal law had to be enforced. Students and other protestors rioted when Meredith was admitted to the university in October. Smith blamed Barnett and the Citizens' Councils for the tumult. By defying the desegregation order and calling on the university to do the same, Barnett had set "the pattern of resistance and defiance for the people (and the mob) to follow." The main target for Smith's anger was the Citizens' Councils, which she claimed had infected the young rioters with the spirit of defiance and sought to direct their activities. She demanded that the Councils' role be investigated and those responsible for the riot be "exposed and held accountable."[25]

Events in Holmes County continued to force Smith to speak up for values and beliefs that increasingly aligned her with those of the civil rights movement. The Student Nonviolent Coordinating Committee's voter registration campaign spread to Holmes County in April 1963. Within weeks, vigilantes shot into and bombed the home of aspiring black voter registrant Hartman Turnbow while the occupants slept inside. Miraculously, no one was hurt. Smith condemned the bombing as "a vicious and criminal act," and noted that at least two white men were known to have been involved. She identified the motive for the attack when she added, "If the bombing victim had committed a crime it was that of trying to qualify to vote."[26]

By the summer of 1963, Smith had begun referring to civil rights activity in the state as "the freedom movement in Mississippi." In June, she condemned the "shocking, hate-inspired murder" of Medgar Evers, Mississippi Field Secretary of the NAACP, and praised him as "a living symbol of the freedom that Mississippi Negroes are determined to achieve." The more white extremists attacked the federal government and the civil rights movement, the more she recognized the necessity for such external involvement in Mississippi. In 1964 she insisted, "There is no such thing as state sovereignty. The state was never meant to be supreme. That question . . . was settled a hundred years ago in a bloody conflict." Smith warned that if the "so-called 'good white people' " failed to speak out, then the only solution to Mississippi's racial problem was "occupation of the state by Federal troops."[27]

Her work won Smith the Pulitzer Prize in May 1964, making her the first woman to achieve that honor for editorial writing. Smith insisted that she had never intended to become a controversial figure but revealed what had made her so: "My fight has been to defend and protect the freedom of all Mississippians to say and do what they want to do without taking dictation from the White Citizens Council, the Ku Klux Klan or any other extremist organization." Buoyed by the award, Smith personally welcomed thirty civil rights workers in July 1964 when they entered Holmes County as part of the Freedom Summer voter registration project. "These young people," she wrote, "wouldn't be here if we had not largely ignored our responsibilities to our Negro citizens." During the summer, Smith entertained Martin Luther King Jr. as a houseguest.[28]

She also supported the federal civil rights bill that desegregated public accommodations. When it passed in July 1964, Smith argued that Christians had to speak out against injustice: "It is not enough to be good ourselves—to not hate, or discriminate. . . . Not until we Christian people of Mississippi speak out and thereby create an atmosphere in which laws are obeyed and those who break them are swiftly and surely punished, can we claim we are doing our duty as good citizens. . . . We must let our faith in God be stronger than our fear of our fellowman and the Citizens' Council." She endorsed the bill's champion, Lyndon Johnson, "a man big enough to be president of all the people of the United States," for election as president. She also supported his War on Poverty program. Smith wrote: "It is our moral responsibility, as well as good business, to do something about improving economic conditions for all of our people. Therein lies in large measure the solution of other problems which we face, such as Mississippi's budget and tax structure, and the continuing racial situation."[29]

In both her editorials and her speeches, Smith continued to deny that she promoted integration, but by 1965 she said racial intermarriage, illegal in Mississippi, should be allowed. She argued that African Americans were not seeking "social" mixing but rather "full equality under the law." Smith also welcomed the Voting Rights Act passed in the wake of the Selma, Alabama, demonstrations and described "the deliberate disenfranchisement" of blacks as "a sordid chapter in the history of our state."[30]

Following the passage of the Voting Rights Act, twenty-eight hundred African Americans in Holmes County registered to vote, most of them assisted by federal examiners. Holmes County schools desegregated grades one through four in September 1965 under federal court order. Most whites, however, created new private schools to evade desegregation, and militant segregationists pressured other whites to send their children to these new schools, which were aided by state tuition grants. Smith warned whites not to endanger Mississippi's future by abandoning the public school system. In vain, she wrote: "It is time for the white people of Holmes County to throw off the claims of petty would-be dictators with which they have long been bound—it is time for the white people to cry FREEDOM!"[31]

Smith still suffered from the advertising boycott and had debts of $100,000 by 1965. The African American community raised $2,852 at an Editor's Appreciation Day in November, held at Saints Junior College, a private black institution in Lexington. African Americans also organized efforts to break the white merchants' boycott of the *Lexington Advertiser,* as well as to secure equal employment opportunities for themselves. Saints Junior College teacher Robert Clark led the efforts to end the boycott but encountered stiff resistance from white leaders who told him that "this is one thing off limits."[32]

Clark worked closely with Smith. Holmes County elected Smith to its newly formed antipoverty committee in 1966, which, in turn, elected her and Clark to serve on the board of directors of Central Mississippi, Inc. The organization operated a federally funded community action program, sponsoring training and adult education across six counties, as well as Head Start centers for preschool children from deprived backgrounds. Equally concerned about poverty, Smith's husband served as the first director of Mississippi Action for Progress, Inc., a state-approved biracial group established in the fall of 1966 with a $3 million federal grant to operate a Head Start program in selected counties.[33]

Smith's commitment to the federal antipoverty program and the rule of law made her critical of America's military escalation in Vietnam. In May 1966, she announced that "our Congress has not declared war. . . . Today there are more than one quarter million American men engaged in an undeclared and from our viewpoint an illegal war in Viet Nam. More than 20,000 young Americans have already died or been wounded in this conflict." She complained that America's expenditure on Vietnam had been funded at the expense of poverty programs. Smith wrote in January 1967, "This nation cannot afford to provide $30 billions for armaments to destroy and rebuild a country for the brown skinned people of South Viet Nam—and forget about the white and black poor of America." By March, Smith urged a negotiated settlement, affirmed that Asia would have to be run by Asians, and protested that "the United States is supporting and propping up a military coup regime imposed on the people of South Viet Nam."[34]

Her concern about poverty also led Smith to enter the Democratic primary race for state senator in 1967, seeking to represent Holmes and Humphreys Counties. Her main campaign themes centered on quality education, industrial growth, greater access to welfare for the needy, and impartiality in law enforcement. Smith beat her nearest rival, Ollie Mohamed, by 2,266 votes to 2,096 in Holmes County, but trailed him by 803 to 2,468 in the Belzoni merchant's home county of Humphreys. As many African Americans did not vote in the primary, Smith drew the majority of her votes from whites. There was sufficient white opposition, however, to ensure her defeat in the runoff election, which she lost, 4,264 votes to 6,616. The increase in Smith's vote came mostly from blacks who had not voted earlier.[35]

A few weeks after the election, African Americans organized a selective buying campaign to protest against police brutality, achieve employment opportunities, and secure publication of the county's legal advertisements and public notices in the *Lexington Advertiser*. They declared that they would not support or trade with businesses that advertised in the *Holmes County Herald* and urged local merchants to patronize Smith's paper. Smith disclaimed any responsibility for the campaign but told her tormentors, "Now it's your turn." Although blacks supported the boycott, whites remained intransigent, and it did not achieve its main aims.[36]

Robert Clark, who helped organize the boycott, won the election in 1967 to the Mississippi House of Representatives, making him the first African American to serve in the state assembly since Reconstruction. Reapportionment had reduced the county's representation in the House from two seats to one. In the general election, Clark beat J. P. Love, who had defeated Wilburn Hooker in the Democratic primary. Smith offered Clark her "warmest congratulations" and deemed it "significant that those who have been fighting this editor the hardest went down in defeat."[37]

Her own situation improved when a four-and-a-half month African American selective buying campaign finally led twenty-three Lexington merchants to agree in December 1969 to upgrade job opportunities for blacks, support equal justice under the law, and advertise in Smith's paper. The Holmes County Board of Supervisors voted unanimously in February 1970 to award a two-year contract to the *Lexington Advertiser* for publication of legal notices. Smith gained renewed national recognition when she received the National Education Association's Abraham Lincoln award in July for public service, and the National Federation of Press Women's Woman of Achievement award for her "abiding courage and strength of character in the face of difficulty and opposition" in May 1971. She won the Democratic party nomination for the state senate in August but lost the five-county general election to Republican Ray H. Montgomery by 9,644 votes to 13,677. To her delight, she received a majority vote in her home county.[38]

Thereafter, Smith's career declined. She lost the county contract to publish legal notices to the *Holmes County Herald* in 1972 and compounded her financial difficulties by borrowing to complete her home, Hazelwood. Local blacks also broke with her when she began criticizing their leadership. Smith attacked a black boycott of Lexington's white merchants in 1973 and accused it of intimidating other African Americans. Robert Clark sadly recalled, "She never really accepted black people not doing what she wanted done." Still not reconciled with whites either, Smith proved unable to compete with the *Herald,* and eventually farmed out her printing. After her husband died in 1983, Smith's health declined. Her printer cut off her credit in 1985, and she filed for bankruptcy two weeks before publishing the last edition of the *Lexington Advertiser* on September 19 of that year. Smith's belongings and property were sold at auction, and she returned to Alabama to live with her sister.[39]

In 1993, afflicted by Alzheimer's disease and living under the care of her niece in a nursing home, Smith won the Fannie Lou Hamer Award. A year later, she was the subject of a made-for-television movie, *A Passion for Justice: The Hazel Brannon Smith Story,* although neither she nor her family had been consulted. Near death, she watched the film from her bed and died a few weeks later on 14 May 1994.[40]

Accounting for Smith's gradual conversion to civil rights champion, Hodding Carter III said, "Hazel, who was a nice segregationist white woman, just decided that her Christianity, her moral and political beliefs, couldn't allow her to support what was being done."[41] Smith's religious beliefs contributed to and meshed with her basic values: a commitment to the impartial rule of law, freedom of thought, and educational and economic progress. Faced with a challenge to her values by the Citizens' Councils and the rise of massive resistance, she chose to defend them even at the risk of economic ruin. The treatment she received from white supremacists, together with the burgeoning civil rights movement, forced her to confront the discrimination African Americans habitually encountered and then to face their discontent. Smith's values enabled her to accept desegregation and endorse racial equality, although she, herself, could never fully overcome her paternalism toward African Americans.

NOTES

1. *Lexington Advertiser,* 7 May 1964.

2. Ibid., 5 May 1966; Hazel Brannon Smith to George Mitchell, 30 July 1956, folder 40, box 48, Administrative Records, Southern Regional Council Papers (henceforth SRC Papers), Atlanta University Center; Donald Cunnigen, "Men and Women of Goodwill: Mississippi's White Liberals" (Ph.D. diss., Harvard University, 1987), 581–82.

3. Smith to Mitchell, 30 July 1956, folder 40, box 48, SRC Papers; *Chicago Tribune,* 27 March 1986.

4. *Lexington Advertiser,* 22 November 1951, 6 November 1952, 6, 20 May, 10 June 1954, 16 August 1956.

5. Hodding Carter II, *First Person Rural* (Garden City, N.Y.: Doubleday, 1963), 219.

6. Neil R. McMillen, "Development of Civil Rights, 1956–1970," in *A History of Mississippi*, vol. 2, ed. Richard Aubrey McLemore (Hattiesburg: University and College Press of Mississippi, 1973), 154–58.

7. *Lexington Advertiser*, 20 May, 1 July 1954.

8. Ibid., 20 May, 10 June, 8, 15, 22 July, 14 October 1954, 10 November 1955.

9. T. George Harris, "The Eleven-Year Siege of Mississippi's Lady Editor," *Look* 29 (16 November 1965): 122; *Lexington Advertiser*, 18 November, 16, 23 December 1954.

10. *Lexington Advertiser*, 13 January, 9 June 1955, 29 January 1959.

11. Carter, *First Person Rural*, 221.

12. Hodding Carter III, *The South Strikes Back* (Garden City, N.Y.: Doubleday, 1959), 148–54; *Lexington Advertiser*, 14 October 1954, 4 August 1955.

13. *Lexington Advertiser*, 15 December 1955; Smith to Mitchell, 30 July 1956, folder 40, box 48, SRC Papers.

14. Carter, *First Person Rural*, 222–23; Smith to Mitchell, 30 July 1956, folder 40, box 48, SRC Papers.

15. *Lexington Advertiser*, 4, 11, 18 December 1958; Carter, *First Person Rural*, 223–24.

16. *Lexington Advertiser*, 16, 23 July 1959.

17. Ibid., 30 April, 6 November 1959.

18. Ibid., 28 July 1960; *Jackson Clarion-Ledger*, 31 July 1960.

19. *Holmes County Herald*, 21 July 1960; Hazel Brannon Smith to Hodding Carter II, 2 December 1960, Hodding and Betty Werlein Carter Papers, Mississippi State University, Starkville; *Lexington Advertiser*, 10 November 1960.

20. McMillen, 159–60; *Lexington Advertiser*, 5 January, 23 February 1961, 11 January 1962.

21. Hodding Carter II to the Tri-Anniversary Committee, 18 July 1961; "Progress Report as of 10/25/61," Carter Papers.

22. *Jackson Clarion-Ledger*, 5 January 1986; Hodding Carter II to Francis S. Harmon, 12 October 1961, Carter Papers.

23. *Lexington Advertiser*, 6 April 1961, 11 January 1962; Cunnigen, 586.

24. *Lexington Advertiser*, 13, 20 April, 14 December 1961.

25. Ibid., 13, 20 September, 4 October, 8 November 1962.

26. Ibid., 11, 18 April, 9 May 1963.

27. Ibid., 13 June, 15 August 1963, 5 March, 2 July 1964.

28. Cunnigen, 586; *Memphis Commercial Appeal*, 5 May 1964; *Lexington Advertiser*, 2 July 1964.

29. *Lexington Advertiser*, 2 April, 9 July, 13 August, 29 October 1964.

30. Ibid., 14, 21 January, 25 March 1965; *Boston Globe*, 16 March 1965.

31. *Lexington Advertiser*, 10, 24 June, 9 September, 30 December 1965, 24 March 1966.

32. Ibid., 25 November 1965, 17 March 1966; *Jackson Clarion-Ledger*, 31 May 1993.

33. *Lexington Advertiser*, 9 September 1965, 24 February, 10, 17 March, 7, 28 April, 9, 23 June, 13, 27 October 1966.

34. Ibid., 12 May 1966, 26 January, 16 March 1967.

35. Ibid., 8, 15 June, 10, 17, 31 August 1967; *Holmes County Herald*, 3 August 1967.

36. *Lexington Advertiser*, 21 September, 12, 19 October 1967.

37. Ibid., 3, 10 August, 5 October, 9 November 1967, 4 January 1968.

38. Ibid., 25 December 1969, 1 January, 5 February, 9 July 1970, 3 June 1971; *Holmes County Herald*, 4 November 1971.

39. *Lexington Advertiser*, 5, 12 April, 3 May 1973; *New York Times*, 31 March 1986; *Jackson Clarion-Ledger*, 5, 11 January, 3 March 1986, 31 May 1993, 7 May 1994.

40. *Jackson Clarion-Ledger*, 31 May 1993, 13, 24 April, 7, 15 May 1994.

41. Ibid., 5 January 1986.

Margaret Walker Alexander

(1915–1998)

Voicing Form

ROBERT A. HARRIS

Although she spent a number of her writing years outside the American South, Margaret Abigail Walker Alexander always considered herself a southerner. Shaped by her early experiences in Alabama and New Orleans, she studied at Northwestern University at the urging of her teacher—and of Langston Hughes. It was in the South, however, that she completed the majority of her work, using the southern landscape and folkways as grist for her rich storytelling and poetic endeavors.

Margaret Walker's work spans six decades. Her earliest work, in poetry, was sustained throughout that time, while her later work in fiction and in essays continued through to her death in 1998. Walker's literary voice is tinctured by several important influences. She was the eldest of four children born to a Methodist minister and professor, the Reverend Sigismund Walker, and music teacher Marion Dozier Walker. Family history, religion, and the metered strands of song provided the fertile bed in which her work took root. Hers was an imagination nourished by the stories of her great-grandmother as told to her by her maternal grandmother. Recounting a scene from her early life, Walker writes:

> We moved from Birmingham to New Orleans when I was a small child, and my mother recalls how often she and my father came in from night school well past bedtime and found me enthralled in my grandmother's stories. Annoyed, she would ask, "Mama, why don't you let that child go to bed? Why will you keep her up until this time of night?" And grandmother usually answered guiltily, "Go to bed, Margaret. Go to bed right now." My father would add, "Telling her all

MARGARET WALKER ALEXANDER

1970. Wilson F. ("Bill") Minor Papers, Special Collections
Department, Mitchell Memorial Library,
Mississippi State University. Public Information Office,
Jackson State University, Jackson, Mississippi.

those harrowing tales, just nothing but tall tales." Grandma grew indignant then, saying, "I'm not telling her tales; I'm telling her the naked truth."[1]

The "naked truth" sparked young Margaret's imagination. It fueled her creative endeavors and gelled into a cohesive story. Years later, Walker recalled these stories and crafted them into her acclaimed historical novel *Jubilee* (1966). Her continuing efforts to reveal the truths of the American South yielded subjects for her writing. Her first volume of poetry, *For My People* (1942), delves into the struggles of the southern existence. Using the biblical prophets as a backdrop, Walker's *Prophets for a New Day* (1970) casts civil rights leaders as mirrored images of the prophets Jeremiah, Isaiah, Amos, Joel, Hosea, and Micah. *October Journey* (1973), the third of her poetic volumes, is a tribute to the men and women whose actions and written work inspired a race. Finally, *This Is My Century* (1989) represents Walker's swan song of poems. It is as much a look back on her life as it is a statement of accomplishment and mature resolve.

When asked about the literary influences on her writing, Walker looked to family, religion, and music for her answer. In a 1975 interview with Charles Rowell she stated, "My father had many books, and my mother read poetry to me when I was a child. My mother read such diverse poetry as that of Paul Dunbar and John Whittier's 'Snowbound.' My father taught us bits of doggerel. I memorized pieces from the Bible and from Shakespeare. . . . I remember I read Langston Hughes' poetry when I was about 11 or 12 years old."[2] Countee Cullen and James Weldon Johnson were among the other writers of the Harlem Renaissance whose works Walker read and memorized. She counted them among her earliest literary influences.

Maryemma Graham, Walker's student and biographer, notes, "To become a poet, a novelist, a scholar . . . meant rigorous and continuous training. Reading books from her father's library brought with it his bias: nineteenth- and twentieth-century British classics were more familiar to him than the fledgling American literature she would later come to love."[3] With this firm grounding in classical British and American literature and rhetoric, Walker was poised to embark on a lifelong career of writing and teaching.

On her tenth birthday Walker's father presented her with a daybook in which to record the budding writer's numerous poems. According to Walker, her father told her each poem should contain three elements: they should tell a story, be filled with imagery, and reflect the rhythms of her life. Young Margaret took this to heart and instilled these characteristics into her poetic efforts as well as her novel *Jubilee*. This is evident earliest in her poem "Daydream" (later published as "Why I Write") and in her signature poem "For My People," where she captures the realities of southern life and the writer's obligation to sing the songs of the people. Published in *Crisis* magazine when Walker was nineteen years old, "Why I Write" establishes her commitment to humanistic concerns— concerns she addressed throughout her writing career.[4] Later in her life, she called herself a humanist and asserted that the humanistic perspective, more than any other, framed her work. This vision permeates "I Want to Write," for in it she set the foundation for her desire to document the trials of southern life and the strength and faith required to overcome the various obstacles set before southerners, both black and white.

> I want to write
> I want to write the songs of my people.
> I want to hear them singing melodies in the dark.
> I want to catch the last floating strains from their sob-torn throats.
> I want to frame their dreams into words; their souls into notes.
> I want to catch their sunshine laughter in a bowl;
> fling dark hands to a darker sky
> and fill them full of stars
> then crush and mix such lights till they become
> a mirrored pool of brilliance in the dawn.[5]

"I Want to Write" signifies the creative process. It is as though Walker stipulates, through these lines, that through writing she will make possible the "mirrored pool of brilliance in the dawn." She believed that through writing, she could reflect what was around her with new hope and thereby offer a different vision of humanity. Like James Weldon Johnson's creator in *God's Trombones*, Walker used the imagery of hands raised toward a dark sky to suggest the placement of the stars that serve to inspire those who marvel and wonder at their beginnings. This image signals both Walker's keen awareness of the plight of those enduring the poverty and racial oppression of the Jim Crow South as well as her nascent attempts to connect with that awareness and to treat that emerging consciousness as theme in written expression.

W. E. B. Du Bois, founder and editor of *Crisis* magazine, encouraged Walker to submit "Daydream" for publication. Du Bois, a well-known writer and social activist, heard in Walker's work the whisperings of a gifted voice. Her talent was confirmed eight years later when she won the Yale Series of Younger Poets Award for the poem "For My People."[6] The poem had been published earlier in *Poetry* magazine and in Sterling Brown's *The Negro Caravan*. Walker had submitted the poem to the Yale contest on two previous occasions; her perseverance was rewarded. "For My People" became her signature poem, appearing in print more than thirty-four times. It is by far her most anthologized poem and the one she was asked to read at each of her numerous speaking and reading engagements. The poem, all but the last stanza of which Walker says was "written in fifteen minutes on a typewriter," resonates with the cultural awareness expressed in "Daydream" and also provides an insight into the poet's growing racial activism. This activism explains in part why Walker and "For My People" were embraced by leaders of the civil rights movement.[7]

The religious influence on Walker's writing is nowhere more evident than in the opening stanza to the poem.

> For my people everywhere singing their slave songs repeatedly: their dirges and their ditties and their blues and jubilees, praying their prayers nightly to an unknown god, bending their knees humbly to an unseen power.[8]

This striking, candid glimpse of the faith of a beleaguered people extends through the second stanza, where Walker begins a journey through time and place, conjuring communal memories of

> people lending their strength to the years, to the gone years and the now years and the maybe years, washing ironing cooking scrubbing sewing mending hoeing plowing digging planting pruning patching dragging along never gaining never reaping never knowing and never understanding.

This instance of invoking a community's memory is the first of three litanies in which Walker sculpts meaning from the ordinary. In these lists she elevates the mundane events of a typical day's labor to the status of symbols that create meaning by pointing to shared experiences of the past. Part of the power of this effort rests in what is absent as much as what appears on the page. In these lines the reader discerns not only a catalog of the mundane but also the absence of any punctuation, which might serve to separate those tasks in any real or artistic sense. Her license in this regard serves to unify the stanza further and contributes to the unity of the text as a whole. Missing too are references to the tools and implements that might otherwise soften the presentation. The text is rich with verbs. It is direct, unadorned, and determined. It summons the reader to conjure images Walker has embedded between the words. Her litany lauds the efforts of the rural and urban underclass of laborers whose presence is implied only through the tasks each endeavors to complete. The universal nature of Walker's reference is extended in the third stanza when she invokes her

> playmates in the clay and dust and sand of Alabama backyards playing baptizing and preaching and doctor and jail and soldier and school and mama and cooking and playhouse and concert and store and hair and Miss Choomby and company.

Walker recalled playing a game with her sister in which they would pretend to be "Miss Ann and Miss Choomby." This constitutes but one of the many instances in which the poet intertwines elements from her life with poetic and fictional literary situations. Yet, this litany dissolves assumed geographic barriers. Her poem is for all her people, not just those in Alabama backyards, but also those in neighboring and distant states. It is for all who ever played at the games she lists, who are united through their play under one umbrella of disfranchised citizenry.

These words are at once affirmation and motivation. They resonate in the final call to

> Let a new earth rise. Let another world be born. Let a bloody peace be written in
> the sky. Let a second generation full of courage issue forth; let a people loving free-
> dom come to growth. Let a beauty full of healing and a strength of final clenching
> be the pulsing in our spirits and our blood. Let the martial songs be written, let
> the dirges disappear. Let a race of men now rise and take control.

In "The 'Etched Flame' of Margaret Walker," R. Baxter Miller argues that this resistant poem "sets the white oppressor against the black narrator." Walker, however, insisted that the poem was not written in anger but was an attempt to relate the trials of a people. Baxter's noted tension was but a portrayal of the agonies of the South, a depiction of a reality capable of shearing hope from a racial psyche.[9]

Walker graduated at fourteen years of age from Gilbert Academy in New Orleans after only three years of study. She then enrolled at New Orleans University, now known as Dillard University, for two years. Then she transferred to Northwestern University near Chicago. It was in Chicago that Walker honed her writing skills. By the end of her studies, at age twenty, she had completed three hundred pages of the novel *Jubilee*. She later presented the manuscript for review by the members of the Southside Writers' Group—the same group that counted among its members such renowned writers as Marian Minus, Arna Bontemps, Fern Gayden, Theodore Ward, St. Clair Drake, Frank Marshall Davis, and Richard Wright.[10] When the Southside Group disbanded in the late 1930s, Wright left Chicago for New York. Walker's friendship with Wright continued for two years after his departure, and it was on the strength of that association that, years later, Walker penned the biography *Richard Wright, Daemonic Genius* (1988).[11]

In 1935 a family friend who had worked with Black Nationalist and poet Marcus Garvey found Walker a job with the New Deal's Federal Writers' Project as a junior writer. This job paid her eighty dollars a month and enabled her to continue writing. During her tenure with the Writers' Project, Walker had the opportunity to work with other African American luminaries such as poet Gwendolyn Brooks, author Frank Yerby, and dancer Katherine Dunham. Walker, however, found it difficult to write while she was in Chicago, and in 1939, on the advice of Arna Bontemps, she enrolled in the writing program at the University of Iowa, where she earned a master of arts degree in 1940.

By 1940 Walker's promise as a poet had been recognized. "For My People" had won the coveted Yale award, and the book of poems bearing the same title had been published. At this point in her life, Walker yearned to return to the South, where she thought she would be rejuvenated. After a short stay in New Orleans, Walker accepted a teaching position, her first, at Livingstone College in Salisbury, North Carolina. There she met and married Firnist James "Alex" Alexander.

Over the next seven years, the demands of married life and the births of three children made it almost impossible to write. In 1949 she accepted a teaching position at Jackson State College, now Jackson State University, in Jackson, Mississippi, where she spent the remainder of her professional life. Walker says of that time that she "had a very great struggle . . . to try to be a writer, as well as teacher, and a wife, and a mother, and to go on lecture tours."[12]

Although these difficulties were (and are) common for women writers, the seven-year period was not lost time for Walker. During that time, she continued to write in her journals, a practice she had continued from the time of her father's gift. Although the *Jubilee* manuscript was virtually untouched during this time, Walker was able to continue her research on the historical period and to reorganize her ideas for the novel. In this way, *Jubilee* was a constant companion. Walker later remarked that she lived with the novel, rewriting and revising its chapters, for thirty years. This served her well when she returned to Iowa to begin studies for her doctorate. She completed *Jubilee* on 9 April 1965 and submitted it as her creative dissertation. Later that same year she received her doctorate and returned to Jackson State.

Jubilee, Margaret Walker's only published novel, met with acclaim in 1966. It was marketed for its unique perspective and was compared in the publisher's cover note to Margaret Mitchell's *Gone with the Wind:* "This stunningly different Civil War novel boasts a heroine to rival Scarlett O'Hara."[13] But there is more to note in this "difference" than the apparent contrast to *Gone with the Wind.* Like many of the neo–slave narratives, Walker's portrayal of the South revises, in significant ways, the understanding of antebellum and early Reconstruction southern life. Walker achieves this in part because much of the story focuses on her protagonist, Vyry.

In *Jubilee* Walker extends the slave narrative tradition through her choices of slave narrative conventions—those she employs and those she revises. These conventions are sites of intertextuality, which connect Walker's work to the body of writing by other black women who have addressed slave life. *Jubilee* adds onto the slave narrative tradition, and does so with a difference. At both the narrative and textual levels, Walker favors oral storytelling traditions over written ones, extending that privilege into the realm of authentication. Generally, an author points outside the story to verify the text. Walker, however, took her family's oral tradition and used her family's own stories to authenticate her text.

One might expect to find in a neo–slave narrative many of the markers that historians and critics identify as distinguishing characteristics of the tradition.[14] In *Jubilee,* however, these conventions are rarely used. In lieu of an opening "I was born" statement, Walker opts for third-person narration, which necessarily precludes the use of that conventional device. This move would appear to divest the text of an authorial voice, a presumptive or critical "I" in which to vest the validity or authenticity of the narrative. This is not, however, the case in *Jubilee*—in part because the omniscient narrator's voice carries with it the authority of a multiplicity of first-person accounts and also because the initial scene does present a scenario in which birth and being are significant.

In the opening scene, Vyry is taken to visit her mother, Sis Hetta, who is in childbed and dying. Sis Hetta has sent for her daughter, telling Granny Ticey, "I wants to see my youngun Vyry, fore I dies."[15] This scene signals that *Jubilee* is as much about human transitions as it is about the expected odyssey from slavery to freedom. This progression also marks a historical and literary change. In the American literary canon *Jubilee* transcends earlier perspectives on the Civil War era (as posited by Mitchell and others) by using multiple voices to impart the views of all the actors on the stage, not just those of the dominant community.

In this way, Vyry's "existential statement of being" simultaneously expresses both loss and gain. Sis Hetta is lost to Vyry forever, but she is not an orphan. She gains an extended family and is raised, significantly, by two women who occupy central roles in both the slave community and in the "Big House." Through their tutelage, Vyry learns the ways of the community and her expected role in the master's home, including her peripheral place in the Dutton family as the daughter of her master, John Dutton. This overt nod to miscegenation, while consistent with earlier characterizations of slave life, marks a departure from its usual use. Perhaps because of previous treatments of the matter, Walker offers only a tacit negative critique through the voice of John's wife, Salina Dutton. On the morning Vyry is to begin her duties as her half-sister's maid, John, who knows nothing of the arrangement, confronts his wife. "What the hell is going on around here? Why the devil wasn't I told about what's happening in my own house?" he asks. Salina's measured response indicates both her knowledge of John's sexual escapades and her determination to exert power over Vyry in the only way available to her. "You was going to bring her in here anyhow when you got good and ready," she responds, "just like you've brought all your other bastards."[16] This brash reply both indicts Dutton and indicates Salina's reign over the household. Her dominating presence in the house, and later over the plantation, proves to be the principal source of Vyry's suffering.

Publishing as she was during a period of heightened sensitivity to injustice and oppression, Walker had only to include the reference to Dutton's paternity to invoke her readers' critical response. Stephen Rascher suggests that intertextuality binds these kinds of allusions to a set of oral and literary traditions. His discussion, centering on definitions of intertextuality by Henry Louis Gates and Michael Awkward, creates a context for collective recall. Gates's definition of intertextuality, or "literary signifyin[g]" is "a process of repetition and difference or repetition and reversal."[17] Awkward's more semiotic approach describes intertextuality as "a paradigmatic system of explicit or implied repetition of, or allusion to, signs, codes, or figures within a cultural form."[18] Each of these definitions applies to the present discussion. Walker's nearly silent nod to miscegenation, and the subsequent appeal to the reader's collective memory of similar situations, relies on depictions of miscegenation treated in texts preceding Walker's. She signifies on this particular trope by simultaneously repeating and revising it. Whereas earlier narrators have related the distance mistresses sought to keep between themselves and their husband's biracial progeny, Salina orders Vyry nearer.

Walker incorporates an even bolder move later in the novel when Vyry continues to serve Lillian even after emancipation. This service to her half-sister could easily have been grounds for consternation among readers. Where other slave narrators express little or no allegiance to the master's family after emancipation, Vyry remains on the plantation to cook for Lillian and her children. She nurses Lillian as well, hoping the continued care will deliver Lillian from agitation and confusion. When asked by Innis Brown, the freed slave whom she will later marry, why she will not leave with him, Vyry answers, "I can't leave Miss Lillian here by herself. You knows I can't leave her helpless like and sick in her mind!"[19]

Vyry's stand reflects her personal strength because she has the confidence to remain. An alternate reading would position Vyry among the mindless, doting "mammies" caricatured in novels by white authors. Walker characterizes Vyry in a way that rewrites the traditional white novel, for her characterization runs counter to that of the formulaic descriptions of slave women in those novels. In Walker's novel, it is Lillian, the white mistress, who is raped, which inverted other pieces in the slave narrative. Walker's inversion of the rape of Vyry's mother signals both revision and repetition as she relates textually to early slave narratives and antithetically to early white fiction. This link is noted by Elizabeth Beaulieu, who sees *Jubilee* as a "transitional [text], linking nineteenth-century slave narratives to the fictionalized slavery and freedom literature of the late twentieth century."[20]

Walker's treatment of rape establishes a third link to convention. Lillian's fragile condition, occasioned by her rape by a marauding soldier, suggests that both white and black women were precariously situated in the southern milieu. Just as Sis Hetta was powerless to deny John Dutton's sexual advances, so too was Lillian prey to the sexual violence perpetrated by white men. This thread runs a similar course in a novel by Sherley Anne Williams, *Dessa Rose,* published in 1986.[21] Similar too, in the two novels, are the protagonists' reactions to rape. Williams's protagonist becomes more sensitive to Ruthel's plight as a woman after an attempted rape, and Vyry, after years of estrangement necessitated by the hierarchies of the slave system, rekindles her affection for her half-sister and childhood playmate. This recognition of sisterhood as victims of rape signifies a departure from the customary presentation of mistress/slave relationships while also marking, in traditional terms, a known space where race and gender intersect.

It is important to note here that Vyry has other motivations for remaining on the plantation. Shortly before her emancipation she marries Randal Ware, a free Negro and artisan. Ware's role in the community as itinerate blacksmith gives him access to several slave populations. He feels his stature as a freedman carries with it a responsibility to assist slaves in their escape to freedom, and he takes on this responsibility with a determined zeal. As the rumors of civil war escalate into actual warfare, Ware decides to leave the South and urges Vyry to accompany him—but without their children. "I got to go," Ware tells her. "Go away from here; get out of Georgia, maybe get clean outen the South. . . . I can take you with me if you've got the will to go."[22] But Vyry is reluctant to leave their children behind. "How I'm gwine run away with tow children?" she asks. "You know I wants my freedom, but I ain't leaving my younguns."[23] Ware's reasoning, that, "they'll be safe. Leave them like I say, and you'll get your freedom and your babies" is meaningless to her. Unwilling and unable to leave the children behind, she is captured in the woods, returned to the Dutton plantation and given "seventy-five lashes on her naked back."[24]

As in the slave narratives preceding *Jubilee* and the neo–slave narratives following it, instances of physical cruelty abound. Vyry's lashing constitutes the height of her physical punishments. Previous to the whipping, she had been slapped by Mistress Salina, had a chamber pot poured over her head, and, at the conclusion of a most volatile scene, she is hung by her thumbs in a closet, where she loses consciousness and is ultimately rescued by John Dutton. These instances of cruelty, while constituting significant portions of much of antebellum literature, are particularly salient features of the slave narrative. While several narrators—Frederick Douglass, for instance—include vivid descriptions of whippings and beatings, the victims are most often men. Most, Douglass being a notable exception, elide the details of the horrors experienced by women. Historicity, perhaps, bears significantly on these descriptions. Nineteenth-century (predominantly male) narrators were loath to confront their audiences—either in print or in oratory—with the details of the rape, disfiguring, or mutilation of slave women. To do so would be an affront to "proper society." Quite often, mere allusion to the treatment of women, offered with a parenthetical, self-abnegating disclaimer, was sufficient to engage the imagination of the reading or listening audience as to the severity of the ordeal. Writing with benefit of temporal distance from the historical period and in a distinctly changed historical moment, Walker could more effectively include these details.

The effectiveness of Walker's narrative is enhanced not only by temporal distance, but also by the form she employs in presenting the narrative. Like Margaret Mitchell, and perhaps because of Mitchell, Walker structures *Jubilee* within the framework of a historical novel. What differentiates Walker's work, however, is that the foundational elements of her narrative spring as much from the realm of oral tradition as from any fictive elements wrought by her imagination. *Jubilee* is, in part, her family story. Quoting Georg Lukacs's seminal essay on the historical novel, Hazel Carby writes, "Margaret Walker's *Jubilee* has been heralded as a reaffirmation of 'the critical importance of oral tradition in the creation of [Afro American] history.'"[25] What Lukacs and Carby affirm here is the authenticity of the narrative voice, one Walker attributes to her maternal grandmother, Elvira Ware Dozier, who told her the story we encounter in *Jubilee*. Reflecting on her thirty-year quest to complete the novel, Walker writes, "Long before *Jubilee* had a name, I was living with it and imagining its reality. Its genesis coincides with my childhood."[26]

The understood authority of childhood stories permeates Walker's text. Instead of offering an explanatory prologue, Walker allows the text to substantiate itself. Offering, as she does, a new perspective on the era through a strong, determined female protagonist, Walker unfolds narrative simply by allowing a seldom-told story to be told: "As I grew older and realized the importance of the story my grandmother was telling, I prodded her with more questions. . . . I was already conceiving the story of *Jubilee* vaguely, and early in my adolescence, while I was still hearing my grandmother tell old slavery-time stories and incidents from her mother's life, I promised my grandmother that when I grew up I would write her mother's story."[27]

For Walker, her grandmother's voice was authentication enough. Yet, after years of capturing the stories on paper, she realized that others might regard *Jubilee* as just another fictional work, one failing to carry with it the real gravity of her great-grandmother's experience. Although she researched the stories thoroughly, Walker chose not to offer her readers any documentation of the events, trusting instead that her use of language and folk references would sufficiently authenticate the narrative. While consistent with the weight that earlier narrators gave to their texts, Walker's determination to subordinate written records in favor of handed-down stories denotes her refusal to yield to any conventional authenticating strategy, save that contained in the oral tradition. This authorial decision, coupled with her re-presentations of and revisions of conventional slave narrative structures, facilitates American literature's transition to the neo–slave narrative form.

Mammy Sukey and Aunt Sally, the women into whose care Vyry falls after Sis Hetta dies, give her a folk education in the gathering and use of the leaves, roots, and berries that slaves used as medicines. Indeed, Vyry's skills as a midwife ultimately secure for her family a protected existence outside the white town where they eventually settle. Because she is able to offer a needed skill that is based in part on the townspeople's racially stereotyped notion that a black midwife is superior to a white one, Vyry and her family are able to live peacefully near whites without the attendant fears of the Ku Klux Klan and white exploitation they had experienced earlier.

Walker's recognition as an adept essayist is warranted given the diverse treatment of themes in her two published volumes, *How I Wrote* Jubilee *and Other Essays on Life and Literature* (1990) and *On Being Female, Black, and Free: Essays by Margaret Walker, 1932–1992* (1997). Although the publication dates might suggest that Walker came late to the essay form, her first published essay appeared in 1932. Like her poetry and *Jubilee*, Walker's essays—even those of a more personal nature—address the important issues of the times in which they were written. They are both personal and pointed in their treatment of social and political matters. A reading not only offers a glimpse into Walker's life but also provides insights of her relationships with those around her. In "Richard Wright," for example, she employs the same authoritative "I" that exposes the genuine nature of her literary relationship with Wright. After his move to New York, Walker would send him gifts "of food and wine, and cigarettes, and perhaps, what he valued most, an exchange of ideas, moral support, and a stead-fast encouragement."[28] Likewise, her essay "The Humanistic Tradition of Afro-American Literature" made a candid argument for the classification of African American literature as a world literature at a time when talk of literatures of the diaspora lacked the full, scholarly development they enjoy today.

The published essays reflect her journey through her portion of the twentieth century. They deal with race and gender as they impact black women writers, the legacy bequeathed by her literary predecessors, and the trials of juggling writing when other commitments and obligations compete for time. During the period of the black arts movement, the literary counterpart to the Black Power movement, Walker turned her critical eye to the discipline itself. She delineated the cultural and folk elements shaping African American literature and possible methods for mining these influences for the fruitful study of the genre. In these volumes, she includes essays that offer insights into the role of the artist as an interpretive and animating presence during turbulent social and political times.

In one of her final interviews, Walker told Alferdteen Harrison, a colleague at Jackson State University, "I'm like the cat with nine lives. I have had five surgical operations, five pregnancies, and a stroke, but I am very optimistic about the future and I don't think I am going to die before my work is done."[29] Walker died six years later, having completed five volumes of poetry, two of essays, one novel, and the Richard Wright biography. Her autobiography was unfinished at the time of her death.

Walker's legacy belongs to a future generation to assess. Since her death, a handful of scholars have begun to dissect her numerous journals and to revisit her poetry and fiction. Walker, who remarked to interviewer Jerry Ward Jr. that "Mississippi is the epicenter of my life," surveyed the southern landscape and allowed all she perceived to permeate her writing with a rich, distinctive cultural patina.[30] She still has much to offer the contemporary reader, and her place in American literature becomes more firmly cemented with each new investigation into her work.

NOTES

1. Margaret Walker, "How I Wrote *Jubilee*," in *How I Wrote* Jubilee *and Other Essays on Life and Literature,* ed. Maryemma Graham (New York: Feminist Press, 1990), 51.

2. Charles H. Rowell, "An Interview with Margaret Walker: Poetry, History, and Humanism," *Black World* 25, no. 2 (1975): 4–17.

3. Maryemma Graham, introduction to *Fields Watered with Blood: Critical Essays on Margaret Walker,* ed. Graham (Athens: University of Georgia Press, 2001), 11–12.

4. Walker, "Daydream," *Crisis* 41, no. 5 (1934): 129.

5. Margaret Walker Alexander, "I Want to Write," in *October Journey* (Detroit: Broadside Press, 1973).

6. Graham, ed., *Fields Watered with Blood*, xx.

7. Walker, interview by John Griffith Jones, *Mississippi Writers Talking*, vol. 2 (Jackson: University Press of Mississippi, 1982), 131. "For My People" appeared first in *Poetry* (October 1937) and later in *The Negro Caravan*, ed. Sterling A. Brown, Arthur P. Davis, and Ulysses Lee (New York: Arno Press and the *New York Times*, 1941), 409–10.

8. Walker, "For My People," in *For My People* (New Haven: Yale University Press, 1942).

9. R. Baxter Miller, "The 'Etched Flame' of Margaret Walker," in *Fields Watered with Blood*, ed. Graham, 83; Walker, interview, 113.

10. Graham, ed., *Fields Watered with Blood*, xx.

11. Walker, *Richard Wright, Daemonic Genius: A Portrait of the Man, a Critical Look at His Work* (New York: Warner Books, 1988).

12. Alferdteen Harrison, "Looking Back: *For My People* at Fifty," introduction to *Margaret Walker's "For My People": A Tribute*, by Roland L. Freeman (Jackson: University Press of Mississippi, 1992), 5.

13. Walker, *Jubilee* (1966; reprint, New York: Bantam, 1967).

14. A detailed presentation of these conventions appears in James Olney's " 'I Was Born': Slave Narratives, Their Status as Autobiography," in *The Slave's Narrative*, ed. Charles Davis (Oxford: Oxford University Press, 1985).

15. Walker, *Jubilee*, 7.

16. Ibid., 19.

17. Stephen Robert Rascher, "The Neo–Slave Narratives of Hurston, Walker, and Morrison: Rewriting Black Woman's Slave Narrative" (Ph.D. diss., University of Connecticut, 1998), 1.

18. Ibid., 2.

19. Walker, *Jubilee*, 252

20. Elizabeth Ann Beaulieu, "Femininity Unfettered: The Emergence of the American Neo–Slave Narrative" (Ph.D. diss., University of North Carolina, 1996), 16.

21. Sherley Anne Williams, *Dessa Rose* (New York: W. Morrow, 1986).

22. Walker, *Jubilee*, 137.

23. Ibid.

24. Ibid., 137, 142.

25. Georg Lukacs, quoted in Hazel Carby, "Ideologies of Black Folk: The Historical Novel of Slavery," in *Slavery and the Literary Imagination*, ed. Deborah E. McDowell and Arnold Rampersad (Baltimore: Johns Hopkins University Press, 1989), 129.

26. Walker, "How I Wrote *Jubilee*," 51.

27. Ibid.

28. Ibid., 34.

29. Harrison, "Looking Back," 7.

30. Walker, "A Writer for Her People," interview by Jerry W. Ward Jr., *Mississippi Quarterly* 41 (fall 1988): 520.

Fannie Lou Hamer

(1917–1977)

A New Voice in American Democracy

LINDA REED

❀ ❀ ❀

Listen to the voices of three African American women who tell us about black women and social reform in the United States in the middle of the twentieth century. Fannie Lou Hamer, the renowned mother of the Mississippi civil rights movement, reflected, "When I liberate myself, I'm liberating other people."[1] Daisy Bates, who nurtured the Little Rock Nine students as they desegregated Central High School in Little Rock in 1957–58, insisted that "through the struggle and victory, Negroes tested their own strength, and won. They learned unmistakably that they possess irresistible power if they become conscious of it and unite to secure their inalienable rights."[2] Rosa Parks, the genteel lady who unleashed a political tiger through the Montgomery, Alabama, boycott in 1955 wrote that "I had no idea when I refused to give up my seat on the Montgomery bus that my small action would help put an end to the segregation laws in the South. I only knew that I was tired of being pushed around."[3]

In her own way, each of these women tells us that the goal of attaining freedom and equality for African American women and the quest for democracy for all citizens are entwined. As black women worked to improve and liberate themselves and their communities, they also sought to link their individual advancement with their race's economic, political, and social struggles. The contributions of Fannie Lou Hamer to the civil rights movement, therefore, are best understood within the broad context of other black women and organizations that worked for social and political reform in the South. Long before emancipation, African Americans sacrificed to gain greater freedom for themselves and their people. The civil rights movement resembles earlier struggles, especially from the perspective of the leadership of influential women, the use

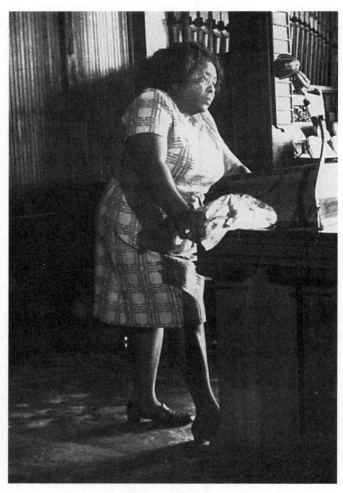

FANNIE LOU HAMER

1971. Tougaloo College,

L. Zenobia Coleman Library, Archives.

of songs and oratory, the importance of religious beliefs, and efforts of black consciousness-raising through self-help organizations.

Throughout America's history, black women have been at the center of two of the nation's most important political movements: the quest for black equality and the demand for women's rights. Mississippi's Fannie Lou Hamer, Rosa Parks of Alabama, and Daisy Bates in Arkansas shared a tradition of inner strength born from centuries of opposition to oppression as expressed in these twin struggles. It was a black woman from Mississippi, journalist Ida B. Wells-Barnett, who initiated the first antilynching campaign in 1892. A black woman, Maria Stewart, had been the first American-born woman to speak in public when it was forbidden for "the gentler sex" to do so. In 1832, she advised black women to "unite and build stores of your own" to achieve economic independence and to "sue for your rights and privileges."[4] Stewart's words foreshadowed Hamer's call for African American self-help over 140 years later: "We have to make it work. Ain't nothing going to be handed to you on a silver platter, nothing."[5] Although it is largely unheralded, the role of black women in the woman suffrage movement was more intense and consistent than that of white women. In addition to sexism from both black and white males, black women had to contend with the burden of racism from white women. Nonetheless, the suffrage movement resulted in all women getting the vote in 1920 with the ratification of the Nineteenth Amendment. Most black women in the South, of course, would not be able to exercise that right for another half century.[6]

For black women, the quest for women's rights has been part of the overall struggle for racial equality. This duality characterized black women's organizations. In 1896 the stated purpose of the National Association of Colored Women (NACW), whose programs served as a model for the National Association for the Advancement of Colored People (NAACP), established in 1909, and the National Urban League (NUL), founded in 1910, was to empower the race, especially its women. The NACW's goals were clear: "To promote the education of women and girls; raise the standard of the home; work for moral, economic, social, and religious welfare of women and children; protect the rights of women and children who work; and obtain for *all* women the opportunity of reaching the highest standards in all fields of human endeavor."[7] These activists believed that their rights as women had to be assured in order for the African American race as a whole to progress.

Recent scholarship agrees that race is a social construction, not a biological determinant. Given America's past, of course, race as an identifier is difficult to discard. In our time, *race,* however, no longer refers exclusively to blackness. Caucasians for example, also are perceived to own a racial identity. In short, people of whatever cultural background are now "raced" in the same sense that the term historically referred to black people."[8]

Several social movements of the early twentieth century enabled the rise of African American women leaders like Hamer in the 1960s. The Progressive Era at the turn of the twentieth century issued in regulations for banking, the food industry, and workers' hours and working conditions and raised questions about delinquency, child labor, and women's status.[9] The New Negro movement, beginning in the 1890s, shattered old stereotypes rooted in slavery in favor of a new vision of African Americans as bearers of a rich cultural legacy. The New Negro movement gave birth to African American literary and artistic achievements known as the Harlem Renaissance, which flourished along side Marcus Garvey's pan-African movement of the 1920s. In the New Negro movement, the Harlem Renaissance, and Garveyism, people of African descent took center stage while those of European origins played supporting roles. These movements framed African American life and culture within concepts of American democracy as America helped to make the world safe for democratic ideals during World War I. The Harlem Renaissance manifested black people's pride in themselves and helped to create a groundswell of enthusiasm for Garveyism, the largest mass movement involving people of African origins prior to the civil rights movement of the 1950s and 1960s.[10]

To understand oppositional culture and what it meant to African Americans in the twentieth century, historians point to the ways through which black people survived and left significant historical markers (including, but not limited to, the Negro spirituals, blues, and gospel) in earlier centuries.[11] Certain laws passed during the Progressive Era paved the way for federal assertion in ways that would later prove advantageous to black people, but reformers during the Progressive Era and progressive legislation in general largely ignored the plight of African Americans. Consequently, Americans of African descent began more aggressively addressing their needs through organizations like the NACW, the NAACP, and the NUL, drawing on a heritage of three centuries of opposition to oppression in America. In the 1910s, 1920s, and 1930s, little changed for African Americans. As African Americans grew more demanding of a more inclusive American democracy in the 1950s and 1960s, the civil rights movement continued to draw from this historical wellspring of communal intelligence and religious faith as well as from cultural expressions of opposition through individual initiative and courage.

African Americans pursued basic human rights during the 1940s, saying that America must make its home front safe for democracy at the same time that it was securing democracy abroad. This concept was symbolized in the Double V campaign, which called for a double victory over tyranny overseas and over racial prejudice in America.[12] During the New Deal administrations of President Franklin Delano Roosevelt, black people played small supporting roles while America underwent major political transformations. Ultimately, in response to the threatened march on Washington in 1941 by African American nationalist Asa Philip Randolph, the Roosevelt administration in May of that year issued Executive Order 8802, which publicly raised issues of importance to African Americans to the national level.[13] Other events and breakthroughs persuaded Harry S. Truman and other presidential administrations that followed that America could not go forward without positively addressing issues of equal justice for all Americans.

The southern conference movement also helped to prepare America for the watershed represented by the civil rights movement. The Southern Conference for Human Welfare, founded in Birmingham, Alabama, in 1938, and its offspring, the Southern Conference Educational Fund, formed in 1946, were interracial organizations often described as "white" because they were southern. The southern conference movement, however, embraced a most significant doctrine in 1938: "races" (read people, regardless of origins) could not live together harmoniously if they could not reap equal benefits from work, political participation, and social accommodations. The southern conference movement brought together people such as Virginia and Clifford Durr, a white couple from Montgomery, Alabama, with NAACP secretary Rosa Parks. In the 1960s, it also brought together white student workers and African Americans in the Student Nonviolent Coordinating Committee (SNCC), which, in turn, attracted such key players as Fannie Lou Hamer.[14]

Born Fannie Lou Townsend to James Lee Townsend, a Baptist preacher, and Ella Townsend on 6 October 1917 in rural Montgomery County, Mississippi, the future civil rights leader shared a birth year with John F. Kennedy, and the two would coincidentally gain national notoriety in the 1960s. Ella and James Lee, who were sharecroppers, moved to Sunflower County when Fannie Lou was two years old, and the child received her six years of education there. School years for sharecroppers averaged about four months a year, and Hamer said she missed many of those because she had very poor clothing.

At the age of six, Fannie Lou began working in the cotton fields, where she continued to chop and pick cotton until the plantation owner, W. D. Marlow, learned that she could read and write. In 1944 she became the time- and record keeper for Marlow and married Perry Hamer, a tractor driver on the Marlow

Plantation. For the next eighteen years of her life, Hamer worked as sharecropper and timekeeper on the plantation four miles east of Ruleville, Mississippi, the place where she and Perry made their home.

Hamer's life forever changed on 31 August 1962, when she unsuccessfully attempted to register to vote in the county seat of Indianola. The usual intimidation amounted to would-be voters' names appearing in the local newspaper. Hamer said that her trouble began immediately. In oral history interviews, she tells of how the landowner, Marlow, appeared at the Hamers' home that same day to "ask" her not to attempt any political activity.[15] Familiar with the physical violence that often followed economic reprisals, and having received the expected threats, Hamer left her family to stay with friends. The move, however, did not stay the violence. Hamer and her friends miraculously escaped unharmed when rounds of gunshots were fired into the friends' home after someone discovered her presence there. Despite the violence and economic intimidation, however, Hamer, by December 1962, had become an active member of the Council of Federated Organizations, a coalition of key civil rights groups including the NAACP, the NUL, the Congress of Racial Equality (CORE), the Southern Christian Leadership Conference (SCLC), and SNCC in Ruleville. In the meantime, Hamer had alternated living with friends and relatives in the surrounding area. A cousin's injury at a plant prompted Hamer to spend two weeks in Chicago, where she assisted in his recovery. SNCC also sponsored her to attend its leadership training conference at Fisk University in the fall of 1962.[16]

Fannie Lou Hamer's life is best framed in a religious and political context. Any discussion of the institutional history of black women would be seriously flawed without examining women's involvement in the black church and black religion. This is particularly true for Hamer.[17] She experienced religion long before she became politically active in a formal sense. She grew up in a household headed by a father steeped in religion who was twice called to become a preacher. She had an intense religious conversion early in life. A cornerstone of Hamer's religion rested on the Holy Bible, whose scriptures were regularly recounted by her pious parents. The Bible, according to her parents, taught Christians to believe by faith and to trust worldly concerns to the righteousness of God. She relied on 2 Corinthians 5.7, "For we walk by faith, not by sight." Hamer's biblical faith included a belief that all people were equal in the sight of God. Her Bible taught in Galatians 3.26, "For ye are all the children of God by faith in Christ Jesus." Ultimately, Hamer's beliefs held hope and promise for all believers, including those who supported white supremacy and the oppression of black people. The Bible, fervently studied by Hamer, stated in Ephesians 3.17–19, "That Christ may dwell in your hearts by faith; that ye, being rooted and grounded in love, May be able to comprehend with all saints what is the breadth, and length, and depth, and height; And to know the love of Christ, which passeth knowledge, that ye might be filled with all the fullness of God." For Hamer, her religious faith went hand in hand with day-to-day survival, providing ways of overcoming and often manipulating an oppressive racial system. Hamer's life and career manifest the way religion and politics merged in African American culture in the United States during the civil rights movement.[18]

Hamer's religious fervor was obvious in her speeches, as when, for example, she denounced abortion (a topic discussed later in this essay). She also claimed and vocalized her religious heritage through singing. The African American singing tradition became a key component of the struggle for democracy as it highlighted the richness of black culture and its role in social reform. A prominent struggle song such as "Before I'll be a slave, I'll be buried in my grave, and go home to my Lord and be free" had origins in the nineteenth century. This song and others like it "proclaimed the sources of their historical lineage." Black activists constructed new dreams "out of the hard materials of black urban life" and sometimes now declared, "Before I'll be a slave, there'll be a Honky in his grave."[19] Hamer recalled that her mother used to sing a song that warned, "I would not be a white man, I'll tell you the reason why. I'm afraid my lord might would call me and I wouldn't be ready to die."[20] Other freedom songs use the river as a metaphor to explain that people of African origins had always struggled for "the right to develop our whole *being*."[21] Fellow activist Bernice Johnson Reagon insists that songs like the ones Hamer sang were essential to shaping the civil rights movement.[22]

Hamer had a signature song, "This Little Light of Mine," which she usually led before her speeches at political rallies.

> This little light of mine, I'm gonna let it shine
> This little light of mine, I'm gonna let it shine
> This little light of mine, I'm gonna let it shine
> Oh, let it shine, let it shine, let it shine!

The words of the song can be viewed as radical. Its fundamental message is that the fight of African American people against injustice will not be stopped. The light (of hope, of justice, of courage, of individuality, of religious inspiration) will never be put out.[23] Often Hamer and other civil rights workers would make up verses about politics. For Hamer, the combination of religious faith and music in such a song as "The Lord Will Make a Way Somehow," for example, became a conduit for the release of built-up anger.

The work of African American women in the twentieth century is directly linked to their foremothers of the nineteenth century, women like Sojourner Truth, Maria Stewart, Harriet Tubman, Anna Julia Cooper, and Ida B. Wells-Barnett. In a chapter entitled "Are We the Women Our Grandmothers Were?" historian Anne Firor Scott expresses her "firm belief that activists of the late twentieth century [could] find inspiration in their history of the forebears."[24] In Scott's estimation, women (black and white) worked diligently to create sustaining institutions that would enrich and enhance the life of their communities—schools, libraries, parks, kindergartens, and other such places. All the while they also did whatever was necessary for women to get the right to vote.[25] With black women, such community work and voluntary associations date back to the African American presence in colonial America.[26] Thus, the twentieth century struggles for equality and freedom merge with a past filled with similar efforts. As late as the 1950s and 1960s, black leaders sustained themselves in the struggle for racial justice by relying on the tools of survival forged by earlier generations.

The most influential women social reformers fit a certain prototype: they were older and their actions became legendary. Their determination and courageous initiative speak volumes. For black women, families and female networks were important institutions that shaped their lives and experiences.[27] In Hamer's world, "network" must include new technological advances that enabled her to be influenced by persons that she might not necessarily have met. Radio and television coverage of the civil rights movement brought to Hamer information on key black women activists before she had the opportunity of meeting them. She found consolation and inspiration in knowing about Ella Baker, a significant SNCC liaison for older and younger civil rights activists.

Looking at individual women leaders whose leadership paralleled Hamer's activism helps us to understand her motives for participation and outspokenness in the 1960s. Rosa Parks, held in high esteem because of her defiance of southern law and tradition, has been called the mother of the modern-day civil rights movement. Hamer and Parks had no direct link through correspondence or work experience, but they both played pivotal roles in their respective communities. In Parks's home of Montgomery, Alabama, as in other parts of the South, public buses were segregated. The front section was reserved for whites and the rear section for blacks. If the front section of the bus became full, blacks were expected to give up their seats until no whites were left standing. On 1 December 1955, Rosa Parks was tired—"tired of giving in," she said—and she refused to relinquish her seat to a white man.[28]

Parks's act of sitting down to stand up for equal rights became legendary for its inspiration to the civil rights movement. In a sustained, concerted effort to defend Parks's position, fellow blacks and their white allies organized the Montgomery Bus Boycott of 1955–56.[29] The boycott led to the successful integration of the city's bus system and made Rosa Parks a symbol of individual courage. Rosa Parks, like Fannie Lou Hamer after her, made it clear that civil rights must also address economic imbalances.

The following year, two states away, a major historical event moved still more blacks and whites to action as another black woman, Daisy Bates, rose to national prominence for her courage and initiative. The Supreme Court decision in *Brown v. Board of Education* of 1954 ended a long struggle for blacks by outlawing the racial segregation of public schools. For the first time since 1896, segregationists were placed on the defensive. In the fall of 1957, nine black teenagers in Little Rock, Arkansas, purposely chosen by School Superintendent Virgil T. Blossom, attempted to carry out the mandate of the Supreme Court by integrating Little Rock's Central High School. The forces of the state, under the leadership of Governor Orval Faubus, prevented their admission and precipitated another internationally observed drama as President Dwight D. Eisenhower federalized the National Guard to guarantee the youths' admittance. Daisy Bates emerged as a rock of strength for her community. Despite virulent attacks from white supremacists, Bates helped the Little Rock Nine make integration an eventual success.[30]

Black women were prominent in leadership roles during the 1960s when southern hostility toward the civil rights movement made open and active participation an increasingly dangerous task. Hamer followed the examples set by other leading women of her time. Like them, she was resourceful and brave. And, like them, she became, not surprisingly, the victim of retaliation from those who opposed equal rights for all people. Economic reprisals, long a successful mechanism to end concerted efforts by blacks who demanded equality, and other forms of intimidation did not deter Hamer. She tried to register to vote several times, an act for which several determined persons had been murdered. In early 1963 she became a field secretary for SNCC and a registered voter.[31]

In joining SNCC, she allied herself with a group advocating equitable economic and political opportunities for blacks, the primary unfinished business after execution of the *Brown* decision. For Parks, Bates, and Hamer, the most important immediate effect of the *Brown* decision had been primarily psychological. All three women increasingly turned their attention in the 1960s to programs promoting economic development for and political participation of their fellow African Americans.

From 1963 onward, Hamer worked with voter registration drives and with programs designed to assist economically deprived black families in Mississippi in circumstances with which she said she felt especially familiar. The youngest of twenty siblings whose parents were seldom able to provide adequate food and clothing, Hamer linked the lack of access to the political process with the poor economic status for blacks. She was instrumental in starting Delta Ministry, an extensive community development program, in 1963.[32]

Hamer did not speak only for African Americans but for all Americans who felt left out of the American Dream. She believed in social change, and she believed in crossing boundaries to accomplish tasks related to social change. Her own poverty did not prevent her from becoming a catalyst for change. Poverty and racial discrimination had kept her uneducated, but she worked side by side with some of America's most educated citizens. In Mississippi, college students from across the nation became some of her strongest friends and supporters. Poverty shaped her worldview, and this perspective compelled her to ask that democracy in Mississippi, the nation's poorest state in the 1960s, include a specific representation of poor people in the state legislature and in the national Congress.[33]

Hamer and others like her in the 1960s entered organized politics when they challenged the Democratic party to live up to its pledge of democracy for all Americans. On 24 April 1964 she helped organize the Mississippi Freedom Democratic Party (MFDP), becoming vice chairperson and a member of its delegation to the Democratic National Convention in Atlantic City, New Jersey, that would challenge the seating of the regular all-white Mississippi delegation. At the Democratic National Convention that August, she addressed the convention's Credentials Committee. Representing the Freedom Democratic Party, she passionately pleaded with members of the Credentials Committee to recognize the biracial representatives of the MFDP as the legitimate delegates from the state of Mississippi. Her speech, televised live, stands as one of the most compelling in American history. In its cadence and use of American symbols, her speech equals Martin Luther King's most famous speeches. Her political rhetoric and personal authority were so powerful that President Lyndon Johnson called a press conference with the exclusive purpose of interrupting her speech. Lyndon Johnson thereby endowed her with a unique distinction: she is the only woman in American history to have had a presidential press conference called to quiet her voice. The 1964 challenge failed, despite a compromise offered through Hubert Humphrey and Walter Mondale that would have seated two nonvoting MFDP members, African American Aaron Henry, president of Mississippi NAACP chapters, and European American Ed King, chaplain at historically black Tougaloo College. Hamer and the other members of the MFDP refused to compromise their principles. The MFDP's actions, however, resulted in an unprecedented pledge from the National Democratic party not to seat delegate groups that excluded blacks at the next convention in 1968.[34]

Hamer's unwillingness to accept the compromise offered by the Democratic party could be read as another example of how religion guided many of her decisions. Although matters did not look promising in 1964, Hamer insisted on standing the moral ground, believing that God would be on the side of righteousness. She chose her Baptist parents' teaching of walking by faith and not by sight. The Democratic party kept its promise in 1968, which reinforced Hamer's religious cosmology.

Hamer in 1964 attempted to run for the U.S. Congress. Since the regular Democratic party disallowed her name on the ballot, the MFDP conceived the Freedom Ballot, which included all the candidates' names, black and white. According to the Freedom Ballot count, Hamer defeated her white opponent, Congressman Jamie Whitten (33,099 to 59). In the official tally, however, Hamer's defeat was a foregone conclusion.[35]

Hamer, Victoria Gray of Hattiesburg, and Annie Devine of Canton in 1964 appealed to Congress, arguing that it was wrong to seat Mississippi's representatives who were all white, when the state's population was 50 percent black. The three women observed as the House of Representatives voted against their challenge 228 to 143.[36]

Hamer founded in 1964 the Freedom Farms Corporation (FFC), a nonprofit venture designed to help needy families raise food and livestock. The FFC enabled Hamer to address her concerns for the plight of poor black and white Mississippians. The FFC also provided social services, minority business opportunities, scholarships, and grants for education. Hamer's efforts with FFC harkened back to efforts by the Populist party in the late nineteenth century to address rural economic needs when poor farmers turned to cooperatives as a way of surviving and helping themselves. During that movement, African Americans had played a significant role in organizing programs and cooperatives that addressed the economic needs of the area's poor, both black and white.[37]

When the National Council of Negro Women (NCNW), an international human rights and self-help organization founded in 1935, started the Fannie Lou Hamer Day Care Center in 1970 in Ruleville, Mississippi, Hamer became chairperson of its board. As late as 1976, even as she struggled against cancer, Hamer served as a member of the State Executive Committee of the United Democratic Party of Mississippi.[38]

Initiative, courage, and selflessness best describe Hamer's life. Her motivation to make a difference in the freedom struggle is best summarized by her repeated remark "I'm sick and tired of being sick and tired." The motto resembled the same sentiment expressed by Martin Luther King Jr. when he began saying in the 1950s that black people had waited long enough for racial justice.[39] In an interview in 1965, Hamer said, "I was determined to see that things were changed," and, paraphrasing John F. Kennedy, she said, "I am determined to give my part not for what the movement can do for me, but what I can do for the movement to bring about a change."[40] On being tired, Hamer put it best when she said, "I do remember, one time, a man came to me after the students began to work in Mississippi and he said the white people were getting tired and they were getting tense and anything might happen. Well, I asked him 'how long he thinks we had been getting tired'? I have been tired for 46 years and my parents was tired before me and their parents were tired; and I have always wanted to do something that would help some of the things I would see going on among Negroes that I didn't like and I don't like now."[41]

Hamer consistently stated that she had *always* wanted to work to transform the South because she saw her parents work so hard to raise twenty children. She spoke often of the hardships of her mother and her enslaved grandmother. She also talked about her father. Once her father bought two mules after much sacrifice, and simply because this meant he might experience semi-independence from the landowner, his mules were poisoned. Hamer never could come to grips with that kind of hatefulness.

What was this unique *something* about Hamer, Parks, and Bates that propelled them to join the struggle for equality in the way they did? Each had been active in community affairs prior to the incidents that brought them to public attention. Like her contemporaries, Hamer had been a diligent church worshipper and volunteer.[42] Unlike many other women who participated in the movement, Hamer, Bates, and Parks were not drawn into politics by children or relatives; they chose to be active of their own accord, and the black community rallied to their support. All three women were middle-aged, which helped them to gain the respect and attention of younger workers when some of the older males sometimes could not. All three women experienced grave hardships or harassment. Parks was jailed. Bates received threats; her house was bombed and shot into. Hamer was severely beaten while in jail after attempting to integrate the bus stations in Winona, Mississippi.[43] From Parks in 1955 to Hamer in the 1960s black women leaders courageously took risks to see if their individual effort could make a difference for their people, their region, indeed the nation. It was Hamer who emphatically said, "the sickness in Mississippi is America's sickness."[44]

Contextualizing Fannie Lou Hamer within the history of African Americans' resistance to oppression, especially in relation to other activist black women, helps to illustrate why Hamer was an angry black woman.[45] Her frustration was the same desperate discontent that had inspired routine resistance to slave labor and full-scale slave revolts in the eighteenth and nineteenth centuries. Recalling her attitude on the day that she first attempted to register to vote, Hamer said, "The only thing they could do to me was kill me and it seemed like they'd been trying to do that a little bit at a time ever since I could remember."[46] Maria Stewart, an abolitionist, had called for the same kind of fearless initiative in 1831 when she said, "We need never to think that anybody is going to feel interested for us, if we do not feel interested for ourselves."[47] Although Stewart often directed specific advice to black women, she made it clear that, in this instance, "we" meant her race of people. Hamer's link to this legacy of African American activism cannot be separated from her work for human rights in the 1960s and 1970s.

Why did Hamer's "little light" suddenly begin to shine so brightly in 1962? Founded in 1960, SNCC had become a recognized force for change by 1962. She attended a SNCC meeting at a church meeting in Ruleville in August 1962 and heard Charles McLaurin and Robert Moses, both of SNCC, talk about political participation and how it could make a difference in the situation of Mississippi sharecroppers. That night, Hamer finally found a group with which she could identify. Parks had already found similar camaraderie with the NAACP and in her association with the Durrs. SNCC, and later the MFDP and the Delta Ministry, helped to sustain Hamer and her democratic principles, in much the same way that the club women's movement had helped women of the Progressive Era to confront problems that otherwise seemed too difficult for them to tackle alone.[48] In 1962, SNCC helped Hamer find her voice.

SNCC's emphasis on economic issues later became a central part of President Lyndon B. Johnson's Great Society programs. This further convinced Hamer that the timing was perfect for public criticism of the desperate situation for blacks in Mississippi. Later, Hamer even voiced her opinion of Johnson's programs in a letter to the president himself. She wrote, "If this is a Great Society, I'd hate to see a bad one."[49]

Hamer's civil rights activism came at a time when many women, especially white women, were beginning to discover feminism. Frederick Douglass spoke eloquently of the tension that black men felt in terms of being American and being black and trying to maintain a balance between the two.[50] Black women spoke of being pulled in three directions, having to come to terms with being American, African American, and female. Most black women chose to work against racism first, recognizing that sexism had to be addressed later. Some chose to address sexism primarily on a personal level all along. Consequently, "black women were the ones to raise the question of women's rights within the black organizations and issues of racism within white women's organizations."[51]

Hamer, however, cannot be seen as a conventional feminist. She fought racial oppression first, and then she wanted justice for all humankind. Her words best illustrate her human rights philosophy: "We have a problem, folks, and we want to try to deal with the problem in the only way that we can deal with the problem as far as black women. And you know, I'm not hung up on this about liberating myself from the black man. I'm not going to try that thing. I got a black husband, six feet three, two hundred and forty pounds, with a 14 shoe that I don't *want* to be liberated from. But we are here to work side by side with this black man in trying to bring liberation to all people."[52]

In this and other of her speeches, Hamer distanced herself from issues that would place her in the camp of mainstream feminists. Despite her well-publicized fury that women were not better represented at the Democratic National Convention in 1968, Hamer later stated that "[black women and men] are in this bag [of discrimination and inequities] together." She further advised black women "not to fight to try to liberate ourselves from the men . . . but to work together with the black man, then we will have a better chance to just act as human beings, and to be treated as human beings."[53] Hamer believed in the family structure. She loved children but was incapable of having her own. Like thousands of poor African American women throughout the South, she had been sterilized without her knowledge or consent during a hospital visit in 1961.[54] Although she was already forty-four years old at the time, this denial of agency in her own life fueled her passion for individual rights as much as it did her desire for children and her reverence for the family. Contrary to mainstream feminist reasoning, however, Hamer did not extend her desire for control over her own body and reproduction to support for abortion, or even birth control. Hamer said, "I believe that legal abortion is legal murder and the use of pills and rings to prevent God's will is a great sin."[55]

Although unable to bear her own children, Hamer raised four girls. One, Virgee Ree, had been badly burned as an infant, and because the girl's parents could not afford to care for her, the Hamers brought her to live with them. Another child, Dorothy Jean, whom the Hamers took from an impoverished single mother, died of a cerebral hemorrhage in 1967. Hamer and her husband, "Pap," then assumed the job of raising Dorothy Jean's two daughters, Jacqueline and Lenora. Hamer felt that her daughters probably needed more of her time and attention than her numerous speaking engagements and public activism allowed.

Although Hamer agonized over the prospect, she did not give up opportunities to speak so that she could spend more time with the girls. She sincerely believed that Pap did all he could to support her as his wife and in the role of parenting.[56]

Hamer received wide recognition for her part in bringing about a major political transition and for raising significant questions that addressed basic human needs. In 1963 the Fifth Avenue Baptist Church in Nashville, Tennessee, presented her one of the first awards that she received; it was appropriately for "Voter Registration and Hamer's Fight for Freedom for Mankind."[57] She received numerous other awards. The National Federation of Business and Professional Women's Clubs, Inc., presented Hamer its National Sojourner Truth Meritorious Service Award as a tribute to Hamer's strong defense of human dignity and fearless promotion of civil rights. The organization's naming of the award also gave credence to the connection between ancestral freedom fighters and those of the twentieth century. Delta Sigma Theta Sorority, Inc., awarded her life membership. Many colleges and universities honored her with honorary degrees, including the nearby Tougaloo College in 1969.[58]

Hamer gave numerous speeches across the country into the 1970s. She had grown weary by this time because she was suffering from cancer. She, however, continued to accept invitations to speak about the subject most dear to her, basic human rights for all Americans. Indeed, she remained tired of being sick and tired until her life ended. She died of cancer on 14 March 1977 at Mound Bayou Community Hospital in Mound Bayou, Mississippi. She was fifty-nine years old.

Fannie Lou Hamer is remembered as a heroine.[59] Personally and politically, she overcame tremendous odds. Hamer relied on what she knew best—religion, song, social activism, and self-help—much of which was rooted in an African American heritage of which she was very proud. She was emboldened by the example of other black female activists like Rosa Parks and Daisy Bates. Perhaps most important, Hamer, like Parks and Bates, attained womanhood at a time that was ripe for reform. Like Parks and Bates, who had the benefit of organizational support from the NAACP, Hamer was fortunate to have the backing of the SNCC, as well as the Mississippi Freedom Democratic Party—and they were fortunate to have her. Like the educated women of the club movement, Hamer used voluntary associations like the Delta Ministry and Freedom Farm to pursue objectives that would have been otherwise difficult to attain.[60]

She became a figure on the national stage of the civil rights movement and a noted orator, despite the fact that she had only about six years of formal education. But Hamer believed that she could compete equally with any high school graduate of the 1970s.[61] As a speaker, Hamer was charismatic. She expressed her thoughts in a unique way, and she had a rich, deep, husky voice. Many Mississippians who heard her speak have said that she was spellbinding.[62] In the context of black women reformers and reformist organizations throughout American history, Fannie Lou Hamer stands out as one of the most unique, courageous, and effective leaders to emerge from the state of Mississippi.

NOTES

The author is grateful to Nell Irvin Painter, Edwards Professor of History at Princeton University, for thinking through some of the issues related to Hamer and her contemporaries in this chapter.

1. Fannie Lou Hamer, "Claiming Our Power," *Essence* 16 (May 1985): 102.

2. Daisy Bates, *The Long Shadow of Little Rock* (Fayetteville: University of Arkansas Press, 1987), 221.

3. Rosa Parks, *Rosa Parks: My Story* (New York: Dial Books, 1992), 2.

4. Maria W. Stewart, "Religion and the Pure Principles of Morality, the Sure Foundation on Which We Must Build," in *Maria W. Stewart, America's First Black Woman Political Writer: Essays and Speeches*, ed. Marilyn Richardson (Bloomington: Indiana University Press, 1987), 38.

5. Hamer, interview by Neil McMillen, 25 January 1973, Mississippi Oral History Program, University of Southern Mississippi, Hattiesburg, 43.

6. Richardson, ed., 38.

7. Hamer, "Claiming Our Power," 101–5, emphasis mine; Rosalyn Terborg-Penn, "Black Women in Resistance: A Cross-Cultural Perspective," in *In Resistance: Studies in African, Caribbean, and Afro-American History*, ed. Gary Y. Okihiro (Amherst: University of Massachusetts Press, 1986), 188–209; Harry A. Ploski and James Williams, eds., *The Negro Almanac: A Reference Work on the Afro-American* (New York: Wiley and Sons, 1983), 1299.

8. Barbara Fields, "Slavery, Race, and Ideology in the United States of America," *New Left Review* 181 (May/June 1990): 95–118; Ann duCille, "The Occult of True Black Womanhood: Critical Demeanor and Black Feminist Studies," *Signs* 19 (spring 1994): 591–629; David R. Roediger, *The Wages of Whiteness: Race and the Making of the American Working Class* (London: Verso, 1991), 3–17, 167–84; Susan Stanford Friedman, "Beyond White and Other: Relationality and Narratives of Race in Feminist Discourse," *Signs* 21 (autumn 1995): 1–49.

9. Noralee Frankel and Nancy S. Dye, eds., *Gender, Class, Race, and Reform in the Progressive Era* (Lexington: University Press of Kentucky, 1991).

10. Irma Watkins-Owens, *Blood Relations: Caribbean Immigrants and the Harlem Community, 1900–1930* (Bloomington: Indiana University Press, 1996).

11. Robin D. G. Kelley, *Race Rebels: Culture, Politics, and the Working Class* (New York: Free Press, 1994), 13; Albert J. Raboteau, *Canaan Land: A Religious History of African Americans* (New York: Oxford University Press, 2001); James F. Findlay Jr., *Church People in the Struggle: The National Council of Churches and the Black Freedom Movement, 1950–1970* (New York: Oxford University Press, 1993). Of course, one of the earliest of scholars to make a clear link of past black resistance to

twentieth-century struggles is Vincent Harding in *There Is a River: The Black Struggle for Freedom in America* (New York: Harcourt Brace Jovanovich, 1981).

12. Linda Reed, *Simple Decency and Common Sense: The Southern Conference Movement, 1938–1963* (Bloomington: Indiana University Press, 1991), 77–79.

13. Harvard Sitkoff, *A New Deal for Blacks: The Emergence of Civil Rights as a National Issue,* vol. 1, *The Depression Decade* (New York: Oxford University Press, 1978), viii–ix, 58–59, 317–23.

14. Reed, *Simple Decency;* Clayborne Carson, *In Struggle: SNCC and the Black Awakening of the 1960s* (Cambridge: Harvard University Press, 1981).

15. Hamer, interview, 1973; Hamer, interview by Neil McMillen, 14 April 1972, Mississippi Oral History Program; Hamer, interview by Robert Wright, 9 August 1968, Civil Rights Documentation Project, Manuscript Division, Moorland-Spingarn Research Center, Howard University.

16. Hamer, "Autobiography of Fannie Lou Hamer," microfilm roll 1, Hamer Papers, Amistad Research Center, New Orleans; "We Want Ours Now!" microfilm roll 1, Hamer Papers; see also Bernice Johnson Reagon, "Women as Culture Carriers in the Civil Rights Movement: Fannie Lou Hamer," in *Women in the Civil Rights Movement: Trailblazers and Torchbearers, 1941–1965,* ed. Vicki L. Crawford et al. (Brooklyn, N.Y.: Carlson Publishing, 1990), 203–32; Chana Kai Lee, *For Freedom's Sake: The Life of Fannie Lou Hamer* (Urbana: University of Illinois Press, 1999), 24, 31–37.

17. Darlene Clark Hine, "Lifting the Veil, Shattering the Silence: Black Women's History in Slavery and Freedom," in *The State of Afro-American History: Past, Present, and Future,* ed. Hine (Baton Rouge: Louisiana State University Press, 1986), 223–49. Hine writes of the need for studies of women in the civil rights movement. Two recent studies on Hamer include Lee, *For Freedom's Sake,* and Kay Mills, *This Little Light of Mine: The Life of Fannie Lou Hamer* (New York: Dutton, 1993).

18. Hamer, "Autobiography"; "We Want Ours Now!" Hamer Papers; 2 Cor 5.7, Gal 3.26, Eph 3.17–19 AV; Aldon D. Morris, *The Origins of the Civil Rights Movement: Black Communities Organizing for Change* (New York: Free Press, 1984), 1–16. See also Charles M. Payne, *I've Got the Light of Freedom: The Organizing Tradition and the Mississippi Struggle* (Berkeley: University of California Press, 1995).

19. Harding, xiii.

20. Lee, 21.

21. Harding, xiv–xv, xix.

22. Reagon, "Fannie Lou Hamer," 203–32.

23. Reagon, "The Songs Are Free," interview by Bill Moyers, videocassette, Mystic Fire Video, 1991.

24. Anne Firor Scott, *Making the Invisible Woman Visible* (Urbana: University of Illinois Press, 1984), 337.

25. Ibid., 345–46.

26. Stephanie J. Shaw, "Black Club Women and the Creation of the National Association of Colored Women," *Journal of Women's History* 3 (fall 1991): 10–25.

27. Hine, 223–49.

28. Parks, 116.

29. J. Mills Thornton, "Challenge and Response in the Montgomery Bus Boycott of 1955–1956," *Alabama Review* 33 (July 1980): 163–235.

30. Reed, "The Legacy of Daisy Bates," *Arkansas Historical Quarterly* 59 (spring 2000): 76–83; Bates.

31. Hamer, "Autobiography"; Payne, 36–39.

32. Hamer, "Autobiography."

33. Reed, "Fannie Lou Hamer: New Ideas for the Civil Rights Movement and American Democracy," in *The Role of Ideas in the Civil Rights–Era South,* ed. Ted Ownby (Jackson: University Press of Mississippi, 2002).

34. Hamer, interview, 1972: Hamer, interview, 1973; Hamer, interview, 1968.

35. Hamer, interview, 1968.

36. Ibid.; Lee, 109.

37. Gerald H. Gaither, *Blacks and the Populist Revolt: Ballots and Bigotry in the "New South"* (Tuscaloosa: University of Alabama Press, 1977); Jane Dailey et al., *Jumpin' Jim Crow: Southern Politics from Civil War to Civil Rights* (Princeton: Princeton University Press, 2000).

38. Hamer, "Autobiography"; "We Want Ours Now!" Hamer Papers; Donna Langston, "The Women of Highlander," in *Women in the Civil Rights Movement: Trailblazers and Torchbearers,* ed. Crawford et al., 157.

39. Jerry DeMuth, "Tired of Being Sick and Tired," *Nation* 198 (1 June 1964): 548–51; Phyl Garland, "Builders of a New South," *Ebony* 21 (August 1966): 27–30; P. Marshall, "Hunger Has No Color Line," *Vogue* 155 (June 1970): 126–27; Joyce A. Ladner, "Fannie Lou Hamer: In Memoriam," *Black Enterprise* 7 (May 1977): 56; Eleanor Holmes Norton, "Woman Who Changed the South: Memory of Fannie Lou Hamer," *MS* 5 (July 1977): 51; Alexis De Veaux, "Going South: Back to Where the Heart of the Civil Rights Movement Still Beats," *Essence* 16 (May 1985): 54, 56, 224; Marita Golden, "The Sixties Live On: The Era of Black Consciousness Is Preserved as a State of Mind," *Essence* 16 (May 1985): 70–71; "Claiming Our Power," *Essence* 16 (May 1985): 101–3; Jean Carey Bond, "From the Bottom Up: Black Women a Source for Liberation of Both Race and the Gender," *Essence* 16 (May 1985): 105–8, 205–7.

40. "Life in Mississippi: An Interview with Fannie Lou Hamer," *Freedomways* 5 (1965), reprinted in *Afro-American History: Primary Sources,* ed. Thomas R. Frazier (Chicago: Dorsey Press, 1988), 357–66.

41. Ibid.

42. Lee, 2, 7, 103, 130–31, 172. See also Evelyn Brooks Higginbotham, *Righteous Discontent: The Women's Movement in the Black Baptist Church, 1880–1920* (Cambridge: Harvard University Press, 1993).

43. Ladner, 56; Norton, 51; Reed, "Daisy Bates," 76–83.

44. "Proceedings of the Democratic National Convention 1964: Credentials Committee," Atlantic City, N.J., 22 August 1964, 32–45, folder 549, box 11, Ed King Papers, Coleman Library, Tougaloo College, Jackson, Miss.; Mamie E. Locke "Is This America? Fannie Lou Hamer and the Mississippi Freedom Democratic Party" in *Women in the Civil Rights Movement: Trailblazers and Torchbearers,* ed. Crawford et al., 27–37.

45. Richardson, ed., 38; Harding, xiii; Scott, 337; Shaw, 10–25.

46. Lee, 26.

47. Richardson, ed., 38.

48. Scott, xxiv–xxv.

49. Lee, 166.

50. Frederick Douglass, *Life and Times of Frederick Douglass, Written by Himself* (Hartford, Conn.: Park, 1888).

51. Hine, 230, 234, 237, 244–48.

52. Hamer, "The Special Plight and the Role of Black Woman," speech given at the NAACP Legal Defense Fund Institute, 7 May 1971, New York City, reprinted in "It's in Your Hands," in *Black Women in White America: A Documentary History,* ed. Gerda Lerner (New York: Vintage Books, 1973), 611–12.

53. Ibid., 613.

54. Mills, 21.

55. Hamer, "Is It Too Late?" 1971, Hamer Collection, L. Zenobia Coleman Library, Special Collections, Tougaloo College.

56. Hamer, interview, 1973.

57. Hamer, "Autobiography."

58. Ibid.

59. Herbert Denmark Jr., "F. L. Hamer Convention Develops Platform, Economic Bill of Rights," *The Atlanta Voice,* 30 July–5 August 1988, 1, 3.

60. Scott, xxiv–xxv; Shaw, 10–25.

61. Hamer, interview, 1973.

62. John Dittmer to author, 22 July 1987.

Mae Bertha Carter

(1923–1999)

School Desegregation in a Delta Town

CONSTANCE CURRY

❀　❀　❀

In January 1966, I drove down a dirt road with cotton fields on all sides, in the heart of the Mississippi Delta. I was based in Atlanta, working as southern field representative for the American Friends Service Committee (AFSC), a Quaker Service organization based in Philadelphia. Jean Fairfax had called from the national office and asked me to visit the home of Mae Bertha and Matthew Carter, black sharecroppers on the Pemble Plantation in Sunflower County, Mississippi. I found their shotgun house on a narrow, dusty road, noted their little vegetable and flower garden, and was welcomed warmly by five-foot-two, intense, blue-eyed Mae Bertha Carter.

Supreme Court Justice Thurgood Marshall, once a leading attorney with the National Association for the Advancement of Colored People (NAACP) Legal Defense and Educational Fund, often referred to Mississippi as "the belly of the beast," indicating the state's long history of racial persecution, violence, and enforced segregation of African Americans. In 1965, Mae Bertha Carter and her husband, Matthew, kicked that belly hard when they enrolled their seven school-age children in the previously all-white public schools in the nearby town of Drew. In 1968, Carl Carter, the youngest, joined them. The Civil Rights Act of 1964 required every public school system wishing to continue receiving federal funds to draw up a desegregation plan. The Drew School System, like many others, submitted a "freedom of choice" plan, which in theory gave all parents a chance to send their children to the school of their choice. In reality, particularly in rural areas of the South, the plan was a snare and a delusion. White supremacists were confident that no black family would dare choose a traditionally white school, particularly not those families trapped in the peonage of the sharecropping system. But, as Mrs. Carter later told me, the white people just didn't know about the Carters out on that farm.

The morning after the Carters submitted their choice forms to the school principals at A. W. James Elementary and Drew High School, the plantation overseer came out to convince them to withdraw the children, hinting at the possible consequences of their action. A few days later, a vigilante shot into the Carters' home in the early morning hours, and their credit was cut off at the local store. The Carter family did not falter. The couple's motivation was simple: they wanted a better education for their children.

During our first visit, I asked Mae Bertha and Matthew why they had made the choice of schools that they did. I knew their house had been shot into, and I had read Carter's letters to the AFSC on the intimidation and economic reprisals against the whole family, as well as the harassment the children suffered in school. Matthew looked me in the eyes and poignantly said, "We thought they meant it."[1] Mae Bertha told me of the poor schools for blacks that she and Matthew had attended, followed a generation later by her five oldest children, who left Mississippi as soon as they graduated from the "colored school." "I was tired of my kids still coming home with pages torn out of worn-out books that come from the white school. I was tired of them riding on these old raggedy buses after the white children didn't want to ride on them anymore. Plus the school board is all white and over both the white and black schools, but that school board isn't concerned about black kids. I just want my children to have a better education and to get out of these fields."[2]

I met the children and heard them tell of the continuing harassment in the schools, by both teachers and students. I also learned what was holding the family together. Each evening the children would gather with their mother and talk about what had happened at school, and they would cry together and often sing freedom songs they had learned from civil rights workers. Mrs. Carter told them, "That is not a white school, it is a yellow brick school, and we pay taxes, so it's your school."[3] Believing that "hate destroys you," she wouldn't let her children say they hated anyone.[4] They also had been taught to finish things once they had started, and as Mae Bertha's son Larry Carter later said to me, "It's like they would have won, if we dropped out."[5]

Following that first visit, Carter wrote the Philadelphia AFSC and thanked them for sending me to visit them. I wrote my report and sent it to Philadelphia. I thought that would be the extent of my involvement with the Carters.

During the antebellum period, in most southern states, it was against the law to teach a slave to read and write. The most obvious rationale for this was that education might lift the aspirations of a slave to a better life and ultimately

MAE BERTHA CARTER
1994. Photo by Ann Curry.
Courtesy of Constance Curry.

free him or her from easy exploitation by white masters. The laws against education for African Americans were lifted after the Civil War, but little changed. There was an apt quote in the black community: "Keep us ignorant and we stay in our place." Or, as Mississippi Governor James K. Vardaman had put it in 1899, "education only spoils a good field hand—it is money thrown away."[6] Throughout slavery, Reconstruction, the years of legal segregation, and thereafter, the quest of the black community for education had been focused and persistent.

In the 1890s, northern white philanthropic groups, including the Peabody Educational Fund, the Anna T. Jeanes Fund, and the Julius Rosenwald Fund, realized the enormous gaps in educational needs and opportunities in the South and began to provide financial resources for building, monitoring, and other assistance for schools for black children. The Rosenwald Fund generally contributed about 15 to 20 percent of the total costs, with the remainder coming from public funds, white philanthropists, and the black school patrons themselves—a practice often described as a system of "double taxation" for blacks. Between 1913 and 1932, the Julius Rosenwald Fund helped establish more than 5,000 schools in the South. In Mississippi, 557 schools for black children received help from the fund, and in the mid-1920s, about one-fourth of all black children attending school in the state went to a so-called Rosenwald School.[7]

Although many of the Rosenwald schools were in the Mississippi Delta, most black children still went to school in one-room school houses or church buildings located on the plantations where they and their parents worked in the fields. The children generally went on a "split session," attending only when the cotton didn't need tending, sometimes receiving only five or six months of schooling a year. The teachers themselves were often poorly educated, and books and equipment were usually old and out of date, generally having been discarded from white schools.

In 1954, the Supreme Court unanimously ruled in the case of *Brown v. Board of Education* that segregated schools were unconstitutional, that the separation of children in the schools was inherently unequal, and it called for states to take steps to remedy this inequality. While the *Brown* decision was a victory for African Americans, white resistance to desegregation quickly intensified throughout the South. The Supreme Court decision fanned the flames of the most primal fear related to educating black people. The anxiety of white elites over losing their low-paid, dependent work force was ever present. A far more sinister threat, especially to whites with school-aged daughters, was the potential for desegregated schools to bring black and white children into new relationships of social equality. Exaggerated visions of miscegenation and near hysteria over the prospect of "race-mixing" at a young age raised white resistance to the *Brown* decision to a fever pitch.

At the local and state levels, white politicians promised their constituents that they would never bow to integration and vowed to thwart the federal government's interference with the southern way of life. In Mississippi, two months after the Supreme Court decision, the segregationist Citizens' Council was organized in Indianola, Mississippi, county seat of Sunflower County and just down the road from Drew. Mae Bertha Carter referred to the lawyers and businessmen in the council as "the uptown Klan." The Mississippi state legislature quickly passed and the state's voters approved a series of laws designed to circumvent the court ruling. The infamous Mississippi State Sovereignty Commission was established in 1956 to preserve segregation at all costs. The state-funded commission investigated and intimidated anyone, white or black, whom it believed might be a threat to the status quo. Meanwhile, white supremacists waged a reign of terror and violence against African Americans that practically immobilized black leaders both in and outside of Mississippi for nearly a decade.

The Student Nonviolent Coordinating Committee (SNCC) and other civil rights workers from outside the South began working in Mississippi in 1961, giving courage and inspiration to local black people. The NAACP filed its first suits for school desegregation in Jackson, Biloxi, and Leake County, Mississippi, in 1962. By 1965, the Carters had gone to mass meetings, had listened to civil rights speakers, and had learned all the freedom songs. Naomi and Ruth Carter had been jailed after marching for voting rights in Jackson. Ruth Carter told me that they really were in the movement: "Going to those mass meetings and marching and going to jail and singing and talking about 'you ain't gonna let nobody turn you 'round.' So that's why we was already motivated when the school integration came."[8]

On the opening day of school in 1965, Deputy Sheriff John Sidney Parker had two cars—four men in each—meet the school bus as it turned off the plantation road and onto the road to Drew. The seven Carter children were on the bus. Ruth, the oldest there, was seated alone; her four sisters and two brothers sat in the three seats in front of her. The Drew City Police and several FBI agents met the bus at the city limits and followed it to A. W. James Elementary School and Drew High School. Crowds of white hecklers stood along the streets or in yards, hollering, "Go back to your own schools, niggers." Officers stood in the school doorways until the Carter children were safely inside and into the principal's office. These precautions continued for a week until it seemed the arrival of the children had settled into a "normal" routine. The FBI reported to Washington on 7 September that seven Negro children registered to attend formerly white schools in Drew, Mississippi, without incident and that local authorities did not intend to have violation of the law on the part of anyone.[9] Their observation in no way could predict the hell that faced those seven children and their parents for years to come.

A civil rights worker in nearby Indianola, Mississippi, visited the Carters soon after the opening of school and notified Jean Fairfax at the national AFSC office about the problems the family faced. Fairfax sent the Carters one hundred dollars from the AFSC to help with food and other expenses and wrote to congratulate them for their courage and to assure them of AFSC support in their struggle for justice. Carter wrote back, "Thank you for the money because we were almost at the end. The children need so much in school. We got it cashed without any trouble at the bank, and I can assure you that we will use it for the kids. I am so happy because the Toms around here say we can't afford it, but people like you will help us do it."[10] Thus began a weekly correspondence between the Carters and the AFSC, which was to last for ten years.

Letters from Carter to the AFSC throughout September told of the family's continuing problems. "My ten year old girl need eye glasses. She can't see the board in school. More talk that we may have to move at the end of the year. The boss called all the people in and ask what all they know about us and why they hadn't told him. He also said he was going to help the ones that wasn't in the mess. So you can see why I was glad to get the money."[11]

Later that same month, she wrote:

I am writing to let you know about the glasses for Pearl and being qualify for free lunches. I called the superintendent of the school and he said only the people on welfare could have free lunches and I couldn't get glasses through the school. He got real nasty when I ask him about it and hung up the phone. I really believe that Drew need some more Negro children in that school. I don't think they should be receiving money with my few little children in there. The school suppose to have been integrate on freedom of choice. A lot of other children could have gone but their parent were afraid of the pressure and someone may shoot in their home just as they did ours. They attitude will probably change since they see my children going on.[12]

In response to a letter from the AFSC, Carter replied:

Yes I have taken Pearl to the eye doctor. She have bad eyes. The test and glasses $40. I paid $15 down and start Nov. l, paying $5.00 a month. We been talking about a place to stay if we do have to move, but we don't know where yet. The people here so mean. We wish we could get a place in Drew but most the Negro people afraid to let us have a place, but we going to try. We need help bad because the boss only let us have $8 when we pick a bale, and we can't pick too much with the kids in school, we have to pick four bales, so that all the cash we had. It hard for the poor to stand up for what is right here. It rains now so no one can pick any cotton. I don't know what we going to do. It is so sad. But I am sure the Lord will take care of us. I try to tell fact. Don't many people know about Mississippi but the ones been here or live here. The whites here are out to get you, like no place to stay, no food, no job. And this will stop the other Negroes. I bath my children everyday and put them in clean clothes. When my little ten-year old Pearl get to school she (teacher) tell her to take a bath and put on clean clothes. I think it need somebody to come to that school and investigate. I think the teacher is cracking up. I cannot report it to the principal because he just as mean as the teacher. All of the people out there in Drew is mean. [13]

Deborah in the first grade, Beverly in the third, and Pearl in the fifth were all at the A. W. James Elementary School. The fifth grade, however, was in a separate part of the school, so Pearl was completely isolated and vulnerable. The unspoken policy of Pearl's teacher was that no white child would have to sit next to Pearl for more than a week. Each Monday, she would move the children seated in front and back of Pearl, take two new children out into the hall and have a talk with them before they took their seats next to Pearl. Even then, the child in front would pull his or her chair up farther and the one behind would push back as far as possible. Pearl later told her mother that the teacher must have kept a list because some of the children had to come back around before school got out. [14]

On the other side of the elementary school, white children called Deborah and Beverly "nigger" and "walking tootsie roll." When the first-graders walked to the high school for special events like a fair or circus, each child had a partner to hold hands for the three blocks. Deborah's partner was always the teacher, and, in her naïveté, she told her mother how proud she was to be chosen from all the others. [15]

Carter continued to correspond with the national AFSC, always expressing her gratitude that people outside of Mississippi were in touch with them. In October, she wrote:

I am thinking about you all. How the Lord have sent you all into our home and I just want to write you. The superintendent call all the kids in to see what was happening to them. My kids are smart. They did it well. Gloria told about the bus driver saying to go on to the back after Stanley start to sit in front. My kids riding up front now. One day Pearl cried when I gave her lunch money. Mother don't make me eat there. She told me how the kids treat her, how she left her food. I wrote the teacher. She took it to the principal. I wrote: "Dear teacher: Pearl found it hard to eat because the kids come up and put their fist in her face. Thank you."[16]

The older children received no better treatment. At Drew High School, spit-balls and name-calling were daily occurrences. They all recall how the white kids jumped away from them, and they usually skipped lunch in the cafeteria because the harassment was so constant and painful. They usually went outside and waited for classes to resume. The situation never improved until the schools were fully desegregated in 1970.

In the meantime, the overseer put a mechanical cotton picker in the Carters' fields and then plowed under the remaining cotton usually picked by the Carters for supplementary income. In addition, someone on a moonless night in November opened the gate to the Carters' animal pen, and their mule, cows, and pigs were gone for good. The AFSC began to send a grant of twenty-five dollars per week for food, and the Colorado Friends sent money for school lunches. Carter's weekly letters continued throughout the fall, describing the harassment of the children.

Concerned about the continuing problems, Jean Fairfax visited the Carters over Thanksgiving. She flew into Memphis, rented a car, and drove down High-way 61 to Merigold. Matthew Carter was sitting on top of his truck at a designated service station and guided Jean back to their house. When he arrived, Fairfax found that efforts to run the Carters off the Pemble land had escalated. Fairfax realized that the Carters needed another place in the school district to live and contacted civil rights leader Amzie Moore in nearby Cleveland as well as Marian E. Wright at the NAACP Legal Defense and Educational Fund Office in Jackson.[17]

The Carters were able to survive November and December without money from the crops. Amzie Moore brought food, the Boulder, Colorado, Friends Meeting sent lunch money, AFSC sent small grants, and a church in New Jersey sent some canned foods. Reverend Maurice McCrackin, a white minister from Cincinnati, Ohio, heard about the Carters, visited them, and sent money from his group, Operation Freedom. When the overseer failed to bring the usual annual fifteen dollars to the Carters for a car tag, Fannie Lou Hamer, by then a leader in the Mississippi Freedom Democratic party, brought the money to Carter.

On 11 December 1965 Carter wrote to Fairfax: "My husband went out today to get the settlement. We owe them $97 and were told to get off the place next week. Mr. Pemble's son-in-law told Matthew that if it had been left up to him we would have been put off in September. We don't have any place to go. Then Mr. Pemble spoke and said we could stay until we found a place, but he was going to sell the house. When you or someone come I will tell you everything. We need help."[18]

As winter set in, the fact that the school bus driver and a teacher asked the children when they were moving confirmed Carter's suspicions of collusion between school officials and plantation owners. With eviction from the plantation looming, Barbara Moffett, Director of the Community Relations Division of the AFSC, wired the U.S. Commissioner of Education:

> URGENTLY REQUEST YOUR OFFICE TAKE ACTION TO ENSURE THAT THE SEVEN
> CHILDREN OF MR. AND MRS. MATTHEW CARTER, R #1, BOX 37, MERIGOLD, MISS.
> CAN REMAIN IN DREW DISTRICT SCHOOLS. SINCE THE CARTERS ENROLLED THEIR
> SEVEN CHILDREN IN THE SCHOOLS THEY HAVE FACED CONTINUAL HARASSMENT
> INCLUDING HAVING THEIR HOME SHOT INTO. THEIR CHILDREN ARE THE ONLY NE-
> GROES IN THIS PREVIOUSLY ALL-WHITE SCHOOL SYSTEM. THE FAMILY NOW FACES
> EVICTION AND NEEDS THE SUPPORT AND HELP OF THE FEDERAL GOVERNMENT IN
> EXERCISING THEIR RIGHTS UNDER THE CIVIL RIGHTS ACT.[19]

Third-grader Beverly, who had agreed during Fairfax's visit to be her "Mississippi secretary," wrote in mid-December: "We have eaten in the lunch room. We had tunafish and peanut butter cookies and green beans and milk for Friday. We had jello and carrots for Thursday. WE WISH YOU A MERRY CHRISTMAS."[20]

The Justice Department sent a representative in early 1966 to talk to Mr. Pemble. Pemble agreed to sign a contract with Matthew allowing him to sharecrop for another year but with his shares reduced to ten acres. With support from Operation Freedom and the AFSC, the Carters were able to make it through the school year. Mae Bertha told me that the children's final report cards showed all of them with an average between 85 and 90 and that not one of them had missed a day of school.

Residents of Drew in general and neighbors on one street in particular awoke to a surprise on the morning of 1 October 1966. The Carters had moved into the one-story frame house with green asbestos shingles at 166 Broadway, a few blocks from the post office and downtown Drew. The journey from the plantation to Broadway had taken over a year after the enrollment of the Carter children and the combined efforts of the AFSC, the NAACP Legal Defense and Educational Fund, and the Unitarian Universalist Association.

When rumors of eviction from the Pemble place began soon after school opening in 1965, and as the harassment continued into the spring of 1966, it was apparent that the best plan to ensure the children's continuing attendance at school was to move into a house in Drew. The Carters along with Marian Wright and other NAACP Legal Defense and Educational Fund staff in Jackson began looking for another place for the family. Various attempts to purchase or rent houses in Drew met with closed doors at the mention of the Carters' name.

In early August 1966, Jean Fairfax asked her staff member Allen Black to go to Sunflower County and find a house for the Carters. Black was young, tall, charming, and black, and under the guise of a worker for the Unitarian Church he was immediately shown eight or nine possible houses. In secret consultation with the Carters, Black chose the Broadway house, and he began the negotiations to purchase the house for seven thousand dollars from Mr. Willie Jones, the owner, who lived in Chattanooga, Tennessee. Black bought the house in his name and legal papers were drawn up later holding it "in trust" for the Carters. Black described the house for AFSC staff:

> The house has a carport and attached utility room and is located on the edge of "the" Negro subdivision. There is an additional lot adjoining which can be used for a small garden. Inside, the house is in good repair. The walls in the living room, hall and all three bedrooms are of nicely varnished pine (just made for kids). There is a complete bathroom, central gas heat (floor furnace) additional gas outlets in each room, a quick recovery water heater and a vent over the kitchen range. The floors had once been painted but were of sufficient quality that a good wax job will make them quite presentable. The house contains furniture and Mr. Jones has offered to sell the whole works for $200.00.[21]

Back in Philadelphia, AFSC staff moved quickly and lined up funding to purchase the house. When Black arrived at the Carters on 30 September, packing was well underway. The family was anxious over the secrecy and elements of deception in the move into Drew. They worried over the prospect of new neighbors in Drew who might not be supportive of them. Mr. Carter was agitated over doing right by Mr. Pemble and gathering the last of the cotton crop he had raised. Mr. Bob, the plantation storeowner, had agreed to take some of Matthew's peas as partial payment of their account. "We have to live with these people," Matthew told Black. Mae Bertha didn't care and wanted to move immediately. They compromised with the family moving that night but with Matthew remaining at the plantation until his cotton was picked.[22]

When they got home from school, Ruth, Gloria, and Larry rode into Drew with Black to clean, turn on the heat, and get the appliances working. Shortly after eight and just after dark, the rest of the family arrived towing a canvas-covered trailer. Since the house was already partially furnished, they had brought only a few items, mostly personal belongings. That night the Carters' oldest son, Larry, went to bed torn between the respect he felt for his father's dedication to honor his sharecropper's contract and his dreadful fear for Matthew out alone picking cotton on a deserted plantation.

The house on Broadway was the nicest one the Carter family had ever occupied, and Black described them as "in good spirits." "I'm always impressed," he wrote, "with the fierce pride they seem to have. Did you know that Matthew subsisted on tomatoes and milk the entire week he spent picking the last of the cotton. Things will be some better because Mr. Carter was able to slaughter a hog last week."[23]

Although the house had amenities unknown to the Carters in previous places, life in Drew was sometimes sad. Beverly wanted to cry at times when she was hurt by her school experiences, but the first time she really cried was after they had moved into Drew and she began to meet black children her own age. They could not understand why she was going to an all-white school and asked her if she thought she was white. Beverly later told me that their reaction hurt her more than any of the bad names the white kids had called her in school.

In December 1966, the Carters signed a contract with the AFSC to repay $3,500 with no interest to begin on 1 August 1967 at the rate of thirty dollars per month. The Carters never missed a payment. In July 1975 they received, in their name, the deed and title to the house on Broadway.

Shortly after my first visit to Sunflower County, we were in touch by letter every week, and either the older children or Mae Bertha would tell me what was going on in the schools or the community. Sometimes Carter would comment on broader political issues like the Vietnam War or on Washington. "Nixon don't need to be President of nothin'," she wrote in 1968.[24]

Our correspondence sometimes called for a visit to Drew. Carter went to work for Headstart in Cleveland, Mississippi, and I often spent time with Matthew, who took care of the house and the children until he too found a job outside of Drew. In 1970, under court order from a suit filed by the Carter family, the dual school system in Drew was abolished and other black children joined the Carters. The black community then had to face slightly different problems with white teachers who often did not understand their children and were quick to discipline them for minor problems. The Carters filed suits several times when they noted unfair treatment.

I took another job in 1975 and lost contact with the Carters and the other families that I had met who also had taken that first step toward school desegregation. Thirteen years later, in 1988, I was attending a conference on women in the civil rights movement, looked across the room, and there was Mae Bertha Carter. We hugged and she brought me up to date. She told me, "You know Matthew died three years ago. . . . [E]ight of our children graduated from Drew

High School and they all went on to college, and seven of them graduated from Ole Miss." This inspired me to record their story and, after interviewing Carter for many hours in her living room in Drew, taping the stories of all thirteen Carter children, and researching the Carter letters and staff reports in the AFSC Archives in Philadlephia, *Silver Rights* was published in 1995.

Mae Bertha and I traveled to fifty-two cities and spoke about her life to colleges, universities, churches, and community groups. It was a privilege and a joy to spend this time with her—she was a very funny woman, and we laughed a lot. She was also one of the wisest people I have ever known, and I used to tell her that I wished she could be president of the United States. She concurred.

Carter always made it clear in her talks that she didn't consider herself a courageous person. "Somebody had to do it," she would say. Nor did she rest on her laurels, which were many, including awards from the University of Mississippi and the NAACP Legal Defense Fund. She was angry that black people were losing interest in voting, and shaking her finger said, "People died so you could vote." In her later years, candidates, black and white, held meetings in her living room, and Willis Simmons, the first black state senator elected from the Delta since Reconstruction, attributes his success in part to Carter.

She continued to work for quality education for "all the children," even after her last child Carl graduated from Drew High School in 1980. For the next twenty years she continued to dog the heels of the Drew school system and in the 1990s bemoaned the slow sinking of its academic rating. Daughter Beverly served on the school board for many years—they told her she might as well since her mother would be at the meetings anyway. Carter was enraged when fellow board members removed Beverly from the board because of her many disagreements with the majority white, male members.

Over time, for Carter, the greatest insult was that some of the white school board members had their children in private, white-only academies but were still making decisions for the majority-black public schools. On our trips, she also talked about punishments, suspensions, expulsions, and overly strict disciplinary measures called zero tolerance policies that affected the children in the now majority-black public schools. She watched CNN and other news programs daily and would tell me her opinions of the mistakes in President Bill Clinton's welfare reform policy as well as the state's prison system that put young black men away at Parchman Penitentiary for minor drug offenses rather than providing rehabilitation.

Mae Bertha Carter fought, literally, until the day she died in April 1999. When she was diagnosed with cancer, she was put on home health care in Drew, and when folks admonished her about never being home, she said, "Well if I have to be home, just take me off the list." In October 2000, at the request of a group of black and white students at the University of Mississippi, a tree was planted in the Circle, the lovely circular lawn in front of the 150-year-old Lyceum building, where bloody riots occurred in 1962 over the enrollment of James Meredith as the first black student at the university. The plaque underneath the tree reads, "In memoriam for Mae Bertha Carter and her seven children who graduated from Ole Miss." Many of the Carter children attended the ceremony, and some grandchildren and great-grandchildren helped dig the earth for the planting of the tree.

When passing through Oxford recently, I went to see the graceful red leaf maple tree, and a cool breeze swept through the steaming July afternoon. I thought of the last time I saw Mae Bertha in the hospital in Jackson. She told me that she wasn't ready to go—there was too much to be done.

NOTES

1. Constance Curry, *Silver Rights* (Chapel Hill, N.C.: Algonquin Books of Chapel Hill, 1995), 11.

2. Ibid., 34–35.

3. Ruth Carter, interview by author, tape recording, Drew, Miss., February 1990.

4. Ibid.

5. Larry Carter, interview by author, tape recording, Drew, Miss., June 1991.

6. Neil R. McMillen, *Dark Journey: Mississippians in the Age of Jim Crow* (Champaign: University of Illinois Press, 1989), 72.

7. Dr. Charles Bolton, E-mail to author, 15 December 2001.

8. Curry, 72.

9. Ibid., 5.

10. Carter to Jean Fairfax, September 1965, Mae Bertha Carter Letters, American Friends Service Committee Archives (henceforth AFSC Archives), Philadelphia, Pa.

11. Ibid.

12. Ibid.

13. Ibid., October 1965.

14. Curry, 123–24.

15. Ibid., 121.

16. Carter to Fairfax, October 1965, Carter Letters.

17. Telephone conversation reports, December 1965, Jean Fairfax Reports, AFSC Archives.

18. Carter to Fairfax, 11 December 1965, Carter Letters.

19. Curry, 137–38.

20. Ibid., 138.

21. Ibid., 150–51.

22. Allen Black, report, October 1966, Allen Black Reports, AFSC Archives.

23. Ibid.

24. Carter to author, October 1968, Carter Letters.

Vera Mae Pigee

(1925–)

Mothering the Movement

FRANÇOISE N. HAMLIN

Vera Pigee wrote a few paragraphs in 1964 that she titled "God Has Always Had a Time, a Place and a People: Mrs. Vera Mae Pigee." In this piece, probably written for a convention speech, she outlined her role in and commitment to the civil rights movement. She stated, "What can a mother, a professional woman and a Christian contribute to the struggle for human dignity?" She offered, "It was my first commitment as a mother to see her [her daughter] more fully equipped to cope with the problems of today. . . . Youth is our greatest resource. Daily, I try to impress this simple truth on parents in my community, and the National Association for the Advancement of Colored People [NAACP] has provided a vehicle whereby I have been able to do this with considerable success. A professional woman in Mississippi is something of a rarity. . . . I think freedom and talk freedom with my customers."[1]

Vera Pigee's life illuminates the importance of black women's local leadership during the civil rights movement in Mississippi and suggests that we look at her experiences in conjunction with the male leadership rather than in competition with it. Doing so invites us to consider the centrality of women's roles as mothers, wives, and daughters to their leadership techniques and styles. Pigee's experiences highlight the overarching theme of gender and organizational collision and collusion that maps the story of the civil rights movement in Coahoma County, Mississippi. Hugging the Mississippi River, Coahoma County is in the Mississippi Delta, straddling Highway 61, eighty miles south of Memphis, Tennessee. This chapter expands upon the concept of African American mothering as a source of resistance and empowerment and sheds light on alternative

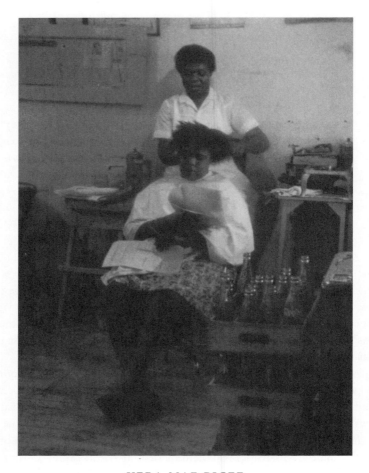

VERA MAE PIGEE

1964. Pigee instructed customers on voter registration
procedures at her beauty parlor in Clarksdale, Mississippi.
From *Powerful Days in Black and White* by Charles Moore.
Courtesy of Charles Moore/Stockphoto.com.

ways of thinking about the broader debate regarding the gendered and racial-
ized leadership of the civil rights movement and social movements in general.

Daughter of sharecroppers from Tutwiler, in Tallahatchie County, Vera Berry
grew up in the Mississippi Delta. Her father had traveled the United States extensively before settling in Mississippi, and he supplemented his farming income as a barber and a tailor. This gave the family extra resources and more
disposable cash than was usually enjoyed by sharecroppers. Vera's mother spent
her time working the farm, raising livestock, growing vegetables, and exercising
her impressive voice in the church choir as well as around the house. Alcoholism
and wanderlust, however, drew her father away when Vera was a small child, and
her mother worked constantly to maintain the family's living standards, raising
two young children and instilling in them the word of God.[2] Vera recalled of
her mother's efforts, "I never really knew we were poor, we always had a lot
of food."[3]

Vera witnessed her mother's faith and strength in the way she stood up for
herself against white men and women in a hostile segregated South. At a time
when black people tended to "take things off of white folks," her mother refused to do so. One day, as she walked along a road in Glendora, Mississippi,
a young white boy on a bike harassed Vera's mother by continuously bumping
into her. After one confrontation too many, Vera remembered that her mother
"gave him a backhand whooping and knocked him plumb off his bike!"[4] Black
Mississippians did not generally take such stances of defiance; alternative modes
of resistance permeated Jim Crow society.[5] Her mother's resourcefulness and
endurance influenced and helped to run the household. Vera grew up fast and
early, marrying at age fourteen Paul Pigee, who was only eighteen. Their daughter, Mary Jane, entered the world a day before Vera's sixteenth birthday.[6]

Pigee helped organize the Coahoma County NAACP chapter with Aaron
Henry in 1953 but left soon after its establishment to study cosmetology in Chicago. Returning to Clarksdale in 1955, she came into the movement by default,
having been elected secretary of the NAACP branch while she was at a church
meeting. "The only thing I knew about the NAACP was that it is something that
is supposed to make these Mississippi white folks act like human beings and I
want to be a part of that monster," she later recounted.[7] Holding that post for the
best part of twenty years, she became active in civil rights struggles throughout
the state.

Pigee owned and ran a beauty shop in the heart of the black neighborhood
in downtown Clarksdale. Black women in Clarksdale, the seat of Coahoma
County, remember her as a leader who had the ability to motivate, some would
say bully, others to act. When veteran civil rights activist Septima Clark was

asked about outstanding vocal black women at the local level, Clark listed Pigee alongside fellow Mississippian Fannie Lou Hamer, who cofounded the Mississippi Freedom Democratic Party, and Daisy Bates of Arkansas, who was instrumental in the desegregation of Little Rock's Central High School.[8] Yet Pigee's story is largely unknown, her presence in the movement ignored. In the two leading books published about the Mississippi movement, and in Clarksdalian Aaron Henry's autobiography, Pigee languishes on the periphery, where she remains a minor actor, the unknown and sometimes unnamed instigator of many of the protest activities in Clarksdale.[9] Vera Pigee, however, always knew her worth. The words she uses to describe herself—a churchgoer, a professional woman, a mother, and an activist—informed her civic life. It is her "self-defined standpoint" that empowered her to maintain and thrive in her "struggle of struggles."[10]

The power of black women to define themselves is crucial to maintaining their resoluteness and to battling the alternative, usually negative, images assigned to them.[11] Replacing the stereotypical images of black mothers—such as the mammy, the matriarch, or the welfare mother—with the image of motherhood drawn by the example of Vera Pigee becomes an opportunity to "express and learn the power of self-definition, the importance of valuing and respecting [oneself], the necessity of self-reliance and independence, and a belief in Black women's empowerment."[12]

Pigee worked principally with local black youth under the auspices of the NAACP Youth Councils. Her leadership is consequently often mistakenly characterized as nonpolitical. The importance of her contributions is also overlooked due to the fact that the national NAACP organization officially opposed direct action—partly due to the costs incurred by bails and trials—and therefore failed to attract the attention of the public. Further, the media machine of the Student Nonviolent Coordinating Committee (SNCC) focused heavily on the efforts of white northern youths to effect change in Mississippi. The Southern Christian Leadership Conference (SCLC) attracted cameras with Martin Luther King Jr., and the NAACP drew attention with its high profile court cases and its visible male leaders. Pigee's work was vital and had far-reaching results, but was also inconspicuous and therefore unsung.

Formal figureheads should be considered separately from community leaders.[13] "Bridge leaders," usually women, work on the ground within the community, using their knowledge and contacts where they can be most effective while holding positions of lesser influence in formal organizational structures. Vera Pigee is located firmly in this model of local leadership. Considering this model with the politics of mothering, we are able finally to render Pigee visible.

In addition to its functions within the household, African American mothering is a political and communal act that socializes and nurtures a variety of public activities beyond the four walls of a narrowly constructed domestic space. The mothering techniques African American women use to inspire resistance are part of a tradition carried forth from slavery and beyond, rooted in some African family structures. Part of this legacy of black women's activism, black women's clubs, most of whose members were middle-class and more affluent, sought to lift their race as they advanced as women. These women became vital leaders in their communities as they worked to establish the NAACP and to recruit members from their sphere of influence. Pigee lived in a community where maternal activism never faltered—rather it morphed to suit the situation and the individual.[14] Rather than limiting and confining the potential of women in society, mothering has been a way for some women to negotiate their communities and, strengthened by their gender, to carry out radical, society-changing work. Throughout the history of the black experience in America, black women have developed a "unique technique of persuasion." While some of the better known black feminists have been noted for their effectiveness as public speakers and "manipulative interpersonal communicators," many more black women have developed their own "uniquely persuasive strategies for interacting and coping with a social enemy."[15] Mothering becomes, for many, the organizing and mobilizing strategy that black women use to persuade others to act.

Gender differences in leadership style and strategy remain a fact of life in many communities. In Coahoma County during the civil rights movement, African American women did not differentiate between their activism and that of men. They also did not identify with mainstream feminism in any way. Yet, when one puts their activities side-by-side with those of self-defined feminists, uncanny similarities emerge. Both groups of women fought for their political rights and recognized the restraints placed on their gender by their pervading society. Both were empowered to organize and demand change. The differences lie mainly in their strategy and self-definitions. Most African American women saw themselves as part of the ongoing overall struggle of the race and used the tools at their disposal as women to exercise their political muscle.

Pigee's identification with mothering manifested itself in her description of the NAACP and its responsibilities to activists. Transferring the nurturing ideal from the individual to the institutional, she fondly christened the NAACP "the grandmother of Civil Rights Organizations." She wrote, "We called the NAACP mother. And mother would be there."[16] In reality, the NAACP leadership acted more like a patriarchal father.

The NAACP was an organization with a reputation for maintaining a rigid hierarchy, male chauvinism among its leadership, and institutional sexism. Adam Clayton Powell Jr. confirmed that "the NAACP stood in the full virility of manhood."[17] The executive branch in Manhattan socialized NAACP members to adhere to their proscribed roles by instituting highly hierarchical decision-making procedures. Every cent spent had to be approved by the appropriate departments in New York before the money trickled into the requesting locale. Staff members in the field were carefully positioned, defined, and constrained, and the content of their speeches was scrutinized, their associations monitored.

Vera Pigee was not a woman to shy away from the spotlight or reject her due accolades. Her historical invisibility and that of other similarly positioned women, despite their centrality in Clarksdale and the state, stems in large part from the omission of her name in organizational reports given about conferences and meetings. The extensive NAACP files located at the Library of Congress may contain a sole letter written in response to several from her that are not filed. In field reports, she is noted only as "an activist." In like fashion, when discussing committees, the reports promote only the recognizable national names, not the local people also present and delegated to perform the groundwork. Pigee was part of the NAACP clique. She regularly corresponded with most of the senior officers and hosted them when they were in Mississippi and during national conventions. She did not, however, share the national spotlight. The only Mississippians fully in the NAACP limelight were Medgar Evers and Aaron Henry. The foot soldiers, mostly women taken for granted, are hard to find. As we move further away from the 1960s and 1970s and memories fade as people die, such activists will be even harder to locate.

Yet Vera Pigee remains unequivocal in her loyalty to the NAACP: the organization gave her the resources and the space to make a place for herself and her activities. To be sure, the NAACP *was* the only national activist group in Mississippi at the local level until the SCLC or the SNCC began organizing in the Delta. Other civil rights groups coming into the state "learned in the various communities that without the support of the local NAACP united the citizenry would not accept them."[18] Groups like SNCC hoped to secure the support of ministers and indigenous leaders, although many traditional black leaders proved too conservative in their approaches to local politics. As the movement progressed, the younger generation of activists felt that the NAACP appealed only to black middle classes bound financially and politically with local whites. Those NAACP activists such as Medgar Evers, Aaron Henry, and Vera Pigee who supported cooperation with other organizations (despite the objections of the national office) may have been an exception to this rule.

Despite the gender-role contradictions, the NAACP embraced Pigee because their new strategy of responding to the growing black unrest in the South called for local leadership and initiation. Criticisms of younger activists plus the student protests erupting nationwide brought organizing children, deemed women's work, to the top of the list of new imperatives. Consequently, "civil rights activism that privileged masculinity [could not] keep black women from claiming their own rights as citizens and mothers."[19] As such, Pigee got the resources and the room to run the NAACP Youth Council in Clarksdale and to advise councils across the state almost without interference. She knew the institutional ropes and so did not press already thinly stretched staff and resources to come in and pep the community, giving her space and monopoly.

The NAACP recognized the importance of women at the grassroots level and encouraged organizers and field workers to exploit the resources women offered. Initiating Mother of the Year awards, banquets, freedom dinners, Christmas seal campaigns, and the like not only served as fund-raising initiatives but also encouraged the attention, involvement, and participation of women. Similarly, the official NAACP publication, the *Crisis,* regularly featured portraits of attractive young women on the cover or in the opening pages as well as accomplished women in their fields and professions and older women serving on local boards and committees. This display and promotion of women, however, was not reflected in the larger organization, where women rarely broke through the male ranks to higher, executive, decision-making positions. Lucille Black and Ella Baker, both prominent NAACP women during this time, served in the national office in New York, in charge of membership and branches, but they had no power over the organization's purse strings.

Pigee's commitment to the NAACP and the movement, through her work with children, started early in the 1950s. In Mississippi, where most adults, especially after the May 1954 *Brown v. Board of Education* decision, feared the recrimination associated with belonging to the NAACP, teenagers joined youth councils as their only safe outlet for expressing their frustration. Pigee attended her first Mississippi NAACP conference in Jackson in 1955, with only two youths present, her daughter, Mary Jane, and fellow youth member Sarah Gaston. At this conference Pigee was elected one of two state NAACP youth conference advisors, despite her objections that in Coahoma County a youth council did not yet exist. She had just been elected secretary of the Coahoma branch in absentia, but started immediately to work to organize the local council.[20]

The Coahoma County Youth Council received its charter four years later in 1959 with thirty-four members, daughter Mary Jane serving as vice president.[21] Mary Jane stayed with her mother, remaining on the front lines in sit-ins and marches for most of her teen years, while Vera labored on the state and regional levels, organizing councils throughout the state and speaking across the nation. Many activists, fearing for their families, kept their children in the background, protecting them from harm and sometimes sending them out of state. Vera Pigee, on the other hand, saw this movement as the ultimate education for her daughter. "Despite the dangers, mothers routinely encourage[d] Black daughters to develop skills to confront oppressive conditions. Learning that they will work and that education is a vehicle for advancement can also be seen as ways of enhancing positive self-definitions and self-valuations in Black girls."[22] It was a lesson in tough love, bolstered by faith. "I know I was doing what the Lord wanted me to do," she said. "And I knew he had his angels captive around me and my family and my house. . . . And I had no right to be afraid."[23]

Pigee treated all in the council as her children, providing siblings for her only child. She held meetings at her beauty salon and at her house and gave the youth keys to her home to find food after they had walked long distances into town to attend events. This is part of activist mothering, where "the blurring of community work and family-based labor by those women frequently meant opening their homes to those in need."[24] Roy Bell Wright, one of the first Coahoma County Youth Council presidents remembered, "She was a mother to hundreds of us over a twenty year period" as she sustained the group with her brand of personal care.[25]

Such alternative kin networks and "othermothering," not uncommon in African American communities, provided young people in Clarksdale with not only a safe space but a nurturing adult to aid in their socialization.[26] Daughter of a strong mother, Pigee already knew the skills of survival, hard work, and female independence. Pigee clearly benefited from her African American foremothers' activism; it became a source of pride, motivation, and inspiration.

Pigee's autobiography opens with accounts of her mother as a role model, just as her convention speech carries that mantel of striving to be a mentor to her own daughter. Through her volunteer work, she added more children to her household by following an African American model of mothering. "The community work of Black women, like that of other women of color, is a complex practice of biological mothering, community other-mothering, and political activism."[27] Furthermore, "*good mothering* [comprises] all actions, including social activism, that addressed the needs of their children and the community."[28] Activist mothering rears activist offspring.

Pigee's work and commitment to the youth of Mississippi ultimately reflected in the council's activities. Clarksdale saw its first public demonstration in the spring of 1960, not long after the Greensboro sit-ins in North Carolina.

The Youth Council, numbering fifty and straining to attempt direct action, prompted Pigee to contact the national NAACP youth director Laplois Ashford, who in sync with institutional policy, dissuaded sit-ins. In Mississippi no resources were available for bonds or attorney support. Pigee, however, hammered out a compromise with the national office whereby a group of youths, including Mary Jane, were allowed to go shopping to buy a Bible and a frame for the Youth Council's charter at local stores known for refusing to serve blacks.[29] The demonstration not only tested the system but also tested the support of Clarkdale's black community for direct action. Served by a nervous white saleswoman, the protest proceeded without incident. Pigee remembered, "We termed this experience a semi-protest, or trial run, and we also watched the action and reaction of the parents and the public."[30] Under Pigee's direction, the council continued to demonstrate with gusto and enthusiasm.

Caught up in the momentum of the movement during their formative years, the youth of Clarksdale labored diligently with the senior NAACP branch members to mobilize their community. Performing tasks that working adults could not or would not execute, they served as ushers in mass meetings; distributed flyers; held raffles, dances, street rallies, workshops, and public programs; sponsored fund-raisers; participated in boycotts and sit-ins; and helped with mailings.[31] The work the Youth Council undertook in the early years, before the influx of SNCC, galvanized the local people. Seeing their own young put themselves on the line in the shadow of Emmett Till's murder in a neighboring county and face massive resistance from white Citizens' Councils, parents were stirred out of their own fears. The mounting activities of the local youth influenced many adults to register to vote and support the movement.[32] Working with the children in the Youth Council, Vera Pigee had immediate contact with their parents.

On 2 December 1963, the Coahoma County Chamber of Commerce, responding to heightened civil rights activities and the notable presence of "outsiders," refused to extend the traditional invitation for two local black school bands to participate in the annual Christmas parade.[33] If officials thought their actions would dampen activities, their plan spectacularly backfired. Attacking children in the festive season provoked angry parents to act when they might not have before. Pigee noted, "This was the straw that broke the camel's back, as far as community involvement."[34] Pigee recounted how the Youth Council met at the beauty shop the same day of the announcement, debating their next step in response. Understanding the increased tension in the air and the risk to their safety, she encouraged them to tell their parents to attend the meeting hurriedly called for the following night. At that meeting, Pigee simply stated, "These are our children." That sentiment, under the slogan No Parade, No Trade, sustained a two-year boycott of downtown Clarksdale businesses.[35] She and other local leaders mobilized a latent constituency of parents to consider the future of their children and make some sacrifices to secure that future. Appealing to their sense of parental responsibility became the battle strategy. Likewise, she trained the children to mobilize their parents through their own activities and sacrifices. The Coahoma County Youth Council became the most active in the state. In essence, Pigee became an intermediary between parents and children, encouraging both to work for freedom, bridging the generational gap to focus on a common goal.

Clarksdale persisted as a hotbed of civil rights dissension through 1963. Since the first youth protest in 1960, sit-ins, marches, and mass meetings had become the norm. Bolstered by a group of volunteering students, mostly from Yale University and including Joseph Lieberman, who would later serve as a U.S. Senator, a massive jail-in punctuated the summer of 1963, inspired by the continual arrests of peaceful demonstrators and the bombing and shootings of the homes of locals. Witnessing the activities of their neighbors and the intensifying national uprising, an increasing number of adults began to take more active interest in the movement. The battle had become personal.

In order to understand Pigee's motivation to act so decisively and with such determination, one must consider her occupation and social position. Long time activist Sheila Michaels described a gathering at the SNCC head office in Atlanta sometime in late 1963. In this meeting, one of the participants noted, "When you organize a town, you have to have two people on your side, the beautician and the midwife."[36] The Highlander Folk School, a training site for liberal activists nestled in the hills of Tennessee, had recognized the true location of power in black communities and the leadership potential of beauticians in the early 1960s and sought to train them in the art of propagating information and strategic organizing. Myles Horton, organizer and director of Highlander, while seeking possible leaders among African Americans in the fifties noted that leaders came from sectors of the workforce not reliant on white patronage or jobs. Hence, he observed, self-employed service providers serving the segregated black population had less to lose and naturally rose to the top in their communities. He discovered, quite by accident, the importance of black beauticians when he noticed the large proportion of professional hairdressers who attended Highlander: "A black beautician, unlike a white beautician, was at that time a person of some status in the community. They were entrepreneurs, they were small businesswomen, you know, respected, they were usually better educated than other people, and most of all they were independent . . . of white control."[37]

Septima Clark, a major organizer of citizenship schools and training work-shops, ran a three-day workshop at Highlander solely for beauticians in January 1961 for the purpose of finding "the things which need to be done in a commu-nity that cannot be done by city and state employees or churchmen. . . . The Beauticians can speak out openly and can publicly promote the cause for justice and equality in the South."[38] Although Pigee never attended Highlander during the organization of beauticians, Clark had already zeroed in on her leadership abilities and encouraged her to attend training sessions for citizenship classes in Dorchester, Georgia, under the auspices of SCLC.[39]

Beauty shop culture aids the dissemination of news. The salon serves as a center of female economy that caters to classes as diverse as its clientele. In such spaces, the beauty shop becomes a kind of public household where the moth-ering of the domestic sphere is renegotiated in a public, yet special place.[40] For working-class women in particular, the beauty shop is a space for economic, po-litical, and social empowerment outside of the man's world. For black women, the black beauty shop is also outside the white world. Pigee's beauty shop shel-tered strategy meetings and activists from the 1950s through the 1970s. Oper-ating a beauty salon provided optimal access to women in the town. It became a safe house for civil rights meetings. It was a space to discuss, cajole, and per-suade. There Pigee could literally hold clients hostage to a continuous barrage of information and persuasion while working on their hair. The beauty shop culture of Pigee's Beauty Salon demonstrated mothering to mothers, while also nurturing techniques and work that fostered activism.

Black women's activism is rendered invisible in many instances because strategies of nurturing are often considered "natural" or the ordinary activi-ties of women in their communities. In fact, this misunderstanding permits many women to engage in subversive activities. They are not suspected; their activities are not prone to arrest for inciting lawlessness or civil disobedience. The space of the female-centered beauty shop, ignored *because* of its seemingly benign, gossip-filled facade, proves to be the ideal space for debate, discussion, and dialogue on current events. Just as Myles Horton stumbled on the reality of black beauticians as community leaders because of their initiative in attend-ing Highlander in large numbers, so too must we recognize that, even in their traditional role as community nurturers, they were also political radicals.

By providing services for the black community, the beauty salon prospered enough for Pigee to be able to employ up to six assistants at one point, allowing her the opportunity to work with the movement full-time.[41] Having the time to invest in the movement, in turn, consolidated her localized power, earning her the respect she needed in order to fulfill her othermother duties. Once this respect was earned, "the community other mother was/is able successfully to critique the behavior of individual members of the community and to provide them with directions on appropriate behavior(s)" and to "affect the well-being of her community," serving "as a catalyst in the development and implementation of strategies designed to remedy . . . harmful conditions."[42]

Pigee knew that the more involved she became in the freedom struggle, the more susceptible her family would become to attack. On the night of 8 June 1963, her house became the target of drive-by shootings. One bullet narrowly missed her bed, and it was found the next morning lodged in her piano on the other side of the wall. She received countless threatening phone calls at her home throughout her activist years and even spent a stint on the official state death list circulated among the movement's more violent white opponents.[43] Pigee felt that her business, located in a prime position in the exclusively black section of town, was protected from white retaliation. When asked if she was wary of unwelcome visitors when she kept her doors unlocked so anyone could enter for shelter, she laughed, "They knew better than to come down there!"[44] Pigee's position as a leader prompted many in the black community to cocoon her business, to protect it as the site of resistance and strategy building.

One of her more vivid memories of harassment during that time stems from daily phone calls at 4:00 A.M. The caller always hung up without speaking. Pigee remembered that this continued for four years. One morning, when she answered the phone she challenged the caller: "You're about ready to talk to me, you keep calling me . . . it's a pity for you to be an old woman and you think that God made this world for you." The surprised caller inquired how Pigee thought she knew she was old. Pigee retorted, "Won't anybody wake up at 4 o'clock every morning, but an old woman! And wake up the whole town. . . . When you woke me up, you woke up the whole town! . . . And it's getting into the evening of your life, you should be on your knees before a mighty God! Because you're going to meet Him one day." Obviously striking a chord, after a few more minutes of conversation, they hung up, and the Pigee household no longer prematurely woke up to the phone ringing.[45]

Her husband, confident in his wife's abilities and determination, supported her, although he stayed in the background. Despite his wife's activities, Paul Pigee never lost his job at a local plant. His boss continually withstood pressure from city officials and the white Citizens' Councils, stating that Paul's work never suffered and his services were invaluable. Paul's support and willingness to share with his wife in such a noble cause should be acknowledged.[46] Parent of just one child, he watched numerous children and adults enter his home, eat his food, and sleep under his roof. Paul Pigee's stamina manifested out of his love for Vera enabled her to go forth with confidence. Talking to an arresting officer in December 1961, when she was booked for conspiring against local business by organizing a boycott, she informed him, "I am *Mrs.* Vera Pigee, a wife, mother, political prisoner, business and professional woman. Wherever I go, even if I am brought in handcuffs, my name is still *Mrs.* Vera Pigee."[47]

Roy Bell Wright later said, she thought like a mother, acted like a mother, and pleaded to mothers. Her confidence convinced others that she would not ask of them what she was not willing to do herself. People saw her struggles and sacrifices and that she could assure them of their children's safety in her care. She encouraged her daughter's desire to agitate and sit-in despite the obvious risks. In fact, in August 1961 Mary Jane and two other youths entered Clarksdale's train station to protest segregation and were duly arrested while grown black men fled the scene. Similarly, Pigee occupied the front line when no one was willing. She and Idessa Johnson, another officer in the local NAACP branch, desegregated the Greyhound Bus terminal after her daughter's sit-in, walking to the window to ask for a ticket, stopping to drink at the water fountain, and visiting the (white) ladies room. Shortly thereafter the *Clarksdale Press Register* reported that all the segregation signs had duly disappeared from both transportation terminals.[48] Pigee presented herself as a woman without fear in the face of violence, a woman willing to speak truth to authorities and hold them accountable for their actions. In short, she practiced what she preached, carrying on the legacy of her mother.

Through Pigee's work and her influence in the community, her activism, church work, and beauty shop, her list of contacts was extensive. When one person lost employment due to his or her movement activity, that person came to Pigee, who would burn up the phone lines to replace that job.[49] Similarly, if the NAACP needed a high profile speaker (like the Reverend Martin Luther King Jr., Constance Motley Brown, or any national officer) to mobilize and revitalize local people in Clarksdale, Pigee would arrange all the details, feeding, protecting, and accommodating them in her home.

Major leaders of the movement recognized her abilities. Retelling a story of good times with the Reverend King, she recalled how he presented himself as down to earth when he visited Clarksdale, usually at her invitation. One morning, King was in town to begin a weekend of meetings in the area, and he and Aaron Henry stopped by her house to collect her for the day's activities. While she pulled on her coat, Henry exclaimed, "Martin hadn't even had any breakfast!" Taking that as a cue, she removed her coat, tied on her apron, and fixed the men a full breakfast of toast, home fries, bacon, and eggs, with juice and coffee. She laughed, "Dr. King came in and sat down and started playing on my piano" until she told them all to get in the car. Once inside, she put down a

paper towel on his lap, "This is your table cloth, now set the plate up there!"[50]
He ate and enjoyed himself in the back of the car as they traveled through the
county's back roads to the first meeting of the day.

The absence of such stories in the existing record of the civil rights movement intensifies the shadow of invisibility that covers the women in the middle.
Carrying out everyday chores such as cooking breakfast for the men before their
exhausting trip, women sustained the movement. In this story, Pigee makes sure
the men are in jovial moods with full stomachs, strengthened, anchored, and on
schedule. Her organization and leadership was different from but equally vital
to that of males. She created a positive atmosphere and attitude that no doubt
reflected the overall tone of the day.

Roy Bell Wright recalled those early pre-SNCC days: "At that time, our
Youth Council and Branch enjoyed a kind of coherence I did not see in any
other branch and youth council in the nation."[51] The highly celebrated arrival
of SNCC volunteers to the Delta beginning in 1963 signaled the end of the
Youth Councils' influence. The "SNCC kid catch," as she labeled it, destroyed
every council in the state except Coahoma County's.[52] These "ego-trippers"
were blamed for going into a town with no resources, creating "unrest toward
the people in the community who had emerged as leaders of the civil rights
movement, who made it possible for SNCC to move into the communities."[53]
Ironically, Pigee, along with Medgar Evers and Aaron Henry, had worked to
organize the Council of Federated Organizations (COFO), which invited the
students in an effort to help the Mississippi movement in its struggle against
massive white resistance. She acknowledged that "we had organized a monster. . . . I was willing to accept my punishment and I was working harder to
kill the monster than I did to give it birth."[54]

Vera Pigee managed to maintain the NAACP's grip on Coahoma County
by keeping a tight rein on the students who volunteered in the area. She made
the SNCC workers sing in the NAACP Youth Council choir and collected their
dues, but remembered, "As soon as they thought the community had accepted
them, they began to tell the NAACP youths to get out of the Freedom House."[55]
Her indignation stemmed from the fact that she had organized the Freedom
House with Dave Dennis after she was elected by COFO as the State Chair of the
Emergency Relief Committee and even paid the rent of the first storefront center
for several months.[56] She commented, "If anyone termed my action or activities
as 'power,' it was well-earned power."[57] Indeed it was power invested in her by
the community as a result of her personal investment into that community. She
continued, stating emphatically, "I didn't like their program, and I didn't have

to put up with it."[58] She expelled a whole group of students overnight by calling on their hosts, her friends, to turn them out.

Many volunteers complained. In a letter to his parents in New York, 30 June 1964, Matthew Zwerling, who stayed with Pigee, criticized her outspokenness while praising her skills in the domestic, typically female, space of the kitchen. "She is something else," he wrote. "Busybody—talks incessantly—strong community leader. (I'm sure she is a leader because she can bully people.) We aren't going to see eye to eye much. It should make the summer a little more exciting and be a good course in diplomacy for me. She is a good cook."[59]

Pigee's heavy-handedness with volunteers like Zwerling made her few friends in COFO, which was staffed primarily by SNCC volunteers. Yet, in her mind, the students were invited to Coahoma County specifically to publicize the Mississippi movement while lending a hand with existing activities. Alienating the students also cut her chances of gaining respect and honor in the organizations they represented. In turn, this kept her potency local and contained, contributing to her subsequent misplacement in the official narratives. Such othermothers were vulnerable because they depended on the will of the community. Once disagreements arose, the position of the othermother became contested. Pigee's position as a community othermother, defending those in her care while relying on community respect and cooperation, became perilous after COFO's inception.[60] Pigee worked hard to maintain her status in the midst of what she considered gross disloyalty.

Years later, she still utilized her initiative and tenacity, making herself an example to others when many were still afraid to take a stand. After most of the threat had dissipated, people began to step forward, realizing that the early participants had not all perished for their efforts. Then everyone wanted the leadership spotlight, "Particularly the ones who had a little smell of education," Pigee complained. Her life philosophy had always been "If one cannot sweep the floor, one can't sit on the stage," and many of those who had recently caught the spotlight had never held a broom.[61]

In the mid-1970s, Vera Pigee moved to Michigan to complete a degree in journalism and sociology at Wayne State University. She commuted to Clarksdale once a month to continue her duties for a while but cut down on her responsibilities. Today, she remains a life member in the Detroit branch of the NAACP and, health permitting, attends the national conference. She spends most of her time traveling to sell her book *The Struggle of Struggles* and speaking, mainly for the National Baptist Convention and the National Baptist Congress.

Vera Pigee's life testifies that a single person with a giant presence within her community can influence lives. Larry Graham, president of the Youth Council in 1973, wrote to James Brown, NAACP national youth director, listing some of Pigee's contributions: "Mrs. Pigee really has helped this youth Council from the beginning until now. . . . [She] organized the Youth Council in 1955. When people was afraid to let [their] children even join. It took her four years to get 35 members." He continued, "The Youth haven't missed a State Conference nor Regional since we were organized. Her first national was in 1959 and she has brought from one to four youth for fourteen years to the National."[62]

Historians of civil rights must make room for the Vera Pigees of the move-ment, God-fearing mothers with the tools to elicit activism from young and old and the audacity and ability to criticize and berate their own as loudly as they did the white opposition. Their leadership was imperative. Without them as agitators, mediators, comforters, and active risk takers, the grassroots resis-tance to white supremacy would not have existed. Their sacrifices and successes demonstrate the practical significance of motherly love and how it immeasur-ably transformed the civil rights movement.

NOTES

1. NAACP Papers, IIIC73, Coahoma County 1964–65 files, Library of Congress, Washington, D.C.

2. Vera Pigee, *The Struggle of Struggles: Part One* (Detroit: Harlo Press, 1975), 13–15.

3. Pigee, interview by author, Detroit, Mich., 12–13 October 2001.

4. Ibid.

5. Robin Kelley, "We Are Not What We Seem: Black Working-Class Opposition in the Jim Crow South," *Journal of American History* (June 1993): 75–112.

6. Pigee, *Struggles: Part One*, 18–19.

7. Ibid., 26.

8. Septima Clark, interview by Jacquelyn Hall, 25 June 1976, Southern Oral History Program, University of North Carolina, Chapel Hill.

9. Charles Payne, *I've Got the Light of Freedom: The Organizing Tradition and the Mississippi Freedom Struggle* (Los Angeles: University of California Press, 1995); John Dittmer, *Local People: The Struggle for Civil Rights in Mississippi* (Chicago: University of Illinois Press, 1995); Aaron Henry, *The Fire Ever Burning* (Jackson: University Press of Mississippi, 2000).

10. Patricia Hill Collins, *Black Feminist Thought: Knowledge, Consciousness, and the Politics of Empowerment* (New York: Routledge, 1990).

11. Ibid., 106.

12. Ibid., 118.

13. Belinda Robnett, *How Long? How Long? African American Women in the Struggle for Civil Rights* (New York: Oxford University Press, 1997).

14. Collins, "Shifting the Center: Race, Class, and Feminist Theorizing about Motherhood" in *Mothering: Ideology, Experience, and Agency,* ed. Evelyn Nakano Glenn et al. (New York: Routledge, 1994), 47; Deborah Gray White, *Ar'n't I a Woman? Female Slaves in the Plantation South* (New York: W. W. Norton, 1985); White, *Too Heavy a Load: Black Women in Defense of Themselves, 1894–1994* (New York: W. W. Norton, 1999); Eileen Boris, "The Power of Motherhood: Black and White Activist Women Redefine the 'Political,' " in *Mothers of a New World: Maternalist Politics and the Origins of the Welfare State,* ed. Seth Koven and Sonya Michel (New York: Routledge, 1993), 213–45; see also Katrina Bell McDonald, "Black Activist Mothering: A Historical Intersection of Race, Gender and Class," *Gender and Society* 11 (December 1997): 773–95.

15. Delindus R. Brown and Wander F. Anderson, "A Survey of the Black Woman and the Persuasion Process: The Study of Strategies of Identification and Resistance," *Journal of Black Studies* 9 (1978): 233, 234.

16. Pigee, *The Struggle of Struggles: Part Two* (Detroit: Harlo Press, 1977), 83; Pigee, interview, 2001.

17. Quoted in Ruth Feldstein, *Motherhood in Black and White: Race and Sex in America, 1930–1965* (Ithaca, N.Y.: Cornell University Press, 2000), 74.

18. Pigee, *Struggles: Part One,* 68.

19. Feldstein, 89.

20. Pigee, *Struggles: Part One,* 25–26.

21. Ibid.; Coahoma County NAACP Youth Charter, 1959, in Vera Pigee's papers in her possession.

22. Collins, *Black Feminist Thought,* 124.

23. Pigee, interview, 2001.

24. Nancy Naples, "Activist Mothering: Cross-Generational Continuity in the Community Work of Women from Low-Income Urban Neighborhoods," *Gender and Society* 6 (September 1992): 450.

25. Pigee, *Struggles: Part Two,* 24.

26. Carol Stack, *All Our Kin: Strategies for Survival in a Black Community* (New York: Harper and Row, 1974); and Stanlie M. James, "Mothering: A Possible Black Feminist Link to Social Transformation?" in *Theorizing Black Feminisms: The Visionary Pragmatism of Black Women,* ed. Stanlie M. James and Abena P. A. Busia (New York: Routledge, 1993).

27. McDonald, 776.

28. Naples, 448.

29. Pigee, *Struggles: Part One,* 45–47.

30. Ibid.

31. Ibid., 31; Pigee, interview, 2001.

32. Stephen J. Whitfield, *A Death in the Delta: The Story of Emmett Till* (Baltimore: John Hopkins University Press, 1988); Dittmer, 127; Charles Payne, " 'Men Led, But Women Organized': Movement Participation of Women in the Mississippi Delta," in *Women and Social Protest,* ed. Guida West and Rhoda Blumberg (New York: Oxford University Press, 1990), 160–62.

33. Pigee, *Struggles: Part One,* 29; Dittmer, 120–23.

34. Pigee, *Struggles: Part One,* 29.

35. Ibid.

36. Sheila Michaels, conversation with author, Oral History Association Meeting, St. Louis, Mo., October 2001.

37. Myles Horton quoted in Aldon D. Morris, *The Origins of the Civil Rights Movement: Black Communities Organizing for Change* (New York: Free Press, 1984), 145.

38. Septima Clark, untitled report, Highlander Papers, State Historical Society of Wisconsin, Madison.

39. Pigee, *Struggles: Part One,* 63.

40. Evelyn Nakano Glenn, "Social Constructions of Mothering: A Thematic Overview" in *Mothering,* ed. Glenn et al.

41. Pigee, interview, 2001.

42. James, 48.

43. Pigee, *Struggles: Part One,* 38.

44. Pigee, interview, 2001.

45. Ibid.

46. Ibid.

47. Pigee, *Struggles: Part One,* 55.

48. *Clarksdale Press Register,* 27 December 1961.

49. Hattie Mae Gilmore, interview by author, Clarksdale, Miss., 12 March 1999.

50. Pigee, interview, 2001.

51. Quoted in Pigee, *Struggles: Part Two,* 25.

52. Pigee, *Struggles: Part One,* 35.

53. Ibid., 35, 72.

54. Ibid., 77.

55. Ibid., 70.

56. Ibid., 70–71.

57. Ibid., 71.

58. Pigee, interview, 2001.

59. Matthew Zwerling to his parents, 30 June 1964, Zwerling Papers, State Historical Society of Wisconsin.

60. James, 48.

61. Pigee, *Struggles: Part One,* 28.

62. Larry Graham to James Brown, 20 July 1973, NAACP Papers; Pigee, *Struggles: Part One,* 35.

For Further Research

Note: The following list is not intended to be comprehensive. For additional sources, consult Joanne V. Hawks, *Mississippi's Historical Heritage: A Guide To Women's Sources in Mississippi Repositories* (Hattiesburg, Miss.: Society of Mississippi Archivists, 1993), individual archives, and the chapter endnotes within this volume. Each entry is followed by the city or county (if applicable) that the item relates to and the principal dates covered, along with a descriptive word or words of the major historical theme(s) that the collection helps to elucidate.

MANUSCRIPT COLLECTIONS

Arthur and Elizabeth Schlesinger Library, Radcliffe Institute for Advanced Study, Cambridge, Massachusetts

Hazen (Elizabeth) Papers (1825–1975) science; Somerville-Howorth Family Papers (1863–1983) social, political, organizations.

Charles W. Capps Jr. Archives and Museum, Delta State University, Cleveland, Mississippi

Howorth (Lucy Somerville) Papers (Cleveland, 1895–1997) political, organizations; Ogden (Florence Sillers) Papers (Rosedale, 1897–1972) political, education; Sillers (Florence Warfield) Papers (Bolivar County, 1854–1958) organizations, social; Warfield (Mary Carson) Papers (1864–1919) literature, social.

Henry T. Sampson Library, Special Collections, Jackson State University, Jackson, Mississippi

Alexander (Margaret Walker) Papers (Jackson, 1940–79) literary, African American; McAllister (Jane Ellen) Papers (Jackson, 1951–73) education, African American; Rhodes (Lelia Gaston) Papers (Jackson, 1969–88) education, African American; Thompson (Cleopatra Davenport) Papers (1971–98) education, African American; Williams (Mildred M.) Papers (1935–86) education, African American.

J. D. Williams Library, Archives and Special Collections, University of Mississippi, Oxford

American Association of University Women, Mississippi Division Records (1927–) organizations; Blanton-Smith Collection (Greenville, 1812–1927) social, domestic; Bondurant

(Emily Morrison) Collection (Oxford, 1837–1925) education, social; Brown (Elizabeth Christie) Diary (Natchez, 1853–63) social, Civil War; Brown (Juanita) Collection (Attala County, 1801–1900) social, Civil War; Buie (Hallie) Collection (Lincoln County, 1920–49) religion, education; Daughters of the American Revolution, David Reese Chapter (Oxford, 1899–) organizations; Eades (Robbie) Collection (Oxford, 1861–1968) education; Freeman (Kate Walthall) Collection (Holly Springs, 1841–64) social; Holly Springs Female Academy Records (Holly Springs, 1836–1901) education; League of Women Voters of Oxford, Mississippi (Oxford, 1962–) political, organizations; Lowry (Beverly) Collection (Greenville, 1976–80) literary; McDowell (Katherine S. [Sherwood Bonner]) Collection (Holly Springs, 1875–1911) literary; Pegues (Harriet) Daybook (Marshall County, 1848–49) domestic, social; Thompson (Lily Wilkinson) Collection (1897–1920) political; Union Female College Collection (Oxford, 1873–82) education; University Dames Records (Oxford, 1927–) organizations, education; Woman's Forum Collection (Oxford, 1948–98) organizations; Zemon (Zoya) Freedom Summer Collection (Clarksdale, 1964) civil rights.

Louisiana and Lower Mississippi Valley Collection, Louisiana State University, Baton Rouge

Applewhite (Cornelia) Papers (Brookhaven, 1877–78, 1924–25) education; Bateman (Mary) Diary (Greenville, 1856) social; Bright (Jane C.) Scrapbook (Yazoo City, 1917–1956) World War I, medical; Buhler (Mary Edith) Papers (Natchez, 1881–1931) literature; Carey (Cora) Family Papers (Holly Springs, 1866–1971) organizations, literature; Dalrymple (C. G.) Letters (Monroe County, 1847) social; Eggleston-Roach Papers (Vicksburg, 1825–1903) Civil War, social; Ellis-Farar Papers (Natchez, 1804–33) education, domestic; Jefferson (Elizabeth) Collection (1867–85) slavery, domestic; Lea (Lemanda E.) Papers (Pike County, 1858–72) Civil War, religion; Lee (Eleanor Percy Ware) and Catharine Ann Warfield Papers (Natchez, 1835–49) literary; Magruder (Eliza L.) Diary (Natchez, 1846–57) social, slavery; McDaniel-Gill Letters (1849–59) domestic; Ratcliff (Olivia J.) Speech (Amite County, 1866) Civil War; Stokes (Joel A.) Family Papers (Pike County, 1863–98) domestic, education.

McCain Library and Archives, University of Southern Mississippi, Hattiesburg

Currier (Lura Gibbons) Papers (1937–83) education, organizations; Daughters of the American Revolution, John Rolfe Chapter (Hattiesburg, 1954–71) organizations, Lost Cause; Gandy (Edythe Evelyn) Papers (1959–83) political; Hardy (William H. and Hattie L.) Papers (Gulfport and Hattiesburg, 1873–1929) social, political; Johnson (Paul B.) Family Papers (Pike, Marshall, and Forrest Counties, 1930s–70s) social, political; Prenshaw (Maude "Leet") Papers (1960–75) literature; United Daughters of the Confederacy, Nathan Bedford Forrest Chapter (Forrest County, 1901–82) organizations, Lost Cause; University of Southern Mississippi Women's Club (Hattiesburg, 1945–90) organizations, education; Wells (Mary Ann) Papers and Photographs (Hattiesburg, 1970–85) social.

Mississippi Department of Archives and History, Jackson

Ayers Family Papers (Natchez, 1809–1992) social, literary; Balfour (Emma) Civil War Diary (Vicksburg, 1863) Civil War; Barber (Bette E.) Photograph Collection (Vicksburg, 1942–68) social; Barksdale Family Papers (1861–1965) social; Beets (Eva Velma Davis) Papers (Marion County, 1918–87) social; Birchett (Raymond) Collection (Vicksburg, 1862–72) Civil War; Bisland-Shields Family Papers (Adams County, 1856–57, 1927–60) social; Bizzell (Pattie) Diaries (Bolivar County, 1934–76) social; Brown (Ann Reagan) Diary (Hinds County, 1883) social; Brown (Mrs. Calvin S. [Maud Morrow]) Papers (Lafayette County, 1922–38) social; Bryant (Clyde) Papers (Holly Springs, 1880s–90s) social; Buck (Charles W.) Papers (Vicksburg, 1852–1922) social; Buie Family Papers (1909–40) social; Cain (Mary) Papers (Pike County, 1920–83) political, social, journalism; Cameron (Jennie Mae Quinn) Papers (Hattiesburg, 1897–1961) medicine, education; Campbell (Clarice T.) Papers (Holly Springs, 1943–81) education, civil rights; Capers (Charlotte) Papers (Jackson, 1943–76) social; Carey (Cora Watson) Papers (Holly Springs, 1855–1914) education, literary; Chapman Family Papers (Newton County, 1830–96) social, religion; Cook (Mrs. Jared Reese [Minerva Hynes]) Diary (Adams County, 1855–59) social; Cooper (Janie Drake) Collection (Brookhaven, 1896–1962) education; Darden Family Papers (Jefferson County, 1853–77) social; Daughters of Confederate Veterans Records (1894–1937) organizations, Lost Cause; Daughters of the American Revolution Records (1900s–1980s) organizations; Davis (Varina Howell) Papers (1847–1905) Civil War, Lost Cause, social; Davis (Varina Howell and Margaret Howell Jefferson Davis Hayes) Letters (1904–8) Lost Cause, social; DeHay (Elizabeth Norton) Papers (Houston, 1857–1930) education, Civil War; Downs (Lettie) Collections (Sharkey County, 1859, 1862–66) Civil War, social; Foote (Helen E.) Diaries (Claiborne and Hinds Counties, 1883–88) education; Foster (Catherine [Kate] Olivia) Diary (Natchez, 1863–72) Civil War; Fox (Tryphena Holder) Papers (Warren County, 1852–85) social, Civil War; Franklin (Eulalia Rogers) Collection (Jackson, 1951–52) literary, education; Gage-Hogg-Young Family Papers (Natchez, 1837–45) social; Garrett (Louisiana Dunlevy) Papers (Madison County, 1860–68) social; Hearn (David Russell) and Family Papers (Madison County, 1873–1909) domestic, social; Heidelberg (Roger) Collection (Attala and Jones Counties, 1911, 1915–24) social, World War I; Henry (Henrietta Mitchell) Papers (Jackson, 1917–27) political; Howorth (Lucy Somerville) Papers (Cleveland, 1900s–1980s) political; Irion-Neilson Family Papers (1843–1911) social, Civil War; Kearney (Belle) Papers (Madison County, 1865–1938) political; Kelly (Peggie Peacock) Letter (Oktibbeha County, 1892) slavery, African American; Lemly (William and Sue) and Family Papers (1836–1950) Civil War, social; Lindsey (Myra Mason) and Family Papers (Jackson and New York, 1922–58) literary; Lindsey-Orr Family Papers (Columbus and New York, 1849–1958) education, literary; Lloyd (Margaret Elise Lott) Family Papers (Columbus, 1921–24, 1937–51) education, social; Lobdell Family Papers (Bolivar County, 1828–1961) education, social; Lockhart-Weir Family Papers (Carroll County, 1833–95) business, social; Lyells (Roby Stitts) Papers (1920s–40s) religion, African American, organizations; Martin (Anne Shannon) Diary (Vicksburg, 1863–64) Civil War, social; Matthews (Burnita Shelton) Papers (Copiah County and Washington, D.C., 1909–88) political; Mayes-Dimitry-Stuart Family Papers (Yazoo City, 1840–1948) social, religious; Mayo (Bettie Black) Diary (Yalobusha and Attala Counties, 1863–78) social, slavery; McArn (Duncan) and Family Papers (Jefferson County, 1902–56) domestic; McNabb (Eliza R.) Papers (Pike County, 1866–76) social; Mississippi Federation of Business and Professional Women's Clubs Records (1929–) organizations; Mississippi Federation of Club Women Records (1915–60) organizations; Mississippi Federation of Women's Clubs Records (1952–56) organizations; Mississippi Nurses' Association Records (1911–77) organizations, medicine; Moman (Zipporah Elizabeth) Papers (Jackson, 1943–64) education, African American; Mottley (Elvira Jeter) Papers (Panola County, 1854–65) literary; Natchez Garden Club Records (Natchez, 1929–82) organizations, social; Natchez Pilgrimage Papers (Natchez, 1930s–80s) organizations, Lost Cause; National Society United States Daughters of 1812 Papers (1907–30) organizations; Navy Mothers' Club Minutes (Jackson, 1941–45) organizations, World War II; Nutt Family Collection (Natchez, 1810–96) social, slavery; Order of the Sisters of Mercy Papers (Vicksburg, 1879–87) religion, organizations; Piney Woods Country Life School Records (Rankin County, 1913–75) education, African American; Polk (Mr. and Mrs. James K., Jr.) Collection (Sunflower County, 1945–73) domestic; Ponder (Eleanor Fox) Papers (1901–63) literary; Posey (Evie S.) Letters and Diaries (Yazoo City, 1930–42) social, travel; Power (Kate M.) Collection (Jackson, 1937–38) political, journalism; Pride (Hannah T. and William W.) Papers (Choctaw Nation, 1821–26) education, religion; Ray (William Henry and Martha Grace) Papers (Holmes County, 1859–76) social, Civil War; Research Club Records (Jackson, 1924–91) organizations; Ricks (Eliza Barry) Papers (Lowndes and Madison Counties, 1847–1900) social; Robinson (Nancy McDougall) Papers (Claiborne County, 1832–73) social, domestic; Skelton (Mrs. Allen) Photograph Collection (Vicksburg, 1976) domestic, arts; Stockwell (Eunice J.) Papers (1833–1913) social, domestic; Stokes (Clara) Papers (Hinds County, 1920s–50s) social; Strickland (Belle) Diary (Holly Springs, 1864–77) social, Civil War; Stuart (Oscar J. E. and Family) Papers (Pike County, 1848–1909) Civil War, social; Sumner (Cid [Bertha] Ricketts) Papers (Brookhaven, 1915–70) literary; Swanson-Yates Family Papers (Hinds County, 1833–79) domestic, education; Taylor-Ballentine Family Papers (Panola County, 1834–1972) business, social; Thompson (Lily Wilkinson) Papers (Copiah and Hinds Counties, 1817–1959) political, organizations; Topp (Mildred Spurrier) Papers (Greenwood, 1948–69) literary, civil rights; United Daughters of the Confederacy Records (1861–1964) organizations, Lost Cause; Walsh (Aimee Shands) and Family Papers (Jackson, 1825–46) social; Walthall (William T.) Papers (Jackson, 1931–43) organizations, race relations; Watkins-Walton Family Papers (Carroll County, 1811–97) domestic, social; Weaver (Gustine Nancy Courson) Papers (Natchez, 1800s) domestic, social; Welty (Eudora) Collection (Jackson, 1909–2001) literary, photography; Wharton (Mary) Papers (Jackson and Port Gibson, 1858–1955) education, religion; Whitehurst (Mary) Papers (Adams County, 1875–89) social, domestic; Williams (Eva Joor) Papers (Copiah County, 1939) religion, literary; Wilson (Margaret) Diary (Adams County, 1835–37) education; Winter (Elise)

Journal (Jackson, 1981–84) political; Woman's Missionary Society Records (Brandon, 1878–90) organizations, religion; Woman's Christian Temperance Union Records (1920–49) political, social; Woodward (Ellen Sullivan) Papers (Oxford, 1925–61) political, organizations.

Mississippi University for Women, Columbus

American Association of University Women, Columbus, Mississippi Chapter (Columbus, 1921–58) organizations, education; Biographical Sketches (1837–98) education; Industrial Institute and College and Mississippi State College for Women Records (Columbus, 1850–85) education, political; Pohl (Emma Ody) Letters (Columbus, 1880–1960) education, arts.

Mitchell Memorial Library, Mississippi State University, Starkville

American Association of University Women, Starkville Branch Records (Starkville, 1930–83) organizations, education; Business and Professional Women's Club Records (Starkville, 1973–89) organizations; Byrd (Elvira) Papers (1866–1964) journalism; Cain (Eyril Edward and Annie Gray) Papers (Starkville, Canton, Natchez, 1785–1965) education, social; Calhoun-Kincannon-Orr Family Papers (Lee, Pontotoc, and Lowndes Counties, 1837–1959) social; Carter (Hodding) and Betty Werlein papers (1872–1979) political, journalism; Cobb (Lois P. Dowdle) Papers (1915–69) organizations, agriculture; Daughters of the American Revolution, Hic-a-sha-ba-ha Chapter (Starkville, 1910–17) organizations; Derian (Patricia) Papers (1947–76) political, human rights; Fields (Norma) Papers (Tupelo, 1960–90) journalism, political; Horn Collection (Choctaw, Scott, and Chickasaw Counties, 1818–71) social, Civil War; Kimbrough Papers (1863–1955) organizations, Civil War, Lost Cause; Lewis (Mary Jane) POW/MIA Collection (Meridian, 1969–78) Vietnam War, organizations; Mars (Florence) Papers (Neshoba County, 1885–1999) arts, social; McRae (Sallie B.) Diary (Kemper County, 1862) domestic, Civil War; Mississippi Extension Homemakers Clubs Collection (Choctaw, Itawamba, Lee, and Pontotoc Counties, 1944–80) organizations, education; Neilson (Sarah) Collections (Lowndes County, 1821–1970) social, organizations; Patterson (Carolyn Bennett) Collection (Kosciusko, 1893–1999) journalism; Red (Abbie Bell Nicholson) Diary (Columbus, 1905–6) education; Rice (Nannie Herndon) Papers (Oktibbeha County, 1824–1963) education, political; Smith (Hazel Brannen) Papers (Holmes County, 1945–76) journalism, civil rights; Starkville Women's Club Collection (Starkville, 1933–70) organizations; Swann and Cavett Papers (Noxubee County, 1884–1929) political, education; Thornton Family Collection (1849–1929) social, domestic; United Daughters of the Confederacy, Lyda C. Moore Chapter Scrapbooks (Lula) organizations, Lost Cause; United Daughters of the Confederacy, Putnam Darden Chapter Records (Starkville) organizations, Lost Cause; Walker (Noverta) Papers (Ripley, 1847–1949) domestic, religious; Wier (Robert and Sadye) Papers (Starkville, 1885–1991) African American, education.

Southern Historical Collection, University of North Carolina, Chapel Hill

Alston (Trudy) Diary (Raymond, 1861–64) Civil War; Burnley (Edwina) and Bertha Burnley Ricketts Memoir (Copiah County, 1830s–60s) domestic, slavery; Edmondson (Belle) Diary (Tupelo, Pontotoc, Columbus, 1861–64) Civil War; Houston Family Papers (Meridian, 1887–1909) social, Lost Cause; Ker Family Papers (Natchez, 1800–1960s) education, religion, social; Mitchell (Mary Elizabeth) Journal (Warren County, 1838–70) Civil War, social; Orr (Jehu A.) Papers (1898–1910) domestic, social; Race (Olivia Corrine Kittredge) Diary (Pass Christian, 1870–73) domestic, religion; Roach (Mahala P. H.) Diary, Roach and Eggleston Family Papers (Woodville and Vicksburg, 1853–1905) domestic, social; Sivley (Jane) Letters (Hinds and Warren Counties, 1862–67) Civil War, social; Smedes (Susan Dabney) Papers (1860–1930) education, religion; Tweed (Robert) Papers (Jefferson County, 1843–98) social, religion; Wadley (Sarah Lois) Diary (1859–84) domestic, social; Worthington (Amanda Dougherty) Diary (Washington County, 1819–78) social.

Swarthmore College Peace Collection, Swarthmore, Pennsylvania

Letters from Mildred Binns Young (Rockdale, 1936–41) civil rights, religion.

ORAL HISTORY

Oral histories within each collection are so numerous that names and descriptors cannot be provided here. Interested readers should consult the collections for that information. "Behind the Veil: Documenting African American Life in the Jim Crow South" Records, Rare Book, Manuscript, and Special Collections Library, Duke University (1940–97) African American, civil rights; "Black Oral History Project on the History of Women in America," Jackson State University, Jackson, Miss. (1974–80) African American; Center for Oral History and Cultural Heritage, Oral History Collections, University of Southern Mississippi, Hattiesburg (1971–) political, social, African American, civil rights, arts, journalism; Gowdy Collection, Jackson State University, Jackson, Miss. (1982) social, African American; Hamblet (Theora) Interviews, Theora Hamblet Collection, J. D. Williams Library, University of Mississippi, Oxford (1955–76) arts, religion; Howorth (Lucy R. Somerville) Oral History, Delta State University, Cleveland, Miss. (1971–74) political; Hudson (Bessie), Virginia Paul, and Susie Fortenberry Interviews, J. D. Williams Library, University of Mississippi, Oxford (1978) social; Hull (Marie) Interview, J. D. Williams Library, University of Mississippi, Oxford (1977) arts; Marshall (Susie) "Church Women United Manuscript and Interview," J. D. Williams Library, University of Mississippi, Oxford (29 October 1991) religion, civil rights; Oral History Collection, Mississippi Department of Archives and History (1960s–80s) social, political; Oral History Collections, Interviews, Mitchell Memorial Library, Mississippi State University, Starkville,

Miss.; Piney Woods Collection, Jackson State University, Jackson, Miss. (1973–79) education, African American; Ralph J. Bunche Oral History Collection, Manuscript Division, Morgan Spingarn Research Center, Howard University, Washington, D.C. (1960s) civil rights, African American; Southern Oral History Program Collection, Southern Historical Collection, University of North Carolina, Chapel Hill (1973–) political, social, religion, African American; Thompson (Sara), "Granny Midwife" Interview, J. D. Williams Library, University of Mississippi, Oxford (1976) medical.

Contributors

DAVID D. CARSON earned a doctorate in biochemistry from Texas A&M University in 1990. He first became intrigued by the story of Elizabeth Lee Hazen while on the faculty of Mississippi University for Women. He is presently associate professor of biology at Louisiana College.

EMILY CLARK received a doctorate in history from Tulane University and has taught at Newnham College, Cambridge, and at the University of Southern Mississippi. She is currently vice president for planning and lecturer in history at Lewis and Clark College in Portland, Oregon.

CITA COOK is associate professor of history at the State University of West Georgia. She received a doctorate from the University of California at Berkeley in 1992. She won the Willie D. Halsell Prize from the Mississippi Historical Society in 2001 and is author of the forthcoming *Growing Up White, Genteel, and Female in a Changing South: Natchez Young Ladies, 1830–1910*.

CONSTANCE CURRY was a member of the Student Nonviolent Coordinating Committee executive committee from 1960 to 1964 and a southern field representative for the American Friends Service Committee from 1964 to 1975. She is the author of *Silver Rights* (1995) and editor of and contributor to *Deep in Our Hearts: Nine Women in the Freedom Movement* (2000). She is a fellow in women's studies at Emory University.

SUSAN DITTO earned a doctorate in 1998 from the University of Mississippi, where she currently teaches American history and writes about gender and domestic space in the nineteenth-century South.

KATE GREENE is a feminist associate professor of political science at the University of Southern Mississippi. Her publications include *Affirmative Action and Principles of Justice* (1989), articles in journals, and several book chapters. She has portrayed Burnita Shelton Matthews in a Chautauqua program for the Mississippi Humanities Council.

FRANÇOISE N. HAMLIN first became acquainted with the Mississippi Delta as a foreign exchange student residing with a family in Clarksdale, Mississippi. Today, she is completing a doctorate in African American studies and American studies at Yale. Hamlin won a Huggins-Quarles prize from the Organization of American Historians in 2002.

ROBERT A. HARRIS is a doctoral candidate in English at the University of Kansas. He currently teaches at historic St. Ignatius College Preparatory School in Chicago.

JOANNE VARNER HAWKS, founder of the Mississippi Women's History Project, earned a doctorate in history from the University of Mississippi, where she served as dean of women from 1972 to 1981 and director of the Sarah Isom Center for Women's Studies from 1981 to 1998. Among the many works that she authored, coauthored, or edited are *Sex, Race, and the Role of Women in the South* (1983) and *Mississippi's Historical Heritage: A Guide to Women's Sources in Mississippi Repositories* (1993).

KATHLEEN MCCLAIN JENKINS earned a bachelor's degree in art history from the University of Mississippi and a master of education degree from Delta State. She is author of the catalog essay "Summers of '96—Shinnecock Revisited: The Inspiration of Kate Freeman Clark by William Merritt Chase" and curator for the National Park Service in Natchez, where she lives with her husband, Edward Bond, and son, Buck.

SUZANNE MARRS is Stewart Family Professor of Language and Literature at Millsaps College. Her many publications on the life and work of her friend Eudora Welty include *One Writer's Imagination: The Fiction of Eudora Welty* (2002) and *Eudora Welty and Politics* (coedited with Harriet Pollack, 2001).

JOHN F. MARSZALEK is William L. Giles Distinguished Professor of History at Mississippi State University. He received his doctorate from the University of Notre Dame. Among his many publications are *The Petticoat Affair: Manners, Mutiny, and Sex in Andrew Jackson's White House* (1998) and the award-winning *Sherman, A Soldier's Passion for Order* (1993). He coedited *The Encyclopedia of African-American Civil Rights, From Emancipation to the Present* (1992).

MARK NEWMAN is a senior lecturer in history at the University of Derby in England. He received a doctorate in history from the University of Mississippi in 1993. Newman is the author of *Getting Right with God: Southern Baptists and Desegregation, 1945–1995* (2002) and the forthcoming *Divine Agitators: The Delta Ministry and Civil Rights in Mississippi.*

ELIZABETH ANNE PAYNE was founding director of the McDonnell-Barksdale Honors College at the University of Mississippi from 1997 to 2002 and was instrumental in securing the resources necessary to bring the Mississippi Women's History Project to fruition. Payne holds a doctorate in history from the University of Illinois at Chicago and is author of *Reform, Labor, and Feminism: Margaret Dreier Robins and the Women's Trade Union*

League (1988). She is currently a professor of history at the University of Mississippi and is writing a book on the Southern Tenant Farmers' Union focusing on the work of Depression-era photographer Louise Boyle.

BRIDGET SMITH PIESCHEL received a doctorate in English from the University of Alabama in 1989. She is a professor of English and head of humanities at Mississippi University for Women and coauthor of *Loyal Daughters: A Centennial History of Mississippi University for Women* (1984).

LINDA REED completed her doctorate at Indiana University. She authored the prize-winning book *Simple Decency and Common Sense: The Southern Conference Movement, 1938–1963* and coedited *"We Specialize in the Wholly Impossible": A Reader in Black Women's History.* Professor Reed served nine years as the director of the African American Studies Program at the University of Houston, where she is currently an associate professor of history.

DOROTHY SHAWHAN is a professor of English and chair of the Division of Languages and Literature at Delta State University in Cleveland, Mississippi. She has published a novel, *Lizzie,* and is currently coauthoring a biography of Judge Lucy Somerville Howorth.

MARJORIE JULIAN SPRUILL received her doctoral degree from the University of Virginia. She taught in the department of history at the University of Southern Mississippi from 1985 to 2002 and is currently Associate Provost for Strategic Planning and research professor of history at Vanderbilt University. Spruill is author of *New Women of the New South: The Leaders of the Woman Suffrage Movement in the Southern States* and editor of several anthologies on the American woman suffrage movement. She is a former president of the Southern Association for Women Historians.

MARTHA H. SWAIN, Cornaro Professor of History Emerita at Texas Woman's University, has most recently taught at Mississippi State University. She is the author of *Pat Harrison: The New Deal Years* (1978) and *Ellen S. Woodward: New Deal Advocate for Women* (1995), as well as many articles. She is a past president of the Southern Association for Women Historians and was honored with the Dunbar Rowland Award from the Mississippi Historical Society in 2002 for lifetime contributions to the study of Mississippi history.

SARAH WILKERSON-FREEMAN received a doctorate from the University of North Carolina and is currently an associate professor of history at Arkansas State University. She has authored a number of articles on the history of women in politics.

Index

abolitionist movement, 44

abortion, 255, 262

Addams, Jane, 49, 165

African American women. *See* women, African American

Afro-Creole women, 15, 16

AFSC. *See* American Friends Service Committee

Alcorn State University, 95, 212

Alcuin Preparatory School for Girls, 90

Alexander, James "Alex," 241

Alexander, Margaret Walker: autobiography of, 247; awards won by, 238, 241; death of, 247; education of, 235, 240, 241; essays by, 246–47; family background of, 235; and Federal Writers' Project, 240–41; and grandmother's stories, 235, 237, 245–46; humanist concerns of, 238; literary influences on, 235, 237; marriage of, 241; as Mississippian, 198–99; photograph of, 236; portrayal by, of southern African Americans, 198–99, 235, 237–38; teaching career of, 241. *See also individual titles of works.*

American Association of University Women (AAUW), 97, 122

American Bar Association, 153, 154

American Friends Service Committee (AFSC), 269, 273–75, 276, 277, 278

American Institute of Chemists, 141

American Missionary Society, 95

Anna T. Jeanes Fund, 271

"Ante-Bellum Southern Woman, The" (W. Davis), 32–33

Anthony, Susan B., 54, 64, 151

Art Students League, 101, 102, 103, 106, 109

Ashford, Laplois, 289

Association for Retarded Citizens (ARC), 213

Association for the Rights of Citizens with Developmental Disibilities (ARC), 218 (n. 40)

Association of Southern Women for the Prevention of Lynching, 170

Attala County, Miss., 115–16

Austen, Jane, mentioned, 33

Author and Agent (Kreyling), 187

Awkward, Michael, 243

Bacon, Sylvia, 156

Bacterial Diagnosis Laboratory, 134

Baker, Ella, 256, 287

Baker, George Pierce, 188

Baker, Josephine, 165

Ball Jar Company, 213

Banner County Outlook, 221

baptism, Catholic, 14; and church-building, 11–12; and record keeping, 6–7, 8

Baptist Church, 95

Barnett, Ross, 226, 228

Barrett, Pat, 226

Barton, Clara, 127

Bates, Daisy, 251, 257, 263, 284; political action of, 260; quoted, 249

Beaulieu, Elizabeth, 244

beauticians, 290–91

Beecher, Catherine, 172

Belhaven College, 95

Benham, Rhoda, 135

Berrien, Laura, 152–53

Berry, Vera. *See* Pigee, Vera Mae

Bethune, Mary McLeod, 154

Bethune-Cookman College, 154

Bilbo, Theodore, 52, 168, 170, 185

birth control, 255, 262

Black, Allen, 277, 278

Black, Lucille, 287

black arts movement, 247